THE WORLD OF

SPORTS STATISTICS

THE WORLD OF

Foreword by Marv Albert

NEW YORK   1978   ATHENEUM

SPORTS STATISTICS

How the Fans and Professionals
Record, Compile and Use Information

ARTHUR FRIEDMAN

With Joel H. Cohen

Library of Congress Cataloging in Publication Data

Friedman, Arthur
    The world of sports statistics.

        1. Sports—Records.   2. Sports—Statistics.
I. Cohen, Joel H.   II. Title.
GV741.F73 1978   796'.02'12   77-76799
ISBN 0-689-10821-4

TO PAT,

who has always been so supportive and who has spent countless nights alone so that I could pursue the work I enjoy so much . . .

And to my late father, Sam, who kindled my interest in sports at a very early age, and who would have been so very proud of this book.

Preface

"POINTS ARE FOR winners; statistics are for losers."

It's been said by countless athletes—superstars, stars and mediocre performers alike.

Yet the truth is that statistics are for *everyone*—winners as well as losers, fans as well as players and coaches. They add zest and invaluable information to any sport.

Certainly, figures can lie (and liars figure), but properly used and understood, an individual's or a team's statistics can be an important instrument of strategy. Properly analyzed and employed, stats can be converted into points (or runs or goals), and losers converted into winners. For fans, stats can be the key to deeper enjoyment and appreciation of the game and of those who play it.

Seldom, of course, are statistics by themselves the *whole* story of a team's or an athlete's performance, and it would be a mistake to base strategy (or adoration) on the figures alone. But placed in the correct context, they can indicate how a pitcher should pitch to a particular hitter in a given situation, who should take what kind of shot when and where, whether to look for the running play or pass, and so forth. Sometimes, they can also indicate who should play or sit, who should be signed or traded.

For some fans, the stats are The Game itself, and more power to them. There is, however, the ever-present danger to both the fan and professional of carrying statistics to such an extreme—categorizing to such a fine point—that they become pointless. A cartoon years ago had a baseball announcer proclaiming something like: ''Jones is only the third left-hander wearing a two-button jersey, who has registered more than one strikeout in each even-numbered inning in the first game of a twi-night double-header played in a western city on a day beginning with the letter *T*.''

But overkill aside, statistics occupy a deserved place of respect, if not honor, in the world of professional sports. Arthur Friedman, who is the official statistician of the New York Mets and the New York Rangers and who has also served as statistician for the New York Knicks and the New York Jets and numerous other teams and sporting events including ''Monday Night Football,'' will guide you through the world of sports statistics. Among the points he will cover are:

- the way a professional statistician works
- how stats have helped coaches, managers, general managers and players succeed (or fail)
- which stats tell the most about a player's value to his team
- thorough-but-understandable ways for fans to score games
- which managers and coaches use statistics to advantage
- anecdotes relating to the use or misuse of statistics by people in professional sports
- changes he'd like to see made in official scoring

Samples of actual professional statistical reports and scoresheets are included.

To those who already appreciate the fact that stats are the fuel that keeps the fires of pro sports crackling—and to those who are yet to be convinced—welcome to Arthur Friedman's World of Sports Statistics.

JOEL H. COHEN

Foreword

E VEN IF Arthur Friedman weren't a close friend of mine since boyhood, even if he hadn't formed fan clubs and imaginary leagues with me, and even if he hadn't discovered my wife for me—I would still be happy to trumpet the praises of this book.

Speaking both as a statistics fanatic and as a broadcaster who considers a statistician essential, I feel this is a book that is long overdue, and I can't think of a person better qualified to have written it than Art. He's the best statistician I've ever known and worked with professionally. He's always thinking from the broadcasting point of view, and his feel for what is significant and interesting is exceptional.

What primarily sets Arthur apart as a statistician is the level of communication he maintains. It's sort of a highly refined ESP. When we worked together directly, Art would invariably know how I'd be thinking; he'd *anticipate* particular statistical insights I'd want to broadcast, and have the pertinent facts ready.

He's not only very knowledgeable, but very quick and very much into his trade. Because of these qualities and his pleasant personality, there's inevitably a pleasant, easy rapport when he's in the booth. I know the Met broadcasters and others he's worked with feel the same way about him.

We go back a long way together, having grown up as best friends in the Manhattan Beach section of Brooklyn, New York. We met as ballplaying opponents in schoolyard games between the kids from Pembroke Street (Art's block) and those from Kensington Street (mine). We played roller hockey, punchball, baseball, basketball and football. (Our street usually got killed because his had older kids playing, but it was fun and you could always get a game.)

To keep the record balanced, I have to say that while Arthur was always a pretty good player, he had a terrible temper—directed against himself—when he didn't do well. He wasn't above hurling a bat against the fence after striking out. I'm happy to report that while he is still intense, he doesn't hurl his calculator out of the booth when he's off by a digit in a batting average.

As youngsters, we were both into keeping notebooks and records of the major league teams and players; we also made up our own leagues with imaginary players who had imaginary statistics, injuries and trades, and we played a complicated dice game that projected a player's full-season accomplishments. At age twelve, all this was more fun than dating girls. We were much more "far-out" in our sports-stats fanaticism than our other friends.

For instance, in order to meet players, get autographs and gain access to ball games, I was always starting fan clubs and drafting Arthur to be my vice-president. We often interviewed athletes for our high school paper, the Lincoln *Log*—and often just for ourselves.

In a sense, the real start of our working together came when, as a high school junior, I was an office boy for the Brooklyn Dodgers. Like other employees, I was entitled to two choice seats at Ebbets Field in the overhanging box right next to the broadcast booth. I'd get to games early with a friend and sit in the first row of the box. I'm sure friends of Walter O'Malley, who arrived later, weren't happy with this or with our exuberant "broadcasts" of the game into a huge tape recorder. I'd do the play-by-play and my friend, often Art, would do "color," read commercials and keep score. After the game we'd go into the booth, where Red Barber and Vince Scully had broadcast, and pick up the discarded commercial messages and use them next game. Kids do that with us now.

It got to the point where our overly enthusiastic "broadcasts" got to be too much for the VIPs in the box, and we were politely given the choice of halting the broadcasts or moving to a booth down the right-field line.

We did a lot of other mythical broadcasting, most of it for my fictitious radio station, WMPA (for Marvin Philip Albert). We had all sorts of programming, from quiz shows to Ping-Pong games played in our basement. The latter were our big events and were very helpful for building speed and accuracy. In our baseball games, we incorporated crowd noises and the crack of the bat.

Arthur was with me, too, as statistician in the first Knick games I ever broadcast professionally, first for WCBS-Radio, then for WHN. I participated as a student panelist on a radio interview show that Howard Cosell hosted for several years, and when Howard asked me to recommend someone to be on the program with us, Art joined as a fellow student panelist.

We worked together more recently on "Monday Night Hockey." I had my own statistician in the TV broadcast booth, while Art was in the control room, preparing information to be flashed on the screen. It was a big plus having him there, because of his ability consistently to come up with interesting facts.

Though I do the Ranger games on radio while he's with the TV end of it, I keep in touch with him, much in the same way that a newspaperman does. He'll often prepare a sheet for me with such material as what streaks to look for, the last time the Rangers won in Los Angeles and who's leading in goals.

He's very serious about his work, but there's a whacky side to Art, too. For instance, he started a fan club for an obscure hockey player, and he had a way of making up nicknames for players, often without rhyme or reason. Man does not live by stats alone.

On that theme, a good statistician is, among other things, perceptive. I learned early that Arthur had that quality when the first night game was played at Shea Stadium. I was doing crowd interviews about the stadium, and Art, ever ready with his binoculars, was helping me find attractive fans to question. "Hey," he said, "there's a great-looking usherette downstairs." Dutifully, I trotted off to interview the girl, whose name was Benita. She was a college student and real baseball fan, and today she's my wife.

But my friend has other things going for him. He knows—and tells—which stats have significance. He knows and talks about the stats the decision-makers rely on. He's *devised* meaningful categories of statistics, and he suggests others, along with changes he'd like to see in official scoring. And much more.

It's true, as Art points out, that certain statistics have no real meaning and that much depends on what you read into them. It's true, too, that there's always the danger of being deluged by stats. Yet for the most part there is great meaning in sports statistics and great enjoyment for those who understand and appreciate them.

Arthur Friedman has made a valuable contribution to both. To my knowledge, this is the first book of its kind, and it's a dandy. I'm confident the hard-core sports fan will devour it eagerly, and that even the reader who isn't a stats fanatic will gain a deeper understanding of many aspects of major sports.

Knowing Art's abilities and background and how he's communicated his insightful knowledge, I'm happy to give his book an enthusiastic "Yes!"

MARV ALBERT

Contents

Contents

HOCKEY

FOOTBALL

BASKETBALL

BETTING AND STATS

NUMBERS FOR FUN AND PROFIT

INTRODUCTION

Welcome to the Big Leagues

IT WAS February of 1966. There I was, sitting on the floor of a bathroom in a St. Petersburg, Florida, motel at midnight, frantically pecking away at the portable typewriter I had placed on top of the toilet seat. I was desperately trying to ignore the shrieking baby in the next room, the spilled correction fluid, the paper caught and shredded in the machine—and complete my mission: cut a stencil that would list the names of forty talented young men and, in well-ordered columns of numbers, tell what they had accomplished thus far in spring training.

Next morning, my eyes would be as bloodshot as those of someone who'd been on an all-night drunk, my back and legs would ache, my nerves would be shattered. But the stencil would be run off and distributed.

And more important personally, I had made it to the big leagues. I had begun my job as statistician for the New York Mets.

The job itself, if not the bizarre setting for that first night, was, I suppose, a natural culmination of a lifelong interest. I grew up in the Manhattan Beach section of Brooklyn, New York, where, as it was for most boys, playing ball was the main thing in my life. I played most of the major sports, participating in baseball and basketball leagues. We kids seldom took off our sneakers.

One of my closest friends when we were growing up was Marv Albert, the same "Yes!" man who today is a premier sportscaster. Our fascination with sports wasn't limited to playing. He and I were such sports nuts that in our middle teen years we invented our own leagues and kept our own records. The

3

other kids laughed at us, but our imaginary leagues had their own teams, cities and players. We traded our make-believe players, gave them imaginary injuries and of course, kept records of their stats.

In addition we collected every baseball and football bubble-gum card we could lay our hands on, and we plotted to meet athletes. We were pretty brazen about it. When athletes came into town, we'd find out what hotel they were staying at, then go introduce ourselves as reporters for the Lincoln *Log,* our school paper (put out by Lincoln High School, on Ocean Parkway in Brooklyn). We weren't actually writing most of these stories for the newspaper, but we would have tried almost anything to meet ballplayers, and the ruse worked. It gave us access to clubhouses and dugouts for our interviews.

One of the first baseball players we got to know was Solly Hemus, a utility infielder. Getting to know Solly was something of a stepping stone for us, and we got to know many athletes. For instance, we did several interviews with Jackie Jensen, who would bring us into the clubhouse or dugout for our talk.

We tried to pick a player who was not the star of his team, figuring there would be less competition for his time and attention. When the Athletics were in town, for example, we called utility catcher Joe Ginsberg, who was just up for a cup of coffee in the majors. He was obliging, as most players were.

Our success with the Hemus Fan Club emboldened us to start the Jim Baechtold Fan Club. Out of Eastern Kentucky, Jim played basketball for the New York Knickerbockers and fit the pattern of the targets of our attention. He wasn't a starter, he averaged 10–11 points a game and he was very friendly. We did so well with the Baechtold Fan Club, drawing a lot of members, that we escalated it into the New York Knickerbocker Fan Club.

You couldn't do it today, but in those days we'd conduct our club meetings right on the floor of Madison Square Garden on afternoons when there were no games. And incredibly, we'd get two or three NBA players to appear at the meeting—even more unbelievably, free of charge! To this day we look back and laugh, in awe of our nerve. Today you can't get a player to go next door for less than three hundred dollars. Yet we got players of the stature of Ray Felix, Harry Gallatin, Sweetwater Clifton and Carl Braun to appear.

Enrollment in the Knicks club hit over 300. In each of the clubs, we published a monthly newspaper *(The Hemus Headliner, The Baechtold Bulletin).* In the Knicks club, we also distributed buttons, held drawings for free game tickets, sponsored a Fan Club Day at the Garden, and gave a Knicks Fan Club player-of-the-year award. It was very exciting.

Marv and I knew we wanted to get into sports in some way, but we really had no specific aspirations, partly because we realized how limited the opportunities were. At that time there were only eight teams in each major baseball league and only six teams in the National Hockey League. No one foresaw the amount of expansion that has since taken place, so I filed away hopes of a sports career under "fantasy," and contented myself with our fan clubs and related activities.

One thing did lead to another, though. Through the people we got to know in 1955, Marv Albert and I landed a six-month radio assignment on what was Howard Cosell's first broadcasting job. It was a national program taped on Thursday nights and called "All-League Clubhouse" or a similar title. It consisted of three teenage panelists—Marv, myself and usually a friend of ours—interviewing a sports star, with Cosell as moderator. Some questions were made up for us; others we thought up ourselves.

The highlight of the show was the appearance of Johnny Podres just after he won the final game of the 1955 World Series, the first Series ever won by the Dodgers. The show was a good stepping stone for us.

Marv went to Syracuse University, where he did broadcasting, while I attended Brooklyn College and bowed out of sports-related work for several years because of lack of opportunity. At that time hardly anyone knew what a sports statistician was, so jobs were scarce. Allan Roth of the Dodgers was the only well-known statistician back then, and is probably the best-known in the business today. He's still active as statistician for the NBC "Baseball Game of the Week" and he has put out various publications.

Marv left Syracuse a year early because he had an opportunity to work at CBS with sportscaster Marty Glickman. One day Marv asked me whether I'd like to help them out by keeping stats at a basketball game. Except for the records I'd kept at home for our imaginary leagues, I had never really done anything like that, but I was game if they were.

So early in the 1962 season, I mustered up my courage, tried to ignore the butterflies in my stomach and went to the Garden to work my very first game as a statistician. Because Marty Glickman had other commitments, Jim Gordon did the play-by-play of the game between the Knicks and the Detroit Pistons. I very proudly accepted my pay—five dollars. Apparently I didn't make any fatal errors, as there were more invitations to fill in as statistician. I accepted with pleasure.

Joining the Jet Set

I got to know Bob Murphy, who was broadcasting for the New York Jets football team in the old Polo Grounds, and for a season (1963) I assisted him with stats.

I had first met Murph when he was broadcasting games for Harry Wismer's old New York football team, the Titans. Sammy Baugh was the head coach and Sleepy Jim Crowley, of the fabled Four Horsemen, was the color man. With Bob Ahrens, I worked for Murphy as a spotter in the old Polo Grounds.

("He [Friedman] was an excellent spotter, as you can imagine," Murphy comments. "He has this steel-trap mind, and it was obvious to me from the very beginning that here was a guy who was really doing a job for me. . . .")

I'll never forget that year with the Jets. Once you got into the broadcast booth, you were so crammed in and busy you couldn't get out to go to the bathroom or anything else, even at half-time. Between the cold of November and December, and the absorption of quarts of hot coffee, nature's call would become insistent, but it would have to go unanswered.

The old American Football League games lasted between three and three and a half hours because of all the scoring, often 100 points. Because you can't write figures while wearing gloves, my fingers would become almost frostbitten from the bitter cold. I couldn't feel my fingertips and sometimes I didn't even know I had a pencil in my hand.

The next year Murph left and Merle Harmon became the play-by-play announcer for the Jets. During a Jets exhibition game at New Brunswick, Bob Ahrens and I introduced ourselves to Merle Harmon. We told Merle we'd both worked with Bob Murphy the year before, doing stats, and asked if we could assist him. He said "Sure," and I did stats and some spotting for Harmon for about eleven years. I worked all the home games and some of the road games. It was excellent experience because, of all the major sports, football is the most difficult to do stats for on an individual-game basis.

What makes football so tough is that there are so many things to note on a single play. If a man carries the ball, you have to record how much yardage he made, who made the tackle, the change of the down, etc. You also have to keep track of all the plays that lead to a score—for instance, you would have to record that the Jets went seventy yards for a touchdown in ten plays.

While I was working the Jets games, I also did some basketball and a little bit of hockey on a freelance, game-to-game basis. The basketball games I worked were both professional and college level. The out-of-town announcers who came into New York would not have a statistician with them, so I worked for them. At just five or ten dollars a game, it was almost a hobby for me. I never expected this labor of love to develop into a full-time occupation because— except for Allan Roth—sports statisticians were an unknown commodity.

In the course of my freelance work, I got to know a lot of broadcasters and athletes. Through that grapevine I learned in early 1966 that the Mets had an opening for a full-time statistician, because Matt Winick, who had handled the job, was moving up to the Mets public relations office. Someone recommended me for the position.

There were about ten of us waiting to be interviewed. Applicants came from different parts of the country and from different occupational backgrounds. Some were accountants or held other well-paying positions. I wondered, "How the heck am I going to get this job?"

My own vocational and academic career was curiously unrelated to statistics. For one thing, I never liked math and was not particularly good at it in school. My parents used to say how terrific it would be if only I had as much interest in algebra as I had in my imaginary leagues. But I wasn't motivated by school the way I was by sports.

In college I took a little bit of everything, then left after two years. In 1960 I went into the army's six-year reserve program and found that the army and I had a mutual dislike. I drifted from job to job: I sold dictionaries, worked as an apprentice window-dresser and then as a clothing salesman, and even considered becoming a barber. I had no real goal in life at the time, except fun. I went back to school for a while, first in the daytime and then at night, but I still had no particular focus.

At the time the Mets job opened up, I was working as bedspread salesman, a job I liked about as much as Charley Finley likes Bowie Kuhn. How fantastic it would be if I could land the statistician's job!

One of the fellows waiting to be interviewed was so nervous he was almost trembling, and I urged him to calm down. "Either you get it or you don't. It's not the end of the world." He told me, "I've been to church every day for the last week, praying. I've just got to get the job. I know I have God on my side." I figured I had some pretty influential references on my side; after all, I'd worked for Bob Murphy and had briefly met Lindsey Nelson, one of the other Met announcers. But this man's references were divine. I wasn't overly optimistic.

Still, when it came time for my interview by the three Met broadcasters and the producer, Joe Gallagher, I told them confidently but not arrogantly that I felt I could do the best job. The interview lasted about forty-five minutes. When it was

7

over they told me they were going to make their decision in two to three weeks and I'd be hearing from them. I went home thinking about all the mistakes I had made, and wishing, "If only I could do it over again. . . . If only I could have said such-and-such."

But I needn't have worried. Two days later I got a call saying that I had the job and they'd give me further information after the team went down to spring training.

I was so high with the exciting news I decided to give my bedspread company my notice in a dramatic way. Immature kid that I was, I drove the company car to a bus stop in front of the showroom on Fifth Avenue in Manhattan and left it there, while I went in to announce, "I quit." As might be expected, the car was ticketed and towed away.

The letter from the Mets (which I still have) arrived shortly thereafter, telling me to report to spring training on such-and-such a day. I was to pick up my own airplane tickets, for which I'd be reimbursed, and fly down to start work.

Now I was scared. I had never really been anyplace, I didn't know anybody in spring training camp, and I didn't know just what I'd be doing. I didn't even know whether I should take my family with me. I called the management and was told it was perfectly all right to bring my family along, providing I paid their air fare. (Jeffrey, my baby son, was young enough to fly free of charge.)

From the Tampa airport, we took a limousine to the Colonial Inn in St. Petersburg, where the Mets were staying. Apprehensively, I asked the desk clerk if there was a room for "Mr. Friedman *of the New York Mets.*" And, to my delight, there was. We checked in, the baby crying and me very frightened. At a loss what to do, I paged Joel Nixon, who was the executive producer of the television broadcasts. Since I was going to be serving as statistician to the broadcasters, he was my boss. We met for the first time in the lobby (he hadn't been at my interview), and he told me, "Make yourself at home and just relax, and we'll talk to you tomorrow morning." In the morning he asked whether I'd like to start and get the feel of things, and of course I said, "Sure."

My first experience would be at an exhibition game between the Mets and the Washington Senators. There were really no stats to keep; it was just a matter of helping the announcers keep track of changes in the field, something you have almost every inning in an exhibition game. And, as you might have guessed, the first one I called was wrong: I had the wrong man playing the position. It was not the last case of mistaken identity of which I'd be guilty in my career.

8

I worked that first game without too many embarrassing incidents, but the worst was yet to come.

Matt Winick, the former Mets' statistician, offered to show me how to type up the stat sheet. In a regular season, there might be fourteen or fifteen columns following each player's name, representing various categories such as RBI's, homers, etc.; but in spring training there aren't as many statistics kept. On the other hand, in spring training you have forty players, each of whom gets a line of stats.

I watched Matt cut a stencil, and the next night it was my turn to update the statistics, based on what had happened that day, and cut a stencil. Working at the desk in our small hotel room, I updated the figures, computed the averages and so forth. Now came the time to type the stencil, which had to be available to be run off the next morning in the hotel office, with copies distributed to the managers, members of the media and anyone else who had an appropriate interest.

The simple mechanical act of centering a stencil and setting up the margins and columns can be incredibly irritating. That night, for me, it was a disaster. Every time I started to type, the baby would wake up screaming. I continually made mistakes. The columns were uneven. I left figures out. When I didn't rip the stencil deliberately, it would get caught and shred accidentally. It was well past midnight. Because of the baby, I decided to abandon the desk and try typing in the bathroom. I put the typewriter on the lid of the toilet seat, and I sat on the ledge of the bathtub, but that didn't work. Then I sat on the floor. The correction fluid spilled, another stencil ripped, my temper boiled over. Three hours later I had it done correctly.

Luckily, the relaxed, cheerful atmosphere of spring training camp is contagious. In spring training everyone is optimistic. Everyone is going to make the team, every team is going to win the pennant.

As spring training progressed players were cut or sent back to the farm team. Accordingly, I would leave the names of those players off the stat sheet. My stat sheet work was becoming easier and more routine. In just four or five days, I had become quite good at updating the stats, cutting stencils, having the updated stat sheets run off and distributing them the next morning.

Players were very eager for the latest stat sheet. After all, their jobs depended on what the stat sheet showed. Not being listed meant you'd been cut. One morning during the first week I was with the Mets, one of the outfielders took a look at the stat sheet and, not seeing his name on it, figured he'd been axed. He went back to the locker room, gathered his belongings and waited for the manager to break the bad news. The news never came, because he had not been cut: I had inadvertently left his name off the sheet. The player, whose name I've forgotten (probably because I'm embarrassed), didn't let me forget how I had "cut" him. Eventually, the team did drop him, but he played for the Mets for part of that season.

Over the years I've mistakenly left a player off the stat sheets several times, and of course, it's always come back to haunt me. The most notable example came in 1969, when I left Ron Swoboda's name off the sheet the day of a game against the Cardinals and Steve Carlton. That night, Carlton struck out nineteen Mets, but Swoboda, the man who wasn't listed, hit two home runs to beat him, 4–3.

Part of the reason for the omission was that at that time I was listing the players in order of their batting average, starting with the highest on top. It's relatively easy to overlook someone with that kind of set-up. Now I list players alphabetically, which makes it much easier to check.

Stats: Only for Losers?

E VERY TIME I hear a ballplayer, broadcaster or newspaper man say, "Statistics are for losers," or that the only stats that really matter are whether you win or lose, I cringe. Those ballplayers are always among the first to crowd around me when I walk into the locker room with the up-to-date stat sheet. And they'll always be the ones sneaking a look at the league stats posted on the bulletin board. All the stats they claim to ignore have a strange way of popping up during contract talks—on both sides of the table, front office as well as ballplayer.

And I'd like to see or hear a play-by-play man in any sport, especially baseball, try to get through a broadcast without citing statistics.

Nicknames

Sometimes stats become part of a player's name—Jerry Koosman becomes "twenty-game-winner Jerry Koosman"; Tom Seaver is frequently referred to as "three-time Cy Young winner Tom Seaver"; Archie Griffin will probably be called "Heisman Trophy–winner Archie Griffin" throughout his career. A statistical accomplishment becomes part of a ballplayer's identity.

Trades

Trades cause new interest in stats on the part of players as well as fans. Players will look at box scores to see what their former teammates are doing, and newcomers to a ball club will want to find out how the man they were traded for is performing. If they see he's gone 3-for-4, they may get more determined, even a little surly.

Beyond Stats

Obviously, statistics are not the whole story of a player's contributions. While effort, desire and other qualities an athlete has inside him can't be measured, they certainly belong in any evaluation of his performance.

In baseball you can't usually tell whether a man is swinging for a home run every time. If a ball is hit to a fielder, he's going to try to throw the runner out. If he's up at bat, he's going to be trying to get a hit all the time. It's a different story if he fails to run out a ball, but otherwise, who's to say he's not giving an all-out effort?

In other sports, however, you *can* tell. In those sports where the need is greater for meshing together as a unit, you can often judge whether a player is giving an all-out effort, especially when his team is involved in a one-sided game. Is the hockey player still going to the boards? Is the football defender still popping the opposition? In other words, is the player still breaking his back to play his best even when the team is so far behind that it's just playing out the string? A man's all-out performance may not show up in such statistics as extra goals or assists in hockey, or anything more than a couple of rebounds in basketball, but it certainly deserves recognition.

Stats Can Mislead

There's no question in my mind about the fact that statistics can be misleading. They tell what already has happened, but they say nothing about *why* it happened, and seldom do they tell you *when* it happened. Most stats have to be considered along with other factors.

For instance, the Mets were always near the bottom of the league when it came to making double plays in the early 70's. Someone looking at this statistic out of context would probably believe that they had to improve the caliber of the men playing shortstop and second base. But the low double-play total of the Mets didn't result from a weak double-play combo. Rather, it was a reflection of the super ability of the Met pitching staff, which was always near the top in best earned-run average. This meant that not as many players were allowed on base by Met pitchers as by other pitchers. Perhaps even more important, Met pitchers were striking out a great many batters, and obviously the more players who strike out, the fewer opportunities there are for double plays, since the batter is not hitting the ball. As you can see, the Mets' double-play statistic taken out of context was fallacious.

Sometimes it's important to know the "when" of a statistic as well as the "why." For instance, fans will say that a particular player has 80 RBI's, which is a very respectable number. But someone with 30 fewer RBI's may have driven in runs in more critical situations and thus be more valuable to the team. An RBI when your team is ten runs ahead or ten behind means little; in a close game, it means a lot.

I feel that a player's game-tying RBI's and go-ahead RBI's are even more important than his game-winning RBI's. Any time you drive in a run that ties a game or puts your team ahead, you're producing at a critical point. These records are kept—I keep them for the Mets—and even though the fans aren't aware of them, the front office and the manager certainly are.

Even though these stats aren't made public, a fan who watches his team closely will pretty much be aware of who performed at his best in critical parts of a game and who got his RBI's when they really weren't very important.

The question of "when" permeates all baseball statistics. Your run scored in the second inning of a game is not quite the same as a run scored in the eighth, yet it affects all subsequent strategy in the game. It may keep your pitcher in the game when otherwise he'd be taken out; it may force the other team to go to a pinch-hitter. It changes a bunt situation; it may change the way the defense plays. Similarly, an early-season winning streak that puts a team in first place is not the same as a September winning streak when the club is already out of the race.

Unfortunately, statistics, by their very nature, can't reflect such things. But the reality of baseball is built on exactly such factors, which I think are part of the beauty of baseball.

Fans are sometimes miffed, or at least surprised, that baseball professionals pay little attention to some stats that the fans treasure. But they shouldn't be. The trick is to keep in mind all the variables that are involved. When you get down to it, all cumulative statistics—homers, RBI's, strikeouts, wins, losses for a pitcher—must be considered in light of the opportunities. Unfortunately, opportunities are kept separately and are unavailable to the public. Consequently, fans are being misled to a certain extent. Knowing only part of a picture often gives a false picture.

There's another side to the subject, however. I think the average fan would be almost overwhelmed if all the accountable items were revealed. So I don't think we can anticipate ever having all the variables made public on a regular basis.

Just remember, despite all the limitations, our enjoyment of sports would be a lot poorer without stats.

BASEBALL

A Statistical Paradise

BASEBALL HAS BEEN CALLED "a small island of activity played in a great ocean of statistics."

Unquestionably, the game sometimes does seem burdened by all the numbers. Yet that weakness is also baseball's strength, because every pitch and every play can be recorded and replayed in pressrooms, barrooms or any other place baseball fans get together.

I don't think it's an overstatement to say that statistics are the lifeblood of baseball, because in no other sport are so many stats available, and in no other sport are the stats studied so carefully not only by fans but also by the players themselves.

Much of the appeal of baseball lies in the opportunity fans have to back up their opinions and arguments with convincing figures. Baseball fans can quote not only well-publicized records but obscure trivia as well. If you asked a Met fan how many games Jerry Koosman won in 1973, he'd probably be able to tell you without hesitation, but if you asked a Jet fan how many touchdown passes Joe Namath had thrown in a particular season, I doubt if he could cite the correct figure. Similarly, a hockey fan would have to think awhile before he gave you Phil Esposito's current goal total. In general, you will get correct answers to comparable questions from a baseball fan more frequently than you will from fans of other sports.

More Valid

Baseball stats are not only more plentiful and better known than the statistics of other sports, they are more valid. In baseball events happen one at a time, and usually through individual effort.

A batter's record is essentially his, and so is a pitcher's record and a fielder's. But when a football running back gets yardage, it's partly as a result of blocking; a basketball player usually scores after someone has passed him the ball at the proper moment; and a hockey player who scores a goal usually has had one or two teammates assisting. As a result, statistics really are more meaningful in baseball than in other sports.

More Precise

Generally, baseball stats are also more precise than those in other sports. The action is clear and easy to follow: it's a ball or a strike, it's a hit or an error.

Compare this with basketball, where three players may go for a rebound, and you can't tell who really deserves credit for the rebound; or football, where there's a question of whether the ball landed closer to the 20-yard line or the 21, or whether the field goal was a 30-yard or 31-yard kick; or hockey, where it's so difficult to determine who deserves an assist. It's more clear-cut in baseball. Sure, sometimes there's a question of whether the error should be given to the player who made the throw or the one who received it, but eventually the question is going to be decided. In baseball you're dealing in specifics.

Make just one mistake, though, and the calls and letters start coming. Early in the 1976 season, Mickey Lolich was pitching for the Mets against the Cardinals. Ralph Kiner, former baseball great who is now a Mets announcer, mentioned that the last time Lolich had pitched against the Cards was in the 1968 World Series, when he hit his only career home run. He hit it, Ralph said, off Bob Gibson. I don't know if I was in the booth at the time—if I had been, I wouldn't have paid much attention, anyhow—but sure enough, the letters came in, most of them addressed to me. The tone was: "Dummy, Mickey Lolich hit the home run in the '68 Series off Nelson Briles." So I checked the record books and asked Lolich, and, sure enough, it *was* Briles. We had to make a correction on the air.

The response from the fans was just another indication of their deep interest in stats.

Time for Stats

One reason that baseball fans are so much more statistics-minded than other sports fans is that the game allows a fan time to contemplate and use his or her imagination. Between pitches, during pitching changes and between innings, there's time to let events sink in and have fans realize, "Hey, this guy's really accomplishing something."

When, on September 1, 1975, Tom Seaver became the first pitcher in major league history to strike out two hundred or more men in eight consecutive years, the fans knew what was happening. People will say, "Aw, statistics, we don't need them. You can't measure anything." Yet Seaver's accomplishment captured the imagination of the forty thousand fans in the park that day and those who were listening at home. The spectators' appreciation reached a crescendo when he struck out Manny Sanguillen to establish the record!

It makes me feel good to see a piece of statistical information used and enjoyed so much.

A Different Type
of Statistician

BECAUSE MY WORK is geared primarily to helping the broadcasters of the Met games, I'm a different type of statistician from most. I sit with the broadcasters and the demands of broadcasting are such that I'm kept busy throughout the game, while a statistician who sits in the press box and serves the writers might be able to complete half his work by the time the game is over. As a result, I have more postgame work to do at home than do most statisticians. There's also a lot of material to prepare for the broadcasters before a game that the print men don't require.

Because I work for the broadcasters, as much as for the ball club, *immediacy* is a must in my job. When a writer asks a press-box statistician, "When's the last time Jon Matlack pitched a three-hitter?" or "When's the last time John Milner hit two homers in game?", the press-box statistician has the luxury of saying, "I'll get that for you in a couple of minutes." But when working in radio and TV, you must have the answer *right away*.

The beauty of a particular piece of information is lost if you don't give it at the precise moment. That's why, over the years, I've learned to anticipate when something special might occur.

A good example of this sixth sense occurred in July, 1976, when the Mets were playing the Cubs in Chicago. The bases were loaded and John Milner stepped to the plate. John had not done well in the series, and in fact, the day before he'd been taken out of the game by Joe Frazier, then the Mets' manager,

20

reportedly for not hustling (though Frazier said it was because Milner's leg was bothering him). Today, he'd popped up twice in critical situations. Now, three Mets took their leads as the count went to 2–0. I just had the feeling that the pitcher would have to come in with the pitch and that Milner was going to hit a grand slam. (I've had feelings like that hundreds of times in my career, but usually what I thought would happen didn't. Still, I always try to be prepared.) So as the pitcher took his stretch, I looked at sheets I'd prepared that list the players' grand slams and noted that Milner had had two in his career. Sure enough, Little Hammer sent the next pitch sailing out of Wrigley Field.

As John began circling the bases, I gave the TV announcer a signal (I held up three fingers and gestured toward the field) that it was John's third career grand slam. Sometimes I'll write out a piece of information, but it's quicker just to give a signal, especially since I also have to give the information to the radio announcer. And I want them to announce it as Milner is circling the bases, not for them to say two batters later, "Oh, by the way, that grand slam by Milner was the third of his career." The beauty of such an item is its immediacy.

My three-finger signal might have been misinterpreted as meaning he had three prior to this one, but the Met broadcasters and I had worked something like eighteen hundred games together, so they were attuned to my signals.

Statistician As Fan

As objective as I try to be in my work, I can't completely suppress the subjective fan in me. I find that, without a doubt, I work better when my team is winning. I ride the crest of partisan enthusiasm.

Early in the 1976 season, for instance, we were playing the Atlanta Braves at Shea Stadium on a cold Tuesday afternoon. We were a run behind in the bottom of the ninth with two men on and two men out. Rookie Bruce Boisclair, a left-handed hitter, was batting against a left-handed pitcher, Pablo Torrealba, who got two sharp-breaking curveballs over on him for strikes. There was no way Boisclair, facing a southpaw, was going to drive in a run. I was so sure the game was as good as over, I wrote down my totals and was preparing to gather up my gear and go home.

But on the next pitch, Boisclair hit a fly ball to right-center field, and, son of a gun, I realized that outfielder Clarence Gaston wasn't going to catch the ball. The ball dropped and rolled to the wall. The first runner came across home plate to score the tying run and the second runner came in to win the game.

There were only about 4,000–5,000 fans in the park, but they were all on their feet screaming and cheering Boisclair, the team was out there mobbing him and, in the broadcast booth, objective statistician Friedman was jumping up and down, yelling, "Way to go, Brucie."

It was bad enough that I'd become a participant, but worse was that I'd forgotten my job. When a game ends, I'm supposed to have my totals ready for the broadcaster. Bob Murphy was doing the play-by-play at the time, and he was involved in the game and excited about the way it had ended, and of course, he was too busy describing the play to put down the totals himself or even to stop and think who the winning and losing pitchers were. That's my job, but I wasn't prepared because I was busy being a fan. It wasn't the first time that's happened and probably won't be the last, because even a statistician gets caught up in the emotions of the game.

Bob Murphy says that when he first started out as a broadcaster, he would let his emotions go and then would have to suffer listening to the playback of what he had done on a tape recorder. "If you start screaming, nobody can understand you," he says. "I think the excitement should be there, but it should be *controlled excitement,* so people can hear and understand each word you're saying, no matter how excited you are."

Another point he makes is that broadcasting in New York is different from anywhere else, because many of the listeners are rooting for the visiting team. "So we don't do any of this 'Come on, gang' or 'We' this or 'We' that," he says. "I try very hard—and I know Lindsey [Nelson] and Ralph [Kiner] do, too—to report the game as though I'm working with a typewriter . . . to be as neutral as I can. . . . But though I try, I can't completely control my own emotions, and Met fans who listen to game after game know darn well who I want to win, even though I don't come out and say 'Come on, gang, let's go out and get them.' "

More Than Numbers

Every statistician is in the information business, and that means more than numbers. I don't provide just statistics, I give information of all kinds. In the course of a year I'll go over the Mets' pressbook or New York Rangers' year-book maybe fifty times, and I'll always find something that I hadn't seen before.

Before a game, I'll look through the opposing team's pressbook, too, and discover little items worth passing along, such as the fact that Freddie Norman of the Cincinnati Reds had a 29–7 lifetime record at Riverfront Stadium. Often it's a personal thing, such as the fellow pitching against Craig Swan is from the same town in Arizona that Swan is. Maybe they went to the same high school or played on the same team, or whatever; I'll try to find out.

In a dull one-sided game I try to find something off the beaten path, a human-interest item, if possible—say, the fact that the same man, Ed Sudol, was the plate umpire in all the longest games the Mets have played.

I'm expected to find out almost anything—from who's going to sing the national anthem and what group or entertainer will perform between games of a double-header, to the gender, weight and name of a baby just born to a ballplayer's wife. Of course, a main concern involves the ballplayers themselves. Was someone hurt in last night's game? If so, will it keep him out of today's line-up? On the road, this is relatively easy to determine, because then I'll get to see the ballplayers on the bus to the ball park, and I can ask John Stearns, for example, whether the injury from the foul tip is going to bench him. At home, though, by the time I get to Shea, the players are already on the field taking batting practice, shagging flies or running laps, and it's not so easy to ascertain the pertinent information.

The accessibility of players on the road makes it easier to obtain all sorts of information—possibly something personal, such as an illness in a player's family; or something specific about his ballplaying, such as a change in batting style. Because there are so many opportunities for informal chats when you're on the road, you're bound to pick up a lot of usable material. Certain things, of course, are off the record, but much of what the players tell you is not, and we may use some of the information weeks or even a month later. A batter may reveal he's contemplating playing winter ball in Puerto Rico, or a pitcher may mention how he pitches to certain hitters.

Picking up this sort of thing is all part of my job, so you can see that being a statistician does not limit one to dealing only with statistics.

Always Something Interesting

Almost every time a batter steps to the plate or a pitcher takes the sign, there is something interesting you can say beyond just "he hits line drives" or "he throws hard."

For instance, Larry Christenson of the Philadelphia Phillies was batting against the Mets in 1976 and Ralph Kiner mentioned that he was the only pitcher in the major leagues to have hit two home runs the year before. That's interesting, and it adds to the enjoyment of the fan listening to or watching the game at home. With a point of interest like that, it's not as if you're inundating anyone with a whole raft of stats. You're just giving a morsel to add to his knowledge and pleasure, and that's what we try to do regularly in our broadcasts.

Trying for Unusual

Whenever possible, we try to call attention to and explain the unusual. One time Gary Nolan, a right-hander, was pitching for the Reds, and Bud Harrelson, a switch-hitter who would usually bat lefty against a right-hander, batted righty. Our broadcasters not only mentioned it, but explained why: Bud was hitting .280 right-handed that season, compared with only a .200 average left-handed. So a question that might have been in the minds of many was answered. True, it wasn't the total answer, because his .280 was basically against left-handed pitching, but it did give a partial explanation for his deviation from the norm.

Ready with the Obscure

We try to be ready with more obscure information of interest, too. For example, one Saturday night in 1976, Montreal pitchers were walking an awful lot of batters, and when the number reached ten I began to wonder whether we were anywhere near a record. Unlike Babe Ruth's home-run total, the record for most walks given by a team in a nine-inning game isn't going to be at your fingertips. You've got to go through a couple of index pages in the record book. I knew if I waited until they walked sixteen, I might be too late. If you say, two innings later, "Oh, by the way, that was a record," you lose the beauty of building up the drama of the situation. So I looked it up right away and found that the record was seventeen, a fact our announcers kept mentioning as the Montreal hurlers walked number thirteen and number fourteen (which was as close as they came to the dubious distinction).

Grasping at Straws

Sometimes, especially when a team has little to cheer about, you really have to scratch for noteworthy items to include in the daily note sheet.

One time I got ribbed in the newspapers for having included the fact that Ron Swoboda and Bud Harrelson had three-game hitting streaks.

"All right, wise guy," I said to one of the needlers, "what would *you* put on a Met note sheet?"

Working for a Losing Team

ONE OF THE THINGS people predicted when I first got the job with the Mets was that I'd have a more difficult job than would a statistician with a winning team. With a losing team, players are being shuffled and you don't get to know them well. Also, the more player changes you have, the more work there is for the statistician. With a team that's winning, everyone is more up for the games, you look forward to coming to the ball park more, and you feel people are paying more attention to what you're doing. And, of course, you become personally attached to some of the ballplayers, so that you're much happier telling positive things about them, such as their accomplishments over a period of time.

But I wasn't to be that fortunate in the first few years I was with the team, though the Mets' record in the 1966 exhibition season was 14–10, which gave rise to some optimism.

The Mets were going to open the 1966 season in the old Cincinnati ball park, Crosley Field. They'd warned me about the way it was set up—that the radio and TV locations were very difficult to get to. The television booth was almost like a photographer's box, in which you had to climb around TV cameras and over barriers. And, because it was right behind home plate, you constantly had to duck foul balls. While the TV booth was almost at ground level, the radio booth was way up on top of the stadium, and it required an elevator to reach. Serving both TV and radio at Crosley would be very difficult.

Because this would be the first regular-season major league game I'd be working, I was understandably very nervous. But Opening Day (traditionally, Cincinnati starts the season a day earlier than the rest of the league) was rained out, and we got rained out the next day and the day after that. So I spent my first three days of the regular season in the Netherland-Hilton Hotel in Cincinnati, just champing at the bit. As each day went by, I got more and more uneasy, more and more apprehensive. It was an unusual situation, comparable, I guess, to going to an office to start a new job and wondering how you're going to do at it, only to have someone tell you, "Come back tomorrow, we don't need you today." Then you go the next day, and the same thing happens.

We flew out of Ohio without playing a game. (It may have been a record for single-season Opening Day rainouts, but that was the least of my concerns.) So my Opening Day had to wait until we got back to New York and met the Atlanta Braves on a Friday. Jack Fisher was on the mound for the Mets and Denny Lemaster was the pitcher for the Braves. There was a crowd of fifty-two thousand at the ball park on a nice, sunny day.

The Mets scored a run in the first, Atlanta tied it in the sixth, and then Cleon Jones homered in the eighth to give us a 2–1 lead going into the ninth. Joe Torre, then with the Braves, doubled. Lee Thomas singled to right, scoring Torre, and when Cleon threw the ball into the Braves' dugout, Thomas wound up on third. Thomas scored what proved to be the winning run when Denis Menke laid down a squeeze bunt.

The Mets came back to win the next day, and again on Sunday. I enjoyed a great emotional high driving home that Sunday afternoon, having completed my first series with the Mets, who for the first time in their history were over .500 with a 2–1 record and in the first division, though only in fifth place. And I thought that perhaps I was not working for a losing ball club. But the Mets lost their next five games in a row, and we never saw the .500 mark again the rest of the season.

A Lot to Learn

As the season wore on, I realized more and more what a novice I was and how much I had to learn.

There were times when the announcers had to scold me because I hadn't taken time to think something out. For instance, I'd rush to get the name of a pitcher coming from the bullpen and would get the wrong name, or I wouldn't be quick enough checking whether the official scorer had ruled a hit or an error, a wild pitch or passed ball.

I was unfamiliar with the people around the league, the ball parks and hotels. The whole business of traveling added to my difficulties.

When I first started with the Mets, I was almost awed by the fact that I'd be living in the same hotels, traveling on the same planes, eating in the same restaurants as major league ballplayers—athletes who until now had been just names in a box score or figures on a television screen.

But baseball traveling isn't always glamorous. It takes you away from your family for long periods. The travel itself is fatiguing, especially in the late stages of the season, if your team is going nowhere in the standings. Your body has trouble adjusting to the time changes and to the long, cramped bus rides to and from airports.

However, there are advantages to being on the road. There are fewer distractions than at home, and my accessibility to the players is greater.

Wes Westrum

The manager during my first year with the Mets was Wes Westrum, a nice man who seemed to be going through a learning period just as I was. I got the impression he used the statistics I gave him almost as a crutch, as if to say, "It's not my fault that we're losing this much, but I haven't got a .300 hitter, I haven't got a twenty-game winner." Wes was basically a shy man who was in the unenviable position of following the legendary Casey Stengel as manager. Casey had been the Mets' manager since their inception.

All in all, it was an experience. Most of the statistics were negative ones, not only one losing streak after another, but items such as, "After five years, the Mets still have never beaten Juan Marichal; they have an 0–17 lifetime record against him." The same was true of their record against Larry Jackson or Sandy Koufax or Bob Gibson over those years. It was just one negative statistic after another.

Book of "Neggies"

Jack Lang, a sportswriter who has covered the Mets since 1962 and has helped me dozens of times, keeps what is referred to as "Jack Lang's Book of Neggies," so called because in the early years of the Mets all we had were really *negative* statistics. Some have carried over to more recent years. For example,

28

when Lee Mazzilli went to center field in 1976, he became the forty-ninth player to play center for the Mets. The same season, Leo Foster became the fifty-third player in Met history to play third base.

Lang has the won-lost record of every single road trip the Mets have made. Because I didn't join the club until 1966, Jack was invaluable in helping me catch up on the first four years.

But by the time I joined the Mets, most of the old jokes about the team had worn thin. People involved with the club were taking their defeats to heart. They no longer had Casey Stengel to throw out a funny one-liner to take their minds off what was happening.

1967

The brightest spot of the 1967 season was the emergence of Tom Seaver as a future star. The most positive statistic I had to follow that season was Tom's pursuit of Al Jackson's club record of thirteen victories.

I had seen a lot of ballplayers coming and going, but 1967 would mark the first dismissal of a manager I had ever experienced. On September 21, Wes Westrum was told that he would not be coming back as manager. Salty Parker, one of his coaches, took over as interim manager. I remember asking myself, "What do you say to a man you have been fairly close with? How do you console him about being fired? Do you wish him good luck? Do you say, 'It wasn't your fault'?" I couldn't find the answers, so I let him slip quietly out of the locker room, without saying anything to him. I've seen him many times since and I've always wondered whether, as touchy as the situation was, I shouldn't have gone over and said something to him the day he was dismissed. But at that point, I just didn't know what to say.

During the 1967 season, the Mets used fifty-four different players, the most ever by a National League team; and we used twenty-seven pitchers, which set a National League record and equaled an American League record. This added to my work as statistician. Every time a new player joined the club, I had to get his record, whether it was in the minor leagues or with another big league team. I needed to get all his particulars: his height, weight, date and place of birth, when he started in professional ball, his entire career record. When a player comes from another major league team, he requires two lines on the stat sheet, one for his total record for the season, and one for his record just with the Mets. It seemed that every day the team was changing players and I was adding new

29

names to the sheets and deleting others and compiling all the information I could find on players coming and going. (When a player leaves, we add his name to a category on the bottom of the batting sheet if he's a hitter, or at the bottom of the pitching stats if he's a pitcher. Some statisticians list these players as "Departed"; I list them as "Others.")

By the end of the 1967 season, I had two years of experience under my belt and I had a good deal of self-confidence, and I think the broadcasters and others with whom I came in contact also had confidence in me. I knew my way around the league and the different press boxes, and so forth, all of which helped my enjoyment of the job and made me better at it.

A Different Kind
of Man

GIL HODGES was different in almost every respect from the previous Met manager, Wes Westrum. Wes was quieter and did not have the imposing physical presence that Hodges had.

I'll never forget the first time Gil met the team. It was at Huggins-Stengel Field in St. Petersburg, Florida. The players encircled Gil, eyeing him almost uneasily. The new skipper of the last-place Mets simply cleared his throat and said, "My name is Hodges."

Gil wasn't the easiest person to get to know, but he was a born leader who commanded respect. Yogi Berra remained as a coach, but Gil brought three coaches with him from the Washington Senators—Rube Walker, Eddie Yost and Joe Pignatano. They became good traveling companions and friends of mine over the next ten years.

Hodges was a different experience for those players, such as Cleon Jones, Ron Swoboda and Ed Kranepool, who had played under Stengel and Westrum. With his great physical strength and huge hands, Hodges made an awesome impression. He projected the image of the old-fashioned father. Though he spoke softly, his rules about behavior, attitude and performance were very, very clear. He communicated more by action than by words.

Gil also had a subtle sense of humor that ran the gamut from deadpan put-ons to outrageous clichés. Though his put-ons often put newcomers offstride, Hodges was sensitive enough not to let them suffer embarrassment.

31

The Longest Game

In Hodges' first season as manager, we opened on the West Coast, first San Francisco, then Los Angeles and finally Houston. In the last game of the road trip, played in the Astrodome, Tom Seaver faced Don Wilson of the Astros and both pitchers were superb. Seaver gave up only two hits in ten innings and Wilson yielded just five hits in nine innings. Neither team could score. The game kept rolling along—twelve innings, fifteen innings, eighteen innings, twenty innings, without a score. In the twenty-second inning, Les Rohr, who seven hours earlier had been pitching batting practice, became the eighth Met pitcher to enter the game. Finally, in the twenty-fourth inning, about 1:30 A.M. Houston time, Norm Miller of the Astros led off with a base hit. Bob Aspromonte hit a perfect double-play ball to Al Weis, but the ball went through Al for an error, and Houston went on to win the longest 1–0 game ever played. It took six hours and six minutes.

Both Tommie Agee and Ron Swoboda went 0-for-10 in that game, losing 100–150 points on their averages, and I don't think they ever recovered.

It was the first time I had ever been through a marathon game like that. As a game wears on and on, a sort of mental fatigue sets in and you get a little giddy. It reaches a point where you begin to hope that nobody scores, so that you'll be able to say you saw and worked the longest 1–0 game in major league history. The announcers felt this way, and so did I.

With five games left to play in the season, we were battling to stay out of last place. (As a matter of fact, we ended up in ninth place, a game ahead of the Astros and only three behind the eighth-place Phillies, which was quite an accomplishment. So was winning seventy-three games—Hodges had said we could win seventy.) But this particular night, September 24, 1968, something happened that obscured the results of the game with the Braves in Atlanta and the year-end standings.

Hodges, who had had a heavy cold for some time, pitched some batting practice before the game. He didn't look well and, as it turned out, he didn't feel well. Soon after the game started, he told Rube Walker, our pitching coach, to take charge of the team, and he went back into the locker room. There he complained of chest pains to Gus Mauch, who was then our trainer, and he was taken to the hospital.

It was hours before the exact nature of his illness was revealed. I went back to the hotel that night, not thinking that Gil was seriously ill. Suddenly the phone began ringing. Reporters were calling from the wire services, the Atlanta papers and the New York papers, asking, "Would you please comment on Gil Hodges' health?" and "We have reports he's suffered a heart attack; would you talk about it, please?" I had no idea of the severity of his illness and I wasn't even certain he had suffered a heart attack, so I really couldn't comment. And I wasn't about to call the hospital.

The next morning, the newspapers and wire services were noting that "Art Friedman, club official, could not confirm whether or not Hodges had suffered a heart attack." By the time the papers came out, though, it was known that he had suffered a heart attack.

The calls I was getting ordinarily would have been received by Harold Weissman or Matt Winick of our public relations department, one of whom would travel with us and answer reporters' questions. But because we were so near the end of the season, neither one was with us in Atlanta, and so I was the one who took the calls. I don't think I slept half an hour at a time that night. When I wasn't on the phone with someone asking about Gil, I was lying awake thinking of him.

1969

Gil recuperated over the winter and was back at the helm for the 1969 season, which developed into certainly one of the most incredible ever in professional sports. It was tremendously exciting for me to be part of it.

The season began on a real downer. The Montreal Expos, playing their first game ever in the National League, beat us, 11–10, in a wild affair. The winning pitcher was Don Shaw, a former Met. Fortunately, it was no indication of what was to come.

Starting in mid-August, we realized we were in a pennant race. The Mets were the talk of the baseball world, and by the time we played the Expos in a twi-night double-header on September 10, the tension was thick in the Met office. Matt Winick's and Harold Weissman's phones in our P.R. office never stopped ringing. I was busier than I'd ever been, and loving every minute of it. I was getting to Shea Stadium as early as four hours before the game. I was ecstatic that every bit of work I was preparing was being read and seen, not by just five or six writers in New York, but by dozens and dozens of writers all over the country. The Mets had captured the imagination of the sports world.

On the night of September 10, we finally reached the Promised Land. Ken Boswell singled to center to drive in the winning run in a 3–2 victory over

Montreal, and we moved .001 percentage points ahead of the Cubs into first place. Two days later, we enjoyed a remarkable double victory in a twi-night double-header over the Pirates. Each game was won by a 1–0 score, and amazingly, our winning pitchers—Koosman, who pitched the opening shutout, and Don Cardwell, who pitched the second—drove in the runs. It was probably something that had never happened before in major league baseball. I tried desperately to find out for sure, but there was no record kept on anything so obscure as that.

On September, 15, we were part of another amazing story. Steve Carlton struck out nineteen Mets, breaking the major league record of eighteen held by both Sandy Koufax and Bob Feller—but Carlton still lost the game, as Ron Swoboda hit two two-run homers for the Mets.

Bob Moose of the Pirates no-hit us on September 20, cutting our lead to four games, but we came back to beat Pittsburgh in a double-header.

When, on September 24, we defeated the Cardinals, 6–0, we clinched the National League Eastern Division title. The champagne we drank—and spilled, and bathed in—was the first of three such locker room celebrations. The second came, of course, after we swept the Braves for the National League pennant; and the third, after we beat the Baltimore Orioles, four games to one, to win the World Series.

Looking Back

It wasn't until a month after the season ended that I could look back calmly and reflect on the amazing events of 1969. Though I had had a lot more work and responsibility, it never seemed like drudgery. I had enjoyed being sought after in any city that the Mets went to, even cities where the teams were out of contention. Question after question would be directed to me: "What's that incredible hitting streak Clendenon is on?" "What has Shamsky done in the last six weeks?" "Tell us about Seaver's last half dozen performances." "What's the Mets' magic number?"

Fan Club and Other Recognition

It was during the 1969 season with the enormous interest in the day-to-day activities of the Mets that people began to recognize me. Before this, some people may have known my name because it was mentioned on every radio and TV broadcast involving the Mets. But now I was besieged by autograph-seekers every time I entered or left Shea Stadium. (To be honest, they were satisfied with the autograph of *anyone* connected with the Mets.)

But recognition took other forms, too. For years I had cashed my checks at the same bank in Brooklyn, where I was living at the time. The checks always bore the Mets emblem, but until '69 nobody gave it a second thought. Artie Friedman is probably a clerk or some kind of maintenance man, they thought. But once the Mets caught fire in 1969, people became aware of everyone's connection with the team, and it reached the point where if there was a long line when I came into the bank, the assistant manager would take me aside and ask, "Mr. Friedman, can we cash that check for you?" And I would go right to the head of the line and have it done. I enjoyed the same kind of response in grocery stores and other such establishments. Even when I'd walk around in Manhattan, people would recognize me. It was very flattering to my ego to come out of the background and share and bask in some of the glory reflected by the Mets.

During the middle of the season, I became the first, and probably the only statistician to have his own fan club. Organized by a group of young fellows on Long Island, the Art Friedman Fan Club lasted for about two years. At its peak, the club had a membership of about seventy young people who went to baseball, basketball and hockey games. Like the clubs Marv Albert and I had formed when we were teenagers, this group held meetings and even put out a publication. It was nice while it lasted, and I don't suppose any other statistician has ever been fortunate enough to receive such an honor.

1970

The longest winning streak of 1970 was only seven games, and though the Mets were in the race until the final weekend of the season, it didn't have the excitement of 1969.

The highlight of the 1970 season came early, when, on April 27, Tom Seaver became the first pitcher ever to strike out nineteen batters in a day game. He finished with an incredible flourish, striking out the last ten San Diego batters in a row. Unfortunately, because it was a weekday afternoon game, there was only a small crowd on hand. But for those who were there, Seaver's performance was a supreme thrill, one of the most exciting things I've ever watched.

Otherwise, the season was a letdown for the Mets. The only thing that

35

didn't disappoint us was the attendance—we hit 2,697,479, the second highest in the history of baseball and the highest ever for a New York team. The daily big crowds fired everyone up and made everyone work harder. The charismatic feeling of '69 carried over to every game, but the glow wasn't enough.

1971

Another disappointing season followed. In 1971 we finished in a tie for third with a record of 83–79, fourteen games out of first place.

Again, Tom Seaver was almost the whole story. Every time he went out to pitch, there was excitement. He established the league record for strikeouts by a right-handed pitcher with 289, and led the league with a fantastic 1.76 ERA.

Bud Harrelson was an All-Star selection at shortstop that year; we also had a super bullpen in Tug McGraw and Danny Frisella. We had great crowds again, but our hitting fell off. Jerry Koosman, plagued by arm and shoulder miseries, had a disappointing 6–11 record.

After having tasted championship champagne only two years earlier, it was getting tougher and tougher to accept mediocrity again. But that's what confronted us, and by August we were dragging ourselves to the ball park.

1972

In 1972 I missed most of spring training and joined the team in West Palm Beach, Florida, in time for its last few scheduled exhibition games. Arriving at the hotel on Friday night, I learned that the rumored players' strike had become a reality. The remaining exhibition games were canceled and there was no telling when the season would begin. I decided to stick it out, at least over the weekend. The few of us who were left around the hotel—the manager, coaches, broadcasters and newspapermen—decided that if nothing broke, we'd fly back to New York on Monday.

I spent a peaceful Saturday and much of Sunday. About five o'clock I saw Gil Hodges and his coaches walking slowly off the golf course, when suddenly Gil fell over backwards like a fallen oak. Naturally, I ran right over. I'll never forget the sight of that giant of a man, his World Series ring on one finger of his huge hand, lying absolutely still and bleeding profusely from the back of his head, which had struck the pavement.

36

Rube Walker and Eddie Yost ran to phone for medical aid. I ran to the nearest motel room and banged frantically on the door until someone opened it. I just pushed right past him and grabbed a blanket and pillow for Gil.

Within two minutes, medical help arrived from a nearby hospital, but by then he had almost turned blue. The medical men massaged his heart and gave Gil oxygen before taking him by ambulance to the emergency ward of the hospital in West Palm Beach. We followed by car and for half an hour, equipment manager Nick Torman, the coaches, Harold Weissman and I paced the floor. Then the doctor came out of Emergency shaking his head, and said we had lost Gil. It was, of course, an awful shock for all of us.

Joe Pignatano and Harold Weissman agreed that media people would have to be made aware of the tragedy. (Until then, no newspaperman had even known of Gil's collapse.) But someone from among us would have to break the sad tidings to the Hodges family before they heard the terrible news on the air. Joe Pignatano, Gil's good friend, eventually made the call to Gil's family in Brooklyn.

The whole episode was an event I wish hadn't happened. It was something I'll never forget.

Yogi

Yogi Berra took over as the Mets' manager, and he was a different experience altogether. In the years I knew him, first as a coach for the Mets and then manager, I was struck by how much he loved baseball and working with baseball statistics. He couldn't talk enough about baseball, and he'd call me every day for some statistical tidbits. Yogi was almost always the first one up in the morning and down to the coffee shop, where he'd carefully examine the box scores and accounts of all the games. He always wanted to know the score of other games in both leagues. The former hitting great and pennant-winning manager of the Yankees just wanted to know what was happening in baseball.

He is always fun to be around, and I could understand why Yogi Berra stories were legend. Because of his love for baseball and for what he was doing, on almost every flight he'd walk down the aisle of the plane and demand, "Hey, kiddo, gimme one of those things." I knew he meant the stats sheet. He'd take it and read it all from top to bottom. Then we'd be on the bus or another plane, and he'd do the same thing again. I always made sure I kept extra copies of the stat sheets with me.

37

In Yogi's first season with the Mets, we got off to a fantastic start. On May 21, we had a 25–7 record and were in first place, six games ahead.

But then we had an incredible run of injuries. Things got so bad that on successive days we had to use two catchers, Jerry Grote and Duffy Dyer, in the outfield. Our team finished with a .225 batting average, the lowest in the league, and we ended up again with eighty-three wins, this time against seventy-three losses (the season had been shortened by the players' strike), and we finished 13½ games out of first place.

Even More Amazing

In some ways the 1973 season was even more amazing than 1969, for the simple reason that we didn't realize what was happening; we just caught the crest of a wave and rode it through the final weeks of the season to the pennant. "You gotta believe," Tug McGraw said, and we did.

The Mets were in last place as late as August 30, when we were 6½ games out of first and ten games below .500. Then we began our move and won twenty out of twenty-eight games in the month of September, finally taking the pennant on the day *after* the season ended (because of some rain delays in Chicago).

Throughout the year, the National League East was known as the "least" division and the "division of mediocrity," because all the teams in it were hanging around the .500 mark and it almost seemed as if no one wanted to win it. (Of course, *everybody* wanted to win it.)

I enjoyed this season more than 1969 because virtually every day we were passing one more team and moving up one more notch. It was the kind of thing you could build up to—more so than in 1969, when everything seemed to happen so fast. We had the schedule for all the teams we were contending with figured out days in advance; we worked on what we thought our pitching rotation would be for the next week or ten days, and which pitcher we expected the Mets to be facing in the next series and the series after that. Up until the day before the season ended, five teams had a shot at winning the flag, so there was an abundance of "magic number" combinations and other statistical mysteries and certainties. September, 1973, was the busiest and most exciting month I have ever been through in all my years in sports.

We took over first place on September 21 and never lost it. We came into Chicago the last weekend of the season and got rained out the first two days we were there. The tension pulled tighter. Finally, on Sunday we got to play a double-header with the Cubs, losing the first game, 1–0, but then winning the nightcap, 9–2, behind Jerry Koosman. A double-header was scheduled for Monday, but we won the first game, 6–4, with Seaver on the mound, and that clinched the pennant, so there was no need to play the second game. By mutual consent it was called off, and we started the celebration.

One player who was unhappy with the cancellation was Milt Pappas, the scheduled Cub pitcher, who was warming up for that game, despite the inclement weather; he was planning to make a bid for his one-hundredth National League win. But umpire Augie Donatelli, in the last regular-season game of his career, declared the game canceled. Pappas stood there, hands on hips, shaking his head as if he knew he'd never get a shot at number 100 in the National League. He was right; he never pitched again in the major leagues.

We had a tremendous playoff series with Cincinnati, which included a melee after Pete Rose slid into Bud Harrelson. The playoff series went the limit, and we won it, three games to two. After that, the World Series against the Oakland A's seemed almost anticlimactic. After leading three games to two, we flew to Oakland and lost the final two games, and the Series.

World Series

IN BOTH 1969 and 1973, I worked the World Series games played at Shea, but I didn't go to the away games in Baltimore in '69 or in Oakland in '73. One of the reasons is that the home team supplies all the statistics and notes about both their own team and the visitors, so there was no need for me to type a stat sheet or provide other information when the games were out-of-town. We didn't have any local (WOR) telecasts of the Series games, which were carried on network television, so I just watched them on TV. I worked the home games, and then updated what had happened in the road games, so I could include those figures in the stat sheets I prepared for the later home games.

Both years, after the hectic pennant races and especially after the tremendously exciting and emotional playoff with the Reds in 1973, I found the Series almost a letdown—even though we went to seven games with the Oakland A's.

Everything takes on an entirely different character when you're involved in a playoff or World Series. The players enjoy being in the national, and even international, spotlight, and I feel as if everyone is examining my work under a microscope. You've got the top media men from all over the country in attendance, which makes you extra careful about your work.

People you've worked with all year who are ordinarily very relaxed and loose seem to tense up when the playoffs and Series begin. You're accustomed to traveling on the plane with your own players and the local writers with whom you've developed a relaxed relationship, but now everyone seems a little uptight. All sorts of people are traveling with you—from owners and front-office people to columnists and magazine writers you've had little contact with all season.

Even the fans at the ball park seem different from the kind you're used to having in regular-season play. Just the change of season, to fall weather, helps make it a whole new experience, one that's difficult to put into words. But I feel fortunate to have been through two post-season series.

1974

The 1974 season was a tremendous downer. We had a terrible year, finishing twenty games below .500, which is incredible for a team that had gone to the seventh game of the World Series the year before. Seaver had a problem with his hip; McGraw had a bad year. We couldn't do anything right. It was the least enjoyable year I spent with the Mets. We never got in contention for the pennant and stayed well below .500 for most of the season.

1975

In 1975 we came within four games of first place in the Eastern Divison in early September, but again we never seriously contended for the title. We finished two games over .500 with an 82–80 record. Yogi Berra was fired as manager in August and replaced by Roy McMillan, the first-base coach.

The season wasn't without its highlights. Tom Seaver, recovered from his hip problem, won twenty-two games and the Cy Young award. Dave Kingman, acquired from the Giants before the season started, set a club home-run record of thirty-six. Rusty Staub became the first player in the club's history to knock in one hundred runs. So we had some interesting things to work with as the season drew to a close.

1976

In 1976 Joe Frazier, a successful manager in the Mets' farm system, was the new skipper. The Mets thought they would be pennant contenders in 1976, but though they finished with a respectable record (86–76), they wound up in third place, fifteen games back of the Phillies. From the second month of the season on, we were never serious pennant contenders.

Under conditions like this, you have to treat every game as a separate event. An important part of my job, possibly the most important part, is to make sure we have enough information about what else is going on in baseball, in order to keep our listeners informed and increase their enjoyment.

In keeping with our policy of informing listeners about other teams, we paid close attention—and gave almost inning-by-inning reports—of every game San Diego's Randy Jones pitched, until he fell off in early August. At the time of the All-Star break he had looked like a shoo-in to become a thirty-game winner. Also, we gave attention to the large crowds that the Padres were drawing whenever Jones (who went on to win the Cy Young award) pitched.

The same thing applied whenever Mark "The Bird" Fidrych took the mound for the Detroit Tigers. This rookie had captured the imagination of most of the country's baseball fans with his flaky mannerisms and excellent pitching skills. He had a chance to become the first American League rookie to win twenty games since Bob Grim did it in 1954. Fidrych did finish with nineteen wins. Late in the season, Minnie Minoso appeared in a major league ball game for the first time in twelve years and, at the age of fifty-three (!) became the oldest player ever to get a base hit, and the third oldest player ever to play in a major league game.

When our broadcasters weren't talking about Minnie, they might be discussing the pursuit by the Oakland A's of the all-time stolen-base record, or the Reds' attempt to be the first National League team to win a pennant without any of its starting pitchers winning as many as fifteen games. We'd dwell on teams with long winning or losing streaks more than we would have, had the Mets been involved in a heated pennant race.

This is not to say there wasn't ample material about the Mets. Dave Kingman was battling Mike Schmidt, last year's winner, for the home-run title. Had he won it, he would have been the first Met ever to win the home-run championship. As it was, he came within one of tying for the lead, though he was out of action with an injury for six weeks. Before the injury, he was hitting homers at a record pace, and had he approached Roger Maris's single-season record of sixty-one homers, it would have been a statistician's dream.

1977

The 1977 season was pretty much a disaster, both on and off the field. The big event was the trade of Tom Seaver to the Reds. For that and other causes, the front office was under constant pressure. Attendance was down by 400,000 from 1976, and there were so many young, inexperienced players in the club, it was like being with some other team.

As always, there were a few bright spots, notably the play of a few of the youngsters—especially Steve Henderson, who came to us in the Seaver trade. If there was one highlight for the team, it was winning three games from the Cardinals the last weekend of the season. That kept us from losing one hundred games (we finished 64–98), which tells you what kind of season it was.

Tools of the Trade

LIKE ANY OTHER specialists, statisticians have tools of the trade. It's probably fair to say that a statistician can be only as good as his tools.

The press guide from each team is always part of the paraphernalia I carry with me, as are the box scores of every National League game of the season and the daily standings. (You might want to make the point that Cincinnati has had a hell of a month in July. Now, how far were they ahead on July 1? You've got it right there.) Some of the information, of course, is never used; a lot, you might refer to only once or twice a year. But you have it handy when it's needed.

I always carry record books with me. There's the *Sporting News* official record book and a record book put out by the Elias Sports Bureau. I go through these books possibly thirty or forty times a year, on a plane or bus, and find different items of interest.

Since it's part of a statistician's job to be familiar with the rules, I carry a rulebook at all times, and there are various league publications I find helpful, too, as well as the day-by-day records of each of the Mets and schedules of both leagues. Looking ahead in the schedule gives the broadcasters the basis for saying something like, "Pittsburgh is going to Philadelphia for a crucial five-game series" or "This is the start of a ten-game road trip" for a particular team coming into Shea.

One book I often use gives every conceivable combination of at-bats, hits and batting averages, so that if a man who was 83-for-265 gets a hit, I can look at

44

a particular column and immediately tell you what his new batting average is
(.317). And if he goes hitless the next two times, I can immediately give you his
up-to-the-minute percentage (.315). I look those up most of the time, but certain
figures don't require it. If he gets his eighth hit in thirty-two at-bats, I know
without looking that he's now at .250. There are times of the season when a base
hit or failure to hit causes a greater change in batting average than others.
Obviously, if a man who was 2-for-4 on the first day of the season and thus has a
.500 average gets a hit his next time up, his average soars one hundred points to
.600. Later in the season, if he has one hundred hits in 321 at-bats for a .312
average, a hit in his next time at-bat isn't going to add more than two points to his
average. Near the end of the season, a hit may not even change his average
appreciably.

In addition to printed material, I keep a calculator and a pair of binoculars
with me. Even though I was a mediocre math student, I don't always rely on the
calculator, partly because often it doesn't work or it causes problems. Occasionally I've had calculators smashed to bits by foul balls.

Binoculars help me see who's up in the bullpen. (They're sometimes used to
get a closer look at an attractive spectator, but that involves statistics of another
variety.) I've been careless watching the bullpen on occasion. I'd seen a particular reliever warming up, and after a few batters, the manager made a pitching
change and I assumed the man coming in was the one I had spotted in the
bullpen. But the manager called in a different reliever, a fact I neglected to notice
until it was too late. The announcer, going by the pitching card I handed him,
sounded foolish when the mistaken identity became apparent.

There's really no excuse for mistakes like that, which are caused by lack of
concentration or laziness. But in a sense, working with people long enough
means never having to say you're sorry. They know I have enough pride that I
feel bad, but there's no point in saying so. I just shouldn't let it happen again.

Probably the most embarrassing thing that's ever happened to me took place
in a Mayor's Trophy game between the Mets and the Yankees in Yankee
Stadium in 1970. I had been to the stadium once or twice before, and I didn't
leave enough time to get there as early as I would have liked. Arriving only about
an hour before the game was due to start, I hurried to the pressroom and was
pleasantly surprised to see the line-ups posted on the wall. *Great*, I thought. *I
won't have to go to the dugout to get them, and so I can go straight up to the
booth.*

Our announcers copied the line-ups from what I had copied from the pressroom wall, including the fact that Thurman Munson was playing first for the

45

Yankees. In the Yankee first, our broadcaster reported, "The ball is well hit by Thurman Munson," and he wound up on second with a double. When he came up again in the third and belted a homer, the announcer said, "I didn't know Munson had that much power. He really pasted the ball."

An inning or so later, our engineer called me over and said, "Listen, we've been swamped with calls. The Mets [broadcasters] have said Thurman Munson has hit a home run, and the Yankees [broadcasters] have said it was Danny Cater who hit the homer. You better check."

I got my binoculars out and sure enough, the number on "Munson" was 10, not 15. I checked further and found that I'd had the wrong guy playing for four innings, and not just playing, but hitting a double and a home run. What was I going to do?

When the inning ended, I took a deep breath and told our broadcasters, "Guys, I really messed up. Thurman Munson is in Fort Dix, New Jersey, serving military time. The man we called Thurman Munson is Danny Cater."

Our announcers went on the air and said simply, "We're sorry, we've given you the wrong information," and proceeded to correct the mistaken identity. But I was so embarrassed and humiliated that it bothered me for weeks. Had it been a National League player, I wouldn't have made that kind of mistake, because I know just about every NL player by his mannerisms and characteristics. I wouldn't have needed to check a uniform number to know who was who.

Lindsey Nelson, who was doing the play-by-play for us when "Munson" first batted, is kind enough to say it wasn't my fault, since Thurman had been listed on the line-up cards and in Lindsey's words, "We wouldn't have known Thurman Munson if he was coming down the street."

After the game, Lindsey was in the pressroom talking with Lee McPhail, who was then the Yankees' general manager, and with Ralph Houk, who was the manager. When Houk asked Lindsey who he thought was the outstanding player in the game, Lindsey answered, "Thurman Munson."

Fortunately, there haven't been many of those. During the '76 season, Al Hrabosky was pitching against us for the Cardinals one inning. In the next inning, we saw a small St. Louis left-hander out there on the mound who looked just like Hrabosky, the Mad Hungarian, with his long hair and mustache. Since there had been no pinch-hitter for Hrabosky, and since we had heard no announcement of a pitching change, we assumed Hrabosky was still pitching.

With two outs and two strikes on him, John Milner lined a hard single to right, and something struck me as wrong. Milner usually isn't able to pull the ball so sharply off Hrabosky, who's such a hard thrower. I took my binoculars out and looked toward the mound. The pitcher certainly looked like Hrabosky—smallish, left-handed, Hrabosky's motion. But no mustache!

I decided I'd better check my scorecard. As I was doing this, the pitcher balked and Milner went to second. Then he walked Joe Torre and threw a wild pitch, so he'd done nothing but call attention to himself. Meanwhile, my heart was sinking and I was in a state of shock. My suspicions were confirmed: the pitcher who had faced four Met batters this inning wasn't Hrabosky, but Doug Capilla, a rookie left-hander who had beaten the Mets last weekend in his first major league appearance. I had to break the embarrassing news to Lindsey Nelson, who was broadcasting the game, that we had announced the wrong pitcher for four batters.

"There was a time," Lindsey comments, "when we wouldn't have acknowledged it, we would have tried to cover it up some way. But everybody realizes that you do make mistakes, so you just say, 'I made a mistake; it's not Hrabosky, it's his second cousin. It's Capilla.' "

Late in the season, when a kind of mental fatigue sets in and new players have come up, it's easy to be fooled, but you try not to let it happen. It was the first time that it had happened to me with my own team, and I promise it will be the last. It upset me and I know it upset all three announcers, because we take pride in our work and hate to make a mistake of that magnitude.

Dee-fense Is Part of the Job

I mentioned earlier how I've had calculators demolished by foul balls. The same thing can happen to the statistician if he's not careful. That's why defense is a vital part of the job.

When I first started out, I got hit several times with foul balls that came into the broadcast booth. Now no matter how busy I am, I always stop what I'm doing and watch the pitch.

There are several stadiums in the majors where it's particularly dangerous to be in the booth, especially if there's a fastball pitcher on the mound. For instance, Jim Maloney, who used to be with Cincinnati, pitched about as fast as anyone in the league. Batters would be swinging late at him, and the balls would come flying into the booth at Crosley Field, where the Reds used to play. That reminded me always to look at the pitch. You save your skin, and you're spared the embarrassment of having missed what happened on the play.

47

Missed Play

There have been times when I didn't follow my own advice and consequently missed events. For instance, we were playing the Cardinals in St. Louis early in the 1976 season and the Cardinal pitcher, Eric Rasmussen, hit a Skip Lockwood pitch to left-center field. As he rounded first base, we knew it was a sure stand-up double.

A rule I try to follow is to watch every play until it's completely finished, until the pitcher is ready to deliver the next pitch. This time, I broke my own rule and didn't watch it to conclusion; neither did our broadcasters. Matter-of-factly, I marked down Rasmussen's double and updated his batting average, and looked back to the action. There wasn't any. The field was clear; the Mets had run in from their field positions, and the Cardinals were starting to come out onto the field. Obviously the inning was over, but none of us knew why. It put the play-by-play man in an embarrassing situation, and it was my fault.

All he could do was give the cue for the after-inning commercial and say, "Well, folks, now back to the station. . . . When we come back, we'll try to explain to you what happened."

Needless to say, while the commercial was on, I hustled to the press box to find out what had happened: Rasmussen had missed first base, a fact that Mets first baseman Ed Kranepool pointed out to the umpire. The Mets' second baseman, Felix Millan, put the tag on Rasmussen, who was declared out by the first-base umpire. We got those facts on the air as soon as the commercial was over, but we should have had them immediately.

I had learned a long time ago—it was put to me in very explicit terms—that when I make a mistake or get careless, I'm not the one who's going to be publicly embarrassed. The broadcaster suffers the humiliation. He obviously can't say, "It's not my fault; Artie Friedman screwed up." He's got to accept the implied responsibility. I must keep in mind at all times that my mistake can make him seem foolish in front of thousands and thousands of people.

Western Union Ticker

A tool we rely on heavily is the Western Union ticker. There is usually one in both the radio and the TV broadcasting booths, and if we're broadcasting on radio and TV, I'll keep both machines going. The ticker is usually close to the

N..PHA...WUPS..NY..KOOSMAN   ...PHA..UNDERWOOD
                    ..21-9   ..10-5.

N..PHA..BATS..NY..KOOSMAN...AND..STEARNS..PHA..UNDERWOOD..AND..BOONE

..N..NY   ...N..NY ..PHA   .N..NY   ..PHA
    .0....   .0   .I...   .000   .100..

N..NY   ..PHA   .N..NY   ..PHA
  .000.I0   .100.0..   .000.I00   .I00.000..

REED   ..PTG..PHA .TH   ..N..NY   ..PHA
  ..8-7   .7 ..   .000.I00.00   .I00.000.00..

        ..N..PHA..GARBER..   ..PTG..PHA .TH
                      .8-3   .9 ..

        ...N..PHA..VUCKOVICH..HHR..NO ..PHA .TH..NONE.ON
                              .I   .9   ..

  .N..NY   ..PHA
      .000.I00.000...I.5.I   .I00.000.001...2.8.I

        ...WP..GARBER   ..LP..KOOSMAN   ..
                  ..9-3   ..21-10

        ..TIME   ...ATTENDANCE
              .I.59   .23.084.

broadcasting location, and the closer it is, the better, since that permits me to get the scores down on paper quickly and then on the air.

On p. 49 are a few samples of ticker tape we work from. In the top row of tape, "N" stands for National League, "PHA" means the game is being played in Philadelphia. "WUPS" stands for "warm-ups," that is, the pitchers warming up for that game. They are Koosman, with a 21-9 record, for "N.Y.," New York, and Underwood, with a 10-5 record, for "PHA," Philadelphia. (Of course, I'd be *at* the Mets game and wouldn't need this. But it's a valid example.)

A few minutes later, Western Union sends additional information—"BATS" for "batteries," the pitchers and catchers for each team. So the second row of tape means that in a National League game at Philadelphia the batteries are Koosman pitching and Stearns catching (New York), and Underwood pitching and Boone catching (Philadelphia).

In the third row, the game has started and New York has failed to score in the first inning, but "PHA—1" means Philadelphia scored a run in the bottom of the first. (The score is transmitted every half inning.) At the end of three innings, you can see New York has three zeros and Philadelphia has just the single run in the bottom of the first.

In the fourth row, you will notice that New York has scored a run in the top of the fourth. (Read the tapes straight across, as if they contained only one line. Each digit represents runs scored in an inning, with the first-inning score given in the first digit, at the left, the second-inning score in the second and so on. Every three-inning unit is separated from the next by a dot, just to make it easier to grasp quickly what inning the game is in.) At the end of six innings, the game is still tied at 1–1.

Now Philadelphia has made a pitching change in the seventh, and the pitcher's name (Reed) and his record (8–7) are given just as they were for the starting pitcher. After eight innings the game is still at 1–1.

In the top of the ninth, Garber is now "PTG" (pitching) for Philadelphia. He has an 8-3 record.

In the seventh row of Western Union strips we see that for Philadelphia Vukovich has hit an "HHR" (home run), "NO 1" (his first), with none on in the ninth, which, it turns out, won the game.

The next strip gives the inning-by-inning scoring and the totals of runs, hits and errors for each team. New York had "1-5-1," meaning one run, five hits and one error, while Philadelphia had "2-8-1," two runs, eight hits and one error.

According to the next strip, the "WP" (winning pitching) was Garber,

..N..CIN...WUPS...ATL...RUTHVEN   ...CIN..NOLAN
                        ..14-16   ..14-9..

..A..BOS...WUPS...BLT...PAGAN   ...BOS...WISE
                        ..2-5   ..13-11..

..N..ATL   ..CIN
      .01   .02..   ...A..BLT   ..BOS
                                    .00   .IQ...

.A..BOS...FISK..HHR..NO   ...BOS .TH..NONE.ON
                  .17   .4   .

..N..CIN..PEREZ..HHR..NO   ..CIN .TH..NONE.ON
                  .19   .4   ..

.N..ATL   ..CIN   ..A..BLT   ..BOS
    .010.00   .020.10..   .000.201   .100.10..

      A..BOS..JACKSON..HHR..NO   ..BLT .TH..NONE.ON
                        .27   .7   .

        ..A..BLT   ..BOS
                .000.201.1   .100.100..

        HOLDSWORTH   ..PTG..BLT .TH
                ..4-0   .7 .

whose record is now 9-3. The "LP" (losing pitcher) was Koosman, whose record is now 21-10. The final entry shows us that the time of the game was one hour and fifty-nine minutes, and the attendance was 23,084.

Reproduced are excerpts of Western Union reports on other games, either during warm-ups or in progress. See if you can decipher them.

Explanations to what the second Western Union illustration tells us:

LINE 1   In the National League at Cincinnati, Ruthven, with a 14-16 record, is warming up for Atlanta, and Nolan, 14-9, for Cincinnati.

LINE 2   In the American League at Boston, the warm-up pitchers are Pagan, 2-5, for Baltimore, and Wise, 13-11, for Boston.

LINE 3   At the end of two innings in the National League at Cincinnati, the Reds lead, 2–1. In the American League at Boston, at the end of two, the Red Sox lead, 1–0.

LINE 4   In the American League at Boston, Fisk hit his seventeenth home run of the season in the Boston fourth with none on.

LINE 5   In the National League at Cincinnati, Perez hit his nineteenth home run of the season in the Cincinnati fourth with none on.

LINE 6   In that Reds-Braves game at Cincinnati, at the end of five innings, the Reds lead, 3–1. In the American League at Boston, the Orioles are ahead, 3–2.

LINE 7   In the American League at Boston, Jackson hit his twenty-seventh home run for Baltimore in the seventh with none on.

LINE 8   In the American League at Boston, Baltimore has added a run in the seventh (Jackson's homer), and, with Boston coming up in the bottom of the seventh, the Orioles lead, 4–2.

LINE 9   In the seventh inning, Holdsworth, with a 4-0 record, has come in to pitch for Baltimore.

On a busy night, such as Friday, or a Sunday afternoon, the Western Union machine is constantly moving and transmitting scores, pitching changes, home runs and so forth. Sometimes there are problems with the ticker. The tape gets jammed or damp and doesn't run through. It may not have enough ink, or it might have too much ink, which results in copy either too light or too dark to be read. I've ruined many a shirt and broken many a nail trying to fix a Western Union machine.

The machine sends along mistaken information sometimes, which we pass along, and then ten or fifteen minutes later, we get a correction on it.

In my first or second season with the Mets, Western Union sent across a line total "0-0-1," and without bothering to check on it, I passed it along as a no-hitter for one of the pitchers. A few minutes later they corrected the totals by putting a "1" before the second zero, meaning the team had *ten* hits, rather than none. That embarrassing incident taught me a lesson I've never forgotten. If a line score comes across indicating a no-hitter or even a one-hitter, before I use it I'll attempt to check with our radio station, or the other team's broadcast booth if we're on the road, to confirm whether it was indeed a no-hitter or one-hitter. If it was a one-hitter, I can also find out how many batters had been retired before the one hit was given up, and whatever other particulars I can. Then when we give the score, we'll give information that is as complete as possible. Our attitude is that we're in business to inform the fans and listeners about anything that's happening in baseball, not just with the Mets. We do it, and the fans appreciate it.

Accumulating as much pertinent detail as possible for out-of-town games requires a great deal of time. In fact, it's probably one of the most time-consuming aspects of my job. I spend more than an hour a day reading as many newspapers as I can, carefully looking over the box scores and noting the highlights of last night's games. On a Sunday morning it's difficult to find a paper that can tell you what happened in the games played Saturday night, especially those played on the West Coast. Often I resort to calling the National League office. People there are always helpful; they'll tell me not only who won the game, but also the highlights.

Fans know that if they tune us in on Sunday afternoon, we'll tell them anything of note that took place Saturday night in the major leagues that they may not yet have heard or read.

When I arrive at a ball park on the West Coast, I usually have a lot to catch up on, especially if we're playing a night game, because of the time differential between the East and the West. When I get to the park at six o'clock Los Angeles, San Francisco or San Diego time, it's nine o'clock in the East and all the games there are underway already.

As the scores come in on the ticker, I'll transfer them to out-of-town score sheets (see illustration, p. 57) for the announcers.

On the road, I have to keep two sets of score sheets, one for radio and one for TV. Updating them neatly gets to be difficult, in light of all my other duties. Sometimes I don't get them updated until we're on the air.

At home, I make up three sets of out-of-town scores, but I update only one, the one I keep with me in the radio booth. A second set goes to the TV booth, but there is someone there, usually a college student hired by WOR-TV or the stage

53

manager, to update that set. Of course, I'll check them periodically during a game to make sure they've got everything correct. The third set of scores is kept and updated down in the control room for use by Ralph Kiner on his postgame TV show, "Kiner's Korner."

When the out-of-town scores are given is usually left up to me, since the announcers have enough other matters to worry about. Baseball fans, who are so aware of details, love to hear the out-of-town scores. So, I seldom let our game go more than two or two and one-half innings, or twenty or twenty-five minutes, without having the announcers do a rundown on scores in both leagues. If we don't have time to run them all down, we give at least a good portion of them. Almost always we'll give the National League scores first, since the Mets are in that league and our listeners, most of them Met fans, are National League–oriented.

On a night when pennant races are involved—and on September 23, 1976, three division titles were in contention—we may give scores of "big" out-of-town games as often as the end of every half-inning.

A determining factor of how often we'll give the out-of-town scores is the closeness of the Mets game. If it's one-sided, we tend to give the scores more often because the pace of the game is so slow and free of tension. In a dull game, sometimes the most interesting things an announcer can talk about are the happenings in games around the league. In a tight game, where the outcome hangs on a single pitch, we won't give the scores as often.

In general, we prefer to give a rundown of the scores when the opposing team is at bat. Our fans hate to have anything disrupt the play-by-play of the Mets' turn at bat.

We will only interrupt a crucial Mets situation with league updates if a pitcher has pitched a no-hitter, a team has clinched a division title, or someone's hit a dramatic homer, say, a grand slam in the ninth. Otherwise the updates can wait until the inning is over or the play is completed.

Sometimes I need the time between innings to explain something to a broadcaster that would be too long or too complicated while he's giving the play-by-play. For instance, in a game between the Cardinals and Phillies, Pete Falcone, who started the game for St. Louis, left the game when he was hit on the left arm by a line drive off the bat of Garry Maddox and was taken to the hospital for X-rays. It would have been difficult to whisper this to the play-by-play man or write it out for him while he was broadcasting, so I waited for a commercial break between innings.

In the case of an important run in an out-of-town game, I'll attempt to find out how the run scored. And I'll also write down anything noteworthy about a team's victory.

Items such as winning and losing streaks and "magic" numbers (the combination of a team's wins and their opponents' losses needed to win the pennant) are put on the out-of-town scoresheets before the start of action in the leagues, and they can easily be updated when the game is completed.

In most instances, I don't have to list the first name of National League players because we're familiar with just about every player in our league. In the case of the American League, more often than not I will note a player's full name, as we're just not familiar with many of them.

We feel that relaying out-of-town baseball scores is one of the most important parts of a broadcasting team's job. Others apparently don't share these sentiments. Sometimes I'll listen to a Yankee game on the way home from Shea Stadium, and it seems to me their broadcasters don't even bother to keep the out-of-town scores. I feel that's not really fair to their listeners, the majority of whom are doubtless Yankee fans, but many of whom are also just plain baseball fans. Baseball fans want to know what's happening in games everywhere; that's why they pore over the box scores in the morning papers. The fans are being cheated when broadcasters just go through the motions—either ignoring the out-of-town scores or giving the seventh-inning score of a game for which we'd given the final score forty-five minutes earlier.

I get bugged when broadcasters are unfamiliar with players' names. In some cases there is obviously very little preparation. They'll almost joke about the fact that they don't know the name of a player who has just come into an out-of-town game. One will say, "It's Autry," and the other will say, "Who the hell is that? Maybe it's Gene Autry." It happens to be Al Autry, a rookie pitcher called up by Atlanta, who pitched in his first major league game a few days before. To them, not knowing is funny; to us, it's not. Knowing correct names and proper pronunciation is an important part of the job, and we try to be as well informed as we possibly can. Both the National and American leagues issue books with the phonetic spelling of their players' names.

Come September 1, the rosters are increased from twenty-five players to forty players, and, as a result, strange names crop up all over the majors. It keeps me on my toes. I have to check the transactions in the *Sporting News,* the daily papers and the news releases issued by the teams, so that we can give a player's full name, pronounced correctly. I also try to get some background information about a newcomer, such as where he played in the minor leagues and what his pitching or hitting record was.

55

Sample Out-of-Town Scoresheets

These are samples of actual scoresheets we use. You'll notice that the Pittsburgh-Chicago game, an important one because the Pirates were chasing the Phillies for the Eastern Division flag, was an afternoon contest. St. Louis-Philadelphia, San Diego-Cincinnati, Atlanta-Houston and Los Angeles-San Francisco all were night games, as indicated on top of each line score.

The Cubs beat the Pirates, 4–3, and the line totals—4-19-0; 3-9-0—are pretty much self-explanatory. Medich started for the Pirates. Tekulve came in in the eighth inning, as indicated by the "8" in parentheses, and was the losing pitcher ("LP"). His record, including the defeat, is now 5-3. Bonham was the starting pitcher for Chicago and Coleman came into the game in the eighth and was the winning pitcher ("WP"); his record is now 2-7. The only home run of the game was by Richie Hebner. The "1/0" indicates the homer came in the first inning with nobody on base. The number of home runs he has for the season is shown on top, "8."

Obviously, the winning run was scored in the bottom of the ninth, and so I made it a point to find out how that came about. It was a one-out single by Joe Wallis that drove in the winning marker.

To the left of the word Pittsburgh, it says, "lost four of five." Since that was before this game, the Pirates have now lost five out of six. Farther down, you'll see that the magic number of Philadelphia is eight.

In the St. Louis-Philadelphia contest, Falcone, 12-14, started for the Cardinals. Walker came in the third, Hrabosky in the eighth and Solomon in the eighth. The starter for Philadelphia was Jim Kaat, 11-13. Note the comment that he had lost five in a row. Schueler relieved in the first, Twitchell in the third, Reed in the fifth, Garber in the seventh and McGraw in the ninth. Garber was the winning pitcher and now has an 8-3 record. The only home run in the game was by Brock in the first with nobody on, his fourth of the season.

Cincinnati won its game, 4–3. Strom started for the Padres and lost. His record is now 11-16. Gullett was the winning pitcher for the Reds. Home runs in the game: Doug Rader, his eighth, in the second with nobody on; Mike Ivie, his sixth, in the third with one man on. For this game, I provided some notes about Cincinnati's win—among them, that the Reds were the first National League team ever to have seven 10-game winners. I also noted the fact that Eastwick picked up his twenty-fifth save, which was noteworthy because at that point he was leading the league in saves.

There is no final score for the Atlanta-Houston game, because our game

Wed. Sept. 23 National — sample #2

lost 4 of 5

[redacted]

	1	2	3	4	5	6	7	8	9	10	11	12	R	H	E
Pit	1	0	0	0	0	1	0	1	0				3	9	0
Chi	0	0	1	1	0	1	0	0	1				4	10	0

Medich
TeKulve (8) — LP (5-3)

Joe Wallis Singled in Winning run With one out in 9th inning

Bonham
Coleman (8) — WP (2-7)

Hebner *8 1/0

Nite	1	2	3	4	5	6	7	8	9	10	11	12	R	H	E
St.L	4	0	0	0	0	0	0	0	0				4	7	4
Pha.	1	0	0	0	0	0	0	8	X				9	13	0

magic # is 8

Falcone 12-14 (left game when hit on left arm by Maddox line drive)
Walker (3)
Hrabosky (8)
Solomon (8) — LP (1-2)

Kaat 11-13 (has lost 5 straight)
Schueler (1)
Twitchell (3)
Reed (5)
Garber (7) — WP (8-3)
McGraw (9)

Brock *4 1/0

Nite	1	2	3	4	5	6	7	8	9	10	11	12	R	H	E
SD	0	1	2	0	0	0	0	0	0				3	13	1
Cin	2	0	0	0	1	1	0	0	X				4	10	1

Clinched title

Strom 11-15 — LP (11-16)
Friesleben (6)

Gullett 9-3 — WP (10-3) (1st N.L. team to have 7 10 game winners)
Eastwick (9) (25th Save)

Rader *8 2/0 Ivie *6 3/1

Nite	1	2	3	4	5	6	7	8	9	10	11	12	R	H	E
Atl	0	2	0	0	0	0	0								
Hou	3	0	0	0	2	0	0								

Lacorte 3-9 Andujar 8-10

Nite	1	2	3	4	5	6	7	8	9	10	11	12	R	H	E
LA	0														
SF	0														

Sutton 19-9 (seeking first 20 win season of career) Bob Knepper 0-1

	1	2	3	4	5	6	7	8	9	10	11	12	R	H	E

Wed. Sept. 23 American

T.N.D

1st	1	2	3	4	5	6	7	8	9	10	11	12	R	H	E
Balt	0	0	0	1	0	1	0	0	0				2	7	1
N.Y.	0	0	0	0	0	0	0	0	0				0	4	2

magic # is 3

Palmer — WP (22-13) 1st 22 game winner in majors

Ellis — LP (16-8)

2nd	1	2	3	4	5	6	7	8	9	10	11	12	R	H	E
Balt	0	0	0	0	0	0	0	4							
N.Y.	1	0	0	0	0	1	0								

Rudy May 13-10
Tippy Martinez (8)

Figueroa 19-8
Jackson (8)

Nite	1	2	3	4	5	6	7	8	9	10	11	12	R	H	E
Mil	2	0	0	0	0	0	0	1							
Bos	1	0	0	1	1	0	1	2							

Won 7 of 8

Jerry Augustine 8-11
Ed Rodriguez (5)

Dick Pole 5-5
Jim Willoughby (8)

Fisk *16 8/1

	1	2	3	4	5	6	7	8	9	10	11	12	R	H	E
Clev	1	0	1	0	0	1	0	0	0				3	8	2
Det	0	0	0	0	0	0	0	0	0				0	3	1

Bibby — WP (13-6)

Ray Bare — LP (7-8)
Steve Grilli (8)

Nite	1	2	3	4	5	6	7	8	9	10	11	12	R	H	E
OaK	3	1	0	0	0	4	3								
K.C.	1	0	0	0	0	0	0								

Swins
magic # is 5

Blue 16-12

Marty Pattin 8-12
Hall (6)
Bob McClure (7)

Phil Garner *8 6/2 Rudi *13 7/1

Nite	1	2	3	4	5	6	7	8	9	10	11	12	R	H	E
Min	0	1	1	0	0	4	0								
Chi	0	0	0	2	0	0									

Singer 11-9

Bart Johnson 9-15
Pete Vuckovich (6)

Butch Wynegar *9 2/0 Carew *8 6/1 Wynegar *10 6/0

Nite	1	2	3	4	5	6	7	8	9	10	11	12	R	H	E
Tex															
Calif															

ended when that contest was in the eighth inning with the score 5–2.

The Dodgers and the Giants were only in the second inning when we completed our game, since they were playing on the West Coast. There's a note that Don Sutton was seeking the first twenty-win season of his career. And I noted the name of a San Francisco rookie pitcher, Bob Knepper. I used his first name because he was unfamiliar.

On the American League scoreboard, "TND" in the left-hand corner of the Yankee-Baltimore game is an abbreviation for twi-night double-header. You'll notice, also, that the Yankee magic number starting that night was three.

The Yankees and Dock Ellis lost the first game, as Jim Palmer of the Orioles became the first twenty-two-game winner in the major leagues. The second game was in the bottom of the eighth when we went off the air.

In the Milwaukee-Boston game, you'll see that I used first names for all four pitchers because we're not nearly so familiar with players in this league as in the National. At the bottom, there's the notation that Boston had won seven out of eight.

A final score for the Cleveland-Detroit game, which was played in the afternoon, is listed, while the Texas-California game had not yet started. Because Oakland and Kansas City were neck-and-neck for the Western Division title in the American League, we kept giving the score of their game every inning or so. In the Minnesota-Chicago game, Butch Wynegar had two home runs.

Statistician's Staples

VARIOUS TYPES of record sheets and cards comprise a statistician's staples. Chief among them is the basic stat sheet.

Stat Sheet

A stat sheet lists the names of all of a team's players. Next to each batter's name are columns for the number of games he's played in, his at-bats, runs, hits, doubles, triples, home runs, RBI's, walks (and how many of them were intentional), strikeouts, sacrifices and sacrifice flies, stolen bases and times caught stealing, errors he committed, double plays he hit into and how many times he was hit by a pitch.

All the statistics on the sheet are totaled to give the team's record. The team batting average is figured by dividing total hits by total at-bats. Pitchers' hits and at-bats are listed in a paragraph below.

The stat sheet then gives each pitcher's won-lost record; his earned-run average; games in which he's appeared; games started; complete games; innings pitched; what he has allowed in the way of hits, runs, earned runs, walks and intentional walks; his totals for strikeouts, wild pitches, batters hit by pitches and home runs allowed; plus how many games he's saved. Listed below are pitchers who have thrown shutouts.

NEW YORK METS

Public Relations Department, Shea Stadium, Flushing, N.Y. 11368 (212) 672-2000

Friday Night   August 13, 1976

Game No. 117   Home Game No. 57   Cincinnati at New York

BATTING	AVE.	G	AB	R	H	2B	3B	HR	RBI	BB-I	SO	S-SF	SB-C	E	GDP	HP
Boisclair	.272	75	173	22	47	6	0	0	4	13-1	31	4-0	9-3	1	3	0
Brown	.241	43	54	8	13	3	0	0	2	2-0	3	0-0	1-3	0	2	0
Dwyer	.177	58	102	9	18	3	1	0	5	13-1	11	0-1	0-0	1	2	0
N.Y.	.100	8	10	2	1	0	0	0	0	2-1	1	0-0	0-0	0	0	0
Foster	.250	5	16	3	4	2	0	0	6	2-0	3	0-0	0-0	0	0	0
Grote	.258	87	279	25	72	8	1	3	19	35-2	17	3-1	1-2	5	14	1
Harrelson	.217	82	249	17	54	9	2	1	20	46-3	47	6-0	6-1	16	1	0
LH	.196	–	168	–	33	5	1	0	14	36-1	33	4-0	–	–	0	0
RH	.259	–	81	–	21	4	1	1	6	10-2	14	2-0	–	–	1	0
Hodges	.276	46	123	20	34	6	0	4	24	24-1	11	1-1	2-0	7	3	0
Kingman	.234	91	363	56	85	11	1	32	72	19-4	92	0-2	5-3	7	3	5
Kranepool	.280	94	321	36	90	14	1	7	37	28-1	33	2-3	1-0	3	8	0
Mangual	.236	88	288	42	68	12	3	3	22	58-2	71	4-1	22-8	5	0	2
N.Y.	.164	22	73	3	12	3	2	0	6	8-0	22	0-0	5-1	0	0	0
Millan	.262	99	382	37	100	18	2	1	20	30-4	14	5-1	2-3	9	11	4
Milner	.260	90	316	38	82	15	3	12	57	40-1	46	0-3	0-3	3	9	0
Phillips	.258	64	198	26	51	4	5	3	25	23-6	19	2-4	1-2	10	2	0
Staiger	.256	55	168	15	43	6	1	2	14	15-4	23	1-2	2-2	4	2	1
Torre	.311	89	241	29	75	8	2	4	23	12-1	25	2-1	1-2	6	14	4
Vail	.259	31	81	6	21	3	1	0	6	4-0	12	0-1	0-0	3	0	0
LOLICH	.146	23	41	5	6	0	0	1	5-0	18	9-0	0-0	5	0	0
Others	.215	–	587	67	126	21	3	10	56	73-5	73	6-3	11-10	2	11	3
TOTALS	.245	116	2910	443	957	142	24	79	411	401-36	572	73-22	47-36	99	96	19

PITCHERS BATTING: Apodaca 2-14; Espinosa 0-3; Koosman 14-51; Lockwood 5-13;
Lolich 6-41; Matlack 12-63; Myrick 0-2; Sanders 0-2; Seaver 5-57;
Swan 3-30.

PITCHING	W-L	ERA	G	GS	CG	IP	H	R	ER	BB-I	SO	WP	HB	HR	SV
Apodaca	2-5	2.84	32	3	0	72.2	55	29	23	22-8	38	0	2	3	3
Espinosa	0-3	1.69	4	2	0	16.1	12	5	3	5-0	11	0	0	1	0
Koosman	14-7	2.18	24	22	9	163.2	145	62	58	49-5	119	3	1	12	0
Lockwood	6-7	2.78	40	0	0	68.	45	23	21	28-7	78	2	2	5	13
LOLICH	7-10	2.88	23	22	5	143.2	134	60	46	43-1	102	10	0	5	0
Matlack	12-6	2.76	25	25	11	186.	159	64	57	41-2	114	10	2	13	0
Myrick	1-0	3.79	15	0	0	18.2	24	9	8	9-1	9	0	0	0	1
Sanders	1-2	2.31	27	0	0	39.	30	11	10	8-2	14	0	0	3	1
Seaver	9-8	2.70	26	25	8	197.1	157	62	59	59-7	174	10	3	10	0
Swan	5-8	3.55	17	17	2	104.	98	50	41	33-3	80	0	4	8	0
TOTALS	59-57	2.94	116	116	35	1045.	893	392	341	318-40	756	35	18	63	17

SHUTOUTS: Matlack 4; Lolich 2; Seaver 2; Koosman 1; Swan 1;
combined: Swan-Lockwood 1.

Won-Lost Records	Home	Road	Totals
Day	15-16	11-10	26-26
Night	14-11	19-20	33-31
Vs. RHP	19-20	22-23	41-43
Vs. LHP	10-7	8-7	18-14
One Run Games	13-15	4-8	17-23
Extra Innings	2-6	1-2	3-8
Shutouts	8-8	3-8	11-16
Vs. East	12-17	16-15	28-32
West	17-10	14-15	31-25
Cincinnati	2-1	2-4	4-5

Double Plays: Mets 88; Opponents 117

Att:	Home	1,083,240 (56 games, 52 dates)
	Road	1,078,846 (60 games, 57 dates)
	Totals	2,162,086 (116 games, 109 dates)

Team Highs - 1976
Runs Game - 17 (4/17) vs. Pit.
Hits Game - 21 (4/17) vs. Pit.
HR's Game - 4 (6/4) vs. LA
Runs Inn. - 8 (6/27) vs. Chi.
Win Streak - 10 (6/23-7/4)
Losing Streak - 4 (5 times)

Player Highs
Hits Game - 4 Grote, Kingman,
Phillips, Harrelson
RBI's Game - 8 Kingman (6/4) vs. LA
HR's Game - 3 Kingman (6/1) vs. LA

Doubleheaders: 1 Win   1 Loss
5 Splits

Pinch-hitting: 1/2 AB 39 Hits
1 HR 17 RBI

NEW YORK METS

Public Relations Department, Shea Stadium, Flushing, N.Y. 11368 (212) 672-2000

GAME NO. 117--METS PRESS NOTES--AUGUST 13, 1976

NATIONAL LEAGUE
EASTERN DIVISION

	W	L	PCT.	GB
Philadelphia	74	38	.661	–
Pittsburgh	60	52	.536	14
METS	59	57	.509	17
Chicago	52	64	.448	24
St. Louis	47	63	.427	26
Montreal	40	68	.370	32

WESTERN DIVISION

	W	L	PCT.	GB
Cincinnati	75	40	.652	–
Los Angeles	61	52	.540	13
Houston	58	59	.496	18
San Diego	56	61	.479	20
Atlanta	53	62	.461	22
San Francisco	49	68	.419	27

THURSDAY'S RESULTS
San Diego,3; Mets,0
Cincinnati,8; Chicago,3
Atlanta,4; Philadelphia,3

AMERICAN LEAGUE
EASTERN DIVISION

	W	L	PCT.	GB
New York	67	44	.604	–
Baltimore	56	53	.514	10
Cleveland	55	56	.495	12
Detroit	54	58	.482	13½
Boston	53	57	.482	13½
Milwaukee	47	61	.435	18½

WESTERN DIVISION

	W	L	PCT.	GB
Kansas City	68	44	.607	–
Oakland	61	53	.535	8
Minnesota	56	56	.500	12
Texas	54	58	.482	14
California	55	65	.435	19½
Chicago	48	63	.432	19½

THURSDAY'S RESULTS
New York,12; Minnesota,5
Cleveland,5; Texas,4
Boston,2; California,1
Oakland,4; Milwaukee,3

OTHER NL GAMES TODAY: LA@Chi(2); SD@Mtl(tn); StL@Atl(n); SF@Pha(n); Pit@Hou(n).

TONIGHT'S PITCHERS:

Mets: Mickey Lolich(7-10 this season and 214-183 lifetime) is 0-1 this season
and lifetime against Cincinnati. Lost to Reds 5-1 on May 14 at Cincinnati, allowing
3 hits and 4 runs, 1 earned, with 2 walks and 4 strikeouts in 6 1/3 innings(only appearance vs Reds this year). Has won in 3 of last 6 starts with 3 no decisions,
giving up 14 earned runs in 45 innings (2.80 ERA).

Reds: Jack Billingham(9-8 this season and 106-83 lifetime) is 1-0 vs. the
Mets this season and is 8-4 lifetime against New York. Had complete game victory
against Mets in 5-1 Reds win on May 14(vs Lolich) in Cincinnati. Allowed 4 hits and
1 run, with 2 walks and 3 strikeouts in only appearance against Mets this year. Has
won two in a row beating the Giants on August 3, and the Dodgers last Sunday, allowing
only 2 earned runs in 17 2/3 innings.

***

REMAINDER OF SERIES:

Tomorrow afternoon: Nino Espinosa(1-2) vs. Pat Zachry(11-3).

Sunday afternoon: Jerry Koosman(14-7) vs. Gary Nolan(10-7).

***

Joe Torre has hit safely in 10 straight games with 18-37 (.486), raising his average from .279 to .311...Roy Staiger has hit in 8 of his last 11 games with 14-37 (.3..
raising his average from .221 to .256...Felix Millan has hit in 7 of his last 8 games
with 12-30 (.400).

***

Mets' pinch hitting: Apodaca 0-1; Boisclair 9-17; Brown 1-5; Dwyer 1-5;
Grote 3-7 (1 RBI); Harrelson 1-5; Hodges 2-6 (1 RBI); Kranepool 2-7 (1 RBI); Millan
Milner 5-10 (4 RBI); Phillips 0-5; Staiger 0-1; Torre 7-29 (3 RBI); Vail 3-12.
TEAM 39-142, .275, 1 HR, 17 RBI.

***

Game winning RBI: Kingman, 11; Milner, 8; Kranepool & Millan, 4 each; Grote,
Harrelson, Hodges, Phillips, Torre and Vail, 2 each; Boisclair, Koosman, Mangual and
Staiger, 1 each.

New York Mets   Monday Night   Sept. 13, 1976

Game No. 142   Road Game No. 74   New York at Pittsburgh

Batting	AVE.	G	AB	R	H	2B	3B	HR	RBI	BB-I	SO	S-SF	SB-C	E	GDP	HB
B.Baldwin	.077	5	13	2	1	0	0	0	2	1-0	1	0-1	0-0	0	0	0
Boisclair	.276	97	254	36	70	12	2	1	10	20-3	51	4-0	9-4	2	3	0
Brown	.214	56	70	11	15	3	0	0	2	3-0	4	0-0	1-3	0	3	0
Dwyer	.173	60	104	9	18	3	1	0	5	13-1	11	0-1	0-0	1	2	0
N.Y.	.083	10	12	2	1	0	0	0	0	2-1	1	0-0	0-0	0	0	0
Foster	.224	18	49	7	11	2	0	1	14	7-1	5	0-0	3-0	1	0	0
Grote	.269	95	305	28	82	13	1	4	25	38-3	17	1-1	1-2	5	15	1
Harrelson	.233	102	309	30	72	11	2	1	24	56-4	53	7-0	9-2	17	1	2
Hodges	.238	54	147	21	35	6	0	4	24	27-2	14	1-1	2-0	7	4	0
Kingman	.231	105	412	61	95	12	1	34	77	20-4	109	0-2	6-3	8	10	5
Kranepool	.285	109	372	41	106	16	1	7	41	13-4	34	2-3	1-0	3	10	0
Mangual	.231	102	303	47	70	13	3	3	24	58-2	76	5-1	24-8	5	6	2
N.Y.	.159	36	88	13	14	4	2	0	8	8-0	27	3-0	7-1	0	0	0
Masilli	.111	5	9	2	1	0	0	0	1	1-0	1	0-0	1-0	0	0	0
Millan	.280	119	454	45	127	23	2	1	24	47-5	16	5-1	2-4	11	14	6
Milner	.276	113	398	49	110	23	4	13	71	5-7	49	0-3	0-6	3	10	0
Phillips	.260	78	242	29	63	4	6	4	28	24-7	25	3-4	2-2	11	2	0
Staiger	.245	75	237	20	58	8	1	2	21	19-4	30	1-4	3-3	5	7	1
Stearns	.304	17	56	10	17	2	0	1	7	3-0	1	0-1	1-1	1	1	0
Torre	.309	106	285	32	88	9	3	4	28	16-1	31	2-2	1-3	7	16	5
Vail	.224	45	125	8	28	5	1	0	9	6-0	16	0-3	0-0	4	3	0
SEAVER	.099	31	71	5	7	0	0	0	1	1-0	30	0-0	0-0	1	1	0
Others	.214	–	583	68	125	21	3	10	55	75-6	74	6-3	11-10	12	10	2
Totals	.248	141	4745	542	1175	179	29	88	495	474-47	686	85-29	60-45	112	119	25

Pitchers Batting: Apodaca 2-14;   R.Baldwin 1-2;   Espinosa 0-6;   Koosman 17-68;
                Lockwood 0-15;   Lolich 7-50;   Matlack 14-75;   Myrick 0-2;
                Sanders 0-2;   Seaver 7-71;   Swan 3-32.

Pitching	W-L	ERA	G	GS	CG	IP	H	R	ER	BB-I	SO	WP	HB	HR	SV
Apodaca	2-7	3.16	38	3	0	77.1	60	33	27	24-9	39	0	3	4	4
R.Baldwin	0-0	2.65	8	0	0	17.	12	5	5	10-1	9	0	2	0	0
Espinosa	3-3	3.86	8	3	0	28.	25	14	12	9-2	21	0	0	3	0
Koosman	19-8	2.83	30	28	14	216.	182	73	68	59-5	161	3	1	15	0
Lockwood	7-7	2.89	49	0	0	83.2	57	30	27	32-7	92	3	2	6	16
Lolich	8-12	2.93	29	28	5	180.2	169	73	59	49-1	117	11	0	12	0
Matlack	15-8	2.82	31	31	14	230.1	198	79	72	52-2	133	11	3	15	0
Myrick	1-0	3.43	18	0	0	21.	28	9	8	10-1	9	0	0	1	0
Sanders	1-2	2.80	30	0	0	45.	37	15	14	11-3	15	0	1	3	1
Seaver	12-10	2.50	31	30	11	238.	187	71	66	71-9	209	12	3	12	0
Swan	5-8	3.58	18	18	2	108.	103	52	43	35-3	82	0	5	8	0
Others	1-2	4.71	–	–	–	20.2	22	12	11	12-2	9	0	2	2	0
Totals	74-67	2.92	141	141	46	1266.2	1080	466	411	374-46	896	40	22	81	21

Shutouts: Matlack 6;   Seaver 4;   Koosman 3;   Lolich 2;   Swan 1;   combined: Swan-Lockwood

Met Records	Home	Road	Totals
Day	19-19	16-12	35-31
Night	17-13	22-23	39-36
Vs. RHP	25-23	28-27	53-50
Vs. LHP	11-9	10-8	21-17
One Run Games	18-16	6-12	24-27
Extra Innings	2-6	1-2	3-8
Shutouts	11-8	6-8	17-16
Vs. East	14-18	21-16	35-34
West	22-14	17-19	39-33
Pittsburgh	1-4	4-3	5-7

Team Highs – 1976
Runs Game – 17 (4/17) vs. Pit.
Hits Game – 21 (4/17) vs. Pit.
HR's Game – 4 (6/4) vs. LA
Runs Inn. – 8 (6/27) vs. Chi.
Win Streak – 10 (6/23-7/4)
Losing Streak – 4 (5 times)

Player Highs
Hits Game – 4 Grote, Phillips, Stearns, Harrelson, Kingman
RBI's Game – 8 Kingman (6/4) vs. LA
HR's Game – 3 Kingman (6/4) vs. LA
Hit Streak – 16 Milner (4/11-5/26)

Att:			
Home	1,337,651	(68 games, 64 dates)	
Road	1,273,209	(73 games, 70 dates)	
Totals	2,610,860	(141games,134 dates)	

Double Plays: Mets 104   Opponents 143

Doubleheaders: 1 Win   1 Loss   5 Splits

New York Mets   Monday Night   Sept. 13, 1976

Game No. 142   Road Game No. 74   New York at Pittsburgh

Tonight's Pitchers:

METS: Tom Seaver (12-10 in 1976 and 180-106 lifetime) is 0-1 against the Pirates in 1976 and 18-11 lifetime vs. Pittsburgh. Lost 12-3, August 7, at Pit. (5 IP, 8 H, 5 R, 5 ER, 2 W, 7 K). Started against Pirates on July 28 at Shea without a decision in game won by Pittsburgh, 1-0, in 13 innings (10 IP, 7, 0 R, 4 W, 10 K). Has won his last two starts over the Phillies and Cubs. In five of Seaver's ten defeats the Mets were shutout. Is making his 31st start of the season. Tom leads the National League in strikeouts and ERA.

Strikeout Leaders		ERA Leaders	
SEAVER	209	SEAVER	2.50
Richard	179	Rau	2.56
Koosman	161	Jones	2.66
Montefusco	157	Norman	2.67

PIRATES: Larry Demery (10-4 in 1976 and 23-15 lifetime) is 0-0 against the Mets in 1976 and 3-0 lifetime vs. New York. In his only appearance of the season against the Mets he pitched two innings of relief on April 17 at Pit. in game won by New York, 17-1 (2 IP, 2 H, 2 R, 0 ER, 0 W, 0 K). Demery has won his last four starts over the Dodgers (2-1), Giants (5-2), Padres (5-0) and Phillies (5-1). Is making his 12th start of the season.

****

Tomorrow night's probable pitchers:
METS: Craig Swan (5-8). Is 0-1 against the Pirates in 1976 and 0-1 lifetime.
PIRATES: Jim Rooker (13-7). Is 0-1 against the Mets in 1976 and 3-3 lifetime.

****

The Mets' pitching staff leads the NL in ERA with a 2.92 mark (Philadelphia, 3.13); complete games with 46 (San Diego, 42); strikeouts with 896 (Philadelphia, 780) and shutouts with 17 (Houston, 16).

****

John Milner has hit safely in 10 of his last 11 games with 19-for-43 (.442) and nine RBI over that stretch. His 71 RBI is one short of his career high of 72 in 1973. He has str"ruckout only three times in his last 107 offical at bats, while drawing 21 walks over that span.

****

Bruce Boisclair has hit safely in six straight games, 11 of his last 12 and 18 of his last 21...Bud Harrelson has hit safely in six of his last seven games with 11-for-23 (.478)...Felix Millan has hit safely in 16 of his last 18 games with 27-for-69 (.391)...John Stearns has started 11 straight games since rejoining the Mets on Sept. 1 and has hit .390 over that stretch (16-for-41)...The Mets are 5-1 on the current road trip...Ed Kranepool has a five-game hitting streak and has hit safely in 14 of his last 16 games.

****

Pitching coach Rube Walker left the team this morning to attend the funeral of his father-in-law, F.J. Annis, who passed away yesterday in Lenoir, N.C. at the age of 72.

****

Mets' Game-Winning RBI:

Kingman	11	Boisclair	2
Milner	9	Hodges	2
Millan	5	Vail	2
Staiger	5	Mangual	1
Kranepool	4	Koosman	1
Phillips	3	Foster	1
Grote	3	Stearns	1
Harrelson	3	R.Baldwin	1
Torre	2		

Also included on a stat sheet is a given team's record in such categories as day games, night games, against righties and against lefties. Also, its record in one-run games, extra-inning games, shutouts, double-headers and double plays, and its won-lost record against the Eastern clubs and the Western clubs. There are attendance figures for at home and on the road, and team highs for the year in such categories as runs in a game, home runs in a game, biggest win streak and biggest losing streak. And there are individual high achievements, such as Kingman's eight RBI's in a single contest against the Dodgers.

For home games, using data I provide, Tim Hamilton of the Mets' P.R. department, makes up a separate sheet for notes and for standings in both leagues, along with the results of the previous day's games and the current day's schedule. In baseball it's the obligation of the home team to supply current standings on stat sheets. The notes will always include a detailed paragraph about each of the starting pitchers. There will be a variety of information about each of them, such as his season and lifetime records against the team he's facing today, his most recent accomplishments, his career and season won-lost record and his ERA. Probable pitchers for the next several games will also be listed, along with such notes of interest as players on streaks and unusual guests in attendance at today's game.

Master Book

I also keep a master book of miscellaneous information which does not appear on the stat sheet but is strictly for reference. It's something the general manager likes to look at.

Contained in it is a page for each Met player that has his day-by-day record, the opposing team, his average, his cumulative game total, his at-bat total, his runs, hits and so forth. Figures for home games are written in red, and those for road games in blue, to make it easy to distinguish at a glance.

If somebody says, "Henderson's been hot. How many hits has he had lately?" by looking at Henderson's page, I can quickly answer, "He just went 2-for-4, which gives him six hits in his last fifteen at-bats."

The same sort of information is kept for the team as a whole and for pitchers. In addition, there are separate pages for everyone's pinch-hitting record, and a breakdown of how each batter has hit against righties and lefties. There's a page listing how the Mets have done against each opposing team, and this includes the score, whether the Mets won or lost, the winning and losing

NEW YORK METS

Public Relations Department, Shea Stadium, Flushing, N.Y. 11368 (212) 672-2000

GAME 149--METS PRESS NOTES--SEPTEMBER 19,1976

NATIONAL LEAGUE						AMERICAN LEAGUE				
EASTERN DIVISION						**EASTERN DIVISION**			
	W	L	PCT.	GB			W	L	PCT.	GB
Philadelphia	89	58	.605	-		New York	91	55	.633	-
Pittsburgh	85	62	.578	4		Baltimore	81	66	.551	10½
METS	78	70	.527	11½		Cleveland	73	72	.503	17½
Chicago	68	81	.4563	22		Boston	72	76	.486	20
St. Louis	67	80	.4557	22		Detroit	67	80	.456	24½
Montreal	50	96	.342	38½		Milwaukee	63	84	.429	28½
WESTERN DIVISION						**WESTERN DIVISION**			
Cincinnati	95	55	.633	-		Kansas City	86	63	.577	-
Los Angeles	83	66	.557	11½		Oakland	80	68	.541	5½
Houston	73	77	.487	22		Minnesota	76	75	.503	11½
San Francisco	70	81	.464	25½		California	69	81	.460	17½
San Diego	68	81	.456	26½		Texas	67	81	.453	18½
Atlanta	66	85	.437	29½		Chicago	63	87	.420	23

SATURDAY'S RESULTS	SATURDAY'S RESULTS
METS,6;Pittsburgh,2	New York,5;Milwaukee,3
Philadelphia,4;Chicago,1	Cle,5;Balt,1(1st);Balt,3;Cle,2(2nd)
StL,4;Mt1,1(1st);StL,7;Mt1,4(2nd)	Boston,5;Detroit,4
San Francisco,5;Cincinnati,0	Oakland,3;Texas,2
San Diego,4;Houston,1	Kansas City,6;Chicago,5
Atlanta,5;Los Angeles,4	California,6;Minnesota,0

OTHER NL GAMES TODAY: Pha@Chi;LA@At1;SF@Cin;StL@Mt1(2);SD@Hou.

TODAY'S PITCHERS:

Mets: Craig Swan(5-8 this season and 7-15 lifetime) is 0-1 this season and lifetime against Pittsburgh. Lost to Pirates 7-5 on April 18 at Pittsburgh, allowing 6 hits and 6 runs, 3 earned, with a strikeout in 3 2/3 innings. Had no decision in Mets 4-3 win last Tuesday at Pittsburgh, allowing 5 hits and 2 runs, with 2 walks and 2 strikeouts in 7 innings. Last win was on July 4, allowing 4 runs in 6 innings in Mets 9-4 win over Chicago. Has started only 2 games since July 27 game with Phillies when he left game with strained right elbow. Has 1 loss and 4 no decisions since win on July 4.

Pirates: Jim Rooker(13-8 this season and 72-80 lifetime) is 0-2 against the Mets this season and 3-4 lifetime against New York. Had no decision in Mets 2-1 win on July 29 at Shea, allowing 7 hits and no runs, with 3 walks and 5 strikeouts in 6 innings. Lost to Mets 7-4 on August 8 at Pittsburgh, allowing 5 hits and 4 runs, with 1 walk in 1/3 of an inning. Lost to Mets last Tuesday 4-3 at Pittsburgh, allowing 7 hits and 4 runs with 3 walks and 4 strikeouts in 8 1/3 innings. Has won 3 of his last 4 decisions with 2 complete games(SF, 8/28;Pha,9/8), allowing 9 earned runs in 32 innings(2.53 ERA) over that span.
*****

TOMORROW'S PROBABLES(4:05 PM):

Mets: Mickey Lolich(8-13). Is 1-1 this season and lifetime against Pirates.

Pirates: John Candelaria(15-6). Is 1-0 this season and 3-1 lifetime against Mets.
*****

PROBABLES FOR UPCOMING SERIES IN MONTREAL:

Tuesday night: Jerry Koosman(20-8) vs. Dan Warthen(1-8).
Wednesday night: Jon Matlack(15-9) vs. Larry Landreth(1-0).
Thursday night: Tom Seaver(14-10) vs. Gerald Hannahs(1-0).
*****

The members of the New Jersey Division of the Motor Vehicles Inspection Force were scheduled to attend today's game in celebration of their 70th Anniversary(1906-1976).
*****

Felix Millan has hit safely in 9 straight games with 12-34(.353), and in 23 of his last 25 games with 36-96(.375)...Ed Kranepool has hit safely in 10 straight games with 14-36(.389)...Jerry Grote has hit safely in 8 straight games with 13-28(.464) raising his average from .255 to .274...Bruce Boisclair has hit safely in 15 of his last 17 games, and in 22 of his last 26 games.
*****

Mets' pinch-hitting: Apodaca 0-1; B.Baldwin 0-1(1 RBI); Boisclair 10-19(1 HR,1 RBI); Brown 1-7; Dwyer 1-7; Foster 0-2; Grote 4-9(1 RBI); Harrelson 0-1; Hodges 2-6(1 RBI); Kingman 0-1; Kranepool 3-8(2 RBI); Mangual 0-2; Mazzilli 1-2(1 HR,3 RBI); Millan 1-4; Milner 5-10(4 RBI); Phillips 3-14; Staiger 0-1; Stearns 0-3; Torre 8-34(3 RBI); Vail 4-16. TEAM 48-175, 3 HR, 23 RBI, .274 AVE.

NEW YORK METS

Public Relations Department, Shea Stadium, Flushing, N.Y. 11368 (212) 672-2000

SUNDAY AFTERNOON SEPT. 19, 1976

GAME NO. 149   HOME GAME NO. 75   PITTSBURGH AT NEW YORK

Batting	AVE.	G	AB	R	H	2B	3B	HR	RBI	BB-I	SO	S-SF	SB-C	E	GDP	HB
B.Baldwin	.077	5	13	2	1	0	0	0	2	2-0	1	0-1	0-0	0	0	0
Boisclair	.281	102	270	38	76	12	2	2	13	23-4	52	4-0	9-5	3	3	0
Brown	.214	57	70	11	15	3	0	0	2	4-0	4	0-0	1-3	0	3	0
Dwyer	.173	60	104	9	18	3	1	0	5	13-1	11	0-1	0-0	1	2	0
N.Y.	.083	10	12	2	1	0	0	0	0	2-1	1	0-0	0-0	0	0	0
Foster	.226	21	53	8	12	2	0	1	14	7-1	5	0-0	3-0	1	0	0
Grote	.274	97	310	29	85	14	1	4	27	38-3	17	3-1	1-2	5	15	1
Harrelson	.231	107	325	31	75	11	2	1	26	53-4	53	7-0	9-3	17	1	2
Hodges	.232	55	151	21	35	6	0	4	24	27-2	15	1-1	2-0	7	4	0
Kingman	.229	109	428	63	98	12	1	35	78	20-4	117	0-2	6-4	8	10	5
Kranepool	.290	115	389	44	113	17	1	8	43	33-4	36	2-3	1-0	3	10	0
Mangual	.232	103	306	47	71	13	3	3	24	59-2	77	5-1	24-8	5	0	2
N.Y.	.165	37	91	13	15	4	2	0	8	9-0	28	3-0	7-1	0	0	0
Mazzilli	.143	11	28	3	4	0	0	1	3	6-0	1	0-0	3-1	0	0	0
Millan	.283	126	481	48	136	24	2	1	29	38-5	16	6-1	2-4	12	14	6
Milner	.271	118	417	51	113	24	4	13	72	58-7	50	0-3	0-6	3	11	0
Phillips	.260	81	246	30	64	4	6	4	29	24-7	25	3-5	2-2	11	2	0
Staiger	.232	82	263	21	61	8	1	2	22	20-5	31	1-4	3-3	5	8	1
Stearns	.271	22	70	11	19	3	0	1	7	9-0	3	0-1	1-1	2	2	1
Torre	.308	109	295	34	91	10	3	5	30	19-1	32	2-2	1-3	7	16	5
Vail	.227	48	132	8	30	5	1	0	9	5-0	17	0-3	0-0	4	3	0
SWAN	.118	19	34	3	4	0	0	0	1	3-0	14	5-0	0-0	2	0	1
Others	.214	–	585	68	125	21	3	10	55	75-6	74	6-3	11-10	12	10	2
Totals	.247	148	4969	563	1226	185	29	92	515	503-49	717	87-30	62-49	115	122	26

Pitchers Batting: Apodaca 2-15; R.Baldwin 1-2; Espinosa 0-6; Koosman 17-72;
                   Lockwood 6-16; Lolich 7-51; Matlack 14-77; Myrick 0-2;
                   Seaver 7-77; Swan 4-34.

Pitching	W-L	ERA	G	GS	CG	IP	H	R	ER	BB-I	SO	WP	HB	HR	SV
Apodaca	2-7	3.11	39	3	0	81.1	63	34	28	25-10	42	0	3	4	4
R.Baldwin	0-0	2.84	9	0	0	19.	13	6	6	10-1	9	0	2	0	0
Espinosa	3-4	4.35	9	4	0	31.	31	17	15	11-3	24	0	0	3	0
Koosman	20-8	2.76	31	29	15	225.	186	74	69	62-5	174	3	1	16	0
Lockwood	8-7	2.93	50	0	0	85.2	58	31	28	33-8	94	3	2	6	16
Lolich	8-13	3.16	30	29	5	185.1	175	79	65	51-1	119	11	0	13	0
Matlack	15-9	2.84	32	32	14	238.1	207	82	75	53-3	140	11	3	15	0
Myrick	1-0	3.00	20	0	0	24.1	29	9	8	11-1	9	0	0	1	0
Seaver	14-10	2.39	33	32	13	256.	197	73	68	74-9	225	12	3	12	0
SWAN	5-8	3.52	19	19	2	115.	108	54	45	37-3	84	0	5	9	0
Others	2-4	3.44	–	–	–	67.2	61	28	26	24-6	25	0	3	6	1
Totals	78-70	2.92	148	148	49	1329.2	1128	487	432	391-51	945	40	22	85	21

Shutouts: Matlack 6; Seaver 5; Koosman 3; Lolich 2; Swan 1;
           combined: Swan-Lockwood

Met Records	Home	Road	Totals
Day	20-19	16-12	36-31
Night	18-16	24-23	42-39
Vs. RHP	26-25	29-27	55-52
Vs. LHP	12-10	11-8	23-18
One Run Games	18-16	7-12	25-28
Extra Innings	2-6	1-2	3-8
Shutouts	11-9	7-8	18-17
Vs. East	16-21	23-16	39-37
West	22-14	17-19	39-33
Pittsburgh	2-5	6-3	8-8

Team Highs - 1976
Runs Game - 17 (4/17) vs. Pit.
Hits Game - 21 (4/17) vs. Pit.
HR's Game - 4 (6/4) vs. LA
Runs Inn. - 8 (6/27) vs. Chi.
Win Streak - 10 (6/23-7/4)
Losing Streak - 4 (5 times)

Player Highs
Hits Game - 4 Grote, Phillips, Stearns,
            Harrelson, Kingman
RBI's Game - 8 Kingman (6/4) vs. LA
HR's Game - 3 Kingman (6/4) vs. LA
Hit Streak - 16 Milner (4/11-5/16)

Att: Home 1,383,269 (73 games, 68 dates)
     Road 1,288,968 (75 games, 72 dates)
     Totals 2,672,237 (148 games,140 dates)

Double Plays: Mets 107;
                 Opponents 147

Doubleheaders: 1 Win   2 Losses   5 Splits

pitchers, where it was played, who hit the home runs and how many men were on base when the homers were hit. If you want to see how many home runs Kingman had hit against the Braves, for instance, you could see that midway through the 1976 season, he had hit eight, five of them at Atlanta Stadium.

The team's day-by-day record is also kept in the master book, so that you can tell the last time we were first in our division, or how many games out of first the team was on any given day. This record also tells how the team has done in night games, day games, double-headers, one-run games, shutouts, extra-inning games. There is a breakdown of double plays against each team by the Mets, and by each team against the Mets.

Among the special categories I keep for the general manager is the ratio of runners batted-in to runners in scoring position (on second or third base). This will tell you something. If a batter has had thirty-six men in scoring position, and he's batted-in four, he hasn't done very well. I would expect my third-, fourth- and fifth-place hitters to have a 40 percent mark. This is what I told the Mets' general manager, Joe McDonald, when he asked me to give him a guideline. Interestingly, before Wayne Garrett was traded away, he had a 39 percent RBI's/opportunities ratio. John Milner at one point had a 49 percent mark, and Ron Hodges' was even higher. Of course, you also have to consider how many RBI's are involved in the percentage. Few statistics can be judged in isolation from other factors.

Games Started/Games Team Won

A statistical category I started keeping recently is the number of games each player started that the team won. Bruce Boisclair, at one point in 1976, had started seventy-three games, of which the Mets won thirty-nine. That doesn't tell you an awful lot, but it might have some worth for a general manager at the end of the season.

Grand Slams

Because it's such a spectacular feat, I keep the record of all grand slams in the majors up-to-date. No matter what team the hitter is with, I'll note down what career number the grand slam represents.

When a player comes up against the Mets with the bases loaded, I'll look quickly to see whether he's ever had a grand slam and, if so, how many. When a grand slam is hit, the first thing a fan likes to know is whether it was the batter's first.

Special Sheets

Before the season starts, I prepare sheets that have readily available such information as each career shutout by each Met pitcher; each Met pitcher's strikeout high in the major leagues; each Met club record for most hits in a game, most runs in a game, most home runs in a game. I'll list the career home-run total of every major league player who has hit 300 or more. Willie McCovey, for example, started the 1977 season with 465 career four-baggers and each time he hit one, I just added to the updated total. Because it was on a sheet, I didn't have to take the time to look it up in a record book, and thereby risk missing something that was happening in the bullpen or on the field.

Can you imagine what a void there would be if nobody ever kept track of home runs in major league baseball? What would have happened to Hank Aaron's record, and all the others that preceded his?

I think one of the major trivia questions twenty years from now will be what pitcher Hank Aaron hit the record-tying home run (number 714) off of (Jack Billingham of Cincinnati), and whom he hit the record homer (number 715) off of (Al Downing of the Dodgers). If nobody stopped to keep records of such things, the significance and the surrounding excitement would be lost.

Batting Sheet

Here is Ed Kranepool's batting sheet for the early part of the 1976 season.

As you can see, his first game was April 9 against Montreal.

In the line for each game, the data given are, from left to right, the date of the contest, the team the Mets played, the player's average after that game, what game of the season it was for that player, and the number of at-bats, runs, hits, doubles, triples, home runs and runs batted in. Then bases on balls, including the number of intentional ones, strikeouts, sacrifices and sacrifice flies, stolen bases and times caught stealing, safe on errors, grounded into a double play, hit by a pitch. After the first game, cumulative totals are entered into the appropriate box for each category, along with how many of those items happened in that game. You'll notice, for example, that on April 9, Krane had three at-bats. On April 11, he also had three at-bats, so a "3" is entered in the upper half of the at-bat box,

DATE	TEAM	AVE.	G	AB	R	H	2B	3B	HR	RBI	BB-I	SO	S-SF	SB-CS	E	GDP	HR
Apr. 9	Mtl	220	1	1/2							1	1					
11	Mtl	000	2	3/6							1						
13	Chi	111	3	3/9		1						3/3					1
14	Chi	231	4	4/13		3/3											
15	Chi	222	5	5/18		4					3/3		2/3				
16	Pit	189	6	4/22													
17	Pit	214	7	6/28	4	2/6			1	5/6							
19	St.L	226	8	3/31		1/7						1/4					
20	St.L	235	9	3/34	1	3/8	1										
21	St.L	256	10	5/39		2/10				1/7							
23	Hou.	233	11	4/43													
24	Hou.	229	12	5/48		1/11											1/2
25	Hou.	231	13	4/52	6	1/12											
26	Atl.	268	14	4/56	7	3/15											1/3
27	Atl.	259	15	8/53						1/8			0-1				
28	Atl.	274	16	4/62	8	2/17											
29	Atl.	273	17	4/66		18						5					
30	Hou.	257	18	4/70								6					
May (1) 2	Hou.	284	19	4/74	3/11	3/21			1	1/9		7					
(2) 2	Hou.	286	20	3/77	12	1/22					2/5						
4	Cin.	300	21	3/80		2/24	2			1/10	1/6	8					
5	Cin.	282	22	5/85								9					1/4
6	Cin.	290	23	4/89		1/25	3			2/12		1/10					
7	SD	280	24	4/93	13	1/26											
8	SD	281	25	3/96		1/27				2/14	1/7						
9	SD	273	26	3/99													
11	Atl	272	27	4/103	14	1/28					1/8						
12	Atl.	271	28	4/107	15	1/29					1/9						1/5
14	Cin.	270	29	4/111		1/30	4										1/6
15	Cin.	261	30	4/115								1/11					
(1) 16	Cin.	267	31	5/120	2/17	2/32			1	2/16							
(2) 16	Cin.	265	32	1/121													1/7
19	Pha.	266	33	3/124	1/18	1/33					1/10						
20	Pha.	276	34	3/127		2/35											

and a "6" (for the number of at-bats altogether in the season) is written in the lower half of the at-bat box. The same kind of thing is done in the hit box, home-run box, RBI box and any others.

In his second game, he had one RBI so a "1" is placed in the RBI box for that game. In Kranepool's next appearance, April 13 at Chicago, he went 1-for-3, so a "1" is put in the hit box, a "3" is put in the top part of the at-bat box, and a "9," for his season's total of at-bats, is put in the lower half. At the end of the game, he was 1-for-9 and had a batting average of .111.

I don't fill in a box unless the player has done something in that category on that day. For instance, none of the boxes relating to hits, runs or RBI's are filled in for the first game.

By leaving boxes blank in categories in which nothing happened, I have a clear picture of how long it's been since a player did do something. For instance, it's easy to see that Kranepool had no walks from April 13 until the second game of a double-header May 2, when he drew two against Houston.

To indicate a double-header, I put a small "1" in parentheses to indicate it's the first game, and a small "2" in parentheses to indicate the second game.

In the first game on May 2, Kranepool went 3-for-4 and scored three runs, so I put a "4" in the top of the at-bat box and a "74," for his cumulative at-bat total, in the lower half of the box. The "3" and "11" in the runs column indicate he scored three runs that day, bringing his season's total to 11. And the "3" and "21" in the hit box reflect his hits for the game and the season.

The abbreviations I use are slightly different from the standard ones. For the sake of expediency and to help fit in all the columns, I'll use just "S" for sacrifice hits rather than "SH" and "GDP" rather than "GIDP" for "grounded into double play." The "I" after "BB" tells how many of the bases on balls the man received were intentional. Through May 20, Kranepool hadn't received any intentional passes, so we know all his walks were unintentional.

Kranepool's average went from .257 on April 30 to .300 on May 4, but then it slipped back down to .276 on May 20. Being easy to read, the batting sheet enables me quickly to trace a hitter's streaks and slumps over the course of a season.

Pitching Sheet

As you can see from the pitching sheet on page 70, which was kept on Tom Seaver in the 1976 season, a pitching sheet gives the date of the game, the Mets' opponent, the pitcher's won-lost record after the game, his earned-run average after the game, what number game it is for the pitcher this season, what number of starts it represents, how many complete games he's pitched, how many innings pitched, and how many hits, runs and earned runs the pitcher has allowed. Also, how many bases on balls he gave and how many of them were intentional, how many he struck out, how many wild pitches he threw, how many batters he hit, how many homers he yielded, how many games he's saved, and how many shutouts he pitched.

As with the hitting sheets I do, two figures are entered in some boxes, the top one to give the number in the particular game, the lower one to give the cumulative total in that category. Figures for home games are written in blue, road games in red.

Seaver's first appearance of the season was on April 9 against Montreal. He won the game, so his record was 1-0. He gave up one run in seven innings pitched, giving him a 1.29 ERA. The run he gave up was earned. He allowed five hits and one walk, made one wild pitch and hit one batter with a pitch. Tom struck out eight and gave no home runs. It was neither a save nor a shutout for him, so those boxes are left empty.

Tom's second appearance of the season was a start on April 14 at Chicago. In that game, he pitched five innings, so I entered a "5" in the top portion of the innings pitched (IP) box, and a "12" in the lower portion, which indicates the total innings pitched thus far this season. Similarly, he gave up five hits, so a "5" is put in the top of the hit box, and a "10" in the lower half, because that's how many hits he has allowed this season. In this game, he allowed three runs, all of them earned, bringing his total to four earned runs allowed for the season. His ERA was 3.00 after the game. He gave up two walks, neither one intentional, bringing his total to three for the season. Five strikeouts brought his total to thirteen in that category. He gave up his first home run of the season.

You can see that Seaver had a winning streak from June 13 to 23, during which time he won three straight starts, beating San Francisco twice and St. Louis once. Two of those victories were complete games. He then went two more starts without winning before beating Atlanta on July 8. The nine innings he pitched that day brought his total innings pitched to 150⅔. (In this instance, the numeral to the right of the decimal point refers to thirds of an inning.) You'll notice that in the next game, he pitched only one-third of an inning, bringing his total to 151.

It's easy to see how his ERA fluctuated during the course of the season. It reached its low point of 1.89 after his fifth start of the season, went up to 3.43 on

DATE	TEAM	W-L	ERA	G	GS	CG	IP	H	R	ER	BB-I	SO	WP	HB	HR	SV	SHO
Apr. 9	M+l	1-0	1.29	1	1		7	5	1	1		8	1	1	1		
14	Chi.		3.00	2	2		5	5	3	3	2	5			1		
							12	10	4	4	3	13					
19	St.L		3.15	3	3		8	5	3	3	3-1	8	2	3			
							20	17	7	7	6-1	21					
24	Hou	2-0	2.48	4	4	1	9	3			5	5					
							29	20	8	8	11-1	26					
29	Atl	3-0	1.89	5	5	2	9	5				9					1
							38	25				35					
May 4	Cin	4-0	2.05	6	6		6.1	6	2	2	7-1	4	1				
							44.1	31	10	10	18-2	41	4				
9	SD	4-1	2.21	7	7	3	7	10	4	3		5					
							53.1	41	14	13	22-3	46			2	2	
15	Cin	4-2	2.25	8	8		7	5	2	2	4-1	9					
							60.1	46	16	15	22-3	55					
20	Pha	4-3	2.61	9	9	4	9	7	5	5	3	8		1	1		
							69.1	53	21	20	25-3	63	5		3		
25	Pha	4-4	3.24	10	10		6	15	7	7	3	5		1	1		
							75.1	68	28	27	28-3	68	6		4		
30	St.L		3.43	11	11		8.2	8	5	5	5	2					
							84	76	33	32	33-3	70					
June 4	LA	5-4	3.10	12	12	5	9	3			1	8					2
							93	79			34-3	78					
9	SD	5-5	3.06	13	13		7		2	2	1	7					
							100	88	35	34	35-3	85					
(2) 13	SF	6-5	2.88	14	14		8.2					3					
							108.2	93	36	35	36-3	88					
18	SF	7-5	2.82	15	15	6	9					6			1		
							117.2	95	38	37	38-3	94	7		5		
23	St.L	8-5	2.91	16	16	7	9	8	4	4	1-1	11					
							126.2	103	42	41	39-4	105			6		
28	St.L		2.78	17	17		6	5	3	3	1	6					
							132.2	109	45	44	40-4	111	9				
July 3	Chi.		2.92	18	18		9	10	2	2	2-1	8					
							141.2	118	47	46	42-5	119			7		
8	Atl	9-5	2.80	19	19	8	9	6	2	1		8					
							150.2	124	49	47		127					
11	Atl		2.80	20			1.1				1-1	1					
							151				43-5						
17	Hou	9-6	2.72	21	20		8	3				11					
							159	127	50	48		138			8		
23	M+l		2.68	22	21		9	6	2	2	2-0	8			2		
							168	133	52	50	45-5	146	9		10		
28	Pit		2.53	23	22		10	7			4-1	10					
							178	140			49-6	156		3			
Aug. 2	M+l		2.48	24	23		8	4			4	8					
							185	144	54	51	53-6	164	10				
7	Pit	9-7	2.65	25	24		5	8	5	5	2-1	7					
							190	152	59	56	55-7	171					
12	SD	9-8	2.70	26	25		7.1	5	3	3	2	3					
							197.1	157	62	59	57-7	174					
18	LA	9-9	2.62	27	26	9	8.2	7	3	1	1	5					
							206	164	65	60	62-8	179	11				
24	SF	10-9	2.51	28	27	10	9	4				8					3
							215	168			63-8	187					
29	LA	10-10	2.50	29	28		8	7	2	2	2	7					
							223	175	67	62	65-9	194			11		
Sept 3	Pha	11-10	2.41	30	29	11	9	4			3-1	8					4
							232	179			68-9	202	12				
8	Chi.	12-10	2.50	31	30		6	8	4	4	3	7					
							238	187	71	66	71-9	207			12		

70

NO.	GAME	DATE	TEAM	PITCHER	MOB	INN	NOTES
1	4	4-13	Cubs (at)	Knowles (L)	0	8	
2	7	4-16	Pirates (at)	Medich (R)	0	4	
3	11	4-20	Cardinals (at)	McGlothen (R)	1	2	
4	34	5-16	Reds	Gullett (L)	0	4	
5	45	5-29	Cardinals	Forsch (R)	0	4	
6	46	5-30	Cardinals	McGlothen (R)	1	6	
7	54	6-6	Dodgers	Sutton (R)	1	3	
8	66	6-18	Giants	Dressler (R)	0	4	
9	73	6-26	Cubs	Bonham (R)	3	3	3rd Career Grand Slam
10	77	7-1	Cardinals	Wallace (L)	3	6	4th Career Grand Slam
11	104	7-31	Phillies (at)	Christenson (R)	0	1	
12	112	8-7	Pirates (at)	Tekulve (R)	1	8	
13	120	8-17	Dodgers (at)	Rhoden (R)	2	1	
14	156	9-27	Expos	Landreth (R)	1	3	
15	156	9-27	Expos	Lang (R)	3	6	5th Career Grand Slam

May 30, and then stayed under 3.00 for the entire season after June 13.

As with a batting sheet, you'll notice that I don't fill in a box unless the player has done something in that category that game. For instance, on June 4, when Seaver pitched a shutout, I filled in nothing in the runs or earned-runs column, because there was nothing to fill.

Home-Run Cards

The home-run card I keep on each of the Mets tells you everything you might want to know—the date each homer was hit, whether at home or on the road, against what team and pitcher, whether the pitcher was a lefty or righty, how many were hit with men on base, what field they were hit to. The card will also show how many career homers the player had at the start of the season, so that by simply adding that figure to how many he has to date for the season, I can quickly give his up-to-date career total.

This is John Milner's 1976 home-run card. As you can see, he had only seven homers in 1975, and a lifetime total of 67 coming into the 1976 season. Home runs hit in home games are marked in blue and those in away games are marked in red. "At" tells in whose park the Mets' away game was played.

John's first homer of the 1976 season came in the Mets' fourth game (not necessarily Milner's fourth) of the season, on April 13 against the Cubs. Darold Knowles was the pitcher he hit it off, and the "L" in parentheses indicates a left-handed pitcher. "MOB—o" means there were no men on base when Milner homered, in the eighth inning ("INN").

You can quickly tell when Milner had slumps and when he was on a good hitting streak by noting the dates and numbers of the games in which he hit his home runs.

Milner's streak of grand slams is readily apparent on the card. On June 26 he hit one off Bill Bonham of the Cubs in Chicago in the third inning. Then, four games later, on July 1, he hit a grand slam in the sixth off Mike Wallace, a lefty. On September 27 he hit another grand slam, this one against right-hander Chip Lang of the Expos. Earlier in that game, he hit a "plain" homer against Larry Landreth, with one man on.

The home-run card fully spells out a batter's homer record. In just a glance, you can calculate how many he's hit on the road and at home, off lefties or righties, how many men were on base, how long since he hit his last one, how many he's hit this season and in his career, etc.

I keep the home-run cards of the Met players right alongside me so that when a drive starts out looking as if it might be a home run, I get the batter's card right out. Our broadcaster can give all the particulars as the hitter is rounding the bases, not when the next batter is at the plate.

Pitching Cards

I keep a pitching card for every pitcher in the National League. It's a system I set up when I started with the Mets. A pitcher's card lists every appearance he has made this season. It tells who his opponent was, at home or away, whether he won or lost and by what score. It also tells how many runs and hits he allowed in each of those appearances.

If a pitcher has been traded, the card would show when that happened, and the broadcaster would be able to give specifics about the pitcher's record with each of the clubs for which he played. A pitcher's career record is, of course, part of the information on his card.

With the aid of a pitching card, a broadcaster will be able to tell fans a lot more than simply, "Sosa is a right-hander with a 6-3 record."

As an example, look at the 1976 pitching card of Jim Lonborg of the Phillies, on page 74.

At the top of the card you'll see that his record in the previous season, 1975, was 8-6. His lifetime record in the major leagues was 120-112, while his record against the Mets was 1-0 in 1975 and 5-4 lifetime. In his listing of 1976 appearances, the number "1" indicates it was his first appearance and the "S" means it was a start.

He first appeared in a game on April 14, against the Expos at Montreal. The "W" tells us he got a win. The score was 8–2. The "1" indicates it was his first complete game of the season. He pitched nine innings, gave up six hits, two runs (one of which was earned), three walks, and struck out six. ("K" is a traditional symbol for strikeouts.) His won-lost record for the season was now 1-0.

We know that his second appearance of the season was in relief because of the "R." In that game he pitched just a third of an inning and got no decision.

Coming into the month of June, before his start on June 4, Lonborg had a perfect 8-0 record. His two starts against the Mets on May 20 and May 25 are indicated in red to make them stand out.

If there's something outstanding that ought to be noted, such as a no-hitter or save, I'll add it in the "notations" column.

When a pitcher is starting against the Mets, his card is included in the clipboard I provide for each of the announcers (as is a card for the Met starter). The announcers can look over the visitor's card either before the game or once it's under way. As soon as a reliever comes in, I pass his pitching card over to the broadcaster, and he has a pretty good picture of what this man has done this season and through his career.

I keep the pitching cards up-to-date by checking the box scores of all National League games every day and adding pertinent information to the cards that same day.

Pitching Chart

A pitching chart is kept for every game of the season, usually by the pitcher who's slated to start the next day's game. He charts each pitch thrown in the previous game (by his team's pitcher) in such a way that whenever you study the

JIM LONBORG

1975 8-6
LIFE 120-112

1975 vs NY 1-0
LIFE vs NY 5-4

APPEAR-ANCES		DATE	TEAM	DECISION	SCORE	COMPLETE GAMES	IP	H	R	ER	BB	K	NOTATIONS	RECORD	
														W	L
1	S	4/14	At Mtl	W	8-2	1	9	6	2	1	3	6		1	0
2	R	4/17	At Chi	-	14-16		1/3	0	0	0	0	0		1	0
3	S	4/23	Atl	-	5-6		6 2/3	5			3	4		1	0
4	S	4/28	Cin	W	7-6		5	8	4	4	4	1		2	0
5	S	5/4	Hou	W	5-0	2	9	7	0	0	0	3		3	0
6	S	5/9	LA	W	10-3	1	8	6	3	3	2	7		4	0
7	S	5/15	At Hou	W	2-1	3	9	4	1	1	1	4		5	0
8	S	5/20	At Mets	W	5-3		6 1/3	9	3	3	0	2		6	0
9	S	5/25	Mets	W	8-4		7	8	4	4	2	4		7	0
10	S	5/30	Mtl	W	7-1	4	9	5	1	0	3	3		8	0
11	S	6/4	At SF	L	1-5		6	10	5	5	0	3		8	1
12	S	6/9	LA	L	2-3	5	8	10	3	2	1	7		8	2
13	S	6/13	At SD	L	0-5		7 2/3	9	4	4	2	2		8	3
14	S	6/18	Cin	W	6-5		8	9	4	2	4	6		9	3
15	S	6/22	Mtl	L	3-8		5	6	4	4	3	3		9	4
16	S	6/27	At StL	W	6-2		5 2/3	6	2	2	2	6		10	4
17	S	7/5	LA	L	0-6		6	7	3	3	0	5		10	5
18	S	7/10	SD	W	4-2		7	4	2		2	4		11	5
19	S	7/18	At LA	-	2-1		7	7	1	1	2	5		11	5
20	S	7/23	Pit	W	11-1	6	9	6	1	1	0	5		12	5
21	S	7/27	Chi.	-	2-5		9	5	2	2	1	7		12	5
22	S	8/2	At Chi.	L	2-4		6	8	4	4	2	3		12	6
23	S	8/6	At St.L	L	2-6		6 1/3	5	2	2	2	2		12	7
24	S	8/13	Atl.	L	3-4		3	8	4	4	2			12	8
25	S	8/19	Mtl.	W	5-4		7 1/3	9	4	4	3	4		13	8

chart, even a year later, you can tell whether a particular pitch was a ball or strike, what kind of pitch it was (fastball, curve, etc.) and if the ball was hit, where it went and whether it was a base hit or an out.

The best way to learn the details of a pitching chart is to study one. The chart reproduced on page 76 is of a game played September 22, 1976, between the Mets and the Expos at Montreal. Jon Matlack was the Mets' starting pitcher.

As the printed portion at the top of the sheet explains, an "X" stands for hit-and-run, "S" for swing, "1" for fastball, "2" for curve, "3" for slider, "4" for a change of pace, "5" for screwball and "6" for knuckleball. A line drive is symbolized by a straight line, a ground ball by a dotted line, and a fly ball by an arc.

This chart was prepared by "#41," Tom Seaver. The catcher ("C") was Stearns, the plate umpire ("U"), John McSherry. The temperature was 52° and the game started at 8:05.

Within the large box for each batter's turn at bat are a series of very small boxes, one row following the letter "B," for balls, and the row below following the letter "S" for strikes. The box in the lower left portion of the big box represents the diamond. Should the batter hit the ball, its trajectory will be drawn here. The small box in the lower right portion of the big box contains the number of the inning in which that at-bat took place. The numeral above that lower right-hand box is the cumulative total of pitches thrown in the game.

The first pitch to Bombo Rivera, leading off in the bottom of the first against Jon Matlack, was a fastball low and on the inside corner. How do we know that? The "1" stands for fastball. The dot to the left of the "1" indicates the location of the pitch, high and inside. (Since the dot is to the left of the numeral, the pitch was inside. If the pitch had been outside, the dot would have been placed to the right.) Since the number is written in the row next to the letter "S," we know it was a strike. The second pitch was a curveball ("2") inside, for a ball. And so was the third pitch. The fourth pitch was a fastball. The little check mark indicates the batter swung. The fifth pitch was another fastball for a ball. The fact that the dot is in the upper right-hand corner indicates it was high and outside.

With the count 3-2, Rivera swung at the sixth pitch and, as the straight line drawn through the box in the lower left-hand corner tells you, it was a line drive to center field. The "L-8" indicates it was a line drive caught by the center fielder.* The "1" in the circle means he was the first out of the inning.

* As most baseball fans know, each fielding position has a number for scoring purposes. The pitcher is number 1; the catcher, 2; first baseman, 3; second baseman, 4; third baseman, 5; shortstop, 6; left fielder, 7; center fielder, 8; and right fielder, 9.

75

X – HIT – RUN
S – SWING
1 – FAST BALL
2 – CURVE
3 – SLIDER
4 – CHANGE
5 – SCREW BALL
6 – KNUCKLE BALL

Date **9·22·76**

N. Y.
at
MONTREAL

PREPARED BY **#41**   C. STEARNS
U: McSPERRY

BATTING PRACTICE
1. ....
2. ....
3. ....

LINE DRIVE ——————
GROUND BALL · · · · · · ·
FLY BALL   52°
7:05

BATTER

RIVERA — L8 — E4 — 1B — 63 — (fielding marks)

FOLI — F3 — 1B — DP 543 — 53

DAWSON — 53 — F8 — F8 — Ks

VALENTINE — F1 — F8 — HR — F8

WILLIAMS — HR — 1B — Ks — F8

PARRISH — 1B — DP F83 — 1B — 1B

MACKANIN — F3 — F8 — F9 — FC

FOOTE — 53 — 2B — F1 — 1B

MORALES·9⁴ᵗᴮ
THORNTON·7ᶜ'ˢ
FREED·5ᵗ²
LANGE·3ᴿᴰ

LANDRETH — 53 — Ks — L4

P.H.   P.H.   P.H. LOCKWOOD

N.Y. 030 010 000 – 4
MONT. 010 001 000 – 2

PITCHER		FAST BALLS	CURVES	CHANGE	SLIDER	SCREW BALLS	KNUCKLE BALLS	H	R	SO	BB	TOTAL
MATLACK 1.2	BALLS	18	20	2				10	2	3	0	40
	STRIKES	50	18	9								77
LOCKWOOD .1	BALLS	3						0	0	0	0	3
	STRIKES	2										2
	BALLS											
	STRIKES											
	BALLS											
	STRIKES											
	BALLS											
	STRIKES											
	BALLS											
	STRIKES											
	BALLS											
	STRIKES											
	BALLS											
	STRIKES											

W.P. MATLACK
L.P. LANDRETH

Tim Foli was next up, and the first pitch to him was a curveball on the outside corner of the plate for a strike. The second pitch was a curveball on the outside part of the plate, and, as the slash reveals, was fouled off for a strike. The third pitch was a change-up (''4'') on the outside corner of the plate, which was also fouled off. The fourth pitch was a fastball inside—ball one. The next was a fastball outside, so now the count was 2-2. On the sixth pitch to Foli, a fastball inside, he swung and hit a pop foul to the first baseman, as indicated by the trajectory drawn in the lower left-hand corner and by the ''F-3.'' The ''1'' inside the box in the lower right-hand corner means it was the first inning. The ''12'' above that box represents the cumulative total of pitches Matlack had thrown up to that point. The circled ''2'' indicates the second out.

In the second inning, Ellis Valentine led off for Montreal. The first pitch to him was a fastball on the outside corner of the plate for a strike. The next pitch was another fastball, a little lower than the previous one (note the position of the dot) and on the outside portion of the plate, in the strike zone. Valentine swung and hit a fly ball to the left fielder. The ''1'' in the circle indicates he was the first out of the inning. The ''2'' in the lower right-hand box indicates it was the second inning. The ''16'' is the total number of pitches thrown by Matlack. The next batter, Earl Williams, took a curveball outside and a fastball high and outside for a 2-0 count. The next pitch was a fastball on the inside portion of the plate and Williams hit a home run. You can trace the trajectory of the ball by following the line outside the box. The slash marks inside the box indicate he scored a run, and the ''HR'' stands for home run. Since he did not make an out, no number is circled.

Larry Parrish, up next, took a fastball inside. The next pitch was a change-up that he fouled off. He then swung and fouled off an inside fastball, then fouled off a breaking pitch on the outside of the plate. A curveball outside brought the count to 2-2. On the sixth pitch he blooped a base hit to right field on an inside fastball. The ''1B'' stands for a one-base hit. And so forth.

In the sixth inning, you can see that when Valentine hit his home run, Matlack had fallen behind him, 3-1. He had also fallen behind on the count to Williams on his first-inning home run.

In the sixth inning, Williams struck out swinging (as noted by the ''Ks''). But Matlack had already thrown eighty-six pitches and was still only in the sixth inning, a lot of pitches for that number of innings.

A pitching chart is particularly valuable when you have a pitcher returning after an arm injury. For instance, Craig Swan missed a lot of time with a tender elbow in the 1976 season. When he came back to pitch, Joe Frazier and pitching coach Rube Walker decided that he'd throw only 70–75 pitches in his first appearance. The pitching chart being kept that day told them when he had thrown the prescribed amount.

It's also valuable for the manager and pitching coach to know how many pitches someone has thrown at a given point in a game early in the season. When a pitcher has just come out of spring training, and the weather is still cool, they might decide that he'll come out of the game when he's thrown one hundred pitches—no matter what the score of the game is.

On the same sample pitching chart, we can see that Skip Lockwood came in to pitch to pinch-hitter ("P.H.") Jose Morales with two out in the ninth inning. Pinch-hitters and substitutes are listed in the last box, above the name of Landreth, the Montreal pitcher.

Lockwood threw all fastballs to Morales, the first three for balls and the next for a strike. He then threw a fastball outside that Morales lined to the second baseman ("L4") for the final out of the game. A circled "3" indicates Morales was the last out of the game. The "5" on top of the lower right-hand box is the total number of pitches Lockwood threw. The "9" in the box indicates it was the ninth inning.

Everything is totaled at the bottom of the sheet. The inning-by-inning score for both teams is given. Matlack, in 8⅔ innings pitched, threw 68 fastballs, 38 curves and 11 changes, allowing 10 hits and 2 runs. He struck out ("SO") three and walked ("BB") none. Fifty of his fastballs were strikes, as were eighteen curves and nine changes. Lockwood threw five fastballs, three for balls and two for strikes (including the pitch that Morales lined for the final out). The winning pitcher ("W.P.") was Matlack and the losing pitcher ("L.P.") was Landreth.

The compiled pitching chart is given to pitching coach Rube Walker, who keeps all the charts on a clipboard. After the season Rube takes all the charts home with him (Jerry Koosman kiddingly says that it gives Rube something to do during the winter). In the off-season Rube will study the pitches a particular pitcher has thrown, and try to find a pattern of performance. One pitcher may get hurt a lot when he's behind, because then he comes in with a fastball rather than a breaking pitch, and the batters have come to expect it. Or Rube may come up with something else a pitcher may not have been aware of. During the season, pitchers will refer to the charts and sometimes they'll get photocopies of the pitching charts to take home and study over the winter.

Batting Order Card. This is a copy of the official batting order card that Joe Torre handed to the plate umpire prior to the Mets-Pirates game on September

ON ROAD—OFFICIAL BATTING ORDER

CLUB **NEW YORK**   DATE 9/27/77

#	ORIGINAL		CHANGE	ALSO ELIGIBLE
1	RANDLE 5	B	Norman	NORMAN
		C		MANGUEL
2	MAZZILLI 8	B		STAIGER
		C		VAIL
3	BOISCLAIR 9	B	Staiger	FOSTER
		C		ROSADO
4	HENDERSON 7	B		HODGES
		C		KRANEPOOL
5	MILNER 3	B		HARRELSON
		C		MATLACK
6	STEARNS 2	B		KOOSMAN
		C		SWAN - TODD
7	YOUNGBLOOD 4	B		ZACHRY
		C		JACKSON
8	FLYNN 6	B		MEDICH
		C		PACELLA
9	ESPINOSA. 1	B		BALDWIN
		C		APODACA
		D		LOCKWOOD
		E		SIEBERT
				MYRICK

MANAGER'S SIGNATURE J Torre

OFFICIAL BATTING ORDER

CLUB **PITTSBURGH**   DATE 11/27/77

#	ORIGINAL		CHANGE	ALSO ELIGIBLE
1	TAVERAS	B	Edwards	BERRA
		C		FOSTER
2	GARNER	B		EASLER
		C		EDWARDS
3	PARKER	B	Easler	DYER
		C		EASLER
4	ROBINSON	B	Berra	DUFFY
		C		MENDOZA
5	OLIVER	B	Gonzalez	DYER
		C		HARLSON
6	OTT	B		BIBBS - KIRKER
		C		FORSTER
7	MACHA	B		JACKSON
		C		HOLLAND
8	MORENO	B		CANDELARIA
		C		GOSSAGE - DEMERY
9	KISON	B		TEKULVE
		C		ROBINSON - TERRELL
		D		
		E		D. JONES

VISITING MANAGER'S COPY C. Tanner

27, 1977. The original was kept by Torre; a carbon copy was given to the opposing manager and another copy to the plate umpire. The back lists the ground rules.

Batting order cards come in three different colors. The Mets fill out a white one for home games, a blue one when they're on the road, and a green one in spring training. Except for the difference in color, all are the same.

There is room for changes when someone is replaced in the course of a game, in which case the manager crosses out whoever was in that batting spot and fills in the replacement's name in the "Change" column.

There is an "Also Eligible" category for players who are on the bench, available to play, but not starting the game. A quick look by the manager can tell him what players he has left to use as pinch-hitters, pinch-runners or anything else.

One of the Mets' coaches pastes the batting order slip on the wall of the dugout right where the manager sits. The coach will list the available hitters according to which side of the plate they hit from—first the right-handed pinch-hitters, then the lefties. If there's a switch-hitter on the bench, he'll write "SH" next to his name. As a player is used in the game, his name is crossed out, so a glance will tell who is available as the game goes on.

1976

SHEA STADIUM

GROUND RULES

Ball hitting above amber line on ledge of wall in right and left field in fair territory — HOME RUN.

Ball hitting edge of amber line of wall in right and left field in fair territory and bouncing into bull pen — TWO BASES.

Ball rolling under any part of field boxes and staying out of sight — ONE BASE on throw by pitcher from rubber — TWO BASES on throw by in-fielder.

Ball hitting side of facing of dugout considered IN DUGOUT.

Ball going into dugout — ONE BASE on throw by pitcher from rubber — TWO BASES from field.

Fair ball bouncing over fence — TWO BASES.

Fair ball bouncing over temporary fence in foul territory in left and right field — TWO BASES.

Typical Day at Shea

IT MIGHT BE of interest for you to know what happens in the broadcast booth before, during and after a game. Let's take the game between the Reds and the Mets on August 13, 1976.

A normal day at Shea Stadium starts for me about two and a half hours before a game, which means about 5:30 P.M. when there's a night game, 11 or 11:30 A.M. before a day game. When I get to the park, I take my updated stats stencil to my second-floor office in the public relations department. While Tim Hamilton is having the stencil run off downstairs, I'll catch up on various things. For example, I'll skim the sports section of one or two afternoon papers I haven't yet seen, to cut out box scores or other items of interest that can be given to our broadcasters. If I'm out of scoresheets or other blanks I use in my work, I'll stop in the supply room to replenish my supply.

About six o'clock, I pack my case with mimeographed stat sheets and other materials and begin my rounds. After I get a copy of the line-up, which has been posted in the dugout by one of the coaches, my first stop is the manager's office, where I give the Mets' manager two copies of each of the Mets' stat sheets and two copies of each of the visitors' stat sheets. The visitors' sheets are especially important before the first game of series. They tell you such things as which visiting player is hot and which isn't. It's important to know how opposition players have been doing *currently*. The fact that someone on the Reds, for instance, has a .280 average isn't as important as how well he's been hitting in

81

the week or two before the Reds play the Mets. Whether he's hot or cold *now* is the story.

While I'm there, I'll ask the manager why a particular player is out of the line-up—whether he's injured, or whatever. The manager's answers will provide information that I'll pass on to our broadcasters, who often will have spoken to the manager themselves. My question might be as general as "what's new?" or as specific as "why isn't Mike Vail in the line-up against the lefty who's pitching tonight?" If I happen to run into a player, I'll ask him how he's feeling, or why he isn't in the line-up, or whatever might provide some background information.

What this serves to emphasize is that the statistician is a reporter of information that may not necessarily be related to statistics. You get into injuries, personalities and general matters affecting your own club and your opponents. If the Mets are playing a team we haven't seen in quite a while, I'll go into the pressroom and chat with the visiting team's broadcasters to find out what's new with their club—who's hot, who's in a slump, who's injured, who's being rumored about for a trade, and so on. If they've brought up a kid from the minors, I try to find out from their broadcasters or their P.R. man what his record was with the farm team. If you wait until the newcomer is at bat or in the bullpen during the game, it's going to be very difficult to get the information and transmit it to both your TV and radio broadcasters in time.

During the course of a game, too, we'll share player and team information with the visiting team's broadcasters, whose booth is right next to our radio booth. Cincinnati's duo, Marty Brennarman and Joe Nuxhall—the former pitcher who was the youngest pitcher (age fifteen) ever to appear in a major league game—are especially cooperative.

From the manager's office, I go to the TV control room, where I leave off a copy of all the stat sheets, plus a copy of the out-of-town schedule and scores. There I'll visit the executive producer, Ralph Robbins, and the director, Jack Simon, and we'll exchange information about the day's game. The TV control room needs copies of the stats so that throughout the game they can update batting averages and other stats for the Videograph machine to flash on the TV screen as each batter comes to the plate.

I also give stat sheets to the radio broadcast booth and to the TV broadcast booth, and keep a set for myself.

My visits to the manager's office, the visiting broadcasters, the television control room and TV and radio broadcast booths takes me to about 6:30 or 6:45. At least an hour before game time, I want to be at my post in the radio broadcast booth, which is up behind home plate. The first thing I do when I arrive there is to get the Western Union ticker going for the out-of-town games (such as those at Wrigley Field, where there are only daytime games).

The statistician should always be there and set by the time the broadcasters arrive. Since they're often delayed by meetings with sponsors' groups, or by pregame presentations, I want to have everything ready for them. Consequently, I discourage people from stopping by to chat with me before the game.

I make up a sheet for the broadcaster containing the batting order and all the important statistics, such as hitting streaks that players have going for them. I put this on a sheet because it's easier for them to read it that way rather than constantly having to refer to stat sheets. With a team such as the Cincinnati Reds in 1976, there are a lot of things to check out—how many Reds are among the top ten National League hitters, which of them are among the RBI leaders and so forth. That season, on one of the Reds' visits to New York, they had won thirteen of their last fifteen games and this fact was, of course, noted on the sheet I prepared for the broadcasters.

When the Mets are at home, I normally am prepared early. About an hour before game time I will get the visiting team's line-up. I have to be careful with the visitors' line-up, even though I may be very familiar with their uniform numbers, and so I'll always double-check it with the scoreboard. About five minutes before the game begins, the line-ups are announced on the public address system, and I automatically check off that line-up against mine, in case there has been a late substitution because of injury or illness. Sometimes this happens without anyone having said anything, and the new entry will just appear on the scoreboard or be announced over the public address system. In several instances, we've looked at the on-deck circle and seen a batter we didn't have listed in the line-up. Occasionally I get so tied up doing something else that I get careless with the line-up.

Friday nights are almost always more hectic than other nights because all teams play and there are more out-of-town scores to keep abreast of throughout the game than there would be on Saturday, for instance. Friday night games also tend to attract bigger crowds, which means more noise and more strain; and if it's the first game of a series, as Friday night games usually are, that adds to my preparation time. Sundays, too, are hectic, but there's something about a night game that is more exciting than an afternoon game. This is especially true during the hot months, when the heat slows the pace of an afternoon game.

Members of the press are served by one of the Mets' public relations staff—Arthur Richman or Tim Hamilton—who will occasionally turn to me for an answer to a question. Sometimes a newspaperman will come directly to me.

83

And when I have a piece of information that I think is newsworthy, I'll call Arthur or Tim to remind him to announce it to the newspapermen covering the game. But I'll make sure that our radio and TV, the media that need data immediately, get it first.

Almost anything can come up in the course of the game concerning rules, records or anything else, and I'm always available to look it up for the sportswriter. If things are hectic, it may take a few minutes until I can get back to him, but the writers understand.

Game Time:
August 13, 1976

BACK IN THE broadcast booth before the game, Bob Murphy asks what's happening in the double-header between the Cubs and the Dodgers in Chicago, and I tell him that the Cubs were winning big, but the Dodgers just scored three runs and it's now 7–5, Chicago. It's amazing, but after a fifteen-inning first game, it seems as if they're going to be able to finish the second game, even though they have no lights at Wrigley Field. It's 6:50 in Chicago now, but if the weather is good and the skies are clear, they might be able to get the game in, Bob says. It's the top of the ninth inning there.

Bob asks who the winning pitcher in the first game was, and I tell him it was Joe Coleman. "The Cubs are getting surprisingly good pitching," he says. "I can't understand it." He asks what the Cubs' record is, and I tell him they've won seven out of ten coming into today's second game.

During home games, my headquarters is the radio booth, because at Shea there are people in the TV booth to help me keep score, change averages and so forth. I'm close enough to the TV booth that if they need something quickly, I can supply it, either by going there, or by leaning out of the radio booth and gesturing.

TV is really the more important medium, because then people can see what's happening and they need the corresponding information immediately— for example, the name of the pitcher the fans at home see warming up. So on the

85

road, when I don't have people helping out in the TV booth, I make sure I am located there.

Now I walk a few steps to the TV booth, which is located next door to the radio booth (on its third-base side) at Shea, and share with Lindsey Nelson the information I just discussed with Bob Murphy and Ralph Kiner. I take with me a copy of the out-of-town scoresheet containing the details of the unusually long 15-inning afternoon game in Chicago. (Incidentally, a stage manager sits alongside our TV broadcasters at home and assists them with identifications, giving out the scores, etc.)

Before and during the game, there will be occasions when I'll give a piece of information to the color man (Ralph Kiner) rather than to the play-by-play man (Lindsey or Bob), either because it's something he can use better, or because I don't want to disturb the play-by-play broadcaster. Also, it gives the play-by-play man a moment to catch his breath. An example of this would be if shortstop Dave Concepcion were to make an error, and rather than break in on Bob Murphy, I would tell Ralph Kiner that it is Dave's twentieth of the season, an unusually high number.

Bob Murphy asks whether Ken Griffey is leading the league in hitting, and I tell him that Griffey is still a point behind Bill Madlock. On the data sheets I give the broadcasters, I put down what Madlock was hitting coming into today's double-header in Chicago, so they can relate it to what Griffey does in tonight's game. If I have the time and feel it's sufficiently important, I'll try to get information about what Madlock did in this afternoon's games. That can be done in several ways, such as calling someone in the Cubs' public relations department or at WNEW-AM, the local New York radio station that broadcasts our games, and, of course, checking the wire for box scores.

Ralph Kiner asks about Pete Rose's on-base percentage, and I get to work finding it out—dividing his total appearances at the plate by his hits and walks. Ralph asks, "Rose leads in hits and runs, right?" I confirm that he does, and add that Morgan leads in stolen bases; Griffey is second by a point in batting; Foster is third in batting, first in homers and first in RBI's.

The scoresheet that Ralph and the other broadcasters use contains a diagram of the field, on which they write in the names of the men playing the defensive positions. Ralph's scoresheet is bigger than the one I use. The reason I use a small one is that I have so many other papers that I try to conserve space where possible. I don't recommend that anyone else use a small scoresheet.

Ralph uses different color markers to underscore any outstanding play or

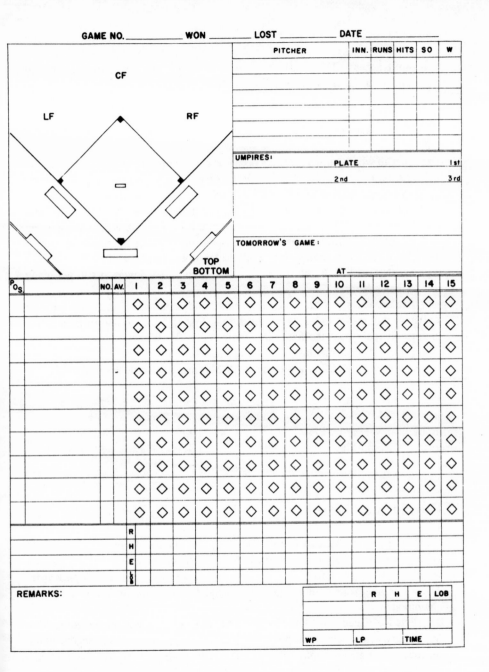

POS.		NO.	AV.	1	2	3	4	5	6	7	8	9	10	11	12	13	14	15
				◇	◇	◇	◇	◇	◇	◇	◇	◇	◇	◇	◇	◇	◇	◇
				◇	◇	◇	◇	◇	◇	◇	◇	◇	◇	◇	◇	◇	◇	◇
				◇	◇	◇	◇	◇	◇	◇	◇	◇	◇	◇	◇	◇	◇	◇
			-	◇	◇	◇	◇	◇	◇	◇	◇	◇	◇	◇	◇	◇	◇	◇
				◇	◇	◇	◇	◇	◇	◇	◇	◇	◇	◇	◇	◇	◇	◇
				◇	◇	◇	◇	◇	◇	◇	◇	◇	◇	◇	◇	◇	◇	◇
				◇	◇	◇	◇	◇	◇	◇	◇	◇	◇	◇	◇	◇	◇	◇
				◇	◇	◇	◇	◇	◇	◇	◇	◇	◇	◇	◇	◇	◇	◇
				◇	◇	◇	◇	◇	◇	◇	◇	◇	◇	◇	◇	◇	◇	◇
				◇	◇	◇	◇	◇	◇	◇	◇	◇	◇	◇	◇	◇	◇	◇
		R																
		H																
		E																
		LOB																

REMARKS:

	R	H	E	LOB
WP		LP		TIME

rally—not necessarily to call attention to it during the game, but possibly to highlight it on "Kiner's Korner."

Order of Broadcasters

The order in which our announcers broadcast Met games is rotated. Bob Murphy will start on radio one day and on TV the other. Whichever he doesn't start on, Lindsey Nelson will. Ralph Kiner does color for two innings on TV, then does the third and fourth innings of play-by-play on radio, while the broadcaster who did the first two innings on radio takes two innings off. There is no TV colorman in the third and fourth innings. Whoever opens on TV does the first four innings there, then takes two innings off, while Ralph does the fifth and sixth innings of play-by-play on TV. In the seventh inning, Ralph goes downstairs to get ready for "Kiner's Korner."

The broadcaster who did the first two innings on radio returns for the fifth and sixth innings on radio. Whoever did the first and second and fifth and sixth innings on radio does the final three innings on TV. Whoever did the first four innings on TV does the last three on radio.

If you were charting a typical day's coverage, it would look like this:

	1	2	3	4	5	6	7	8	9
Kiner	TV Color		Radio Play		TV Play		Off		
Murphy	TV Play-by-Play				Off		Radio Play		
Nelson	Radio Play		Off		Radio Play		TV Play		

During the Game

Now the game's about to begin, and the game itself, of course, is the most enjoyable part of the job for me, as well as for the broadcasters and anyone else who loves baseball. Once you lose your feeling for this, it's time to pack it in. There's more excitement tonight than usual because the Reds are the world champions.

Pete Rose leads off for the Reds, and to indicate how well Pete's going, Bob Murphy mentions that he's got more hits than any other player in the major leagues. Rose grounds out, Millan to Torre. Ken Griffey, who's also having a

88

fine year—and Bob gives some statistical evidence to support that statement—is up next and he grounds out, first baseman Torre to the pitcher, Lolich, covering.

Next up is Joe Morgan, the league's Most Valuable Player. There are so many things you can say about him you don't want to overdo it. He comes to bat leading the league in stolen bases with thirty-eight; he's drawn an incredible eighty-three bases on ball while striking out only twenty-six times, which reflects what a super ballplayer he is. He's hitting .325, has scored ninety-two runs—and you can go on and on in praise of his talents and statistics. Bob selects just a few to talk about, as Morgan draws another walk.

In 1975 the Reds set a National League record for victories at home. At this point in the 1976 season, they've compiled a 34-21 home record, which is pretty fair, but their record on the road is a remarkable 41–19. An interesting statistic, and Bob mentions it.

Lolich throws over to first, and Morgan is picked off. Torre throws down to Phillips, the shortstop, who tags Morgan for the final out of the inning. I scramble through my records and come up with the fact that it's the fifth time this season that Lolich has picked a man off, which is certainly above average. If I had anticipated the possibility of a pickoff, I would have been ready with the statistic, instead of having to rush to get it in before the commercial. Bob also mentions that Morgan is charged with a "caught stealing," because if Torre's throw had been off line or whatever, and Joe made second safely, he would have been credited with a steal.

The Western Union ticker reports that San Diego and Montreal have almost finished the first game of their twi-night double-header, which started at six o'clock, New York time. All I can do about that is wait for Western Union to send across a summary. The second game of the Dodger-Chicago twin-bill is in the ninth inning right now. Later in the season, there will be days, especially Saturday afternoons, when the ticker will be sending across reports of hockey, basketball and football, in addition to baseball games.

Bruce Boisclair hits a smash to Morgan, which the second baseman can't handle. Over the public address sytem, I hear the official scorer announce that he's charging Morgan with an error. There is so much noise and the broadcasters are concentrating so hard, they may not have heard the announcement, so I form my thumb and index finger into a circle to indicate to them it was an error. I make the gesture to Lindsey Nelson in the TV booth as well.

Boisclair goes to second when Millan is hit by a pitch, and John Milner flies out to center field. Joe Torre is coming up now and Bob Murphy will mention that Joe has hit safely in ten straight games and has a batting average of .345 in that period. This lends documentation to any general statement about Torre's "hot bat lately."

In between pitches, I keep up-to-date on the out-of-town scores. But when the pitch comes in, I stop checking the ticker tape to see what happens on the field. With two runners on base, I have to be ready for anything, including a double steal. I look up how many steal attempts and successes Boisclair has had, just in case. But Torre grounds into a double play, and the inning is over. I total up the runs, hits, errors and men left, and get set for the Cincinnati second.

Up first is George Foster, who's having a fabulous season, including 102 RBI's, which is more than any left fielder in the Reds' history. He leads the league in that department and is third both in the league batting race and in home runs. If he were on the Mets, I'd calculate what he'd finish up with if he kept to his present RBI and home-run pace, but I don't generally go to the trouble of doing it for visitors.

Western Union gives a score of the Montreal-San Diego second game. The Expos have been doing very well lately and picking up ground on the Mets in the battle for third place.

Bob Murphy makes an interesting point that demonstrates how dominant Cincinnati is over its opposition. The Reds have scored two hundred more runs than their opponents have against them, at this point in the season.

Foster and Johnny Bench ground out, and Tony Perez lines out. To update their averages I check the book that has every conceivable batting average for every possible number of hits and at-bats. I can look across and see what a hitter's average will be the next four times up. I change Perez's season's average from .263 to .262, but he's been up so many times already this year that his average may not change next time up. On the batting sheet, I put a slash through the average at which Perez started the game and fill in the new percentage. (I do this for every player in the game as he comes to bat and hits or makes out.)

The Mets traded Wayne Garrett on July 20, and since Roy Staiger took over the third-base job, he's been hitting at about a .330 clip. Bob Murphy makes this point when Staiger comes to the plate in the Mets' second. Again, the specific statistic tells more about the player's performance than just the general statement that he's been hitting the ball well over the past twenty games.

Between innings the broadcasters skim through the data on the clipboards I've prepared for them. Included are bits of information about the starting pitchers, such as their height, weight, age, place of residence and their record this season, last season and lifetime in the majors. In the case of the opposing starting pitcher, I include his record against the Mets this season and lifetime. This

PLAYER	G	AB	R	H	2b	3b	HR	RBI	AVG
8 Boisclair	75	173	22	47	6				4	272 270 279 278 277 *7 or 8 games*
4 Millan	99	382	37	100	18	2	1	20	262 361 360
7 Milner	90	316	38	82	15	3	12	57	260 258 258 260 *10 games*
3 Torre	89	241	29	75	8	2	4	23	310 307 308 307 310
9 Vail	31	81	6	21	3	1			6	259 268 265 274 271
2 Hodges	46	123	20	34	6			4	24	276 274 272 276 276
5 Staiger	55	168	15	43	6	1	2	14	256 254 253 256
6 Phillips	64	198	26	51	4	5	3	25	258 256 256 259
1 Lolich	23	41	5	6					146 143 146
Kranepool	94	321	36	90	14	1	7	37	280
Brown	43	54	8	13	3			2	241
Dwyer	58	102	9	18	3	1		5	177
Foster	5	16	3	4	2			6	250 235
Grote	87	279	25	72	8	1	3	19	258 *6 of 7 games*
Harrelson	82	249	17	54	9	2	1	20	217
Mangual	88	288	42	68	12	3	3	22	236 235

information is also available on the stat sheets, but if the broadcasters have it condensed for them in the clipboards, they have the information right in front of them and don't have to poke through a lot of papers.

Concepcion leads off the Reds' third and Ralph Kiner mentions that he was the National League's starting shortstop in this year's All-Star Game. Just after Ralph's comment, Concepcion homers to left field. Ralph immediately notes that this is the sixth homer Lolich has allowed in 146 innings, which is better than average.

As Pete Rose steps to the plate, an announcement from the Mets P.R. department comes over the loudspeaker in the broadcast booth, stating that Rose had been hitless in nineteen at-bats coming into tonight's game and is 0-for-1 so far tonight—the man with the most hits in the league is hitless tonight. Ralph Kiner mentions that fact on radio, and I go over to the TV booth to make sure that Lindsey Nelson is aware of it, too. He hasn't heard the announcement, so my visit is worthwhile.

This time Rose singles, and as he makes the big turn around first, the fans get all fired up. Another announcement from the P.R. department: "Here's some more information about Pete Rose. That single was the two-thousandth single of his career, and his next base hit will be his twenty-seven–hundredth base hit. 2-7-0-0." Pete's dream is to reach three thousand hits. (He did in 1978.)

Griffey, who came into tonight's game just one point behind Madlock for the league lead in batting average, forces Rose at second. Had he hit safely, I would have quickly calculated his average, so we could say, "As of this moment, he is leading Bill Madlock, who was hitting .332 starting today's action."

Ralph makes the point that the pitcher doesn't seem as fast as he usually is. That's Ralph's own observation, though there are times I will mention things like that to him. It may be that a pitcher is throwing more breaking pitches than usual, or a batter seems to have adopted a new stance. If Ralph agrees with my observation and thinks it's worthwhile, he'll mention it on the air.

If a pitcher has gone to a 3-2 count often, Ralph will mention that, as possible evidence of a control problem or, certainly, that a man is throwing a lot of pitches. He'll say the pitcher has gone to 3-2 on six batters so far and retired five of them. It's an interesting sidelight.

It's not all serious business in the broadcast booth. When they're not on the air—say, during a commercial break or rain delay—Bob Murphy may do a soft shoe and Lindsey Nelson may sing the words to the song Jane Jarvis is playing on the organ. Or Ralph Kiner may chat about some character of a ballplayer, while Joe Aiello, the radio soundman, needles me about something.

John Milner walks in the Mets' third. Some broadcasters, including Ralph, note down what the count was when the man drew his base on balls. Then, next time up, he'll say Milner walked on a 3-1 pitch.

Ralph is one broadcaster to whom it's easy to convey information, because he has a delightful, low-key kind of personality and a gentle sense of humor, and he very seldom gets rattled.

The broadcasters usually leave it up to me to decide when to give them the out-of-town scores. If they've gone a couple of innings lasting half an hour without having given the scores, they'll ask me for them.

Torre is hit by the pitch, and I mention to Ralph that's the third time Joe has been hit by a pitch in his last five games. It well might be connected with how well Torre has been hitting lately (he's had safeties in ten straight games). I don't think Billingham would *try* to hit him in this spot, but he might be trying to pitch him tighter than he normally would. I look up Billingham's record of hit batsmen. Torre is only the third batter he's hit all season.

When Torre is hit, it loads the bases. This is one obvious time when I would never interrupt an announcer with out-of-town scores or anything else, unless it was really pertinent information. Even if somebody should start warming up in the Cincinnati bullpen, I would not break the broadcaster's rhythm by telling him. Vail grounds out, and the Mets fail to score.

With one out in the Reds' fourth, Foster singles, and I immediately look up how many steals he has this season, so I'll be ready in case he breaks for second. Only if Foster tries to steal will I give the figures of his past steals to our broadcaster.

The count on the batter, and the type of hitter he is, helps you anticipate whether the runner will be moving on the pitch. Bench has flied deep to center, and so there are two outs and Tony Perez is up. Perez, of course, is a power hitter. If Lolich should fall behind him, 2-1 or 3-1, and has to come in with a pitch, there's a good chance Foster will be running, hoping to score from first on even a long single. An oddity in a defensive alignment can also help alert you to the probability of a runner going.

Perez doubles down the right-field line; Foster races around third and digs for the plate, but the throw from right fielder Vail to Hodges nabs him for the third out, as Perez makes it to second. Sometimes on a play like that, the batter is credited with a single because the scorer feels he took second on the throw. But in this case, it's the scorer's judgment that he would have made it safely to second had there been no other baserunner and no throw to the plate, so Perez is credited with a double.

93

Hodges strikes out leading off the Met fourth. Some broadcasters or writers will note on what kind of pitch the batter struck out, so that in their summaries, they can say, "Billingham struck out eight men, seven on fastballs."

After each at-bat, I adjust the batter's batting average. Sometimes there's no need to consult the average book or use a calculator, because, for instance, I know automatically that fifty-two hits in two hundred at-bats is a .260 average.

The ticker tells me that the Cardinals have just scored six runs against Atlanta in the top of the fifth inning, and I pass that item along to Bob Murphy, who will mention it on the air, along with the fact that San Francisco's John "Count" Montefusco has just defeated Philadelphia, 2–0. It occurs to me that the Count has been pitching very well lately, so I check his card (as you know, I have a card for every pitcher in the league) and I see that he has won five of his last six games. That, too, is worth mentioning. I write that on the blue out-of-town sheets, which I'm constantly updating from the ticker, and which I periodically hand over to the broadcaster.

In the bottom of the fifth, the Mets rally for two runs to go ahead, 2–1. I feel the excitement, and I'm pleased when things go well for the team, but I don't stand up and cheer or applaud. Some visiting broadcasters do it, and so do general managers visiting in the press box, but in my opinion—and maybe I'm too cosmopolitan—I think it's kind of bush. The broadcast booth is a working area and if you can't contain your emotions, you shouldn't be sitting there; you should be sitting with the fans. Clapping, cheering, yelling is for the fans, not for the people working the game.

During the rally, John Milner came to the plate with a man on and one out. I knew he'd hit a couple of home runs lately. If he had swung and the ball was heading for the fence, I could have had his home-run card out by the time he reached second. Then, if it was a homer, our broadcaster could quickly relate how many homers John had hit lately, and against whom.

In the Cincinnati sixth, the Reds mount a rally as Griffey leads off with a single. Lolich throws over to try to pick him off, but the ball gets away. As soon as I see the play developing, I turn up the sound on the public address loudspeaker in the booth, so I can hear the scorer's decision about who gets the error. It's charged to the pitcher, who made the throw, so I form a circle with my thumb and index finger and make a throwing motion. I do this for our radio broadcaster, then lean out of the booth and do it in view of our TV announcer next door.

The scoreboard is running a quiz right now. I have nothing to do with anything on the scoreboard, except for the out-of-town games. I give the schedule of the out-of-towns to the scoreboard electricians the day before, so that the schedule is posted by the time the fans start coming into the ball park.

This is a big hitting game with lots of action, and I enjoy working this sort of game, as opposed to one that drags. I've worked no-hitters against the Mets pitched by Bill Stoneman, Bob Moose and Ed Halicki. When a no-hit bid reaches the sixth inning, I begin looking up how often the team has been no-hit; whether the particular pitcher has ever pitched a no-hitter; and if so, when and against whom; or the closest he's ever come to pitching one.

When Perez hits a triple to the right-field corner, a reliever, Ken Sanders, gets up in the Mets' bullpen. I get ready with his pitching card.

Concepcion, at bat next, hits the first pitch into the left-field stands for his second homer of the game. He also has a double. All three of his hits were on first pitches, and our broadcaster reports that.

In the Mets sixth, Jim Dwyer pinch-hits for Lolich. Dwyer and Pepe Mangual came to the Mets from Montreal in return for Wayne Garrett and Del Unser. I learned that the new Mets got the others' uniform numbers here, while Garrett and Unser got their former numbers at Montreal. No big deal, but sufficiently interesting to mention.

In the Reds' seventh, Sanders comes in to pitch for New York. From his pitching card, I'm able to tell Lindsey Nelson, who's now broadcasting on radio, that this is the fifth time Ken has appeared against Cincinnati, which is a high number since the teams have met only ten times thus far. He's pitched four innings against the Reds and allowed three hits and three runs, so he hasn't been that effective.

I take Sanders' pitching card over to the TV booth to give our broadcaster there the pertinent data about Ken's record against Cincinnati. While there, I update the batting averages, and check the out-of-town scoresheets for accuracy and spelling.

Since Sanders is a right-handed pitcher, Pete Rose bats left-handed for the first time in the game. I call attention to the fact that before tonight's game, he was hitting .332 right-handed and only .293 left-handed. For any switch-hitter, we have stats available about his hits from both sides of the plate.

Lindsey mentions again that five of the batters in the Cincinnati line-up are among the top ten hitters in the league. It's a fact worth repeating, but not too often.

At this point in the game, we can anticipate the announcement of the night's

95

official attendance figures. If the team is closing in on a particular milestone, I would total them up. Tonight's attendance puts us over the 1,100,000 mark, so I tally it.

Griffey gets his second hit of the night and Foster gets his third, and they're now both hitting .333, which conceivably could put them in first place in the National League batting race depending on what Bill Madlock of the Cubs did this afternoon. When Joe Torre comes up in the seventh, our broadcaster notes that his ten-game hitting streak is in jeopardy. He may not get up again this game. I notice that Pedro Borbon is warming up in the Cincinnati bullpen; and I pass on the information. Torre strikes out swinging, to end the inning. In the top of the eighth, Joe Nuxhall, one of the Reds' broadcasters, comes into our radio booth to ask Ralph which Cincinnati player he wants to have on "Kiner's Korner." Because Joe's team is winning at this point, he'll have first choice for his postgame show. He's probably going to have Dave Concepcion, who has just had his fourth hit of the game, including two home runs. Ralph will probably use George Foster, and then Concepcion will come on midway through the program.

Mike Vail doubles to open the Met eighth and when Hodges singles him to third, immediately two pitchers start warming up in the Reds' bullpen. Staiger singles to left, driving in one run, and now we can anticipate a pitching change for Cincinnati. I see Sparky Anderson making a motion with his left hand, which means he's calling for a left-hander, so I know that would be Will McEnaney. I get out his pitching card and give it to Lindsey, who's now our radio broadcaster. Leo Foster is coming in to pinch-hit for Phillips, so I write his name in the appropriate box on my scoresheet, and I draw a heavy line at the top of the box to indicate that he's the first man the new Reds pitcher, McEnaney, is facing. He hits a fly ball to center, and the runners hold. Now Pepe Mangual is going to pinch-hit for Ken Sanders and I write his name in the appropriate box. Since Sanders is coming out of the game, the official scorer announces his line totals for the game, over the pressbox intercom. According to the announcement, Ken yielded two hits, but my stats show he gave up three. I would call the discrepancy to the official scorer's attention, but somebody in the press box has already told him, and he changes his total to three hits.

After Mangual strikes out swinging, Jerry Grote comes up to swing for Boisclair. He hits a good shot to left, but it's caught, and the inning is over. There were three successive hits, but then three pinch-hitters were retired, and the Mets pick up just one run.

Mangual and Foster stay in the game, and we enter their names, the inning they came into the game and whom they replaced on the scoresheet. Foster, playing short, will hit in Phillips' spot, and Mangual will play center and hit in the ninth spot. The new pitcher, Bob Myrick, will hit in the lead-off position.

Above Rose's box we draw a solid line to indicate he's the first man Myrick is facing. Pete lines to first. Griffey singles to center, but Morgan flies to center and Foster flies to right, ending the top of the ninth.

Millan leads off with a pop fly to the second baseman. Milner singles to right, and Torre singles to left. Joe has now hit in eleven straight games, and that fact is duly reported. Now the potential tying run is up in the person of Mike Vail, and the Reds change pitchers, bringing in Rawly Eastwick. Vail grounds to the second baseman, Morgan, who flips to Concepcion for the force on Torre, and the throw to first doubles Vail, to end the game.

I remind Lindsey on radio and Bob on TV that the win for the Reds is their fourteenth in sixteen games and that they've increased their first-place margin to 13½ games over the Dodgers in the National League West on their way to the 1976 championship. I also mention that the Mets have now lost two in a row after winning seven of their last eight. I give them the game totals, the home runs and the winning and losing pitchers, and mention that McEnaney will be credited with the save—but I have to correct the latter. Even though he faced only one batter, Eastwick gets the save, since the tying run was then at bat.

The official scorer tells us that the length of the game was two hours and twenty-eight minutes, and the Reds left six men on base and the Mets, eleven.

If there's something particularly interesting on the out-of-town scores, I'll pass it along to our broadcasters. But the scores themselves were just given in the eighth inning and, since there's a postgame show coming, on which my updated scores will be given, I don't bother; though as a courtesy to Chip Cipolla, who's doing a postgame radio show on WNEW, I'll keep updating scores for him until we leave.

Schaefer Award

It's my task to award points in the competition for the Schaefer Met players-of-the-game award. Every game, a total of up to ten points for outstanding Met play is credited. The points are shared by up to four players who, in my opinion, are deserving of points that game. At the end of the season, the player with the most points gets a Leroy Neiman painting. Tonight no Met pitcher has qualified for points, but I'm awarding three points to Vail, who had 2-for-3 and drove in one of the Mets' three runs with a sacrifice fly, and two points to Boisclair, who had two hits and scored a run. Our broadcasters announce who's leading in the Schaefer competition, which we update periodically. (In 1976, Jerry Koosman won the award, narrowly edging Dave Kingman. Lenny Randle won in '77.)

After the Game

After the game is over, I normally pack all my paraphernalia very carefully in my case and head for home. Very rarely do I stay and work at the park. I prefer an hour or so to clear my head before starting to work at home. On occasion, rather than battle the postgame traffic, I might stay for a while and try to get some of my work done.

From the time this game ends until the next game begins tomorrow afternoon, I have about three hours' worth of work to do. I try to do about half of the required homework as soon as I get home from the game—because I'm still keyed up and the game is still fresh in my mind—and the rest of it the following day.

Definitions

EVEN FOR veteran baseball fans, it might be helpful to go over the precise definitions of the various categories for which statistics are kept. Some are not so well known as you might imagine.

Batting Average

To determine a player's batting average, you divide the number of times he has been at bat officially into the number of hits he's made and carry it three decimal places. For instance, if a player has been at bat 120 times and had 30 base hits, you divide the 30 by 120 and come out with .250. A player who gets a hit on every official time at bat is hitting 1.000. A player who has no hits is batting .000. Strictly speaking, a .300 batting average means a player has hit safely 30 percent of the time, and a 1.000 average is the equivalent of 100 percent.

At-Bat. An official at-bat is registered when a player has had an opportunity to get a hit. It is *not* an official time at bat when a batter walks, is hit by a pitch, makes a successful sacrifice bunt to advance the lead runner, hits a sacrifice fly to score a man from third base, or is awarded first base because of interference by the catcher.

Hit. A base hit is given on any ball hit that enables the batter to reach first base

99

safely without the aid of an error by a fielder (providing he does not reach first base safely while a teammate is being put out without advancing a base. For example, if there were a man on base, and the fielder decided to try to retire *him*, rather than the batter, and the batter reached first safely on the play, the batter would not be credited with a hit).

A single, double, triple or home run counts as one hit when you're computing a batting average.

Batting Championship. In order to qualify for the batting championship of either major league, a player must have had at least 502 *appearances* at the plate. Appearances differ from at-bats, in that they include not only the official at-bats, but also the number of walks the batter draws, the number of times he was hit by a pitch, any sacrifice bunts or flies he hit, and the number of times he was awarded first base on catcher's interference.

Slugging Percentage

To calculate a batter's slugging percentage, divide his total official times at bat into the total bases made on all of his hits.

Total Bases. A batter gets one total base for a single, two for a double, three for a triple, and four for a home run. If a batter is called out for having failed to touch a base, the last base he reached safely will determine whether he's credited with a one-base hit, two-base hit, three-base hit or home run. For example, if he is called out because he didn't touch second base, he is credited with a one-base hit. If he's called out for missing first base, he is charged with a time at bat and not credited with a hit or any bases at all.

If a batter ends a game with a safe hit that drives in as many runs as are necessary to put his team in the lead, he's credited with only as many bases as are advanced by the runner who scored the winning run—and then, only if the batter runs out as many bases as are advanced by the runner who scores.

Let's say, in the bottom of the ninth inning, with the score tied, a runner is on second base, and the batter hits the ball up the alley for a base hit that scores the runner with the winning run. If the batter reaches second base safely, he can be credited with a two-base hit. But if in a similar situation, the runner is on third and the batter hits the ball equally well, even if he makes it to second he is credited with only a one-base hit, since the lead runner had to advance just one base to win the game.

An exception to this principle comes when the batter hits the ball out of the playing field. Then he and any runners on base are entitled to score, and he's credited with a home run—four bases.

Slugging Championship. It's usually a power hitter who will lead the league in slugging average, and generally the same hitters are up among the leading sluggers every year. The top man in each league ordinarily has a slugging average well over .500 and sometimes over .600.

Recent slugging leaders in the National League were Mike Schmidt of Philadelphia in 1974 with a percentage of .546; Dave Parker of Pittsburgh in 1975, .541; and Joe Morgan in 1976, .576. In the American League, Dick Allen, then of Chicago, led in 1974 with .563; Fred Lynn of Boston in 1975, .566; and Reggie Jackson, then of Baltimore in 1976, .502. In 1977 Jim Rice of Boston won in the A.L. with .593, and George Foster of the Reds won in the N.L. with .631.

In the course of a season, the leaders in slugging are not usually printed in the newspapers or talked about on the air, as are the top hitters in percentage, runs batted in and home runs. But a good baseball fan usually is aware of who they are because he knows the leaders in doubles and triples as well as homers.

On-Base Percentage

An informal listing that most teams keep is a player's on-base percentage. It is calculated by taking a man's total appearances at the plate and dividing it into the times he has been on base (except for fielder's choice or safe on error). To get a player's *on-base total,* you add up his base hits, his walks, the number of times he was hit by a pitch, and the number of times he reached first on interference. (Don't include the times he got to first safely while another man was being retired on a fielder's choice; this would simply count as an at-bat.) Divide the on-base total by the total appearances to get his on-base average.

Let's say a batter had the following appearances:

400	official at-bats
36	walks
18	sacrifice bunts
4	sacrifice flies
3	hit by pitch
1	interference
462	total appearances

In those appearances, he had:

122	hits
36	walks
3	hit by pitch
1	interference
162	total on-base

Now you divide the on-base total (162) by the appearances (462), and you get a .351 on-base percentage. (This same man has a batting average of .305.)

What the on-base percentage does, is assess more accurately the value of a player who doesn't have a high batting average but who draws a lot of bases on balls. Bud Harrelson of the Phils, for instance, has less than a .250 lifetime batting average, but because he draws perhaps forty or fifty more walks a season than many players with higher averages, he will probably attain an on-base percentage as good as that of a player whose batting average is thirty points higher.

A player of the caliber of Joe Morgan will hit .320 over the course of a season on 151 base hits (as he did in 1976). When you realize he also drew 114 walks, you can see what a fantastic on-base percentage he had and why he was selected MVP in the National League.

Earned-Run Average

In the minds of some, the initials ERA stand for the Equal Rights Amendment, but to a baseball fan, they're the abbreviation of earned-run average, one of the highly regarded indicators of a pitcher's value.

An earned-run average is computed on the basis of a nine-inning game, so to arrive at a pitcher's ERA, you multiply his total of earned runs by nine, and divide that result by the number of innings he pitched. Say Jim Palmer gave up two runs in a game in which he pitched eight innings. To get his ERA for that game, you'd multiply the runs by nine, and divide that total (eighteen) by the number of innings he pitched (eight). The result (2.25) is his earned-run average.

In figuring out an ERA, round off thirds of an inning (which are given for each man retired in an inning). For instance, if he's pitched 110 and *one*-third innings, you just use 110 in computing his ERA. If he's pitched 110 and *two*-thirds innings, carry it to the next complete number—111—and use that in computing his ERA.

ERA Championship. To qualify for the earned-run average championship, a pitcher must work at least the same number of innings as the number of games on his team's schedule. Since most teams play 162 games over the course of a season, he would then have to have pitched at least 162 innings. If a game was rained out and never replayed, then the minimum total for innings pitched would be 161.

Earned Run. An earned run is one for which a pitcher is held accountable by his own pitching, whether it's the result of a base hit, a base on balls, balk or wild pitch or a combination of these. They're considered the pitcher's fault and if they result in a run, that run is earned.

However, if an error or passed ball contributes to a particular run, which otherwise would not have scored, it is an *un*earned run and is not figured in a pitcher's earned-run average.

Once a defensive team has had an opportunity to make three putouts in an inning, but the inning has been prolonged by one or more errors, all the runs that come in afterward in that inning are unearned, even a home run.

With two outs in the ninth inning of a game in 1977 in Dodger Stadium, Boisclair dropped a long foul fly hit by Davy Lopes and was charged with an error for prolonging Lopes's life at the plate. Lopes then hit a three-run homer to give the Dodgers a 5–3 win over the Mets. The three runs were unearned.

What if it's the pitcher who makes the fielding error? It's treated exactly the same as when any other fielder commits a miscue: the resulting run is not computed as an earned run. The pitcher does get charged with an error, of course, but if he's like every other hurler, he's a lot more concerned about his ERA than his fielding average.

Fielding Average

To calculate a fielding average, you divide the number of chances offered into the number of chances accepted by the fielder.

Chances Offered. Putouts, assists and errors constitute the number of chances offered.

Chances Accepted. The total number of putouts and assists make up the number of chances accepted.

A player who made no errors would have a 1.000 percentage. Someone who had 500 chances offered and made 25 errors would have 475 chances accepted. When you divide the chances accepted (475) by the chances offered (500) you find he has a .950 fielding average.

Putouts. A fielder is credited with a putout if he catches a fly ball or a line drive, whether it's fair or foul; if he catches a thrown ball that puts out a batter or a runner; if he tags a runner when a runner is off a base to which he legally is entitled or if he's the fielder closest to a runner who is hit by a batted ball. A catcher also receives a putout when the batter is struck out, unless he drops the ball and has to make a throw to first base.

Assists. An assist is given to a fielder if he throws or deflects a batted or thrown ball in such a way that a putout results, or would have resulted except for a subsequent error by another fielder. Even if he handles the ball several times, only one assist—and no more—is credited to each fielder who throws or deflects a ball in a rundown play that results in a putout or that would have resulted in a putout except for a subsequent error.

A pitcher does not get an assist when he strikes out a batter unless he fields an uncaught third strike and makes a throw that results in a putout at first base.

Errors. An error is charged for any misplay—fumble, muff or wild throw—that prolongs the life of a runner or permits a runner to advance one or more bases.

A player cannot be given an error for his slow handling of a ball if the play did not involve a "mechanical" misplay. Mental mistakes or misjudgments cannot be scored as errors unless they're specifically covered in the rulebook, such as a pitcher being late in covering first base.

Fielding Championship. To qualify for the fielding-average championship, a player must take part in two-thirds of the games scheduled, unless he's a pitcher or catcher. A pitcher, to qualify for a fielding championship, must pitch in at least as many innings as there are games on the schedule; a catcher must play in half the games scheduled.

Major leaguers generally have a season's fielding average of well over .900. There have even been cases of outfielders finishing a season with a fielding average of 1.000, after having played 100 or more games. Three outfielders in the history of the major leagues played 150 or more games in a season and finished with a fielding average of 1.000. The most recent player to do that was

Curt Flood of the Cardinals in 1966. He played in 159 games without making a single error!

First basemen usually finish with very high fielding averages, well up in the .990's, though none has ever played in at least 150 games and finished with a 1.000 average.

Baserunning Average

Baserunning averages are arrived at by dividing the number of attempted steals into the number of bases stolen. For example, a player who steals fifteen bases and is caught stealing five times is successful fifteen out of twenty times, and he would have a percentage of .750—or, to use the phrase more commonly employed in a baserunning average, 75 percent.

Stolen Base Credit. A player is credited with a stolen base whenever he advances one base unaided by a hit, putout, error, forceout, fielder's choice, passed ball, wild pitch or balk.

If a runner starts for the next base before the pitcher delivers the ball, and the pitch results in what ordinarily would be charged as a wild pitch or passed ball, the runner *is* credited with a stolen base, and you do not charge either a wild pitch or passed ball on this play. The runner is also credited with a stolen base if, when he's attempting to steal, the catcher receives the pitch and then makes a wild throw to the base.

When a runner who is attempting to steal—or one who's been picked off base—evades a putout in a rundown play and advances to the next base without the aid of an error, he's credited with a stolen base.

When a double or triple steal is attempted, and one runner is thrown out before holding the base (getting there safely), the other runner is not credited with a stolen base either; he simply advanced on the throw that resulted in the putout of the first runner.

A runner is not given credit for a stolen base if he is put out when oversliding the stolen base in attempting either to return to it or to advance to another base.

When a runner advances solely because of the defensive team's indifference to his advance, he is not credited with a stolen base. Let's say a team batting in the ninth is ten runs behind and there are two out. If a runner should reach first base, the pitcher isn't going to worry about him at this point in the game. He just

105

wants to get that last out, and so sometimes he won't even use a stretch motion. If the pitcher uses his regular wind-up, it's very easy for the baserunner to go to second. If nobody pays any real attention to him, and no throw is made, he is not credited with a stolen base. His advance is attributed, in scoring, to a fielder's choice.

Caught Stealing. A runner is charged with being caught stealing if he is put out, or would have been put out by an errorless play when he tries to steal, when he is picked off a base and tries to advance or, as mentioned, if he overslides when stealing.

You do not charge a player with having been caught stealing unless he had the opportunity to be credited with a stolen base when the play began.

Team Standings

To determine a team's won-lost percentage you divide the total number of games played to a decision into the number of games won. For example, if a team plays one hundred games and wins fifty and loses fifty, divide one hundred into fifty and, of course, the percentage would be .500. If a team wins all its games, it has a 1.000 percentage; if it loses all its games, the percentage is .000.

The same method is applied to figuring out won-lost percentages for a pitcher. If a pitcher has twenty decisions, of which he wins fifteen, his percentage is .750.

Games Ahead/Games Behind. To determine how many games one team is ahead of the other, add the differences of the two teams' wins and losses and divide by two. For instance:

	W	L
Mets	28	10
Pirates	24	16

The Mets have won four more games and lost six fewer games. (Scheduling differences and postponements account for differences in number of games played.) Add the four and six together, which gives you ten, then divide by two for the number of games by which the Mets lead (five).

It isn't always this simple, because often a team that has won more games than the next may have lost more than that other team, too. In that case, instead of adding the two figures (more games won and fewer lost), you would subtract one figure from the other before dividing by two; for example:

	W	L	GB	Pct.
Pirates	26	13	−½	.667
Mets	30	16	—	.652

The Mets have won four more games than the Pirates, but have also lost three more. So you would take the three from the four, leaving you one. Then, as always, divide by two, to find out how many games ahead the Mets are. In this case, the answer is one-half game. (The reason the games-ahead total is a fraction is that the teams have played a different amount of games.)

Incidentally, there have been occasions when a team has been ahead in games but has had a lower percentage. In such an instance the team considered to be in first place is the one with the best numerical percentage, as in the above standings.

To reiterate, the determining factor for first-place is a team's won-lost percentage, not how many games ahead it may be. It is possible to be even a game behind another team and yet still have a better percentage. That could have happened at season's end in 1972, when because of the players' strike at the beginning of the year, teams played an unequal number of games. If such an anomaly were to happen, the team with the better percentage would win the pennant.

Even during the season, many broadcasters make the mistake of saying two teams are "virtually" tied for first, when there's no such thing. Very rarely at a given stage of the season do teams have exactly the same record (the identical percentage).

Magic Number. As the baseball season nears conclusion in the final weeks of September, you hear the term "magic number" used. What it means is the combination of the leading team's victories and the second-place or other team's defeats that will clinch a championship or pennant for the leading team.

To figure the magic number in a pennant race, just add one to the number of games left to be played by the lead team, then subtract the number of games the team is ahead in the loss column over its nearest opponent.

Here's an example. On the morning of September 20, 1976, the Cincinnati Reds were in first place in the National League West:

	W	L
Reds	96	55
Dodgers	84	66

The Reds have played 151 games, which means they have eleven left to play in the regular season. Add one to the number of games left, which gives you a total of twelve. Now, the Reds have lost eleven fewer games than the second-place team, so you subtract that figure (eleven) from the total of games left to play plus one (twelve), and that gives you the magic number—one.

The magic number can be arrived at from different directions, too. You could look at the record of the second-place team and see that the Dodgers have played 150 games, leaving them twelve to play in the season. If they were to win all twelve, the maximum number of victories they could have would be ninety-six. Cincinnati already has ninety-six victories, so all the Reds have to do to clinch is win just one more game.

Or you could look at the loss column, where you notice that the Reds have lost fifty-five to the Dodgers' sixty-six. If Cincinnati were to win only one of their eleven remaining games, the most they could lose in the entire season would be sixty-five games, which, again, would give them the division championship.

Let's look at the American League East on the same day, where the Yankees are in first place:

	W	L
Yankees	92	55
Orioles	81	68

We see that the Yankees have played in 147 games, which means they have fifteen left to play. Add one to that figure, for a total of sixteen, then subtract the number of games the Yankees are ahead in the loss column, which is thirteen. The remainder is three—the magic number.

Again, you can approach it in different ways. You can look at the win column and calculate that if the Orioles win all thirteen of their remaining games, they would end up with ninety-four victories. If the Yankees were to win just three more, they would end up with ninety-five victories, thus eliminating Baltimore from contention.

Or look at the loss column, and notice that if Baltimore were to win all of its remaining games, it would still have sixty-eight defeats. (You can't improve your loss column.) To keep ahead of the Orioles, all the Yankees would have to do would be to win three of their remaining fifteen games, because twelve losses would give them a total of only sixty-seven defeats, one better than Baltimore's sixty-eight.

How to Score
a Baseball Game

THERE ARE a number of ways to keep score at a baseball game. There's no one "right" way. I learned how to keep score from Ralph Kiner, who eventually changed his way of doing it. But both systems are certainly valid.

No two people keep score exactly alike—and that includes writers and broadcasters as well as fans—but in almost all cases, any writer or broadcaster can read the other's scoresheet and be able to tell what happened.

If you look around the ball park, you'll see that at least half the fans keep score during the game, but most of them, I would imagine, do it very casually, just for their own enjoyment. Some don't even bother to mark down *how* a batter makes out; they're content just to put an "o" to symbolize he's been up, made out and gone. They're not interested, but of course, we are.

The best way a fan can conveniently score a game is not necessarily the way a broadcaster, newspaperman or statistician would do it. Still, it might be helpful to go through part of a game, to see how it's done by the professionals. You can adapt it to your own preference.

The most important thing in keeping score is that you can understand it. It doesn't matter what your system is, so long as you can read back your scorecard, even weeks or months after the game has been played, as clearly as if you had written down every play in longhand. A sportswriter or broadcaster isn't likely to hold on to a particular scorecard beyond the series, but a statistician who keeps records has to make sure every box score is complete and legible, so he can read it and get the significance even two years later.

Each defensive position is given a number. The pitcher is number 1; the catcher, 2; the first baseman, 3; the second baseman, 4; the third baseman, 5; the shortstop, 6; the left fielder, 7; the center fielder, 8; and the right fielder, 9. (This system goes back a long time, possibly to the turn of the century.) If a batter hits a grounder to the shortstop, for example, and the shortstop throws to the first baseman to retire him, a simple notation, "6–3," tells the story. Some writers and some broadcasters will make a notation to show how hard the ball was hit, but for my purposes that's not necessary.

Incidentally, since you're using numbers for defensive positions, it's a good idea *not* to use numbers any other way in your scoring. I do in some cases, though I don't think it's the best way to keep score. But I've been doing it for so long I can't shake the habit.

Let's score an actual game—the one I discussed in *Game Time:* August 13, 1976, between the Mets and Reds at Shea Stadium:

Pete Rose, first up in the Cincinnati first, grounds out, second to first. So in the first-inning box alongside his name, I put "4–3." Although dashes are not used on the scorecard, we use them to separate numbers here, for purposes of clarity.

Ken Griffey, next up, grounds to the first baseman, who throws to the pitcher covering for the out. In the first-inning column in the box next to Griffey's name, therefore, I write "3–1."

Joe Morgan walks, a fact I indicate in the first-inning box next to his name with a "W," which I place in the lower right-hand corner of the box to explain how the batter reached first. (Some scorers use "BB" to indicate base on balls, but I prefer to use one letter, "W." If it's intentional, I'll add an "I.") When the pitcher throws to first, Morgan breaks for second; the first baseman throws to the shortstop, who tags Morgan out. I then put "P.O. 3–6" above the "W" to indicate what happened—a pickoff, with the first baseman then throwing to the shortstop.

By the way, that play will count as a pickoff in the record of the Met pitcher, Mickey Lolich, while in Morgan's record it will count as "caught-stealing" because, in the opinion of the official scorer, had Morgan made it to second on that particular play, he would have been credited with a stolen base. Since you were going to credit a man with a stolen base if he made it (though, in Morgan's case, it wasn't *really* a try for a stolen base), then you have to charge him with a "caught-stealing" when he didn't make it.

The Mets are now up in the first, with Bruce Boisclair leading off. He hits the ball to the second baseman, and when the second baseman can't handle it, he's charged with an error. So in the lower right-hand corner of the first-inning box next to Boisclair's name, I put "E-4."

BOISCLAIR
```
┌─ ─ ─┐
│     │
│  E-4│
└─ ─ ─┘
```

Felix Millan was hit by the pitch, so I simply put "HP" in the lower right-hand corner of his first-inning box. (Some broadcasters and writers would use the symbol "HBP" for "hit by the pitcher.")

MILLAN
```
┌─ ─ ─┐
│     │
│   HP│
└─ ─ ─┘
```

When Millan goes to first, Boisclair, of course, moves to second. How do I indicate on the scorecard how he got there? I do it by a notation in the upper right-hand corner of his box. You could use "FM" to indicate that Boisclair got to second on what Felix Millan did; or "SB" to show he got there on what his second baseman (Felix Millan) did. But here's an instance where I use a number (which I understand, but which might be confusing to someone else). The number I put down is "4," which represents the position that Millan plays, second base. In other words, Boisclair went to second on the basis of what his team's second baseman did at the plate. As I mentioned above, it might be clearer for you to put Millan's initials in the upper right-hand corner of Boisclair's box, "FM" rather than the number of the position he plays. Note the column to the left of the batters' names is one headed "Pos.," meaning the positions they play. Now the scorecard looks like this:

Pos.		I
8	Boisclair	4 E-4
4	Millan	HP

John Milner, up next, flies out deep to center field. Boisclair tags up and goes to third after the catch. In Milner's first-inning box, I put "8" with an arc over it, to indicate fly to the center fielder. (If it had been a line drive, I would have put a straight line above the 8.) And in the upper left-hand corner of Boisclair's box, I account for how he reached third base by writing in a "7," to indicate he got there on the basis of what his own left fielder, Milner, did that inning. You might prefer to use "JM," Milner's initials. The first-inning part of the scorecard now looks like this:

Pos.		I
8	Boisclair	7 4 E-4
4	Millan	HP
7	Milner	⌢ 8

Joe Torre then grounds to the second baseman, who steps on second to force Millan and throws to first to double-up Torre. In Torre's box, I put "4-3." In the upper right-hand corner of Millan's box, I write "4uX," indicating he was put out by the second baseman unassisted ("u") and he was forced out ("X"). And I draw a line to connect Torre's box and the upper part of Millan's. The first-inning box score for the Mets now looks like this:

Pos.		I
8	Boisclair	7 4 E-4
4	Millan	4uX HP
7	Milner	⌢ 8
3	Torre	4-3

The totals for the first inning are 0 runs ("R"), 0 hits ("H"), and one error ("E") and one man left on base ("L").

In the Reds' second, George Foster grounds out to shortstop, so I put "6-3" in the second-inning box after his name. When Bench grounds out to third, I put "5-3" in his second-inning box; and when Tony Perez lines to left, I put a "7" with a straight line over it in his second-inning box. For a broadcaster, it's important to know whether a ball a man hit was a fly or a line drive; although it's of no particular consequence to me as a statistician, it does add a dimension.

Mike Vail leads off the Met second inning with a single to right, which I indicate with a slash from the bottom of his second-inning box up to the right.

	I	2
Vail		/

If the single had been to center I would have put the slash straight up; if it had been to left field, the slash would have slanted to the left. It's all very practical, and most people I've observed keeping score have done it on that sort of basis.

When Ron Hodges flies out to center, I put an "8" with an arc over it. It was a routine catch. I don't indicate a spectacular catch in any particular way, but a broadcaster or writer may use an asterisk, arrow or different-color pen or pencil to call attention to the out-of-the-ordinary play. I try not to clutter my scoresheet with anything that isn't really pertinent to a permanent record.

Roy Staiger grounds to the shortstop, Dave Concepcion. Concepcion throws to second baseman Joe Morgan for a force play on Vail. Accordingly, I put "FP" in the lower right-hand corner of Staiger's box, to indicate he reached first on a force play. In the upper right of Vail's box, I put "6–4X," meaning he went out on a force play from the shortstop to the second baseman.

Mike Phillips grounds out to the first baseman unassisted, a fact I indicate by "3U."

For the Mets in the second inning, it was no runs, one hit, no errors and one man left on base.

In the Cincinnati third, Concepcion leads off with a home run, which is designated simply by "HR." I also draw two circles in Dave's third-inning box, one of them blacked-in to indicate that he scored a run, the other undarkened to indicate a run batted in.

If you want to indicate to what field a home run was hit, you can draw an arrow or slash in the appropriate corner or middle of the box. Some broadcasters and writers will indicate where a homer was hit. The tiny "L" indicates this one was hit to left.

Just about everyone uses "K" to indicate a strikeout, and so that's what I put in Cesar Geronimo's box. I also add a small "s" to indicate he struck out swinging. If it had been a called third strike, I would have put a small "c" after the "K." Billingham grounds out, first baseman to the pitcher covering, so I put "3–1" in his box.

Rose singles to center field, so I draw a slash straight up and put a little line under the slash to keep it from looking too much like the number 1.

Then Griffey grounds to the second baseman, who steps on second to force Rose.

In the Mets' third, Lolich strikes out swinging (Ks), but Boisclair singles to center. ⌐⊥⌐(Boisclair's hit was a grounder, but I don't distinguish between a base hit that is lined and one that is grounded. Some writers and broadcasters might do it by adding "L" for a liner and "G" for a grounder, or with some other symbols. Ralph Kiner, next time Boisclair comes up, will want to mention what kind of hit Bruce got.) When Millan goes out, third baseman to the first baseman, I put "5–3" in Millan's box and "4" in the upper corner of Boisclair's box—to signify he got to second on what his own second baseman, Millan, did. Milner walks, so I put "W" in the lower right-hand corner of his third-inning box.

Torre is hit by the pitch, so I put "HP" in the lower right-hand corner of his box, and accordingly, the other runners move up a base on what the Mets' number-3 fielder (the first baseman, Torre) did. Mike Vail then grounds to the third baseman, who steps on third, forcing Milner to end the inning. I put "FP" in Vail's box, to indicate he hit into a force play, and in the top left-hand corner of Milner's box, I put "5uX," to indicate he was forced out by the third baseman, unassisted.

With two out in the Reds' fourth, Foster is on first. Then Perez doubles to right, and Foster rounds third and heads for home, but he's out at the plate on a throw from the right fielder to the catcher. To score the play, in the upper right-hand corner of Perez's box I draw two slash marks, signifying a double, and slant them to the right, to show the hit was to right field. In Foster's box, I put a "3" in the upper left-hand corner, because he reached third on the basis of what his team's first baseman, Perez, did; but then he was out trying to score, so in the lower left-hand corner I write "o-St," for "out stretching," and "9–2," to show the putout was made by the catcher on a throw from the right fielder. I also put a little arrow from the upper left-hand corner of the box to the lower left-hand corner, to indicate it was all part of the same play. Foster's box looks like this:

```
┌─────────┐
│ 3       │
│ o-St    │
│ 9–2     │
└─────────┘
```

Except for a single by Phillips, the Mets go out without a threat in the bottom of the fourth. The Reds get a leadoff double to left by Concepcion in the fifth, but then go down, one-two-three.

In the Mets' fifth, Boisclair singles to right. After Millan flies out and Milner walks, Torre grounds to the shortstop, who throws the ball past the second baseman, allowing Boisclair to score and Milner to take third. In Boisclair's box, therefore, I put "E-6" in the lower left-hand corner, to show he scored on the shortstop's error, and a darkened circle, to indicate a run scored. In the upper left-hand corner of Milner's box, I put "E-6," to show he reached third on the shortstop's error. Torre, safe on a fielder's choice, has "FC" written in the lower right-hand corner of his box. He's not credited with an RBI on this kind of play, so I don't put a circle in his box. Mike Vail then flies to center, scoring Milner, so in the lower left-hand corner of Milner's box, I put "9," to indicate he reached home on the basis of what his right-fielder, Vail, did; and I add a filled-in circle to represent a run scored. Torre takes second on the throw to the plate, so I put "T" in the upper right-hand corner of his box. Vail gets a circle placed in his box, to represent a run batted in, and I also place an "8" under a line, to indicate the fly was caught by the center fielder. The "SF" indicates sacrifice fly. Hodges grounds out, second to first, so that requires just "4–3."

The Mets' fifth inning looks like this:

Pos.		4	5
8	Boisclair		● E-6 /
4	Millan		7
7	Milner		E-6 ● 9 W
3	Torre		T FC
9	Vail		SF 8̂ ○
2	Hodges		4–3

There is no room to indicate that the runs are unearned, so I simply make a notation to that effect in a space at the bottom of my scoresheet: "2 U.E.R. off Billingham."

In the Reds' sixth, Griffey singles to right and moves to second when the pitcher, attempting a pickoff, throws the ball away. This is indicated in the upper right-hand corner of Griffey's sixth-inning box by "E-1" and, to indicate that it was on a pickoff attempt, "P.O." The latter makes certain that I somehow don't think the pitcher made an error on his single. Morgan flies to right, and Griffey goes to third after the catch, so I put "4" in the upper left-hand corner of Ken's box.

When Foster homers to right, the Reds regain the lead, 3–2. After Bench lines out to center, Perez triples to right, so three slash marks slanting to the right are drawn in the upper left-hand corner of his box, explaining how he got to third. Concepcion follows with a two-run home run to left field. Geronimo ends the inning by flying to left.

As pinch-hitters come up, I write the name of the batter in the appropriate box. For instance, Dwyer comes in to pinch-hit for Lolich with two out in the bottom of the sixth, so the name Dwyer is written in and underlined at the top of the sixth-inning box in the row alongside Lolich's name. He ends the inning by grounding out.

In the top of the seventh, Ken Sanders comes in to face the Reds. At the top of the seventh-inning box of the man leading off the inning (Billingham), I draw a thick black line, to indicate that he's the first batter the new pitcher is facing.

In the Reds' seventh, Billingham goes out, short to first. Rose is hit by a pitch. Griffey singles him to third and takes second on the throw in. Morgan is walked intentionally, loading the bases. Foster singles to center, scoring Rose and Griffey. Bench is out on a foul pop to the third baseman, and Perez flies to left. How do you score it?

Pos.		7
5	Rose	9 ● 7 HP
9	Griffey	T ● T 7 ⊥
4	Morgan	7 IW
7	Foster	○ ● ⊥ ○
2	Bench	F 5
3	Perez	7
6	Concepcion	
8	Geronimo	
I	Billingham	6–3

The entire scorecard for that game is reproduced on p. 118. Notice that nowhere on it do the players' uniform numbers appear.

The tempo of a baseball game allows fans to keep score. The game is slow, and there are enough pauses that allow you to sit and reflect on everything that's happened.

In other sports, things happen too fast, and that's why you may see a basketball fan keep score of points by player, which is relatively easy, but not keep track of rebounds or assists, which is difficult. The average fan won't keep score of a football game. Hockey is simple, because there are just a few goals, assists and penalties to note. Yet everything happens very quickly, and I find that one of the beauties of working hockey games in the TV control room is that I get to see replays.

BASEBALL

Scorecard — Top half (Reds):

Umpires: Quick, B. Williams (2nd), Wendelstedt, Stello (3rd) — Game 117 — Friday (N) Aug. 13 — Att. 32,370 — Time 2:28

Pos		Ave	1	2	3	4	5	6	7	8	9	10	11	12
1	5 Rose (Flynn-5 9th)		43				43		HP					
2	9 Griffey		31		FP									
3	4 Morgan		W		8		9	IW		8				
4	7 Foster		63		1		HR	1		9				
5	2 Bench		53		8		8	5						
6	3 Perez		7				7							
7	6 Concepcion		HR				HR							
8	8 Geronimo		Ks		7		7		3					
9	1 Billingham		1		63		63	6						

PITCHER	Inn	R	H	SO	BB	R	0	0	0	0	4	2	0	0
Lolich	6					H	0	0	2	2	4	2	0	0
Sanders	2					E	0	0	0	0		0	0	0
Myrick						L	0	0		1	0	2	0	

WP Billingham LP Lolich Save Eastwick

TOTALS	R	H	E	LOB
Reds	7	13	2	6
Mets	3	9	1	11

Scorecard — Bottom half (Mets):

Pos		Ave	1	2	3	4	5	6	7	8	9	10	11	12
1	8 Boisclair (Myrick-1 9th)		E-4		1		E-6	7	31	Grote 9				
2	4 Millan		HP		53		7		W	4				
3	7 Milner		8		W		W		31	3				
4	3 Torre		43		HP		FC		Ks					
5	9 Vail				FP		08			463				
6	2 Hodges			8	Ks	43								
7	5 Staiger			FP	53		Ks		01					
8	6 Phillips (Foster-6 9th)			34		1	43		Foster 8					
9	1 Lolich (Mangual-8 9th)				Ks	Ks	Dwyer 43		Mangual Ks					

PITCHER	Inn	R	H	SO	BB	R	0	0	0	0	2	0	0	1	0
Billingham	7					H	0	0	0	0	0	0	3	2	
McEnaney	1/3					E	0	0	0	0	0	0	0		
Eastwick	2/3					L			3		0		2		

2 U.E.R. off Billingham

TOTALS	R	H	E	LOB

Official Scorers

To BECOME an official scorer in major league baseball, a sportswriter has to have covered at least one hundred major league games a year for a minimum of three consecutive seasons.

The scorer doesn't determine the outcome of plays—the umpires do that— but rather, how a play goes into the official records. Seated in the press box, the official scorer announces his decision over a microphone, and it can be heard throughout the entire press and broadcast area and at scoreboard control. The decision is then flashed on the board.

Jack Lang, a veteran sportswriter, started covering baseball in 1946 for the *Long Island Press* (since the *Press* folded he's been working for the New York *Daily News*). At first he covered just the home games of the Brooklyn Dodgers (as well as the Yankees, when the Dodgers were on the road. Occasionally he covered the Bushwicks of the Negro League, which boasted some great black ballplayers, some of whom became major leaguers and a few, Hall of Famers). So he saw more than one hundred games a season without leaving New York. In 1947 he started traveling with the Dodgers. Jack has seen every World Series since 1946.*

* Jack Lang believes he's covered more no-hitters than any baseball writer in history. According to Red Foley of the *New York Daily News,* who looked it up, Lang covered thirteen, including Don Larsen's perfect game in the 1956 World Series, and not including the two or three he witnessed in spring training. When Jack broke into covering big-league baseball in 1946, he saw two no-hitters in one week, one by Ed Head in Brooklyn's Ebbets Field and one by Bob Feller in Yankee Stadium.

Since he started serving as an official scorer, he has scored thousands of games. When Jack first started scoring, official scorers were paid twenty dollars a game; now the figure is fifty dollars a game.

In almost every instance, a scorer is a qualified member of the Baseball Writers Association.

There was a time when there was no problem getting official scorers, since each big-league city had plenty of experienced and qualified writers to fill the position. That isn't the situation any more. The number of daily newspapers whose writers cover home and away games has dropped sharply. A lot of newspapers aren't sending their baseball writers on the road, and among newspapers that do, some, including major ones in Philadelphia, Atlanta and Milwaukee, as well as the *New York Times* and *Newsday,* don't allow their staffers to serve as official scorers.

According to Lang, the papers prohibit their writers from scoring because they feel it's a conflict of interest. "They're wrong," he comments, "because we're not working for the ball club, we're scoring for the league. There's no relationship whatsoever with the ball club."

He says that in his twenty-eight years of scoring, no one connected with a team's front office has tried to pressure him about any scoring decision. Players are another matter, since they feel that scorers' decisions affect their livelihood. "If they harass umpires who call them out, they're going to harass official scorers, too," he observes.

Possible conflict with players is another reason some newspapers won't allow their people to be scorers. The contention is that if a ballplayer gets angry at the scorer, he won't cooperate with the man in his capacity as reporter. Obtaining an interview with a player who feels a writer deprived him of a hit or cost him an earned run an hour or so before, could have obvious difficulties. But Lang doesn't consider that a problem, because "if I don't get the story from one ballplayer, I'll get it from another. . . . If I fail to get a quote from a ballplayer who may not be talking to me, someone else who's covering for the papers will give it to me, because they know the situation and they feel it's unfair that a ballplayer should hold a scoring decision against you."

In Atlanta, neither paper will allow its writers to act as official scorers; according to Lang, a college professor who is a fan and something of an acknowledged baseball expert sometimes does the job. The Writers Association tried to stop that practice, he says, but really was in no position to do so because it had no one qualified to offer as a replacement. In Milwaukee a retired baseball

writer has been the official scorer at some games, and in New York retired
baseball writers (who had scored previously) scored several games in 1976.

A School for Scorers

We're getting to the point where baseball is going to have to face up to this
problem. It's going to have to start hiring qualified scorers from other areas,
perhaps schooling them, paying them a reasonable salary and maybe even rotat-
ing them among cities.

Official scorers can be recruited from the ranks of retired players, umpires
and writers. Candidates could be given a course of instruction about baseball
rules and scoring criteria and procedures, then undergo a test to determine
whether they qualify to become official scorers.

Jack says that the Baseball Writers Association has recommended that the
league assign an extra umpire to travel with a team; every third or fourth day, one
umpire would act as official scorer. This would give the umpire a day of rest,
Lang comments, "and he'd certainly be qualified [to score]. But neither league
wants to do it because of the travel expense for the extra man." He contends that
though fees paid per game to scorers have gone up, the leagues are saving a
fortune by not having to pay traveling or per diem expenses.

Complaining Players

I get heat all the time from players demanding, "Who's the official scorer? How
could he have ruled that?" Whoever it is, and however justified their grievances,
I tell them I'm not getting involved. I tell them, "I sympathize with you, and I
may agree with you, but it's not my decision." A couple of times early in my
career I did get involved, which was a mistake. It's just something I should keep
my nose out of, and now I do.

One day Jesse Gonder, who used to catch for the Mets, came up with the
bases loaded and hit a line drive to center field. The ball hit off the fielder's glove
and bounced out, allowing three runs to score. Gonder was convinced he should
have been credited with a hit and three runs batted in, but Lang scored it as an
error. "Everybody in the park knew it was an error," Jack maintains.

When Lang walked into the clubhouse after the game, Gonder screamed at
him, and according to Jack, "used the magic word that the umpires will not

permit. I just said to him I was the scorer, but not the blank-blank scorer, and 'if you have any complaints, just take them up with the league president.' '' Lang has often pointed out to complaining ballplayers that they should take their gripes to the league president. ''He's the one who appointed me. I'm the same as an umpire, a league official. It says so in the official rules of baseball.'' In fact, Gonder was fined by the league for directing an obscenity at Lang, just as he would have been for using it against an umpire.

Sometimes, on a close decision, Lang, like other scorers, will go to a player he respects to talk over a decision, ''and 99 percent of the time, the ballplayer, speaking off the record, will say, 'you're right.' I'd go to Seaver or Koosman or Torre or Harrelson on the Mets—someone I know has not been a moaner or griper, who will accept the scorer as someone who can be guilty of errors the same way an umpire or anyone else can be when using human judgment.''

In one recent season, Lang points out, a player complained bitterly about a fielding error he'd been given, yet one of his teammates admitted to Jack that while the player griped about the error to the scorer, he had come into the dugout and acknowledged, ''I should have had that.''

Occasionally a scorer will change a decision (he has twenty-four hours in which to notify the league scorer of the change before the original decision becomes permanently recorded). In 1976, Felix Millan hit a ball hard to the third baseman and Jack Lang ruled it an error immediately. But upon reconsidering the play, he realized the ball had been well hit and that the fielder played it after one hard hop. He checked with a couple of sportswriters, who said that while they had no disagreement with the scoring, still, the ball had been well hit. Lang decided to make it a hit.

It turned out that Lang's changed decision kept a hitting streak alive, but Jack says that when the ball was hit, he didn't base his judgment on the fact that a hit streak was at stake. ''I think the most important thing in scoring,'' he says, ''is just to use logic and also ignore whoever is involved.''

Jack says he's had about three or four dozen complaints in all the years he's been scoring. ''When you're making several thousand decisions, you're never going to satisfy everybody, just as even the greatest umpires in the world aren't going to satisfy everybody. Any time you're making a human decision, there's margin for error.''

In many instances, complaints from the players are really a result of the players either not knowing the scoring rules or not being able to be objective. A batter thinks everything he hits should be a hit, while the pitcher thinks it should be called an error.

Often one player's unhappiness with a scorer's decision is another's delight.

No-hit bids put added pressure on an official scorer, especially as the game goes into its later stages. The rulebook is cloudy in that it says that an error should be given on a play the fielder should have made with "ordinary effort." As Lang points out, the scorer has a difficult job. "Would the fielder have made the play with ordinary effort? Well, what if it took *extra*ordinary effort? Maybe it should have been a hit; maybe he should have gotten it, maybe he shouldn't have. You've got to use common sense, especially when you're dealing with a no-hitter."

Nothing in the rulebook allows the scorer to charge a mental error. He can't presume that a player should have done something; an error can be given only for an actual act. (As a matter of fact, a proposal was made—but not passed—in the winter of 1976 that the league president or league statistician be permitted automatically to overrule a scorer who gave an error just because he thought someone should have done something, unless it was an actual act.) Some presumptions in scoring are allowed, however, as a result of two major rule changes over the years.

One change involves the sacrifice. It used to be that if a man bunted when a teammate was on first with less than two outs, a sacrifice was automatically awarded, even if his team was behind, 9–0. As Lang points out, common sense would tell you he was bunting not to move the man over but to get on base by surprise. Now in a situation like that, the batter is not credited with a sacrifice.

The other change involves the double play. Say you've got the ordinary shortstop–to–second baseman–to–first baseman (6-4-3) double-play situation. If the second baseman is not hit by the runner, and has all the time in the world to make the throw for the second half of the d.p., but throws the ball away, you can give him an error. It used to be that one out was all that could be required by a scorer on a potential double play.

But though scorers now have the latitude to charge an error in that situation, few do—possibly because they're afraid to incur the wrath of the player involved.

Team Errors

Some of the baseball writers have been fighting to have a new category of errors recognized: team errors. When two fielders collide, Lang says, "it's a crime that you have to give an error to somebody. . . . Some scorers cop out and award a hit, which also is a crime."

Even ballplayers will occasionally say, "That should have been a team error," and I think it's just a matter of time before that category is added. It takes baseball years to make some changes.

Jack recalls one play on which he could have awarded a hit but didn't. That was when Billy Baldwin, in right field, tried to flip his glasses down, but they wouldn't come down, and he missed a catch he should have made. Someone might say, "Well, it wasn't his fault that the glasses didn't come down." But the ball should have been caught, and whenever a ball that should be caught isn't, someone's at fault and has to be charged with an error.

Official Scoresheet

An official scoresheet resembles a box score. As you can see, the pitching summary is at the bottom. The categories that you would find horizontally in a newspaper (stolen bases, hit by pitches, etc.) are added vertically on an official scoresheet.

The scorer has to *prove* a box score—in other words, make sure that the total on one side (of such items as at-bats, sacrifices, bases on balls, hit by pitches and any other way players could have gotten on base) equals the total on the other. If the two totals don't prove out, the scorer can't send in the report until he's found the error.

There is now a rule that the scoresheets are to be filled out by the official scorer and mailed to the league statistician in New York within twenty-four hours of a game's completion. The National League statistician is the Elias Sports Bureau. Headed by Seymour Siwoff, it is one of the most highly respected agencies in the nation. The American League abandoned the Howe News Service in Chicago, which for years was the league's statistician, and now uses a computer service in Boston. Jack Lang believes the computer is no more accurate than the human scorers who work for the Elias Bureau, which, he says, "is probably the best statistical bureau in the country, because they check and double-check and mathematically prove out what the scorers submit to them."

Scorers will usually fill out the official scoresheet right after the game, but sometimes, toward the end of the season when there's no real rush for the information, the sports bureau is reasonably satisfied if the scoresheet is received within a week of the game.

While awaiting official scoresheets, the Elias Sports Bureau uses the box scores that appear in newspapers as unofficial statistics. The people at Elias will then check those against the official scoresheets.

VISITING CLUB PLAYERS
PUT SUBS IN PROPER BATTING ORDER

	Pos	AB	R	H	Total Bases	2B	3B	HR	RBI	Sacrifice Bunt	Sacrifice Fly	Bases on Balls Totl	Bases on Balls Int	HP	SO	SB	CS	Grnd into F DP	PO	A	E	DP
1																						
2																						
3																						
4																						
5																						
6																						
7																						
8																						
9																						
10																						
11																						
12																						
13																						
14																						
15																						
16																						
17																						
18																						
19																						
20																						
21																						
TOTAL –																						

BATTED FOR (Tell how, as:– 'doubled for Smith in 5th')

↓ HOW ↓	↓ NAME ↓		RAN FOR			
a)	for	in	1) for	in	Number out when winning run scored	DP♦ Team Total
b)	for	in	2) for	in	1st Base on Interference	
c)	for	in	3) for	in	Passed Balls	
d)	for	in	4) for	in	Home Run with Bases Full	
e)	for	in				

DOUBLE PLAYS _____
(Give Names)

OPPONENTS

VISITING CLUB PITCHERS' SUMMARY	W L S	IP	H	AB	Totl Bat to Face Pitch'r	R	ER	HR	Sacrifice Bunt	Sacrifice Fly	Bases on Balls Totl	Bases on Balls Int	HB	SO	WP	BK	Check One Start	Check One Finish	BOX SCORE PROOF	
																			Runs ___	At Bat ___
																				Bases on Balls ___
																			LOB ___	Sacrifices ___
																			Opponents Put Outs ___	Hit by Pitcher & 1st by Interference ___
																			TOTAL ___	TOTAL ___
																				Totals should equal

STARTING TIME & DATE MUST BE DUPLICATED ON HOME CLUB SHEET

Comparison made of Visiting Pitching vs. Home Batting Totals ☐

UMPIRES: _____

NOTE: When total of earned runs differs from team total, enter team total and circle it.

OFFICIAL REPORT of BASEBALL GAME for CHAMPIONSHIP of
National Professional Baseball LEAGUE (Sheet 1)

Played in City of _____ on _____ 19 ___

_____ VS _____
Visiting Club   Home Club

OFFICIAL SCORER: _____

FORM AN-3 'Official Report of Baseball Game' — printed in U. S. A. and copyrighted by Baseball Blue Book Inc., originators of the basic form with revisions of December 6, 1939 and others through 1969

GAME STARTED AT

.... AM .... PM

↓ Elapsed time of game ↓

.... Hr .... Min

Weather _____

Grounds _____

Baseball Blue Book, Inc.

PLEASE ENTER ANY REMARKS ON REVERSE SIDE OF THIS SHEET AND CHECK ✓   Remarks ☐   No Remarks ☐

HOME CLUB PLAYERS PUT SUBS IN PROPER BATTING ORDER	Pos	AB	R	H	Total Bases	2B	3B	HR	RBI	Sacrifice Bunt	Fly	Bases on Balls Totl	Int	HP	SO	SB	CS	Grnd into F DP	PO	A	E	DP
1																						
2																						
3																						
4																						
5																						
6																						
7																						
8																						
9																						
10																						
11																						
12																						
13																						
14																						
15																						
16																						
17																						
18																						
19																						
20																						
21																						
TOTAL →																						

BATTED FOR (Tell how, as:- 'doubled for Smith in 5th')

↓ HOW ↓		↓ NAME ↓	inn.	RAN FOR		inn.
a)		for	in	1) for		in
b)		for	in	2) for		in
c)		for	in	3) for		in
d)		for	in	4) for		in
e)		for	in			

Number out when winning run scored _____

1st Base on Interference _____

Passed Balls _____

Home Run with Bases Full

DP ↓ Team Total

DOUBLE PLAYS (Give Names) _____

HOME CLUB PITCHERS' SUMMARY	W L S	IP	H	OPPONENTS AB	Totl Bat to Face Pitch'r	R	ER	HR	Sacrifice Bunt	Fly	Bases on Balls Totl	Int	HB	SO	WP	BK	Check One Start	Finish
Comparison made of Home Pitching vs. Visiting Batting Totals ☐																		

BOX SCORE PROOF

Runs _____	At Bat _____
	Bases on Balls _____
LOB _____	Sacrifices _____
Opponents Put Outs _____	Hit by Pitcher & 1st by Inter- ference _____
TOTAL _____	TOTAL _____

Totals should equal

STARTING TIME & DATE MUST BE DUPLICATED ON VISITORS SHEET

NOTE: When total of earned runs differs from team total, enter team total and circle it

SCORE BY INNINGS	1	2	3	4	5	6	7	8	9	10	11	12	13	14	15	16	17	18	19	TOTAL
Visiting Club _____																				
Home Club																				

Home Club Sheet of Two-Sheet Set

FORM AN-3

Order from the

Baseball Blue Book, Inc.

OFFICIAL REPORT OF BASEBALL GAME (Sheet 2)

Played in City of _____ on _____ 19 __

Between _____ & _____
Visiting Club   Home Club

Game Started At .... AM .... PM

Elapsed Time of Game .... Hr .... Min

Paid Attendance ....

SEE INSTRUCTIONS TO SCORERS ON REVERSE SIDE OF THIS SHEET

The Bureau also gets play-by-play reports of every game from each club's P.R. department (after the AP cut out transmission of play-by-play from the ball parks, the league ruled that each statistician must submit play-by-play reports.) These reports, as well as AP and UPI box scores, are checked against the official scoresheets.

Box Scores on File

Box scores and official scoresheets are on file, kept in some vault at Elias in bound volumes and on microfilm. A researcher can request a game in, say, 1937, and have it run off. A society of baseball historians checks on box scores and if they find a discrepancy, they'll bring it to the attention of appropriate parties. The mistakes will then be corrected, so that record books published annually will have updated statistics.

In 1976, RBI totals for Lou Gehrig and Babe Ruth were changed after errors in addition were uncovered. Mistakes sometimes are discovered when a modern ballplayer approaches a record held by an old-timer. When Mickey Lolich replaced Cy Young on the all-time strikeout list, three different strikeout totals for Young (for whom the coveted pitching award is named) were found. Before the record could be corrected, an official records committee (eight league representatives, sportswriters and broadcasters) had to have proof that the addition and everything else were correct.

Elias Sports Bureau

THE ELIAS SPORTS BUREAU has added considerably to the accuracy, depth and completeness of sports statistics. Many statistics areas in pro sports would be lacking if not for this excellent agency, which is the official statistician for the National Basketball Association and the National Football League, as well as for baseball's National League.

The man in charge of the seven-day-a-week operation is Seymour Siwoff, a friendly, knowledgeable man who has been a professional sports statistician for thirty years, beginning with an old baseball bureau. When that company folded after the principals had died off, he reorganized the company and formed the current organization some twenty-five years ago.

Because Elias is involved in the major leagues, the Bureau issues *The Book of Baseball Records,* a 360-page official record book used by sports broadcasters and writers. Records of both the American and National leagues are included in this book. In addition to serving the professional leagues for which it is official statistician, Elias Sports Bureau also supplies information to television and radio stations, magazines and newspapers.

Elias issues a weekly release on baseball stats (as it does for football and basketball). For daily updates we rely on the wire services.

The Bureau, which moved into football in 1960 and the NBA in 1968 or 1969, now has a dozen full-time staff members and at least six part-timers. The

Bureau works twelve months every year. Siwoff comments, "There's no season."

The Bureau can handle all the sports at one time. I know from visiting the Bureau at 500 Fifth Avenue in Manhattan what an incredibly busy scene it is. Between ten and twelve fellows sit at desks, working with calculators on big charts and ledgers. Some will be working on football, some on basketball and others, even in the wintertime, will be updating baseball stats. The shelves are filled with ledgers and record books dating back years and years.

The demands on Elias are tremendous. The Bureau can't handle phone inquiries from fans, but responds to countless calls from ball clubs, sportswriters and others professionally involved in sports. The Bureau's own extensive phone bills are an indication of the great volume of work it's doing.

I've called on Elias hundreds of times, mainly in the baseball season, and there's always been someone on hand to help, day or night. Very often, a member of the Bureau will be out at the ball park ready to assist. In Cincinnati on a Sunday in 1977, the papers didn't report several Saturday night games, so I called Elias for the scores, pitchers and other details. I learned there had been a 21-inning game between the Padres and Expos at Montreal that lasted five hours and 33 minutes, the longest in Expo history, and also that Cleveland had played a 12-inning affair at Kansas City. All of this we were able to pass on to our listeners, along with details of several high-scoring games.

Ralph Kiner will occasionally raise a question on the air that I can't answer, and the Elias people, who always listen, will call me up in the broadcast booth with the answer. I make sure the Bureau gets credit on the air, of course.

Siwoff: The Value of Stats

Seymour Siwoff feels, as I do, that sports statistics are of value in that they're "a statistical biography of a player." He concedes, "You can overdo anything; you can make it so uninteresting that it just becomes one big blob of numbers. But on the other hand, if you're creative you provide it in a style that people can understand and relate to. . . ."

Knowing Where to Look

Part of the Bureau's success is attributable to the fact that its employees know exactly where to look for information. There is a precise system in the way they compile their information. To keep data current, the Bureau staff talks to the baseball clubs in the National League every day.

The official scorer sends in his scoresheet, and the Bureau reviews it very carefully, since it's the documentary source for the official record. Ball clubs will check the Elias report against their own unofficial figures, so there's a checks-and-balances system. Every Tuesday that the Mets are home, I check every single one of my records against the official records of Elias, which are brought out to Shea by a member of the Bureau. If there are discrepancies, we check to find the error. It doesn't matter who is responsible for the error, the important thing is that the records concur.

There is a constant interchange between the ball clubs and Elias. For instance, a club statistician will call Elias to say, "Look, my at-bats aren't coming out right, can you tell me where I'm off?" Ordinarily, the Bureau can solve his problems very quickly, and is happy to do so. There is also communication between the clubs and Elias on any change that might have been made in an official scorer's decision. Now that his company has grown, Seymour Siwoff has been traveling more to baseball cities, and has found it has paid off tremendously in terms of making helpful suggestions for clubs and scorers.

As thorough as the Bureau is, and as fine a job as it does, I don't think I'd enjoy that type of work. True, I'd be working with stats and, indirectly at least, I'd be involved with sports. But I'd miss the action of being at the ball park. I should think that no matter how much love you have for the game and for figures, working in an office with figures all the time could get a little dry and boring. Elias employees do come out to the ball park and see as many games as they can. But I would still miss the involvement with one particular team and the whole atmosphere of being where the action is.

Ballplayers and Stats

BALLPLAYERS HAVE an inordinate interest in statistics—usually their own.

You can't really blame them. Stats help determine whether they stay with a team, whether they start or ride the bench, how they stack up against rivals on other teams. And, when negotiation time comes around, stats help set their salary levels. Statistics are also a matter of pride and ego.

Players more often will come to a statistician when they're doing well than when they're doing poorly. A ballplayer who is hitting well will say, "What did those hits do to my average?" or "How many points did I go up on that?" But when they're not going well, watch out. When they're in a slump, they don't want to know you. Like the messenger who brings bad tidings, the statistician is their worst enemy.

Some players are remarkable in their awareness of their statistics. Two who stand out in this regard are players no longer with the Mets—Bob Johnson and Donn Clendenon. Johnson, a utility infielder who bounced around several teams, was a fair hitter. After a game, he'd sit next to me on the bus and say, "Boy, that was my seventh career triple" or "I went three for four, so my lifetime average is now .267." He'd have his lifetime mark figured after each game. Clendenon not only was the first player on the bus to ask questions like "What did the 2-for-4 do for me?" but he also knew his record in every category—even how many walks he had that particular season.

Toward the end of a season, players take great interest in their stats, especially if they are close to a noteworthy accomplishment. If a batter is hitting .301 or .298 with just a few games remaining, he'll want to know what he needs in the way of base hits to finish with a .300 average. I'll tell the player and I'll also keep the manager informed of the situation. On the last day of the 1977 season, Steve Henderson needed to go 2-for-4 to finish at .300. A single his first time up brought his average to .299. He needed one more safety in his next three at-bats, but he failed to get it.

If a team isn't fighting for a pennant, a manager can take a man out of the line-up to ensure a batting average, but usually only if the player consents. In 1941, Ted Williams was just above .400 and was offered the opportunity of sitting out the last game. But he asked to play and by virtue of his own efforts that day, finished the season with a .406 average.

In the last game of 1977, Lee Mazzilli doubled his first time up and reached .250. Joe Torre (with whom I'd been on the phone five or six times to keep him posted on players' averages that game) promptly took Mazzilli out of the game. Sportswriters kidded us verbally and in print, noting that this was an example of how far the Mets had fallen—that a player was taken out of the line-up to ensure his finishing at .250! When, in that same game, a hit by John Stearns brought *his* average to .250, I immediately asked Torre whether he wanted to take Stearns out of the game. But Joe said no, explaining that for Stearns, who'd been hitting .280 at the All-Star break, .250 meant nothing, while for Mazzilli it had some significance because he'd been hitting only .221 at the All-Star break and had set .250 as a goal for himself.

A league title can sometimes hinge on fractions of a point, so any player involved in that kind of contest is going to be very, very interested in his precise stats. I've never been involved in something like that. The closest any Met has come to a batting title was Cleon Jones when he hit .340.

Sometimes a player blames a statistician for something that's not his fault. For two months in 1976, Mickey Lolich was driving me crazy because the newspapers that print major league batting and pitching records every Sunday kept giving him a higher earned-run average than he deserved. They had given him two more earned runs than they should have, and instead of the ERA he deserved (2.90), the record read 3.10.

This bothered Mickey more than it would another player because he had just come to the Mets in a controversial trade for Rusty Staub. He knew that one of the first things Detroit fans, players and management would look at in those listings would be his stats. (Similarly, Met fans, including myself, would look at how Staub was doing.)

To make matters worse, Mickey's 4-10 won-lost record was not a true indication of how he'd been pitching. Poor defense behind him or low run-production by the Mets was often responsible for his losses. And then to have his ERA, which belonged among the ten best in the league, listed incorrectly was too much for him.

The mistake resulted from a box-score change from a hit into an error, and that, in turn, converted what had been two earned runs into two unearned runs. The wire service had based its listing on the box score. Finally, the wire services got his ERA right, apparently as a result of a periodic check of teams' official records.

Jerry Koosman had a fantastic year pitching for the Mets in 1976. When I asked him which stats he'd take with him to negotiate a raise, he surprised me by saying he wasn't going to take any stats with him. He felt he didn't have to cite his ERA, his strikeouts or complete games—just the fact that he won twenty-one games was all he needed.

I suspect he was right. The magic phrase "twenty-one victories" should have been enough to guarantee a healthy increase. Only four other pitchers in the National League had won twenty or more games in 1976.

As rare as twenty-game winners were in the league that season, .300 hitters weren't that uncommon. At least thirty batters managed that good an average. Consequently, someone who hit .300 needed additional hitting credentials to bring up at contract time.

In May, 1977, Jerry Koosman came into a game against the Giants needing eight strikeouts to reach fifteen hundred. He defeated the Giants, 8–1, but the seven strikeouts he recorded left him one shy of what he needed. "You trying to delay this?" I asked him. "No," he said. "I want to get number fifteen hundred against a good hitter. I want to strike out Pete Rose." On May 22, he faced the Reds but didn't strike out Rose. In the second inning, losing 4–0, Kooz struck out Bill Plummer, a lifetime .194 hitter, and he never remembered to ask for the ball. When Grote gave him the ball after the game, Kooz didn't even want it.

When Jerry Grote, who goes back to my first year with the Mets (1966), was approaching the thousand-hit mark, I was more than happy to keep track of how many he needed. I'd pass him in the locker room and remind him, "Just nine more to go," and so on. He told me he hadn't saved very many baseballs representing achievements in the course of his career, but he was anxious to retrieve the ball he hit for number one thousand. I predicted he'd probably lose the ball by making hit number one thousand a home run. The ball he did hit for that milestone didn't miss being a homer by very much: it went off the left-field

133

wall for a double. He got the ball back and was very proud of it.

Ed Kranepool is another man who takes a great interest in his stats. The '76 season was particularly satisfying for him because he attained several club records—passing Cleon Jones to become the all-time Met leader in home runs, extra base hits and base hits. Luckily, the one-hundredth home run of his major league career, a game-winner he struck off Joe Kerrigan of Montreal, went over the right-field wall at Shea Stadium and into the Mets' bullpen, where coach Joe Pignatano was able to retrieve it for Krane's trophy case.

As Eddie approached all these club records, I kept him informed of his progress. But he wasn't satisfied. One day he came to me, angrily saying, "Dammit, why didn't you tell me that the base hit I got yesterday was number twelve hundred of my career? I wanted to save that ball." I told him I was sorry, but I hadn't thought of the twelve hundredth hit as a noteworthy milestone and so I hadn't mentioned it to him.

Felix Millan is a player who is both a worrier and a stats-watcher. When things were going well *or* poorly, he was always waiting for me in the locker room to check the stat sheets to see how he was doing.

He always remembers what he does. During the latter part of August, 1976, we had finished our second West Coast trip and Felix had done tremendously well. On the bus taking us to the airport, I sat next to him and said, "Felix, you had a hell of a road trip—eleven hits in six games." He stopped me. "No," he said, "I had *twelve* hits." I looked up the figures, and he was right, which isn't surprising because he's usually on target.

As the 1976 season was winding down to its final three weeks, Joe Torre was battling to bring his lifetime .298 average up to the .300 mark. He had fallen below .300 when in 1975, his first year with the Mets, he had his poorest season in the major leagues. With so many career at-bats—he came into the '76 season with 7,500 of them—it was going to be a tough push for Joe to get enough hits to get those two points back on his lifetime average. As the season drew to a close, I kept him informed of exactly what he needed to do to get to .300 and how close he was to achieving it. (He didn't make it. Though he hit .306 for the season, his career average was still .298.)

Also in 1976 I reminded Tom Seaver of where he stood as he approached his two hundredth strikeout for the ninth straight season. Like many pitchers when it comes to ERA, Tom would stand near me as I worked on my stat sheet and, without saying anything, would look over my shoulder to see what the game had done to his ERA.

Statistics Can Backfire

Statistics may have backfired for Jerry Koosman in 1976. On the way down to an end-of-the-season series with the Phillies in Philadelphia, Jerry and I noted that he needed eleven strikeouts to reach a season's total of two hundred for the first time in his career. If he managed to strike out twelve batters in what was sure to be his final start of the year, he would tie James Rodney Richard of Houston for second place in the league in strikeouts (behind Tom Seaver, who was going to lead the league). These would be positive stats that would help Jerry's case when the writers cast their votes for the Cy Young award.

In a game that meant nothing in the standings—the Phillies had clinched the Eastern Division championship and the Mets were locked into third place—Kooz started and did well. Going into the bottom of the ninth, the score was 1–1, and he had struck out ten men. He then struck out the first batter of the inning, Ollie Brown, to give him his eleventh of the game and two hundredth of the season. Jerry got the ball and walked to the third-base line, where he tossed it into the dugout for one of his players to hold for him as a memento of his first 200-strikeout season.

I'm sure in back of his mind was the fact that he needed one more strikeout to tie for second in strikeouts and improve his chances against Randy Jones for the Cy Young. But I believe achieving the two hundred–strikeout milestone caused him to lose his concentration. Three pitches later, John Vukovich, a light-hitting utility infielder who had never homered in the National League, drove a Koosman pitch out of the park for a round-tripper and a 2–1 Philly victory. (It was only the sixth homer he'd hit in the majors, his first since 1974.) If Koosman had not just struck out his two hundredth man and stepped off the mound to throw the souvenir ball into the dugout, he might have borne down more on Vukovich and not yielded the homer.

Jerry, charged with the loss, ended the season with a 21-10 record. Randy Jones won the Cy Young award.

Cat and Mouse

Contract negotiations, quite naturally, often evolve into a statistical cat-and-mouse game, since general managers use a player's stats to support their own side of salary negotiations, too. For every positive statistic a player can flaunt, a general manager can find a "neggie." For example, when a pitcher emphasizes how many men he struck out, the G.M. rebuts with, "Yes, but you gave so many bases on balls.'' Or if the player points up how few walks he yielded, the general manager will counter with his low strikeout total.

When a .300 hitter justifiably emphasizes his batting average, the general manager is likely to retort, "But look at your RBI's." And if the hitter had a good season in homers and runs batted in, the general manager will probably say, "But you hit only .250."

During spring training in 1977, when Dave Kingman and the Mets' management were at odds over Dave's contract demands, the Mets' general manager, Joe McDonald, cited statistical reasons for the Mets' refusal to agree to the terms Kingman wanted. "Besides the fact that he strikes out a lot [135 times in 1976], he leaves men on base," McDonald contended. "He is not a good hitter with men in scoring position. His record of delivering in the clutch from the seventh inning on in close games is 18 percent." McDonald then noted that Mike Schmidt of Philadelphia had a 42 percent record and Steve Garvey of Los Angeles a 36 percent record in similar pressure situations. According to McDonald, Kingman's overall (for an entire game) run-delivering percentage with men in scoring position was 21 percent, to Schmidt's 29 percent and Garvey's 32 percent. "The overall average for all players in the National League except pitchers is 27 percent," said McDonald.

Kingman, of course, was emphasizing his great home-run production (thirty-seven in 1976, despite missing thirty-three games with a thumb injury— enough to bring him within one of Schmidt for the major league lead that season).

Arnold (Red) Auerbach, president and general manager of the Boston Celtics, in an article recalling the days of basketball pride and integrity when he coached the Celtics, said he had a standard opening statement when he sat down with a player to sign a contract: "Don't bring me your statistics, because I'm not interested in them. . . . Just tell me what you've done to make us a better club."

Said Auerbach in the *New York Times:* "The only statistic that mattered to me was winning, so I paid every player on the basis of what he did to help us win. That meant the man who set the pick was as important as the man who scored from behind it; the man whose tough defense got us the ball was as important as the man who ended up with the easy bucket a few seconds later."

Stats to Determine Trades

As a team's statistician, I'm usually one of the first to know when a club is considering trading or acquiring a player. For instance, in my first nine years with the Rangers, whenever Emile Francis, then the general manager, would ask me for the stats of a particular opposing player, I'd know he was interested in him. The trade might never be consummated, but it alerted me to the fact that he was working on a possible deal.

There's a temptation to pass the word along that a transaction is in the wind, but I resist it. While I might tell it off-the-record to a friend out of sports, I would never divulge it to a player or someone in the news media, where it could get into print or on the air and possibly hurt someone.

When a player is sent down to the minors, it's usually on the basis of the statistics available to the ball club; and when a player arrives at star status, so to speak, it's because of the statistics he's compiled. In the case of the man destined either for stardom or the minors—or anyone else—there are always intangibles that cannot be described by simple numbers. I think everybody involved with baseball realizes that. But still, when it comes down to it, statistics form the critical dimension of baseball.

A trade—that of Tom Seaver to Cincinnati on June 15, 1977—led to the most emotional scene I've ever experienced in professional sports.

Tom, "The Franchise," had expressed a desire to be traded. As the June 15 trading deadline approached, rumors flew like fungoes: he was going to the Dodgers; he was going to the Reds; he was going to the Reds for this group of players; he was going to them for another set of players; he was staying with the Mets, and so on.

As the various deals had unfolded and folded, Joe Torre kept me informed, but of course, I was pledged to secrecy. Then, as the Mets went into their June 15 night game with the Braves, everyone knew Seaver was leaving the Mets.

When the game in Atlanta that night was over—somehow the Mets had managed to keep winning through all the pressures and tensions created by the impending trade—there was still no official word. The Reds' game had gone into extra innings and so no announcement of the trade could yet be made.

Finally the Reds' contest was over. And with nearly a hundred members of the media present—but without Seaver, who had been given permission by Torre to go home before the game—the word came. Arthur Richman, the beleaguered public relations director for the Mets, perspiring profusely in the glare of TV cameras and popping flashbulbs, stepped forward and read from a piece of crumpled yellow paper the details of one of the biggest and most dramatic trades in baseball history. Tom Seaver had been sent to the Cincinnati Reds in return for pitcher Pat Zachry, infielder Doug Flynn and minor league outfielders Steve Henderson and Dan Norman.

137

The Mets greeted the announcement with stony silence. Wordlessly, they boarded the bus for the Atlanta airport. At the airport all nonplaying Met personnel were asked to leave the bus and board the plane. To the players on the bus, Torre read a short farewell note from Seaver, who wouldn't have been able to endure the emotional pressure of a face-to-face goodbye with all his teammates (though he'd exchanged tearful goodbyes with Harrelson and Koosman).

Other Met trades had also been made, and on the plane, before their official announcement, Joe Torre broke the news individually to the players involved in the transactions—Mike Phillips, who was being exchanged for Joel Youngblood; Roy Staiger, who was being sent to the minors; and Dave Kingman, who was going to San Diego for infielder Bobby Valentine and pitcher Paul Siebert. Torre consoled Bud Harrelson, who was almost inconsolable over the trade of Seaver, his roommate and close friend. Aboard the plane, Kingman openly sobbed and the eyes of quite a few others were misty. I got home at four in the morning and like so many of the Mets, spent a sleepless night.

The next day Seaver just joined the names in the "Others" column on the Mets' stat sheet. Joe Torre, his sense of humor intact, commented that "Now Seaver's on the same line as Luis Alvarado." Luis had been with the Mets just for the first few days of the season.

I miss Tom personally and professionally. Just about every time he pitched, he was likely to set one kind of mark or another, and he would make a statistician's pulse throb as he closed in on yet other pitching records. Now, for me, that was all gone.

Tom told me that one of the biggest thrills of his career had come June 7, 1977, at Shea Stadium, when in one of his strongest performances ever, he struck out ten Reds to pass Sandy Koufax and become number twelve on the all-time strikeout list. The two-minute standing ovation the fans accorded him sent chills up his spine and drained him emotionally.

We both were surprised at how aware the fans had been of the strikeout mark he had achieved, as evidenced by their clamor well before the news was flashed on the scoreboard. It was yet another illustration of how attuned baseball fans are to statistical achievements.

Last-Day Decision

An indication of how important statistics are and the effect they can have on a baseball game in the final weekend of the season, even one in which no pennant is at stake, is the way the battle for the batting championship is determined. In 1976 the batting championships in both leagues weren't decided until the final day of the regular season. I don't think there's ever been a situation like this before—where the championships in both leagues came down to the final at-bat for each batter, although there have been similar occasions in both leagues at different times. In 1970, for instance, the batting average of Alex Johnson had to be carried out to four digits before it could be determined that he was the champion.

Don't be deceived by ballplayers' protestations that titles mean nothing to them, or that their only concern is that their team wins. A batting championship is a player's permanent mention in the record books, a monument in agate type attesting to his batting skills. What happened on that last day of the '76 season shows how much a batting title means.

On the last day of the 1976 season, the Kansas City Royals, who were running out the string, getting ready to play the Yankees in the playoffs, were involved in a game that was meaningless except for the fact that two men on the team, George Brett and Hal McRae, were contenders for the American League batting crown.

Hal McRae stood to be the first designated hitter ever to lead the league in batting. As his teammate George Brett came to bat in the bottom of the ninth, with the Twins enjoying a safe lead over the Royals, McRae had a .0004-point lead for the title.

Brett hit a soft fly ball to left field, where Twins outfielder Steve Brye hesitated several times, apparently misjudging the ball. In any case he did not play it very well, and the ball bounced in front of him for a hit, then caromed over his shoulder and into the left-field corner. Brett beat the relay home for an inside-the-park home run.

McRae was up next, and now he needed a hit to win the title, but in his final at-bat, all he could manage was a ground ball to the shortstop, who threw him out. When the averages were carried out to a fourth decimal point, Brett had a league-leading average of .3333 and McRae was second with .3326. Think players don't take the batting title seriously? McRae charged the Minnesota dugout, claiming that Minnesota manager Gene Mauch had instructed Brye to let Brett's ball drop in intentionally so that Brett could win the championship. McRae even suggested racial motives, and the commissioner's office investigated.

In the National League, the batting championship came down to the final day of the season, too, and while the race didn't involve controversy and wasn't between two teammates (a very unusual situation), it was plenty exciting.

Coming into that last day of the season, Ken Griffey of the Reds was leading the league. In second place, trailing Griffey by three points, was Bill Madlock (then of the Cubs), who had won the championship in 1975. To overtake Griffey, he'd need quite a final outing—and he had it, getting four hits in as many at-bats against Montreal.

Griffey, meanwhile, did not start that day for the Reds, but when word reached Cincinnati about the fantastic day Madlock was having, Sparky Anderson, the Reds' manager, inserted him into the line-up. Griffey went 0-for-2, striking out twice. When the calculator stopped flashing, Madlock had a .339 season's average and Griffey a .336.

If proof is needed that statistics are the lifeblood of baseball, just consider the fact that fans stay interested the last weeks of a season even when there is no pennant race. Even though baseball plays twice as many games as any other professional sport, and it can get boring in the absence of a divisional race, fascination with the decimal point keeps interest alive.

Managers and Stats

SOME BASEBALL MANAGERS rely heavily on stats. Earl Weaver of the Orioles, for instance, is likely to shuffle line-ups according to "the charts" so much that one of his players was quoted as saying, "Checking the line-up card any more is like looking for the prize in a box of Cracker Jacks. Every day is a mystery. . . ."

According to an article by Ron Fimrite in *Sports Illustrated,* the statistical charts used by Weaver show him the Orioles' "Weaver-era batting averages against any given pitcher." Therefore, a player with a feeble batting average might be inserted into the line-up because he had a solid percentage against the man pitching for the opposition that day.

"The charts give us an edge," Weaver was quoted as saying. "The point is that certain guys hit certain pitchers better than other guys. It's not always on a lefty-righty basis, either, although it generally works out that left-handed batters hit right-handed pitchers better and vice versa."

Accordingly, players frequently found themselves hitting in various spots in the order and playing at various fielding positions within a short period of time. In one eight-game stretch, only one Oriole was at the same position in every game.

Gene Mauch of the Minnesota Twins is another manager who relies heavily on statistics in establishing his line-up and other aspects of strategy. Mauch told sportswriter Bob Fowler that he and his staff chart every game. Then, before each game, he goes over the charts to "find out who did well in past games against the pitcher we're facing, who did well in that park.

In 1976, his first year as Twins manager, "I had nothing to go on," Mauch told Fowler in *The Sporting News*. "Now I have a lot. I had a very enjoyable winter going over the statistics of each game from 1976 and replaying them in my mind.

"I try to bunch those players who have had success against the pitcher. I try to get them high in the batting order, too. The idea is to try to get something going quickly, and not to give the pitcher any breathers by spreading those who hit him well throughout the order."

In the first thirty-five games of the '77 season, the Twins' skipper used the same line-up in consecutive games only four times. Eleven different players led off; six different players batted clean-up.

When Fowler asked him if there was any pattern to his line-up, Mauch replied, "I sure hope so. When you spend five hours on them, I hope there's some consistency."

I read some years ago that Allan Roth, the statistician, told Charlie Fox, who was then manager of the Giants, that the case for the first and third basemen to guard the lines in late innings of a tied or close game isn't so compelling as many people think it is. He pointed out to Fox that the number of balls hit for doubles down the line was not large enough to make a substantial difference. "More ground balls," Roth said, "go just to the left of the third baseman and the right of the first baseman than past them on the line."

Fox reportedly said that except when the first baseman had to hold a runner on to cut down on the possibility of a steal, he would try out Roth's theory in spring training. I don't know the outcome, but I mention this as an example of statistics affecting managerial decisions.

Of the managers I've known personally, Gil Hodges was the most statistically aware man I've come across in my fifteen years in professional sports. He was incredible in the way he made use of every scrap of intelligence he could lay his hands on.

Gil would look for obscure things on a stat sheet. He wouldn't look for the home-run or RBI totals—he'd know that—but instead he'd look at something as far-out as how the scheduled opposing pitcher was *batting!* He realized that often a team gets burned by a pitcher hitting against it, because the man on the mound tends to relax. Hodges wanted to be aware of that kind of information before the game, so he could warn his pitcher to bear down against the opposing hurler.

Another item Gil would check would be the successful stolen-base attempts against the catcher on the team we were going to play. If the opposition had stolen forty-eight bases and been thrown out only twenty times, Gil would assume the catcher had a poor arm. Stolen bases are often the fault of pitchers not holding the runners on too well, and so you also keep that in mind when you're considering sending a runner down. But you'd be less likely to order a steal against a Johnny Bench, who had thrown out twenty-three of thirty-three runners attempting to steal.

Gil would also check the box scores (I hold on to one for every National League game) of the opposition's past three or four games, to detect certain patterns—for example, has their second-place hitter been sacrificing a lot lately? Now, they might not follow that particular pattern in this game, but Hodges' theory was that by playing percentages you're going to come out ahead in the long run. For instance, it often happens that you intentionally walk a good hitter to get to someone with a .240 average, and then the .240 hitter gets a hit. But if you followed the same strategy ten times, you'd probably come out ahead on seven of those occasions.

Hodges was so exceptionally bright he not only knew what was happening at the moment, but was planning three innings ahead. He'd check to see which of the opposing relievers had pitched a lot recently, so that when the fourth inning came around he'd know whether or not to make a lefty-righty switch. Perhaps Dave Giusti had pitched five days in a row. Then Gil would know the chances of Dave's coming into today's game were slight. Accordingly, he might decide to leave a left-handed hitter in the game although there was a lefty pitcher in now for the other team, because he felt the other team did not have another lefty pitcher on tap.

He would check the bases-on-balls column and try to determine whether the opposing batsman had been looking for a lot of walks lately. He would check the number of wild pitches thrown by an opponent. If the pitcher had thrown a lot of them, he would tell his runners to be extra alert when they were on third base, because this pitcher was inclined to bounce a curveball into the dirt.

Yogi Berra, who became the Mets' manager after Gil's sudden death in 1972, also liked statistics. Before a game in which we were going to be facing a southpaw, he would call me up and ask which of the Mets had been hitting what against left-handed pitchers. I would give him the figures for the players he was asking about, and it would play a big part in his determination of who was going to be in the line-up that particular day.

I would not have the figures broken down to the point where I could tell how John Milner, for example, had done against the *particular* left-hander due to face

143

us, but if managers asked for that information—as they occasionally did—I'd work it out for them.

Joe Frazier, who became the Mets' manager in 1976, didn't use statistics so much as either Hodges or Berra. Frazier was a little more from the old school of managers, who don't rely quite as much on stats. Also, he had managed for many years in the minors, where it might be the traveling secretary, a coach, or even the trainer or nurse who did the stats for a team; and consequently, all that was available was the bare minimum.

In the late 1960's, when some ballplayers had military reserve obligations on weekends, I'd tell Hodges that, say, Richie Hebner of Pittsburgh would not be playing because he was away. Though it's not a black-and-white statistic, it's a piece of information that might be helpful—and I like to think that information is what I'm there to provide.

Joe Torre, who took over the managership of the Mets early in the 1977 season, is astute and blessed with a remarkable memory. Like Gil Hodges, he commands respect, but on a different basis. He is more open than Hodges was. Like Gil, he makes use of all sorts of statistical background information to form his managerial decisions. He has a reason, usually a statistical one, for everything he does in the way of strategy. When he became manager, I opened up all the books to him, to show him statistical records he never saw as a player.

Some information is particularly welcomed by him. For example, Torre made the Mets much more of a running team, and so he needs to know what a particular opposing catcher's record is on throwing out runners trying to steal. I'll also point out such things to him as the fact that one of the Montreal hitters had swung at the first pitch in six of seven at-bats in a current series with the Mets, so that Met pitchers might throw accordingly.

During a series with the Phillies, I was able to inform Joe that a new pitcher the Phils had acquired had been sent to the minors, so that Tug McGraw was the only lefty the Phils had in their bullpen. This would affect what hitters and pinch-hitters Torre might elect to send up.

When I told Joe that Greg Luzinski had an inflamed eye and therefore wouldn't even be able to pinch-hit for the Phils, Torre already knew it. Invariably, he's well prepared with information.

Joe and I have been close, and before he became a manager, we used to discuss what changes he'd make if he were running the team. Now that he's the skipper, I look forward to a long and happy relationship. I expect to enjoy working with Joe more than I have with any other manager.

144

The Most Valuable Stats

SOME STATISTICS are considerably more important in evaluating a player's worth than others, and not all are appreciated by the average fan. In truth, some significant statistical categories are not even known to most fans.

Evaluating Hitters

When I pick up the stat sheet of a visiting team, I scan certain columns very carefully to determine who is really contributing to that ball club.

One category that interests me is "runs scored," something very few fans pay much attention to. It's important. If a man has scored a lot of runs, it means, number one, that he's been on base a lot and, in most cases, that he's got fairly good speed.

Connected with this is the importance of drawing walks. People will point out that you can't drive in a run with a base on balls (unless the bases are loaded), but when you're batting up front in the order, a walk is sometimes more important than a base hit. First of all, you're tiring the pitcher by making him throw a minimum of four pitches—and in most cases five or six—while a hit may have come on the first pitch. And then, of course, you've got him thinking. Since he walked you, he doesn't want to walk the next batter, and so the next batter is likely to get a better pitch to hit than he would if you hadn't drawn a base on balls. A walk is more important for an eighth-place batter than for a man who bats fifth or sixth. If the eighth-place batter walks, he's set up a sacrifice situation for the pitcher, who otherwise represents a probable wasted at-bat.

Evaluating Pitchers

When I examine a pitcher's record—especially a relief pitcher's—I'll always look at the innings he's pitched compared with the hits he's allowed. I'll do this before I look at his won-lost record or his earned-run average. A reliever may have a low ERA, yet not be very effective. He can come in and give up a hit with men on base, but the runs that score are charged to the starting pitcher he's replaced. In that case his ERA stays unblemished though he's given up a crucial hit. If a reliever has allowed more hits than innings pitched—I don't care what his ERA or won-lost record is—he probably hasn't been doing the job. I think most pitching coaches and managers will tell you the same thing.

I'll also look at strikeouts compared with innings pitched, and I'll check out how many home runs he's allowed. Then, maybe, I'll go back and look at the won-lost record and the earned-run average.

Won-lost records can be misleading because a pitcher who yields eight runs when his team scores ten is a winner, while a pitcher who gives up only three runs when his team scores just one is a loser. The latter has been a problem with some of the Met pitchers for a long time.

If we go against the Phillies and I see that Larry Christenson has a 9-5 record, but has given up 118 hits in one hundred innings, it makes me wonder what his record would be with a team that wasn't so good defensively as the Phillies.

Evaluating Fielders

The best way to evaluate a fielder is to watch him every day and note the plays he makes and doesn't make, and why. Some fielders make errors because they have better range and thus get to balls that a slower player won't even get near. A good center fielder, for instance, will chase a drive and just manage to get his glove on it and be charged with an error—just because he got there—while another will just wave at the drive as it goes past him to left-center for a double. So errors don't tell the whole story, and fielding percentage tells you less about how good a fielder is than batting average tells you about his hitting ability.

For instance, you might notice that Rusty Staub has thirteen or fourteen assists and decide he's a great outfielder. But if you were to watch Rusty, who's really a good professional hitter, not a fielder, you'd come to a different conclusion. If you watched him every day in the outfield you'd see how his lack of speed hurts the team. Balls that a better outfielder would get go past him into the right-center field alley or down the right-field line. That's one of the reasons the Tigers now use him almost exclusively as a designated hitter. He doesn't get charged with many errors over the course of a season, but the intangibles make him a poorer fielder than his statistical record indicates.

This is why scouting is so important in baseball; you have to observe a player on an everyday basis.

How many assists a fielder has is of some value in assessing his ability. Usually the good outfielder will be among the leaders in assists, though there's the school of thought that says nobody's going to try to run on the fielder with an especially good arm, while the fielder with a weak arm is going to get a lot of opportunities to throw a player out. If you can break it down to how many assists a player has *per opportunity*, the figures become more meaningful. That kind of statistic involves judgment; did he have a chance to get the runner or didn't he? But it can be done, and is, by most experienced statisticians.

I do that sort of thing with catchers trying to throw out runners attempting to steal. If I don't think the catcher has a chance in the world of throwing out a runner because he got such a good jump, I won't charge it against the catcher's record. I've seen enough baseball to have the sense not to charge someone with something that's not his fault.

Measuring Hitters

There are several rules of thumb that major league managers, general managers and members of the media use in evaluating what a player's performance means to himself and his team. They might be helpful in assisting you to form your own judgments, but keep in mind that no single performance statistic should be considered by itself in judging a player.

A Hit a Game. A player who averages one hit a game over the course of a season is usually an average player, one who hits about .265 or .270. (But Joe Morgan in 1976 had more than one hundred walks in addition to his hit-per-game pace, so his average was considerably higher because he had more than one hundred fewer official at-bats.)

A Homer Every Twenty At-Bats. A player who averages one home run every twenty or fewer at-bats is usually one of the top sluggers in the league and in most cases, will hit between thirty and forty home runs a season.

A player who has only one home run every one hundred at-bats is not considered a long-ball hitter and will usually have fewer than ten home runs in a season. Though he is not considered a power hitter, he might still be a good RBI man.

RBI Percentage. Some teams keep records—I do on the Mets—of how many chances a batter has to drive in runs, in addition, of course, to how many he actually drives in.

To arrive at a man's RBI percentage, take the number of times he comes up with men in scoring position—that is, on second base or third, where a single would usually score them—and divide that total into the number of men he drove in. If a particular batter has had seventy-five men in scoring position when he came up to bat, and driven in twenty, you'd divide twenty by seventy-five and find that his RBI percentage is just under .27, or .266. Driving in about 27 percent of the runners that were in scoring position, this man would probably knock in fifty runs or less in a season.

In figuring a man's RBI percentage, you would not count the run he scores on his own home run, though you would count any others his homer drove in.

A good hitter should be able to drive in between 38 percent and 42 percent of the runners who are in scoring position when he comes to bat.

Walks Versus Strikeouts. A batter who draws more bases on balls than strikeouts is usually regarded as a player with a good batting eye. Most players strike out more often than they walk.

Measuring Pitchers

There are various statistical rules of thumb regarding pitchers, too.

Value of ERA. An earned-run average determines the value of a starting pitcher a little better than it does that of a relief pitcher. The reason I say this is that a relief pitcher may come in with men on base and give up a couple of base hits, but the runs that score will be charged to the record of the man he relieved, not his own. So a relief pitcher with a low ERA is not necessarily having as good a year or pitching as effectively as his ERA would indicate. The number of hits he has allowed per inning pitched is usually a better gauge of how effective a reliever has been, as noted earlier.

Strikeouts. It's an extraordinary pitcher who can average a strikeout an inning. He's one who will be among the top three strikeout pitchers.

Walks. If a pitcher allows one walk or less every three innings—meaning he's allowing about three walks a game—he's considered a very good control pitcher.

Strikeouts Versus Walks. It's considered excellent if a pitcher can strike out two men for every man he walks.

Complete Games. If a starting pitcher can complete half of the games he starts, it's considered very good.

Home Runs. It is excellent for a starting pitcher who pitches regularly in rotation every fourth or fifth day to allow only fifteen home runs or less in an entire season. Most pitchers in regular rotation will pitch at least two hundred innings, so fifteen home runs is a low figure.

Stats of Different Eras

When you're trying to compare figures for different eras, statistical comparisons are never quite equal. The players being compared played under very different conditions, many of which the statistician or fan is not aware of. The ball parks and the game of baseball itself were different in the 1930's and 1940's from what they are in the 1970's.

All-Time Records

It may seem like a contradiction after what I've just said, but I believe that statistics of all-time records are perfectly valid even though they represent accomplishments of different eras.

People still get into value judgments when it comes to records. The most drastic example of this, I think, occurred in 1961, when Roger Maris of the Yankees hit sixty-one home runs to break Babe Ruth's single-season record by one.

About halfway through the season, when it appeared that Maris had a good chance of breaking the mark, Ford Frick, who was then commissioner of baseball, issued his famous and controversial asterisk ruling. He pointed out that in 1927, when Ruth hit sixty homers, teams played only a 154-game schedule, while in 1961 there was a 162-game schedule. He contended that since Maris had eight more games in which to establish a record, unless Maris broke Ruth's record in the first 154 games of the season, it would have to be footnoted with an asterisk, indicating it was a somewhat lesser accomplishment.

In my mind it was a ridiculous decision, because a season's record is either a record for a complete season or it's nothing at all. Look through a record book and you'll find that in almost any record kept, there are differences in the schedules. Granted the obvious fact that a 162-game season is eight games longer than one with 154. But when you compare Ruth in 1927 and Maris in 1961, you find that Ruth came to bat 592 times and Maris 598. So there really was very little difference.

What criterion do you use in judging a record to convince the asterisk-placers that it should go into the books without qualification? Do you use the number of times at bat? The games played? The games scheduled? The official times at bat? You could go on and on.

Interestingly, the same season that Maris broke Ruth's single-season home-run record, Sandy Koufax broke the National League single-season record for strikeouts that had been held by Christy Mathewson. Koufax broke the record in a season of 154 games, while Mathewson's record was set when the schedule called for 140 games; yet nobody suggested putting an asterisk on Koufax's record—probably because nobody paid very much attention to it. Unlike the assault on the home-run record, there was no countdown in the papers on the approaching new mark in strikeouts; you didn't see a chart in the daily papers about how close Koufax was to Mathewson's record, or what pace he needed to break it. But these details were available about Maris and his attempt.

After Hank Aaron broke Babe Ruth's career home-run record, some people contended that Aaron wasn't really the all-time great home-run hitter since he had come to bat more often than Babe Ruth had and therefore it shouldn't count. I don't think the *true* baseball fan would agree with that judgment, since it takes away from the proper appreciation of Aaron's accomplishment.

When Hank Aaron broke Ruth's record, Roger Maris commented, "Henry's going to hear a lot of baloney about times at bat, but he's got the record, and that's all that counts."

If you dig deep, you can find a reason to question almost any record set in baseball on the basis of unequal opportunities or dissimilar conditions.

Tom Seaver struck out 200 or more batters in nine consecutive seasons—the only pitcher in major league history to do so. Would you diminish his accomplishment by saying, "Well, there are weaker hitters now than there were then," or "We play more games now than they did in the 1920's or 1930's, when Cy Young pitched"? If you start getting into these kinds of judgments, you might as well throw out all records, because there is no way that every player (past, current or future) is going to perform under the very same conditions. No two situations are going to be identical. You could look at Lou Brock's single-season record of 118 stolen bases and say he had the advantage of playing on artificial turf, while Maury Wills, the man whose record he surpassed, didn't. And Brock played under much different conditions from Ty Cobb, whose lifetime record he surpassed in 1977; yet no one made a big fuss about the differences.

Though it might be tempting to do so, Ralph Kiner doesn't try to compare, through statistics, ballplayers of his own era with players today. "I think it would be unfair," he says, "to compare, say, Dave Kingman to myself or someone else who was playing in my day. I *will* compare him in style, but he's hitting against different pitchers than we hit against. All I will say is that any great athlete could have played in any era."

Comparing Stats

Comparing the statistics of players on one team is valid, because all of them have played in the same ball parks and pretty much have faced the same pitchers.

There's greater validity in comparing players within the same league than comparing men in different leagues. The hitters in the National League, for instance, play in seven ball parks that have artificial turf, while hitters in the American League play in only three ball parks (K.C., Toronto and Seattle) with artificial turf. Certain types of hitters—those who hit down on the ball and hit a lot of ground balls—seem to benefit from playing on artificial turf, and they'll usually hit for higher averages in those parks than they will on natural grass. So these factors should be evaluated in making comparisons of players who are not in the same league.

Often what seems like a big numerical difference is a relatively small one. Let's say two players have three hundred official at-bats in a season. One hits .333 and the other .290, a pretty sizable point difference. But the difference is only 13 hits (100 by the .333 hitter; 87 by the other). In 300 at-bats, only 12 hits spells the difference between hitting .290 and .250. To make a strictly valid comparison, such factors as lucky bounces, different ball parks, scorers' judgment decisions, and the luck of which pitcher the two players batted against, should be figured in.

ERA Unfair

If I had to pick out just one baseball statistic that I consider unfair, it would be earned-run average. The ERA concept is one-sided. Like saves for a reliever, it measures something only in a pitcher's favor, and ignores the opposite. If a pitcher makes the batter hit an easy ground ball or fly ball that a fielder drops, the pitcher is absolved of earned-run responsibility for any runs that follow in that inning. But if a pitcher gives up a four-hundred-foot shot to right-center field, and the outfielder makes a sensational running catch with men on base, ERA allows for no real corresponding way to measure the pitcher's failure to keep the batter from hitting the ball solidly. In other words, the pitcher receives the benefit of good fielding, and escapes the damage caused by poor fielding in his ERA.

Of course, the pitcher, along with the manager, team and fans, is not concerned very much with anything but runs—earned or unearned—when it comes to winning or losing a ball game. But I'd be willing to bet that the number of hard-hit balls for outs exceeds the number of errors that allow runs. What was a routine fly ball for Willie Mays in his heyday may be a double or triple against a slower center fielder. There really is no way to establish a criterion for "normal" fielding, nor is there any way to equalize the consequences of the fielding behind a pitcher. But in my opinion, ERA has more flaws in it than any other baseball statistic.

A Statistician's View
of Ball Parks

JUST AS BALL PARKS sometimes affect players, they can also affect the performance of a statistician.

For instance, Riverfront Stadium, where the Reds now play their home games, has a terrible set-up. You have to walk two steep flights of stairs to get to and from each booth; and when you get down to them, especially the radio booth, there's no room to walk around. I've come awfully close to flying down those stairs several times, and I usually wear sneakers when we're playing in Cincinnati, because that's the only way I can move around and make my 20–25 trips per game from one booth to another without breaking my neck. The booths are separated by cement walls and are approachable only by steep stairways.

Our broadcasters are constantly changing over from radio to TV. They are allowed only sixty seconds to make the transition, so Riverfront Stadium presents problems. Remember, they have to gather up their jackets, scorecards, books and press guides, go up the stairs, open a heavy metal door, go back outside, open up another heavy metal door, go down the stairs, catch their breath and be ready to open up the next inning. When I make that trip, I occasionally miss a few pitches—which, of course, isn't good.

Pittsburgh's Three Rivers Stadium is a little bit unusual in that our broadcast booth is on a separate level from the regular press box and the home broadcasting booth, and there's no telephone hookup between them. Sometimes, because of the crowd noise, I won't hear a particular announcement from the official scorer—for instance, was it a wild pitch or a passed ball?—and I've got to go down one full level to find out what the official ruling was on that play. Or if I need a bio or the stats of a new player up from the minors, I've got to run down the staircase to where the Pirate P.R. people are located.

By contrast, the Astrodome in Houston is beautifully set up for radio and TV, with the booths next to each other, so that all that's involved in going from one to the other is about four stairs. The proximity of the booths is better here than anywhere else. The Astrodome has some amenities that other stadiums don't, such as the luxury of a pencil sharpener in the broadcast booth. Elsewhere, sharpening a pencil requires a walk to the press box or home TV booth. Also, you never have to worry about wind blowing your papers or rain soaking them.

The Astrodome, as the first of the indoor ball parks, has its own character. The one drawback is that there's a long walk to the clubhouse, where the bus picks us up to take us to our hotel. Because it's a big circular stadium, every entrance and exit looks pretty much the same. One time I came out the wrong exit and missed our bus. Since it was an hour after the game, the fans had left and there were no cabs around. So, loaded down with books, as usual, I trudged a good mile or two back to the hotel in 95° weather.

I also missed the bus in Pittsburgh one time, when the stadium was new, by coming out the wrong entrance. The hotel wasn't far (it's right across the river from the ball park, and the bus takes only about seven minutes, which gives me ten or fifteen minutes more work time than I'd have in other ball parks). But as short as the walk was, it required crossing a bridge, and there I was approached by three kids looking to lift my wallet. I had to use my briefcase as a weapon to scare them away.

Memorial Stadium in St. Louis is set up beautifully. It's probably the easiest ball park for me to work and get around in. The radio and TV booths are about the largest of any in the league. Fifteen people could fit comfortably, so we can get around without bumping into one another. And I have the luxury of spreading my work out.

The elevator runs quickly from field level to the booth. At field level, the elevator lets you off right between the clubhouses, which saves time and makes it easy for me to go about my business.

The Cardinals put out more stat sheets—as many as six or seven—than any other team in the league. The statistical and P.R. staff in St. Louis issues good, clear, easy-to-read sheets with all sorts of information, even some pertaining to the minor leagues.

Wrigley Field in Chicago is the oldest ball park in the National League. It's

154

unique in that all games there are day games—it has no lights, because the team's late owner, Phil Wrigley, had promised area residents he would not let them be disturbed by night games. In other stadiums, most weekday games are played at night, and this is a big adjustment for me.

When we have night games, I can pretty much spread out my workload. But in Chicago, where the games start at 1:00 or 1:30 in the afternoon, the bus will normally leave for the ball park at 10:30 or 11:00 in the morning, or 9:30 before a double-header, and so I don't have that free time to get my work done. When we get back from a game in Chicago, it's usually five or six in the evening, when for some reason it's tough to get working.

A good deal of time in Chicago is spent reading details of last night's games, which hadn't started when we were at the park.

Because Wrigley Field has no elevators, I've got to walk up and down many ramps to get from the clubhouse to where my stencils are run off, then up to the booth, then back down to the field—where I give them to the Mets' manager— and, finally, back up to the booth.

The broadcast booths in Chicago are small, but the worst problem is the ever-present wind. One time I handed the out-of-town scoresheets to Ralph Kiner, but he never got them because a sudden gust of wind swept them out to second base. While moving along a catwalk from the radio booth to the TV booth, I've lost a dozen pitching or home-run cards or scoresheets to the wind. (In Ft. Lauderdale in spring training in 1978, the wind slammed a heavy steel door on Lindsey Nelson's hand, causing a serious injury.)

The ball park in Philadelphia is arranged with our needs in mind, with two rapidly running elevators for the exclusive use of the press. It's an easy matter for me to get down to the field and talk to the ballplayers, and then return to the press level directly in back of the broadcast booths, which are located next to each other.

The Phillies do a marvelous job of putting out stat sheets and getting their work done. In my opinion, Philadelphia has the friendliest and most efficient staff in the league.

The stadium's one drawback is the one steep ten-stair staircase. I've taken several nasty flops rushing between booths, and so, though keeping statistics isn't a contact sport, it has its dangers.

Jarry Park, where Montreal played its home games through 1976, had a certain charm (which carries over to the Expos' new Olympic Stadium) in that stat sheets were done in French as well as English. Announcements over the public address system and in the press box were done in French and English.

Sometimes there was a slight delay in getting postgame totals, because they'd give them in French first.

The park had no elevators. Our bus would arrive in the right-field area, where the clubhouse was located, and the walk to the broadcasting booth was long and involved climbing a steep staircase. Our radio booth was tiny, with room only for two broadcasters to fit comfortably—three, if they squeezed together—so I just stood behind them. Because of the long walk and staircase, I'd get a pretty good workout prior to the game.

Montreal weather has caused a lot of problems over the years. It rains so much and it's so chilly in April, May and September, we sometimes feel as if we're working a football game. We're constantly playing twin-bills, usually twi-night double-headers, because there are so many postponements.

Wind is a problem in Candlestick Park in San Francisco, just as it is in Wrigley Field, and if I forget to put a weight on my papers, they sometimes end up behind home plate.

The park used to be a problem in other ways. Until three or four years ago, it didn't have an elevator, and I hiked miles before and during a game. We'd come into the ball park in the vicinity of the right-field fence, not far from the clubhouse. To get to the broadcasting booth, we'd have to walk through a runway and onto the field. As we walked from right field to home plate, the Giants usually would be taking batting practice, and we had to duck line drives, especially when a left-handed batter was up. I'd make the trip two or three times before the game and when I was heading toward the outfield, I'd make sure to walk somewhat sideways, so I wouldn't be drilled in the back by a line drive.

Dodger Stadium in Los Angeles, in my opinion, is the cleanest and most beautiful ball park in the National League. The elevators are well set up in Dodger Stadium and in San Diego, which also has a beautiful stadium. This allows me to do what I have to quickly, which I greatly appreciate because of the extra work I have to do before a game on the West Coast.

Atlanta Stadium has big broadcast booths—almost the size of those in St. Louis—so that I have plenty of room for spreading out my papers. Because the hotel is perhaps only ten minutes away, I arrive at the ball park earlier and work at a more leisurely pace.

After twelve years with the Mets, I've come to know each ball park intimately and could probably get around them blindfolded. I've learned the most expedient way to operate in particular parks. In some, I found it was best to go to the clubhouse first to talk to the manager or players and to get my line-ups. In other parks, I learned the home team would have its line-up posted by the time we arrived at the ball park, and so I would go to the field and get the home team line-up first. Elsewhere, it's best for me to go right to the public relations office or other office to get my stat sheets run off. Each club has a different way of running off stat sheets. Some use Xerox machines, others use duplicating machines. Because each employs a different kind of stencil, I make sure I've brought the right stencils—whether it's six-hole, nine-hole or whatever—for the cities we're going to visit. The Pirates have their own special duplicating machine, so I have to replace my ordinary typewriter ribbon with a special kind to accommodate it.

I've been burned only a couple of times over the years, when I found myself without the proper stencil. In those instances, I just went to the home team's office in the ball park and typed my stats on a borrowed stencil.

Hotels

Hotels also play a part in how well a statistician performs. You know that in some hotels you're going to have a big desk on which you can spread out your work, while others are cramped. Since I take a lot of books and papers with me on the road, and accumulate others, the larger the room and the more space I have in which to spread my materials out, the easier it is for me to find something and do my work.

The lighting in some hotels is excellent, elsewhere it's poor. Working, as I do, in hotel rooms and on airplanes and in ball parks can affect vision. When I started working with the Mets, I had perfect 20-20 eyesight, but all the work I've done with close figures under lighting that is not conducive to this kind of work, has taken its toll. Because of the strain, I now wear glasses whenever I do my typing or enter my work in a book.

HOCKEY

Hockey

HOCKEY IS probably the easiest of all the sports for keeping statistics and working with a broadcaster. On scoring plays, all you have to do is mark down who scored the goal, who made the assist, and the time of the goal. Because hockey is a low-scoring sport, you get quite a few games where there aren't many scoring plays involved.

Of course, you keep track not only of scoring plays, but also such matters as penalty minutes and shots on goal. And as you do in other sports, you have to be on top of any player records and streaks.

Yet because of the nature of the game, you might sit and watch eight to ten minutes of action without having to make a single notation. And whereas in baseball, football and basketball, you're constantly changing, erasing and up-dating data, in hockey there is hardly ever any reason to erase.

Because keeping stats in hockey is relatively undemanding, a statistician will usually help out in various other ways. When you're working with a broad-caster, you serve as a spotter. Because the action is so fast and frenzied, it's often not clear who scored the goal and who assisted. Many times the puck is deflected into the net off a player's skate, stick or body, and sometimes off a player on the defending team. If you can see the puck change direction and pick up who deflected it, you can be of great aid to the broadcaster in giving proper credit on the score.

Another way a statistician can assist the broadcaster is to be on the lookout for signals by the official, when he's going to call a player for a penalty. Often, the penalty is delayed—in other words, the action is allowed to continue until the team that did not commit the offense no longer has possession of the puck. The reason is simple: If a team is on the attack and a defending player trips one of the attackers, it wouldn't be fair to blow the whistle on what might be a scoring play. So the referee waits until there's a save or offsides, or the defending team gets possession, and then he stops play and gives the penalty. It's helpful if you can pick up the infraction, so the announcer can alert fans to the fact that a penalty is forthcoming. The particular penalty will be apparent in the hand-signal the official gives. There are different ones for slashing, high-sticking, tripping, etc.

The statistician can also help by pinpointing an off-sides violation.

Often, something noteworthy happens behind the action. Say, three players are rushing up ice into the attacking zone to try to score, while in the back of their half of the rink, two players have dropped their sticks and gloves and are now squaring off for a fight. The play-by-play man would naturally have been concentrating on the players with the puck, and so would the color man. Part of the statistician's job is to watch for what's happening behind the action.

A statistician also can be of help to the broadcaster in providing him with the correct pronunciation of players' names. This is especially important in hockey, where there are so many players of French descent whose names are difficult for an English-speaking broadcaster.

Public Relations Help

In almost every case, a statistician who works for a hockey team will be required to do other work in addition to statistics, because even with the sophisticated additions that have been made to keeping hockey records and stats, his team plays only three or four games a week. Consequently, except when there are contests two nights in a row, he has plenty of time to update his information and compile what's needed for the next game. In the Ranger office, I help out with a number of public relations and publicity functions, such as working on the official program. It's a loosely structured, fun office, and we don't mind branching out and doing other jobs as they come up.

Feeding the Videograph

After spending years working right next to the Rangers' play-by-play radio announcer (usually Marv Albert), for the last six years I've been working in the TV control room during hockey games, "feeding" the videograph machine. The videograph is what puts those printed word-and-numeral messages up on your TV screen.

About three or four hours before the game I compile a variety of stats and messages pertaining to that night's game, along with the out-of-town games and the forthcoming schedule for the Rangers and their opponents.

I give these items to John Wiggins, the videograph operator, who programs the data into the videograph computer. Within a half-hour of game time, he's got all these stats and other information keyed to numbers. During the game, when the TV director or someone else in the control booth requests a particular piece of information, John just punches the appropriate number and the information is flashed on the screen.

For instance, let's say there's a stoppage in play and the camera zooms in on a particular player who's drawn a couple of penalties or scored a goal or made a great save. The screen will flash a message pertaining to his stats or his personal history—that this is his thirtieth penalty of the season, or his twenty-sixth birthday, or whatever might be of interest. Or, should the Rangers get a power play going early in the game, we'll try to get a message on the screen telling what the Ranger power-play record is for the season—how many attempts they've had, how many goals they've scored and what their ranking is in the league.

Of course, we're constantly showing the score of the game. As you can see from the reproduced page of messages we had prepared for a game between the Rangers and the Colorado Rockies, the possibilities for videograph messages are wide. And we can make up other messages as needed, in addition to what's been prepared before the game.

A videograph message will usually stay up on the screen between five and seven seconds, possibly as long as ten seconds, to give people at home time to digest it. In addition to informing the viewer, a videograph message relieves the broadcaster of the burden of having to repeat certain data over and over again.

Marv Albert does the radio play-by-play for the Rangers. Schoolteacher Jeff Shermack is an excellent young part-time statistician who sits with the Ranger telecasters, Jim Gordon and Bill "Big Whistle" Chadwick, during the Ranger home games.

The Ranger broadcasters are superb. Generally it's difficult, especially in the New York area, to find competent, knowledgeable hockey broadcasters, because most Americans did not grow up playing hockey. More hockey is being played now than ever before, but ten or fifteen years ago, most of us spent our

RANGERS VS. COLORADO   REFEREE

    MARCH 23, 1977   10 - BOB MYERS

                LINESMEN

             30 - SWEDE KNOX   ATT.   GOALS   PCTG.

             36 - RANDY MITTON   266   56   21.1

                              ROCKIES POWER PLAY

1976-77 SEASON SERIES   ATT.   GOALS   PCTG.

          W.   L.   T.   249   39   15.7

RANGERS   2   1   1

ROCKIES   1   2   1

                        COLORADO HAS A ROAD RECORD OF

OUT OF TOWN SCORES   7-24-6 THIS SEASON.

ISLANDERS   PAIEMENT LEADS THE ROCKIES IN

TORONTO   SCORING WITH 73 POINTS.

BOSTON   GARDNER WAS COLORADO'S FIRST CHOICE

DETROIT   IN THE 1976 AMATEUR DRAFT.

CLEVELAND   HICKEY HAS SCORED FIVE GOALS IN HIS

BUFFALO   LAST FOUR GAMES.

LOS ANGELES   GILBERT LEADS THE RANGERS IN ASSISTS

CHICAGO   WITH 48.

                        McEWEN LEADS ALL ROOKIE DEFENSEMEN

DAVIDSON'S RECORD   IN GOALS WITH 14.

   W.   L.   T.   DEAN LEADS THE ROCKIES IN PENALTY

  13   11   6   MINUTES WITH 90.

    AVG. 3.32   ARNASON IS PLAYING WITH HIS FIFTH

GRATTON'S RECORD   NHL TEAM.

   W.   L.   T.   ESPOSITO LEADS THE RANGERS IN POWER

  10   17   7   PLAY GOALS WITH 15.

    AVG. 4.32   RANGERS NOW HAVE 1,054 PENALTY

PLASSE'S RECORD   MINUTES THIS SEASON AND THAT'S A

   W.   L.   T.   NEW CLUB RECORD.

  12   28   10   PYATT LEADS COLORADO IN GAME WINNING

    AVG. 3.75   GOALS WITH FOUR.

FAVELL'S RECORD

   W.   L.   T.   FOTIU IS THE RANGERS PENALTY LEADER

   7   12   2   WITH 134 MINUTES.

    AVG. 3.97

athletic time in a schoolyard or on a sandlot playing basketball, football or baseball. As a result, we're more familiar with the technical points and the terminology of sports other than hockey.

The same applies to the fans, I think. The American hockey fan is certainly more aware of the finer points of the game today than he was when I first started working for the Rangers in 1967, but still he's not nearly as aware of hockey as a baseball fan or probably even a basketball fan is of their respective sports.

Many hockey broadcasters and sportswriters learned the game as they covered it. Now, with hockey's expansion as a national sport with teams in all parts of this country, in addition to the Canadian teams, broadcasters and writers need more statistics in order to evaluate players and situations accurately. The more stats they have, the less they have to confine their comments to generalities. In the early years, you had to hand-feed some of them with information; now that they have several years of experience under their pads, it's not as imperative as it once was.

Game of the Week

In the 1976–77 season, the National Hockey League inaugurated a television series called the "NHL Game of the Week," which, as the name indicates, is a weekly telecast of a hockey game, originating from a different city each week. The program is shown in most of the NHL cities around the country and about 60 percent of the United States can view it.

The first two games were telecast without anyone feeding stats and information to the videograph operator, but they found that was not the way to operate, especially on national TV. The producers asked me to do it; I was flattered and I accepted. Working on those games brought back memories of some of the other national broadcasts I'd worked on, notably the "Monday Night Game of the Week" in football. I had forgotten what the pressure was like, how tense and involved everyone becomes. Jeff Shermack and I worked hand-in-hand on the "NHL Game of the Week."

The New York Rangers

I started with the New York Rangers in 1967, the first year the National Hockey League had expanded into a twelve-team league from what, for so many years,

had been a six-team league. Now it has eighteen teams. In a decade the league
has tripled in size.

In the days when the league had only six clubs, there weren't that many
statistics kept, and to tell the truth, there wasn't that much use or demand for a lot
of statistical categories. With so few teams, players were well known to spectators. They were identifiable even without the numbers on their jerseys. Most
players who made it to the NHL stayed for a long time, and everyone knew them
and their accomplishments.

So when I joined the Rangers, very little was being kept in the way of
statistics. I was amazed at how little there was in our yearbook and media guide
(which every club issues). I had to add such categories as:

> Most Points by a Defenseman
> Most Points by a Rookie
> Most Goals by a Defenseman
> Most Goals by a Rookie
>
> Most Power-Play Goals
> Most Short-handed Goals
> Most Points by a Line

And that was just a sampling of basic stats that weren't listed in the Ranger
record book. And for that matter, in the forty years the NHL had been in
existence, many team and other statistics had not been kept very carefully,
primarily because there wasn't that much demand.

There were no sheets kept on individual players, when and in what period a
player had scored his goals, against whom, whether on home ice or away. The
same elements were missing in reference to assists.

So many types of stats that I took for granted in other sports were sorely
lacking in hockey. Had there been only six teams when I started in hockey, I'm
sure I would have found it boring compared with baseball, which keeps so many
statistics. Luckily the league then had expanded to twelve teams and as a result
there was more need for statistics.

With the approval of Emile Francis, then the Rangers' coach and general
manager, I gladly added categories. The team's record book now has about fifty
pages of different kinds of statistics and data, such as a listing of every player
who ever was with the Rangers, who made All-Star teams, career goals, hat
tricks (three goals by one player in a single game) and so on.

It took me a good six or seven years of hard work before I was satisfied with

166

the updating of the statistical section of the Ranger yearbook. I had to go through a lot of old newspapers to read up on games that had taken place years earlier.

New Categories of Hockey Stats

So I have introduced several new categories of hockey stats in the last few years. For instance, on my stat sheets I break down leading scorers among the league's defensemen and among rookies. I also keep the averages of the league's leading goaltenders; the leading goaltenders in wins; the leading players in power-play goals and the leaders in short-handed goals. New team stats include the percentage a team has in scoring on power-play opportunities.

Within about six weeks of when I started printing these categories on my stat sheets, I picked up the Canadian newspapers, which we get every day in the Ranger office, and found that they had started printing them, too. Before I knew it, these categories were included in the league statistics.

These statistics help broadcasters. Instead of saying a particular defenseman "is having a terrific year offensively," the broadcaster can now say, "He's the second top defenseman in scoring." Or instead of saying only that this team is "dynamite on the power play" or "the Canadiens will wipe you out," he can now say, "They've scored ninety-two power-play goals and scored on 33 percent of their chances."

There are many more things I'd like to do with hockey statistics. Though I'm not in the Ranger office during the off-season, I submitted a list of ideas to John Ferguson, who took over as general manager and coach of the Rangers toward the end of the 1975–76 season. Several of the ideas have never been tried in hockey before. For instance, nobody's ever broken down how many minutes a player spends on the ice and how many goals he scores per minutes played. We might find that a skater with half the playing time of another skater is more goal-efficient in a per-minute productivity sense.

We now give the ratio of scoring to shots on goal, so that with this percentage you can tell who are the most accurate shooters in the league.

Missing Records

Over the past ten years, the National Hockey League has come a long way in providing new kinds of information and statistics.

But even today, there are still gaps in hockey record-keeping.

For instance, in 1976–77 a rookie defenseman on the Rangers, Mike Mc-Ewen, was scoring goals at a rapid pace, and reporters started asking, "What's the Ranger record for goals by a rookie defenseman?" We had no listing on that category in our record book, and surprisingly enough, I could find no listing for it in the *National Hockey League Guide* either. So I spent a few days going through the Ranger books and records of the fifty years of the club's existence, before I finally discovered that the record had been set a quarter of a century earlier by Hy Buller, who as a rookie defenseman had scored twelve goals.

I wasn't particularly excited about that stat—I didn't think it had a lot of significance—but I was surprised that the league book didn't have a listing for the league scoring record by a rookie defenseman. After I called them, the league P.R. people finally looked it up and found that the record was seventeen, set by Dennis Potvin of the Islanders. It's a category they'll have to add to the record section of the *NHL Guide* in the future.

In the 1976–77 season, while I was working the National Hockey League Game of the Week between the Philadelphia Flyers and the St. Louis Blues, a Flyers rookie by the name of Al Hill, who was playing his first NHL game, scored three goals and two assists for five personal points. I immediately went to the record section of the *NHL Guide,* and found there was no listing for "most points by a rookie in his first NHL game."

So while the game was in progress, I called the NHL office in Montreal. People at the league office weren't sure, but they thought five points was the most ever scored by a rookie in his first NHL game. It was confirmed a day later, but during the broadcast we couldn't report with 100 percent certainty that Hill was the first player to score five points in his first game.

Please understand, I'm not trying to put down the league office, which does a fine job. I mention these things to point out that categories of statistics are still lacking in hockey—and to a lesser extent, in basketball and football. In baseball it would be almost unheard of not to have a record equivalent to the most points scored by a player in his first game, or most goals scored in a season by a rookie defenseman.

Sometimes missing stats are the result of exceptional circumstances. When the Rangers experienced a rash of injuries in March of '77, they called up a goalie I had never heard of before, Dave Tataryn, from our farm club, the New Haven Night Hawks in the American Hockey League. Before that, he had played the first three months of the season in the Southern League, but unfortunately that league folded.

168

On Rod Gilbert Night, March 9, 1977, John Ferguson selected Tataryn to be the Ranger goalie, and naturally, press people wanted to know Tataryn's record in the Southern League. Because the league had folded and the whereabouts of anyone who might have kept records was unknown, his stats were unavailable. We could only talk about his record in the three games he had played for our New Haven farm club.

False Alarms

Every so often, we work hard to prepare stats and charts when a player seems to be making a drive to break a record, only to have the material go unused because of unforeseen circumstances. It happened with Dave Kingman in baseball, when it looked as if he was going to break Hack Wilson's National League home-run record. And it happened with Don Murdoch in hockey.

Murdoch, a rookie right winger with the Rangers in the 1976–1977 season, was on his way to breaking the league record for goals by a rookie (44) set by Rick Martin of the Buffalo Sabres. He had 32 goals in his first 58 games and was far and away the favorite for Rookie of the Year in the league. So I set up charts comparing the scoring pace of both Murdoch and Martin. In response to the press's fantastic interest in Murdoch (he was featured on the cover of the *New York Times Sunday Magazine*), I even kept charts on what part of the ice he scored his goals from and what kind of shots he scored on. Unfortunately, he suffered an ankle injury in February and returned to play only sparingly the last weekend of the season. Nevertheless, he set the Ranger record for most goals by a rookie, but he was never able to touch any of the league records. So all the preparation of charts and data was for naught.

An Emotional Sport

Hockey, a low-scoring and fast-moving game with a lot of action, is an emotionally involving sport. I try to maintain professional cool, but on occasion I've found myself getting carried away while working games. Once, while I was working with Marv Albert at a game the Rangers were playing against an expansion team, with a minute or two left the visitors tied the game and went on to beat us. I got so mad I slammed my fist down on the table. The vibration knocked over a soda can, whose contents soaked all my papers and clothing, and saturated

Marvin. Needless to say, it was embarrassing and messy for me, and awfully uncomfortable for Marv, who had to broadcast the wrap-up of the game with a lap full of cold, sticky soda.

I'll have to check the stats, but I may hold the record for table-pounding among right-handed New York statisticians in close hockey games.

Plus and Minus

THE PLUS-AND-MINUS system, which is a pretty good but not flawless way of evaluating a hockey player's worth, is relatively new; it came about with the league's expansion.

The way it works is simple: a player is given a plus every time he's on the ice when his team scores a goal and a minus every time he's on the ice when the opposition scores a goal. It does not apply if either team has an advantage of one man or more, so that you don't get a plus if your team scores on a power play, and you don't get a minus if the opposition scores when you're short-handed.

At the end of the season, one player may have a plus-20 rating, while a teammate is minus-16. The first player is not necessarily that much better than the second. The flaw in the system is that in many cases it penalizes one player for somebody else's mistakes. For instance, let's say the Rangers have a line of Rod Gilbert at right wing, Phil Esposito at center and Steve Vickers at left wing on the ice together most of the season. To take a hypothetical situation, suppose Gilbert has been doing his job checking the opposing left wing, but Vickers has allowed the opposing right wing to score a lot of goals against the Rangers. Under those circumstances, it's unfair to give both Vickers and Gilbert minuses, when Gilbert has been doing his job and Vickers hasn't.

Some people have suggested that the man who scores the goal should get more than the one plus-point that everyone on ice for the scoring team during the goal gets.

One of the proposals I've made is to break the rating system down even finer, so that you would give the minus only to your right wing if the opposing left wing scores a goal, only to the center if the opposing center he was guarding scored, etc.; and give a minus to the goalie only if you feel he could have stopped the puck. This modification has inadequacies, too, but I think it would give a truer measure of a player's worth than the current system.

In 1977–78, the NHL took the plus-minus statistic a step further, giving a player a percentage in relation to his team's goals for and against. A man on ice for ten of his team's twenty even-strength goals, for example, would have a 50 percent offensive total. If the same man was on ice for eight of the twenty-four even-strength goals against his team, his defensive percentage would be 33 percent. By subtracting the defensive 33 percent from his offensive 50 percent, you find he has a net difference of plus-17 percent.

The advantage of this system is that it indicates a player's on-ice performance in relation to his team's record rather than as a strictly individual figure.

This overcomes the plus-minus discrepancy between players on good teams and players on bad ones. A player with a team that finishes at the bottom of the standings is naturally going to have a worse minus record than someone who plays for a winning team.

Some clubs still don't make the plus-minus figures readily available to the public, because, some say, if a player sees he's in the minus column, he'll start pressing and his playing will be adversely affected. One club says it doesn't release plus-minus figures to newspapermen and broadcasters—and if they don't get them, the public doesn't—because it feels the plus-minus system is not an accurate indicator of a player's performance.

Can you imagine picking up a paper during the baseball season and finding a blank space where you'd hoped to find Tom Seaver's earned-run average, because the Reds felt that his ERA was a misleading statistic? Or if you found a blank space in place of Ken Stabler's interception statistics because the Raiders felt that interceptions were a misleading statistic?

Granted, plus-minus, taken out of context, can be misleading and even severely damaging to a player, but in context and properly understood, it can still be an informative stat.

Since John Ferguson took over as coach and general manager, the Rangers do release their plus-and-minus statistics to members of the media, so that the fans are aware of the system. In my opinion, if these figures are uniformly available, everyone will evaluate the subtleties of plus-minus correctly.

Before the Rangers began releasing plus-and-minus statistics, newspapermen tried to keep those figures themselves. But the average sportswriter doesn't always have the time to note who was on ice for a goal. Usually, the players on the ice will head right for the bench after a score, while the newspaperman is busy writing down such items as who scored, what type of shot was taken, who was responsible for allowing the goal, the crowd reaction and so forth. Also, most newspapermen don't cover every game. As a result, many of the newspapermen who tried to keep plus-minus figures were usually wrong.

Sample Plus-Minus

Let me give you a couple of examples of actual plus-minus figures for particular Ranger players. After forty games played in 1976–77, half-way through the eighty-game season, Greg Polis had a plus-15 rating.

It was arrived at this way: he was on ice for 33 Ranger goals, two of which were on power plays. Therefore he got pluses for 31 of the goals and had a net plus rating of 31. He was on ice when 19 goals were scored against the Rangers, three of which came when the Rangers were short-handed. Therefore, he was given minuses for 16. To get his overall rating, subtract the 16 minuses from the 31 pluses, which gives you his plus-15 rating.

At the same juncture in the season, Phil Esposito had been on ice for 64 Ranger goals, 30 of which were on power plays, so his net plus was 34. He was on ice for 49 goals scored by Rangers' opponents, four of which were on power plays. His net minus, therefore, was 45. By subtracting the plus-34 from minus-45, we find that Phil Esposito had a minus-11 rating at that point.

Goals-Against Average

One measure of a goalkeeper's effectiveness is his goals-against average—how many goals he has allowed for every sixty minutes played.

Twelve or fifteen years ago, teams would carry only one goalie; if he got hurt—unless it was a major injury—he'd get stitched up and come right back into the game. With one goalie, figuring a goals-against average was a simple matter of dividing the total goals scored against the team by the number of sixty-minute games played.

Today it's not quite so simple. With the advent of team expansion and the increased schedule, teams now carry two and sometimes three goalies. Now if a goalie gets hurt during a game or is doing poorly, he's usually replaced. There-fore, to figure a goals-against average, you use the minutes a particular goalie has played and the goals scored against him. (You ignore the number of games in which he's appeared since they are not all complete games.) You multiply the goals scored against him by sixty (since all goalie averages are computed on the basis of sixty minutes played, the playing time of a game). You then divide that total by the number of minutes the goalie has played. The dividend is his goals-against average.

Say a goalie has played 501 minutes and allowed 39 goals. Multiply the number of goals allowed (39) by 60, which gives a figure of 2,340. Divide that by the 501 minutes the goalie has played, and that brings his goals-against average to 4.67.

Another goalie has played in 45 games, for a total of 2,468 minutes, and has allowed 103 goals. Multiply 103 by 60, and divide the answer (6,180) by the minutes played (2,468); his goals-against average is 2.50.

Note Sheet and Stat Sheet

UNLIKE BASEBALL, in hockey it's the responsibility of the home team to supply all the stats and notes for both the home club and the visitors. On the Rangers, we'll sometimes send along notes when our team is on the road, but it's not required. So in preparation for all of our home games, I have to update not only Ranger information but that of the visitors as well. If, say, St. Louis were coming in to play the Rangers on a Sunday, we would take their figures from the league stats we received the previous Monday and update everything pertaining to St. Louis according to what happened in their other games during the week.

The information on both clubs, plus league leaders in various categories and any other bits of information we feel are of interest and value, are put onto stat and note sheets we provide to both teams and members of the media, including our own broadcasters. I do most of the compilation for these sheets, assisted by Ranger office colleagues John Halligan, Janet Halligan and Paul Kanow.

If you look at the example shown of the sheets provided for the game played between the Rangers and St. Louis on December 8, 1976, you'll see the scope of the data given nowadays.

Basic, of course, are the standings, the results of the games last night and the schedule for tonight. Then there are assorted notes, most about the Rangers, but a good number concerning St. Louis. There is even information about the New Haven Night Hawks, the Rangers' top farm club, in the American Hockey

175

NEW YORK RANGERS

MADISON SQUARE GARDEN CENTER
FOUR PENNSYLVANIA PLAZA, NEW YORK, N. Y. 10001/(212) 563-8000

MEDIA NOTES - RANGERS VS. ST. LOUIS, DEC. 8, 1976

Clarence Campbell Conference

Patrick Division:

	GP	W.	L.	T.	PTS.	GF	GA
Islndrs.	27	17	7	3	37	94	64
Phila.	26	13	7	6	32	93	74
Atlanta	27	13	8	6	32	92	81
RANGERS	28	12	11	5	29	109	96

Smythe Division:

	GP	W.	L.	T.	PTS.	GF	GA
St.Louis	27	12	13	2	26	80	99
Chicago	27	10	14	3	23	88	99
Colorado	27	8	16	3	19	76	93
Minn.	27	6	17	4	16	74	122
Vanc.	29	7	20	2	16	75	113

Prince of Wales Conference

Adams Division:

	GP	W.	L.	T.	PTS.	GF	GA
Boston	27	19	6	2	40	107	81
Buffalo	24	14	7	3	31	81	60
Toronto	27	12	9	6	30	103	91
Cleveland	27	6	14	7	19	68	91

Norris Division:

	GP	W.	L.	T.	PTS.	GF	GA
Montreal	29	21	4	4	46	141	62
L.A.	29	9	11	9	27	96	93
Pitt.	27	10	12	5	25	81	90
Detroit	26	8	14	4	20	70	87
Wash.	27	8	15	4	20	78	110

LAST NIGHT'S RESULTS: Islanders 4, St. Louis 2; Pittsburgh 6, Minnesota 2; Washington 4, Vancouver 3.

OTHER GAMES TONIGHT: Atlanta @ Minnesota; Montreal @ Chicago; Buffalo @ Cleveland, Vancouver @ Toronto; Colorado @ Los Angeles.

The Rangers are unbeaten in their last eight games (5-0-3), their longest unbeaten streak of the season. During the streak they have outscored the opposition by a 36-17 margin. The last time New York had a longer unbeaten skein was from Feb. 10, 1974, to March 6, 1974, when they went ten games without a loss (9-0-1).

This is the third meeting of the season between the Rangers and Blues, with St. Louis winning the two previous contests -- 2-1 and 3-1, both in St. Louis. Nine of the Rangers' 12 victories this season have come against Smythe Division teams.

Lifetime, the Rangers have a home record of 21-1-2 against the Blues, out-scoring them 96 to 39. The Blues' only victory in Madison Square Garden came on Nov. 13, 1968, when they used three goalies (Glenn Hall, Robbie Irons, Jacques Plante) in defeating New York, 3-1.

Rod Gilbert has scored at least one point in nine straight games, in 18 of his last 20, and in 23 of the team's 28 outings thus far. He is currently fourth in league scoring with 41 points, behind Guy Lafleur (47), Steve Shutt (44), and Marcel Dionne (43). With seven goals in his last eight games, Rod now has 392 in his career, one short of Bernie Geoffrion's total which is 11th on the league's all-time goal scoring list. He is also 11th on the NHL's all-time point list and is 11th in lifetime assists.

Plans will be announced Sunday for "Rod Gilbert Nigh " to be held in early March. Sunday's contest against the Canadiens will mark Gilbert's 1,000th National Hockey League game, becoming only the 14th player in NHL history to achieve that total with one team. Rod joins Harry Howell (1,160) as the second man to play 1,000 games with the Rangers.

New York's power play continues to lead the NHL with 32 goals in 112 attempts, for a 28.6 scoring percentage. The Rangers have scored six PPGs in their last eight opportunities, while Ranger penalty killers have allowed only three goals in the last 32 shorthanded situations. Overall, they have given up 21 PPGs in 107 attempts by the opposition.

Tonight's officials: referee Ron Wicks; linesmen John D'Amico and Ron Finn.

John Davidson has started ten straight games, allowing only 21 goals in his last 31 periods of action. He has lowered his goals-against average from 3.57 to 2.69, fifth-lowest in the league. Davidson's lifetime record against St. Louis is 2-3-0.

The Rangers are one of four teams not to have been shutout this season. They have gone 54 consecutive contests since last being blanked by Ken Dryden of Montreal on Feb. 8, 1976...Steve Vickers has scored 19 points in his last 16 games...With 711 assists in his career, Phil Esposito is one short of Jean Beliveau's total which is sixth on the NHL's all-time assist list...Don Murdoch is tied for second in the NHL in goals scored with 22. He is the league leader in power play goals with nine, and is tied for the lead in game-winning goals with five...Bill Goldsworthy needs two assists for 250 in his career...Walt Tkaczuk now has 476 points in his Ranger career, only two shy of Camille Henry's total which is fifth highest in Ranger history.

St. Louis is winless in their last four games (0-3-1)...Their road record is 4-8-2 in 14 games...Chuck Lefley is not with the Blues due to a pulled groin muscle...Garry Unger will play in his 671st consecutive game, longest streak in NHL history...The Blues have scored 21 power play goals in 87 attempts, while allowing 19 in 95 shorthanded situations...Red Berenson is 37 years-old today and Ted Irvine is 32...St. Louis has a 2-5-0 record against Patrick Division teams thus far.

The New Haven Nighthawks, the Rangers' AHL affiliate, have posted a 5-2-1 record in their last eight outings and a 15-9-2 mark overall. They are currently in second place, two points behind Nova Scotia. The Nighthawks lead the league in power play goals (34) and have the best defensive record (2.97). Their next game is Friday night vs. Springfield at New Haven. Leading scorers among Ranger-owned players: Jerry Byers (16-13-29); Eddie Johnstone (10-16-26); Larry Sacharuk (13-12-25); Dale Lewis (10-14-24); Jerry Holland (7-13-20); and John Bednarski (3-14-17). Dan Newman has scored 15 points in 17 games since being sent to New Haven on October 28.

The Patrick Division is the only one in which all teams are playing better than .500 hockey, and each team has scored more goals than they have allowed Breakdown of each division by total points: Norris 138; Patrick 130; Adams 120; and Smythe 100.

NEW YORK RANGERS SCORING

	GP	G.	A.	PTS.	PIM	PP	SH	GW	GT
(7) Gilbert	28	15	26	41	22	3	0	1	0
(14) Murdoch	28	22	11	33	8	9	0	5	0
(77) Esposito	28	12	20	32	18	5	0	0	1
(88) Hodge	28	10	18	28	16	4	0	3	1
(8) Vickers	24	9	13	22	2	2	0	0	1
(18) Tkaczuk	28	5	16	21	14	0	0	0	0
(5) Vadnais	28	3	16	19	31	2	0	0	0
(20) Polis	25	7	11	18	26	1	0	1	1
(9) Dillon	26	5	12	17	25	0	0	0	0
(27) McEwen	28	5	11	16	16	3	0	0	0
(4) Greschner	28	3	13	16	37	0	0	0	1
(12) Goldsworthy	28	5	6	11	12	1	0	1	0
(16) Hickey	28	6	4	10	20	3	0	0	0
(3) Farrish	28	0	7	7	32	0	0	0	0
(26) Maloney	23	1	3	4	44	0	0	1	0
(21) Stemkowski	26	0	4	4	2	0	0	0	0
(22) Fotiu	22	1	1	2	38	0	0	0	0
(19) Heaslip	11	0	0	0	2	0	0	0	0
(00) Davidson	20	0	0	0	2	0	0	0	0

GOALTENDERS' RECORDS

	GP	GA	EN	SO	AVG.	W.	L.	T.
(00) Davidson	20	49	1	1	2.69	8	4	5
(33) Gratton	11	46	0	0	4.69	4	7	0

ST. LOUIS BLUES SCORING

	GP	G.	A.	PTS.	PIM	PP	SH	GW	GT
(21) MacMillan	27	7	17	24	4	5	0	0	0
(7) Unger	27	12	11	23	34	4	0	3	0
(25) Lefley	21	3	17	20	4	1	0	0	0
(9) Berenson	27	10	9	19	2	2	0	1	0
(19) Sanderson	21	6	11	17	8	2	0	2	0
(16) Plante	27	10	4	14	23	3	0	2	0
(12) Larose	27	9	5	14	10	1	0	0	1
(27) Irvine	26	6	7	13	6	1	0	1	0
(23) Hess	22	1	12	13	10	1	0	0	0
(6) Patey	27	7	5	12	14	0	0	1	1
(17) Butler	27	3	9	12	32	0	0	0	0
(10) Seiling	26	1	10	11	6	1	0	1	0
(18) Thomson	26	3	2	5	4	0	1	1	0
(4) Affleck	27	0	5	5	4	0	0	0	0
(15) Marotte	24	1	2	3	16	0	0	0	0
(3) Gassoff	27	0	3	3	80	0	0	0	0
(5) Plager	7	0	1	1	2	0	0	0	0
(22) Ogilvie	2	0	0	0	0	0	0	0	0
(11) Sutter	2	0	0	0	0	0	0	0	0

GOALTENDERS' RECORDS

	GP	GA	EN	SO	AVG.	W.	L.	T.
(1) Johnston	12	30	0	0	2.85	5	4	1
(31) Staniowski	19	68	1	0	4.13	7	9	1

RANGER BREAKDOWN:

	HOME	AWAY	TOTAL
vs. Patrick	0-0-0	0-0-2	0-0-2
vs. Smythe	4-1-0	5-2-0	9-3-0
vs. Adams	0-3-1	1-0-0	1-3-1
vs. Norris	1-4-0	1-1-2	2-5-2
TOTALS:	5-8-1	7-3-4	12-11-5

SCORING BY PERIODS:

	1st	2nd	3rd	TOTAL
Rangers:	38	40	31	109
Opposition:	33	34	29	96

RANGER TEAM STATISTICS

Most Goals, Game - 11 (12/4 vs. Minnesota)

Most Goals, Period - 5 (12/4 vs. Minnesota)

Most Shots, Game - 49 (10/12 vs. Minnesota)

Most Shots, Period - 23 (10/12 vs. Minnesota)

Most PP Goals, Game - 4 (10/8 vs. Colorado)

Longest Winning Streak - 2 (3 times)

Longest Unbeaten Streak - 8 (11/22-current)

Longest Losing Streak - 3 (11/10-11/14)

Longest Winless Streak - 4 (11/6-11/14)

RANGER PLAYER STATISTICS

Most Goals, Game - 5, Murdoch (10/12 vs. Minnesota)

Most Assists, Game - 5, Gilbert (10/8 vs. Colorado)

Most Points, Game - 5, Gilbert (twice) & Murdoch

Most Shots, Game - 10, Murdoch (10/12 vs. Minnesota)

Most Shots, Period - 6, Esposito (twice)

Most PIM, Game - 25, Dillon (10/12 vs. Minnesota)

Longest Point Scoring Streak - 10, Murdoch (10/26-11/17)

SHOTS ON GOAL:

Rangers:	941
Opposition:	890

FIRST GOAL OF GAME:

Rangers:	16 times (8-5-3)
Opposition:	12 times (4-6-2)

RANGERS' MONTHLY RECORD

	GP	W.	L.	T.	PTS.	GF	GA
October	13	5	7	1	11	52	52
November	12	5	4	3	13	37	34
December	3	2	0	1	5	20	10

TOP SCORERS IN THE NHL

	GP	G.	A.	PTS.
Lafleur	29	22	25	47
Shutt	29	28	16	44
Dionne	29	14	29	43
GILBERT	28	15	26	41
Sittler	27	12	26	38
McDonald	27	21	14	35
McNab	27	20	14	34
T. Williams	29	17	17	34
Young	27	11	23	34
Robinson	29	7	27	34
MURDOCH	28	22	11	33
Charron	27	18	14	32
Ratelle	25	14	18	32
ESPOSITO	28	12	20	32
Goring	27	11	21	32
Mahovlich	29	6	26	32
Salming	26	4	28	32

DEFENSEMEN'S SCORING

Robinson	7-27-34
Salming	4-28-32
D. Potvin	10-19-29
Turnbull	8-21-29
Park	7-19-26
Lapointe	5-21-26
Bladon	3-18-21

ROOKIES' SCORING

D. MURDOCH	22-11-33
Eriksson	9-11-20
Sharpley	12-6-18
Mulhern	2-15-17
McEWEN	5-11-16
P. Gardner	8-7-15
Chouinard	5-10-15

POWER PLAY GOALS

D. MURDOCH	9
McDonald	8
T. Williams	7
P. Martin	6
R. Martin	5
ESPOSITO	5
R. MacMillan	5

GAME-WINNING GOALS

D. MURDOCH	5
McNab	5
Bergeron	4
Perreault	4
Risebrough	4
Shutt	4
(12 players with 3 each)	

SHORTHANDED GOALS

Clement	3
Dupere	3
Murphy	3
Apps	2
Clarke	2
Henning	2
Harvey	2
McDonald	2

GOALS-AGAINST AVG.

Resch	2.04
Dryden	2.08
Desjardins	2.13
Palmateer	2.67
DAVIDSON	2.69
Gilbert	2.77
Parent	2.83

181

HOCKEY

RANGERS vs. .... Date ....

GOALS	ASSISTS	TIME	PENALTIES

OFFICIALS	SHOTS ON GOAL					SCORE BY PERIODS				
REFEREE		1	2	3	TOTAL		1	2	3	TOTAL
LINESMAN										
LINESMAN	RANGERS					RANGERS				

League. Some of the information is not related to statistics, such as the note that plans are being formulated for a Rod Gilbert Night.

There are separate pages for Ranger scoring and St. Louis scoring, then a page with miscellaneous information containing such items as the Rangers' record against each division and at home and away, total goals, goals scored by period, and then Ranger team and individual stats for the year. In the latter are the season's high in shots, in goals, winning streaks, losing streaks, etc., as well as how the Rangers have done when they've scored the first goal of the game and when the opposition teams have. Following that is a page with the top scorers in the league and then a breakdown of what I call miscellaneous NHL leaders.

Every year I've been with the Rangers I've added items and categories to the sheets that I think are pertinent. I've also deleted categories I've found were not worth the time or effort.

When I started with the Rangers, there were only three columns next to each player's name—goals, assists and points. A few years later, we added penalty minutes, then games played and so on. Now there are nine columns, including power-play goals, short-handed goals, game-tying and game-winning goals. Information about the goalies was also limited to the games played, the number of goals allowed, shutouts, and average. Now, of course, empty-net goals are included, as well as wins, losses and ties.

Game Stat Sheets

This is an example of the form in which each team in the National Hockey League sends its scoring into the league office after every home game. (Ranger scoring is sent by either Janet Halligan or Paul Kanow to the NHL office in Montreal by TWX teletype machine.)

The game referred to here was between the Rangers and Minnesota North Stars on November 28, 1976. You can see on top that the game ended with the score Minnesota, 1, Rangers, 4. Listed are the players who were on ice for each team; then the goaltenders, the minutes they played and the number of goals they allowed. LoPresti played sixty minutes for Minnesota and allowed four goals; Davidson played sixty minutes for the Rangers and allowed one goal.

Scoring and penalties, by period, are also listed. In the first period, no goals were scored. Vadnais and Nantais were penalized at 3:55. The first goal of the game came in the second period. It was by Wayne Dillon. Players credited with assists are named in parentheses (Rod Gilbert and Steve Vickers). The time of

183

MINNESOTA 1 AT RANGERS 4   NOV. 28, 1976

PLAYERS ON ICE

MINNESOTA: BARRETT, O'BRIEN, HICKS, REID, BEVERLEY, SHARPLEY, PIRUS, FAIRBAIRN, JENSEN, HICKE, TALAFOUS, YOUNG, YOUNGHANS, HOGABOAM, ERIKSSON, NANNE, NANTAIS.

NEW YORK: FARRISH, GRESCHNER, VADNAIS, MALONEY, MCEWEN, GILBERT, VICKERS, DILLON, GOLDSWORTHY, MURDOCH, HICKEY, TKACZUK, POLIS, STEMKOWSKI, FOTIU, ESPOSITO, HODGE.

GOALTENDERS

MINNESOTA: LOPRESTI - 60 MINUTES - 4 GOALS AGAINST.

NEW YORK: DAVIDSON - 60 MINUTES - 1 GOAL AGAINST.

FIRST PERIOD

NO SCORING

    PENALTIES: VADNAIS & NANTAIS 3:55

SECOND PERIOD

1. NY, DILLON (GILBERT, VICKERS) 4:23
2. NY, MALONEY (GILBERT, VICKERS) 15:38

    PENALTIES: REID 16:29

THIRD PERIOD

3. MINN, TALAFOUS (YOUNG, HICKE) 9:49 (PPG)
4. NY, DILLON (VICKERS, VADNAIS) 11:39
5. NY, GRESCHNER (TKACZUK, POLIS) 14:26

    PENALTIES: GILBERT 8:24; FOTIU 16:12; NANTAIS-MINOR, GRESCHNER-MINOR, FOTIU-10 MINUTE MISCONDUCT 18:44

SHOTS ON GOAL

MINNESOTA: 8 5 16 - 29

NEW YORK: 16 14 11 - 41.

END

the goal (4:23 of the second period) is also given. The second Ranger goal was scored by Dave Maloney, assisted by Gilbert and Vickers, at 15:38 of the period. Reid had the only penalty, at 16:29.

In the third period, Minnesota scored its first and only goal of the game. It was by Talafous, assisted by Young and Hicke, at 9:49. The "PPG" in parentheses indicates it was a power-play goal. If you look down you can see that goal came while Gilbert was serving penalty time beginning at 8:24.

Dillon, assisted by Vickers and Vadnais, scored for the Rangers at 11:39 and Greschner, assisted by Tkaczuk and Polis, wound up the scoring at 14:26. Penalties in the third period were to Gilbert (as noted above) at 8:24, Fotiu at 16:12, and minor penalties to Nantais and Greschner and a ten-minute misconduct to Fotiu at 18:44.

Shots on goal are then summarized by period: Minnesota, 8-5-16, for a total of 29; and New York, 16-14-11, for a total of 41.

Next come the sheets that are sent to the league office (with copies to the opposing coaches).

On the sheet headed "Official Statistics of Game," note that all the players are listed with the numbers of the jerseys they wore next to their name. Across from each player's name are printed the numbers 1 through 8, which represent possible shots on goal in each period. The official scorer puts a slash mark across the number for any shot taken. The shots are then totaled for each player. For instance, if you look across from Dave Farrish's name, you see that he took only one shot (in the second period) in the entire game, so his total was, obviously, one. Ron Greschner took two in the first period, one in the second and three in the third, for a total of six. You'll notice that the last one was circled and an "X" put in, meaning that he scored a goal on that shot.

Looking down farther, you see that Vadnais had six shots on goal, Maloney, eight—three in the first period and five in the second period, the last of which is circled and marked with an "X" to signify it resulted in a goal.

Shots on goal are tallied across for each player and down, by period, for the team, and then totaled. Vertically and horizontally, the totals should reach the same figure, as they do here (forty-one).

The next two columns deal with pluses and minuses, and again, slashes over numbers are used. Here they indicate a player was on ice when a goal was scored. In the "Goals For" column, you will see by the slash across the number 4 that Dave Farrish was on ice for the Rangers' fourth goal. There are no marks against him in the "Goals Against" column, meaning he was not on ice when Minnesota scored its goal. Therefore, he was plus-one for the game.

NATIONAL HOCKEY LEAGUE
OFFICIAL STATISTICS OF GAME

STATISTICIAN Jack Buckley

DATE Nov 28, 1976

CODE OF SYMBOLS
- / — Under "shots", a shot on goal.
- 9 — Under "shots", a blocked or missed shot.
- ⊘ — Under "goals", a goal scored on shot.
- x — Under "goals for" and "against", the scoring team at a man advantage; both teams cross (but not successsively).
- ⊗ — Under "goals for" and "against", the scoring team playing shorthanded.

HOME TEAM: MINNESOTA

VISITING TEAM: at New York Rangers

PLAYER	No.
FARRISH	3
GRESCHNER	4
VADNAIS	5
MALONEY	26
McEWEN	27
GILBERT	7
VICKERS	8
DILLON	9
	14
HICKEY	16
TKACZUK	18
	20
	21
ESPOSITO	77
HODGE	88

Goaltender: DAVIDSON 00

PLAYER	No.
BARRETT	3
O'BRIEN	5
HICKS	6
REID	20
NANNE	23
BEVERLEY	26
SHARPLEY	7
PIRUS	10
FAIRBAIRN	11
JENSEN	12
HICKE	14
JARRETT	15
YOUNG	17
YOUNGHANS	21
HOGABOAM	21
ERIKSSON	23
NANTAIS	25

Goaltender: LoPRESTI 1

TEAM TOTALS

Carol Vadnais was on ice for the first three Ranger goals and for the Minnesota goal. But as the circle around the slash indicates, the Minnesota goal was scored on a power play, so he is not charged with a minus for that. Therefore, he is plus-three for the game.

Note that in the "Goals Against" column, all four Rangers on ice during the Minnesota goal (except the goalie, who is not involved in plus-minus considerations) have a circle around the slash, indicating the goal came when they were short-handed and so they should not be given a minus. Totals for these columns are carried down. The Rangers had a total of twenty players on ice (excluding the goaltender) for the four goals they scored, each of which came when the teams were at full strength. For the Minnesota goal, they had four men on ice (excluding the goalie) because there was a man in the penalty box.

As mentioned, the four Rangers on ice—Vadnais, Maloney, Goldsworthy and Stemkowski—have circles around the slashes to show they were short-handed, while the five Minnesota players on ice during the Minnesota goal have a slash in a circle to indicate they scored on a power play.

Near the top of the sheet, over from each goaltender's name and "Goals Against" column, is a column for "Empty-Net Goals Against" (when the goalkeeper has been removed for an extra forward in the closing minute of a game). There were none in this contest. Then there is a column for the "Time of Goaltender Removal for Extra Forward." In this game, with Minnesota trailing, 4–1, LoPresti was taken out at 16:06 of the final period, when the referee first signaled a penalty against the Rangers' Nick Fotiu. LoPresti returned six seconds later when the Rangers got control of the puck and play was halted for Fotiu to go to the penalty box.

The "Score Sheet," which goes to the league office, is made out by the official scorer, and concerns itself strictly with scoring—the score of the game; who was credited with goals and assists, by period; the times of the goals; and how many players each team had on the ice when the goals were scored. Notice the admonition to official scorers printed near the top of the card: "Be particular to give credit for assists." Obviously, the contents of this card should jibe with other official reports submitted on this game.

The "Official Report of Match" lists every player who suited up for the game, along with his uniform number, and a "Y" or "N" next to his name indicating "Yes, he did play" or "No, he did not play." The only players to be given an "N" were the back-up goalies, Gratton for the Rangers and Smith for Minnesota. The card also contains such information as the time the game and each of the periods started and ended, and the names of the scorer, the linesmen

This Form must be mailed to the League Office immediately after each Game.

NATIONAL HOCKEY LEAGUE
SCORE SHEET

NOTE:—Official Scorers.—Be particular to give credit for assists.

MINNESOTA   1   at   NEW YORK RANGERS   4

VISITORS   SCORE   HOME TEAM   SCORE

Date Nov 28-1976

CLUB	SCORER	ASSISTANT SCORER		TIME	NUMBER OF PLAYERS WHEN GOAL SCORED	
					VISITING TEAM	HOME TEAM
		1st PERIOD				
		NONE				
		2nd PERIOD				
NEW YORK	DILLON	GILBERT	VICKERS	4:23	6	6
NEW YORK	MALONEY	GILBERT	VICKERS	15:38	6	6
		3rd PERIOD				
MINNESOTA	TALAFOUS	YOUNG	HICKE	9:49	6	5
NEW YORK	DILLON	VICKERS	VADNAIS	11:39	6	6
NEW YORK	GRESCHNER	TKACZUK	POLIS	14:26	6	6

Official's Signature   *Frank Megaffin*

NATIONAL HOCKEY LEAGUE

OFFICIAL REPORT OF MATCH

MINNESOTA vs. NEW YORK RANGERS

Played in MADISON SQUARE GARDEN Rink, Date NOV 28-1976

No.	HOME CLUB	Y or N		No.	VISITING CLUB	Y or N
00	DAVIDSON	Y	Goal	1	LoPRESTI	Y
33	GRATTON	N	Sub-Goal	35	SMITH	N
3	FARRISH	Y	Defence	3	BARRETT	Y
4	GRESCHNER	Y	"	5	O'BRIEN	Y
5	VADNAIS	Y	"	6	HICKS	Y
26	MALONEY	Y	"	20	REID "DC"	Y
27	McEWEN	Y	"	23	NANNE	Y
			"	26	BEVERLEY	Y
7	GILBERT "C"	Y	Forward	7	SHARPLEY	Y
8	VICKERS	Y	"	10	PIRUS	Y
9	DILLON	Y	"	11	FAIRBAIRN	Y
12	GOLDSWORTHY	Y	"	12	JENSEN	Y
14	MURDOCH	Y	"	14	HILKE	Y
16	HICKEY	Y	"	15	TALAFOUS	Y
18	TKACZUK	Y	"	17	YOUNG	Y
20	POLIS	Y	"	29	YOUNGHANS	Y
21	STEMKOWSKI	Y	"	21	HOGANBOOM "C"	Y
22	FOTIU	Y	"	22	ERIKSSON	Y
77	ESPOSITO "C"	Y	"	25	NANTAIS	Y
88	HODGE		"			

Game starting time 7.35 P.M. First period ended at 8.07 P.M. Second period started at 8.23 P.M. and ended at 8.56 P.M. Third period started at 9.12 P.M. and ended at 9.47 P.M.

Won by NEW YORK Score 4 to 1

Official Scorer FRANK McGAIFIN Game Timekeeper BOB McGOWAN

Penalty Timekeeper ED NUBEL - JOE PATRICK

Goal Judges ARTHUR REICHERT - LEE STARK

Linesmen MALCULM ASHFORD - BOB LUTHER

REMARKS:

Signed .... Referee
.... Official-Scorer

SPECIAL INSTRUCTIONS

1. Be sure to indicate with the letter "Y" in the appropriate column all players who *actually played* in the game and indicate those who did not actually play with the "N". This is very important and essential information.
2. Any delay in starting the game longer than fifteen minutes after the advertised time should be reported, stating the cause of the delay and the club at fault. Any unusual incidents occurring in or affecting the conduct of the game should also be reported.
3. This report should be checked, signed and dispatched to National Hockey League, 970 Sun Life Building, by the quickest possible means.

This form should be handed to the Official Scorer or mailed to the League Office immediately after each game.

NATIONAL HOCKEY LEAGUE

PENALTY RECORD

MINNESOTA at N.Y. RANGERS

REFEREE ALF LEJEUNE DATE NOV. 28, 1976

VISITING PLAYER	OFFENCE	TIME	TIME EXPIRED	HOME PLAYER	PLAYER'S NO	MIN.	MAJORS	MIS-CONDUCTS	GAME MIS-CONDUCTS	MATCH
NANTAIS	H. STICK	3.55	5.55		25	✓				
	H. STICK	3.55	5.55	VADNAIS	5	✓				
2ND								PERIOD		
REID	HOOK	16.29	18.29		20	✓				
3RD								PERIOD		
	SLASH	8.24	R9.49	GILBERT	7	✓				
	ROUGH	16.12	18.12	FOTIU	22	✓				
NANTAIS	H. STICK	18.44	—		25	✓				
	H. STICK	18.44	—	GRESCHNER	4	✓				
	MISC.	18.44	—	FOTIU	77			✓		

and the minor officials; and it is signed by the referee (Alf LeJeune) and the official scorer (Frank Megaffin). There is a space for remarks, such as why a game might have been delayed in starting fifteen minutes beyond the advertised time and which club's fault it was, plus any unusual incident that occurred in or affected the game.

The "Penalty Record," as you might guess, records all the offenses, the time and nature of each infraction, and the time when each offending player left the penalty box.

Nantais' first penalty for Minnesota was for high-sticking, at 3:55 of the first period. He left the penalty box at 5:55. Since he served his full two minutes, you can tell there was no power-play goal scored during this time, or else he would have been permitted to leave the penalty box as soon as the other team had scored a goal.

Vadnais went into the penalty box at the same time for high-sticking and also served the full two minutes.

Under the line the penalty timekeeper has drawn to indicate penalties that occurred in the same period, note that Reid served a full two minutes for hooking.

In the third period, Gilbert went into the box at 8:24 for slashing, but returned ("R") to the ice at 9:49, short of two minutes, because Minnesota scored a power-play goal. Nevertheless, he is charged with a full two penalty minutes on his personal record.

Fotiu served a full two minutes for roughing, but notice that players who drew penalties after that (Nantais for high-sticking, Greschner for high-sticking and Fotiu for misconduct) didn't serve the full time, simply because the game ended before their penalties did. Nevertheless, they, too, are charged with the full penalties on their personal records.

Penalties

Just a word about penalties . . .

When a player other than the goalkeeper is charged with a *minor penalty,* he must leave the ice for two minutes, during which time no substitute may be sent in to play in his place. If, however, the other team scores a goal during the course of his penalty, he may immediately leave the penalty box and return to the ice. In that instance, he is still charged with two minutes in his personal penalty total.

For a *major penalty,* a player is ruled off the ice for five minutes, during which his team usually plays at full strength. He may not leave the penalty box before he has served out the full five minutes, even if the other team does score in the interim. Most major penalties are the result of fighting and in most cases where there is a fight, both combatants are charged with a major penalty. In some instances, the player judged to be the aggressor is given a two-minute minor penalty in addition to the five-minute penalty.

When coincident penalties of equal duration are imposed against players of both teams, those players may not leave the penalty box until the first stoppage of play following the expiration of their respective penalties.

A player charged with a *misconduct* penalty is removed from the game for a period of ten minutes, but his team does not play short-handed during that time. As with a major penalty, a player whose misconduct penalty period has expired must stay in the box until the next stoppage of play.

Misconduct penalties are usually awarded for either mouthing off to an official or not following his orders. Sometimes, if a fight has been broken up and a player tries to get it going again, he can be given a misconduct. A misconduct penalty adds ten minutes to the offender's personal penalty total.

A player may also be given a *game misconduct penalty,* which involves his suspension for the balance of that game. However, a substitute may come in for that player immediately. A game misconduct is *automatically* given to the first player to get involved in a fight that is going on between two other players. Though he's not eligible to return to that game, the player given a game misconduct penalty is charged with just ten penalty minutes on his personal record.

Bench penalties, which are not charged to an individual, are given to a team having too many men on the ice, or in cases where an unidentified person on the bench yells something the referee didn't like. They are minor (two-minute) penalties that must be served by one of the players on the ice at the time of the infraction, so that the team will be short-handed. The player who serves the bench penalty is not charged with that time on his personal penalty record.

When the *goalie* is penalized, someone else serves the penalty for him, but it's the goalie who is charged with the penalty on his personal record.

Minor Officials

THE OFFICIAL STATISTICS of a game, which are sent to the league, are kept by so-called minor officials. Their duties are anything but minor; the term is used to distinguish them from the referee and linesmen, the officials who are on the ice during the game.

There are six minor officials—two goal judges, an official scorer, a game timekeeper, a penalty timekeeper and a statistician. They receive no pay for their services during the regular season, and only expense money and transportation from city to city during the playoffs. So theirs is truly a labor of love. Most of these gentlemen are long-time hockey fans who will do just about anything to attend a hockey game, and most have been serving as minor officials for many years.

The home team is in charge of assigning these officials. Clarence Campbell, the NHL president until his retirement in 1977, took a very active interest in their performance, and the overall quality of their work is very high.

The Goal Judges

Seated in a glass booth in the front row of stands behind each goal is a goal judge, whose one job is to signal when the puck has gone completely over the goal line. When this happens, he activates a red light to signify that a goal has

192

been scored. During a season, the judges' record of accuracy is amazingly high.

Precautions are taken to make sure that favoritism isn't a factor in their decisions. A goal judge will alternate ends of the arena from game to game, and sometimes he'll be assigned to do the job of one of the other minor officials. Changing assignments keeps everyone on his toes and makes the officials more flexible in what they are equipped to do.

The Official Scorer

The official scorer, whose work is closely watched by the league president, is responsible for proper crediting of goals and assists and is the man who sends the scoring summaries into the league office after every game.

Awarding goals and assists can be difficult. Some are deflected or tipped in, and even when they're not, there are so many fast-moving skates and sticks on the ice that it requires total concentration throughout the game. Good judgment is important, too, in what is a very demanding assignment.

Official scorers do have TV monitors on which they can see televised replays of the goals, and consequently there are times when they'll make changes in the players they credited with goals and assists. Over the years, I've received many a call in the TV control room from an official scorer seeking to have a certain goal played back between periods, so he can have another look at it, or soliciting my opinion on whether a particular player should be given an assist on a goal.

Qualifying for an Assist. In order for a player to receive an assist, his touch of the puck must have been significant enough for the play's course to be altered. For instance, suppose the left wing's pass to the center was slightly tipped by an opposing player, but the center still managed to control the puck, get off a shot and score. The question the scorer must decide in determining whether the left wing should be credited with an assist is how significantly did the opposing player touch the puck. If the deflection didn't change the course of the puck, the scorer will usually award an assist to the left wing.

A Numbers Game. It may seem like an impossible task for anyone to remember who gave the puck to whom, but it's made possible for the official scorer by a frantic numbers game he plays.

The system involves simply writing down the uniform number of the player who wins the pass from a face-off, and then writing down the number of the man who takes his pass, and so on. When the opposition intercepts the puck, the scorer draws a line under the number of the player who had the puck before the interception. Now the number of the player who made the interception is written under the line, then the number of the man who takes his pass is written below that, and so it goes until there's an interception or goal.

When a goal is scored, all the official scorer has to do (after he determines who scored the goal) is check his list of numbers to see which teammate or teammates touched the puck just before the goal was scored. They are the ones who get credit for the assists.

Sometimes, on a goal that a scorer might have missed because of a pile-up or a puck bouncing off a player or his skate, the referee has the authority to tell the scorer his version of who scored the goal. Sometimes a player will notify the scorer that though he was the skater given credit for a goal, it was another player on his team who had actually scored it. (More often, it's a player complaining that he deserved an assist but wasn't credited with one.) Incidentally, the players are very honest about who deserves proper credit, and most official scorers will take a player's word on it.

Official scorers are, of course, well aware of how important personal points for goals and assists are to a player. Players receive a point each for every goal and every assist, and leadership in scoring can be worth up to two thousand dollars, along with the Art Ross Trophy, to a player. Also, many players have a bonus system as part of their contracts that gives them so much money if they score twenty goals in a season, so much for twenty-five, and an extra bonus for thirty. There's also the element of pride involved, so assist and goal credit is very important.

The official scorer can make changes in awarding credit throughout the game, but once the game is ended and the referee signs the scoresheet, no changes may be made—*even if films of the game show that a mistake has been made!* Then goals and assists must remain as credited. Three copies of the scoresheet are made up, one for each of the coaches and one to be sent to the league office in Montreal.

The league office examines scoresheets carefully, and after each quarter of the season breaks down the ratio of assists to goals, on the road and at home, for every team. If the analysis of scoring shows that a scorer has been giving players a heavy weighting of assists at home, it's brought to the scorer's attention. It has been found occasionally that certain cities in the league award assists to their hometeam players indiscriminately. When this is discovered, the league cracks down. (About a 5 percent to 6 percent variance in the assists-to-goals ratio between home and road games is acceptable.)

The Penalty Timekeeper

In each of the two penalty boxes (one for home players and one for visitors) sits a penalty timekeeper. It is his responsibility to note on an official sheet the name of each player receiving a penalty, the infraction, the duration of the penalty and the time in the period when a penalty began. (The arena scoreboard, of course, displays the number of the player penalized and the duration of his penalty.)

It is also up to the penalty timekeeper to alert a player, when a few seconds are left in his penalty period, to be ready to return to the ice. The timekeeper will generally put his hand on the gate of the penalty box when a penalty period is nearing conclusion and he'll open the gate as soon as the penalty is over. Some players will try to sneak out a second or two before they should, but most penalty timekeepers are veterans who are wise to such attempts. They may even grab a player who tries to skip before his penalty period has expired.

After the game, the penalty timekeeper's records are given to the official scorer, who sends them into the league along with his official stat sheets.

The Statistician

The minor official known as the statistician (not to be confused with statisticians such as myself, who are working *for* a team, either in the TV control room or next to radio or TV broadcasters) must make note of a variety of stats.

He has to record the numbers of the players who were on the ice when each goal is scored and must also tabulate the shots on goal. This is more complex than people think. A lot of judgment is involved in deciding whether a player has gotten off a legitimate shot on goal. Just because a goalie stops a shot doesn't necessarily mean a player receives credit for a shot.

What Makes a Shot. To qualify as an official shot on goal, it has to be a shot that, if not stopped by a goalie, would result in a goal. Thus, a shot to the side of the net deflected by the goalkeeper doesn't count as a shot on goal, nor does a high shot that the goalie gloves above the crossbar of the goal.

Strange as it may seem, not even all shots stopped by a goalie *that would*

195

have gone in the goal are counted as shots on goal. If a player killing a penalty, for instance, shoots the puck from his end of the rink two hundred feet down the ice, the official statistician probably would not award a shot even if the puck were flush on goal. Similarly, if a player's attempted pass to a teammate is too long and winds up hitting the goalie, the player is not credited with a shot.

A goal counts as a shot, but if the puck hits the post without going in, it doesn't count as a shot (after all, it wasn't a shot that was good enough to have gone in).

If a puck caromed off another player before hitting the goalie, it doesn't count as a shot. But say a puck shot forty or fifty feet away hits an opposing defenseman, who actually knocks the puck past his own goalie. Since a goal was scored on the play, a shot on goal must be charged, and it's awarded to the man who shot the puck—in other words, the offensive player who had possession of it last.

If a shot from an offensive player hits another offensive player on the skate or arm and then goes into the net, the player who deflected it in gets credit for the shot on goal—even though it was accidental.

Stats Kept on Officials

Statistics of a sort are kept on officials as well as players. Scotty Morrison, referee-in-chief of the NHL, constantly watches the patterns of penalty-calling by individual referees. If he notes that in a given game the referee calls very few penalties in the first period, more in the second and substantially more in the final period, he might question whether the referee is setting a standard early enough in a hockey game.

What I mean is this: a referee, to do a good job, will set the tone of a game early by gaining full control of it. He'll set a standard or pattern of how close his calls are going to be, whether he's going to call a lot of penalties or just let the players play the game.

If Scotty notes that the number of penalties called declines progressively as the game goes on, it usually indicates to him that that referee has pretty good control of the situation.

196

NHL Stats

EVERY MONDAY MORNING, teams in the league will receive updated NHL stats, sent over TWX machines by Ron Andrews and Mike Griffin, statisticians in the league office in Montreal. Back in 1966, when there were only six teams in the league, these stats were done manually; but the league has tripled in size, and so it's all done by computer now.

An example of league stats is shown here. The standings in the four conferences of the league on January 25, 1977, are shown. There is a column for games played ("GP"), wins ("W"), losses ("L"), ties ("T"), goals for each team ("GF"), goals scored against each team ("GA") and points ("PTS"), which are given on the basis of two for each victory and one for each tie. A team with four wins and two ties, for example, would have ten points.

Another statistic given is the team's percentage, which is calculated by dividing the number of points a team has by the maximum number it could have. Montreal, leading its division as of this date, had played 50 games and, therefore, could have as many as 100 points (two for each victory). Montreal has 79 points. When you divide the 79 actual points by the 100 possible, you arrive at the .790 percentage. The Rangers, too, had a possible 100 points since they had played 50 games. But since they'd picked up only 47 points, their percentage is .470.

The league stats also contain each team's record at home and on the road for

STATISTICS

from Ron Andrews, *Director of Information and Statistician*
& Norm Jewison, *Assistant Director of Information*

Suite 920, Sun Life Building, Montreal, P.Q. H3B 2W2 — (514) 871-9220 — TWX 610-421-3260

Release Number 18

For Release at 6:00 P.M. EST, Monday, January 24, 1977

CAPITALS BY FAR THE MOST IMPROVED TEAM IN NHL

MONTREAL—What a difference a year makes. After missing a playoff berth by a wide margin in each of their first first two seasons in the NHL, the Washington Capitals have vacated the Norris Division basement for the first time since Nov. 15 ---only the second time ever—and are entertaining thoughts of playoff contention in 1977.

Thanks to fine defensive play and inspiration by coach Tom McVie, Capitals have steadily improved to where they are today; fourth in their division with 35 points, three end of Detroit Red Wings and only nine behind third-place Los Angeles Kings. A year ago they were in fifth place, 29 points out of third.

Some of Capitals' accomplishments in 49 games to date: 14 victories, which is three more than they managed all last season and only five fewer wins than they totalled over their entire first two seasons in 160 games; their 35 points is three more than they collected in 1975-76 and 22 more than they had a year ago at this time; their over-all record today is 14-28-7 while after 49 games last season it was 4-40-5; while their goal-production is down slightly--127 compared to 135 a year ago—they have sliced their goals-against total by 74, from 258 to 184. That's more than a goal-and-a-half per game.

Over the last 13 games, Capitals' goaltending duo of Ron Low and Bernie Wolfe has given up 36 goals thus sharing with the New York Islanders the second-lowest total allowed by any team over that span. Only Montreal Canadiens and Boston Bruins, each with 33 goals against in their last 13 games, have yielded fewer. During that period, Capitals held opponents to three goals-or-less in 11 of 13 games. Only League-leading Montreal, with seven goals, Jan. 8 and five last Saturday, managed more.

To date, Washington has yielded seven goals (the highest total) to the opposition in five games, all on the road. By this time last year Capitals' foes had scored seven goals-score in 14 games, including a 14-2 romp by Buffalo Sabres, Dec. 21, 1975.

Another prominent reason for Washington's success recently can be found by glancing at its penalty-killing. Since Dec. 26 (15 games), Capitals have had only two power-play goals scored against them and both were in the same game—last Wednesday's 4-2 win at Buffalo. From Dec. 28 to Jan. 18 they went 12 straight games without a power-play goal against, successfully killing off 32 opposition man-advantages. Over-all, they have given up 28 power-play goals, fourth fewest in the League.

Capitals have only one representative among the NHL scoring leaders. He is center Guy Charron who shares 20th position with 24 goals, 24 assists for 48 points. He was signed by Washington as a free agent from the Colorado Rockies, Sept. 1.

Elsewhere among the leading scorers, Marcel Dionne of Los Angeles scored seven points last week for a total 72 and now trails Montreal's Guy Lafleur by just three. A week ago Lafleur led Dionne by seven points. In third place is Lafleur's linemate, Steve Shutt, who has 67 points. Shutt recaptured the goal-scoring lead from Lafleur last week and now has 38 compared to the right wing's 37. Sophomore center Tim Young of Minnesota North Stars is fourth with 60 points, nine more than he had in 63 games last season.

-30-

FOR RELEASE AT 6:00 P.M. EST, MONDAY · JAN.24, 1977

NATIONAL HOCKEY LEAGUE

SCORING AND PENALTY STATISTICS UP TO AND INCLUDING GAMES OF
SUNDAY, JAN. 23, 1977, COMPILED FROM RECORDS OF OFFICIAL SCORERS

PRINCE OF WALES CONFERENCE

	GP	W	L	T	GF	GA	PTS	PCTG
NORRIS DIVISION								
MONTREAL	50	36	7	7	241	114	79	.790
PITTSBURGH	47	20	19	8	150	154	48	.511
LOS ANGELES	49	17	22	10	159	162	44	.449
WASHINGTON	49	14	28	7	127	184	35	.357
DETROIT	47	13	28	6	123	169	32	.340
ADAMS DIVISION								
BOSTON	48	30	14	4	194	123	64	.667
BUFFALO	47	23	19	5	170	129	51	.543
TORONTO	48	23	17	8	156	156	54	.542
CLEVELAND	48	15	25	8	143	169	38	.396

CLARENCE CAMPBELL CONFERENCE

	GP	W	L	T	GF	GA	PTS	PCTG
PATRICK DIVISION								
NY ISLANDERS	47	29	11	7	173	116	65	.691
PHILADELPHIA	48	27	10	11	173	133	65	.677
ATLANTA	48	22	17	9	160	133	53	.552
NY RANGERS	50	17	20	13	174	182	47	.470
SMYTHE DIVISION								
ST LOUIS	49	21	22	5	141	164	47	.450
CHICAGO	49	17	24	8	155	174	42	.429
MINNESOTA	47	12	25	11	137	191	33	.351
COLORADO	48	12	29	8	133	179	32	.333
VANCOUVER	50	14	32	4	137	195	32	.320

PCTG ARRIVED AT BY DIVIDING POSSIBLE POINTS INTO ACTUAL POINTS.

INDIVIDUAL LEADERS

GOALS: Steve Shutt, Montreal, 38.

ASSISTS: Borje Salming, Toronto, 45.

POINTS: Guy Lafleur, Montreal, 75.

PENALTY MINS.: Dave Williams, Toronto, 202.

POWER-PLAY GOALS: Don Murdoch, Phil Esposito, NY Rangers, 11.

SHORTHAND GOALS: Bobby Clarke, Phil., Lorne Henning, NYI, 5.

GAME-WINNING GOALS: Peter McNab, Boston, 7.

GAME-TYING GOALS: Phil Esposito, NY Rangers, 5.

THREE-GOAL GAMES: Several players, 2.

SHUTOUTS: Ken Dryden, Montreal,6.

GOALTENDER WINS: Gerry. Desjardins, Buffalo, 28.

BEST PERSONAL
  GOALS-AGAINST AVE.: Ken Dryden, Montreal, 2.21.

TEAMS HOME-AND-AWAY RECORD

		AT HOME					ON THE ROAD					
	GP	W	L	T	GF	GA	PTS	GP	W	L	T	GF	GA	PTS

NORRIS DIVISION

	GP	W	L	T	GF	GA	PTS	GP	W	L	T	GF	GA	PTS
MTL.	24	19	1	4	122	52	42	26	17	6	3	110	42	37
PITT.	25	11	8	6	90	80	30	22	7	13	2	80	105	18
L.A.	23	10	9	4	76	57	24	25	7	15	2	86	106	20
WASH.	24	9	11	4	73	75	22	25	4	17	2	55	91	10
TOTAL	120	60	39	21	432	345	141	122	40	65	17	367	439	97

ADAMS DIVISION

	GP	W	L	T	GF	GA	PTS	GP	W	L	T	GF	GA	PTS
BOS.	24	16	4	4	99	71	36	24	14	10	0	85	72	28
BUFF.	25	15	6	4	98	69	34	22	10	10	2	72	60	26
TOR.	24	13	7	4	91	75	30	24	10	12	2	83	81	22
CLEV.	25	10	11	4	95	90	24	23	5	14	4	59	79	14
TOTAL	98	54	28	16	373	305	124	93	42	45	6	298	292	90

PATRICK DIVISION

	GP	W	L	T	GF	GA	PTS	GP	W	L	T	GF	GA	PTS
NY	23	14	6	3	92	57	31	23	15	5	4	81	59	34
PHIL	25	21	1	3	139	62	43	25	6	11	10	69	65	22
ATL.	26	15	6	6	95	66	35	22	7	12	4	65	87	18
NY-R	23	8	11	4	90	89	20	27	9	14	4	98	96	77
TOTAL	97	59	26	13	376	273	129	96	37	32	27	318	311	101

SMYTHE DIVISION

	GP	W	L	T	GF	GA	PTS	GP	W	L	T	GF	GA	PTS
ST.L.	27	13	11	3	97	86	29	26	8	15	3	74	104	19
CHI.	25	11	8	6	96	81	28	24	6	14	4	65	93	16
MINN.	24	7	10	7	75	87	21	23	6	16	2	62	104	18
COL.	24	7	12	5	66	87	19	25	8	16	2	74	104	18
VAN.	24	8	14	2	63	61	14							
TOTAL	123	46	55	19	357	404	110	121	29	76	18	346	497	76

| TOTAL | 119 | | | | | | | | | | | | | |
| OVER ALL | 434 | 218 | 148 | 48 | 1539 | 1329 | 524 | 434 | 149 | 219 | 68 | 1329 | 1538 | 364 |

RESULTS OF GAMES PLAYED DURING WEEK ENDING SUNDAY, JAN. 23, 1977

404	MON.	JAN. 17	MONTREAL	3	BOSTON	7
405	TUE.	JAN. 18	MINNESOTA	3	NY ISLANDERS	7
406	TUE.	JAN. 18	MONTREAL	3	WASHINGTON	0
407	TUE.	JAN. 18	TORONTO	3	LOS ANGELES	6
408	WED.	JAN. 19	CHICAGO	7	COLORADO	2
409	WED.	JAN. 19	NY RANGERS	4	CLEVELAND	3
410	WED.	JAN. 19	WASHINGTON	4	BUFFALO	6
411	WED.	JAN. 19	PITTSBURGH	2	VANCOUVER	3
412	WED.	JAN. 19	PHILADELPHIA	6	CHICAGO	2
413	WED.	JAN. 19	ST. LOUIS	1	BOSTON	3
414	THUR.	JAN. 20	MONTREAL	4	PHILADELPHIA	2
415	THUR.	JAN. 20	PITTSBURGH	3	MINNESOTA	2
416	THUR.	JAN. 20	COLORADO	5	LOS ANGELES	4
417	THUR.	JAN. 20	TORONTO	1	DETROIT	1
418	FRI.	JAN. 21	BOSTON	5	VANCOUVER	3
419	FRI.	JAN. 21	NY RANGERS	4	CLEVELAND	5
420	SAT.	JAN. 22	NY ISLANDERS	2	LOS ANGELES	2
421	SAT.	JAN. 22	PHILADELPHIA	2	PITTSBURGH	3
422	SAT.	JAN. 22	WASHINGTON	4	ATLANTA	4
423	SAT.	JAN. 22	CHICAGO	4	MONTREAL	5
424	SAT.	JAN. 22	BUFFALO	0	DETROIT	4
425	SAT.	JAN. 22	COLORADO	2	MINNESOTA	3
426	SAT.	JAN. 22	NY RANGERS	1	ST. LOUIS	2
427	SUN.	JAN. 23	NY ISLANDERS	7	VANCOUVER	2
428	SUN.	JAN. 23	PHILADELPHIA	1	COLORADO	2
429	SUN.	JAN. 23	ATLANTA	3	BOSTON	3
430	SUN.	JAN. 23	DETROIT	2	MONTREAL	2

432	SUN.	JAN. 23	ST. LOUIS	3	WASHINGTON	4
433	SUN.	JAN. 23	TORONTO	5	MINNESOTA	2
434	SUN.	JAN. 23	CLEVELAND	3	BUFFALO	0

GAMES SCHEDULED FOR WEEK ENDING SUNDAY, JAN. 30, 1977

435	WED.	JAN. 26	MINNESOTA	AT	LOS ANGELES	
436	THUR.	JAN. 27	PITTSBURGH	AT	NY RANGERS	
437	THUR.	JAN. 27	TORONTO	AT	NY ISLANDERS	
438	THUR.	JAN. 27	PHILADELPHIA	AT	ST. LOUIS	
439	THUR.	JAN. 27	DETROIT	AT	BUFFALO	
440	THUR.	JAN. 27	ATLANTA	AT	WASHINGTON	
441	THUR.	JAN. 27	CHICAGO	AT	VANCOUVER	
442	THUR.	JAN. 27	COLORADO	AT	BOSTON	
443	FRI.	JAN. 28	COLORADO	AT	ATLANTA	
444	SAT.	JAN. 29	LOS ANGELES	AT	NY ISLANDERS	
445	SAT.	JAN. 29	DETROIT	AT	PITTSBURGH	
446	SAT.	JAN. 29	BUFFALO	AT	MONTREAL	
447	SAT.	JAN. 29	WASHINGTON	AT	CLEVELAND	
448	SAT.	JAN. 29	CLEVELAND	AT	DETROIT	
449	SAT.	JAN. 29	MINNESOTA	AT	VANCOUVER	
450	SAT.	JAN. 29	TORONTO	AT	BOSTON	2.05 PM EST
451	SUN.	JAN. 30	ST. LOUIS	AT	NY RANGERS	
452	SUN.	JAN. 30	NY ISLANDERS	AT	MONTREAL	
453	SUN.	JAN. 30	PHILADELPHIA	AT	WASHINGTON	
454	SUN.	JAN. 30	BOSTON	AT	PITTSBURGH	1.35 PM EST
455	SUN.	JAN. 30	LOS ANGELES	AT	BUFFALO	2.35 PM EST
456	SUN.	JAN. 30	CLEVELAND	AT	CHICAGO	
457	SUN.	JAN. 30	MINNESOTA	AT	COLORADO	

INDIVIDUAL SCORING LEADERS FOR ART ROSS TROPHY

PLAYERS	TEAM	GP	G	A	PTS	PIM	PP	SH	GW	GT
GUY LAFLEUR	MONTREAL	50	27	48	75	18	10		6	2
MARCEL DIONNE	LOS ANGELES	49	28	39	67	24	5		4	1
STEVE SHUTT	MONTREAL	50	33	24	57	24	5		6	2
PETER MCNAB	BOSTON	47	30	25	55	4	9		7	0
DARRYL SITTLER	TORONTO	46	19	37	56	43	1		6	2
ROD GILBERT	NY RANGERS	47	22	33	55	12	5		6	2
GILBERT PERREAULT	BUFFALO	47	19	36	55	10	4		5	0
RICK MARTIN	BUFFALO	43	25	25	50	18	10		4	2
BOBBY CLARKE	PHILADELPHIA	49	18	36	54	45	3		5	0
BUTCH GORING	LOS ANGELES	47	17	36	53	18	2		3	2
LARRY ROBINSON	MONTREAL	47	11	42	53	23	2		2	0
BORJE SALMING	TORONTO	45	8	45	53	31	1		1	0
DON MURDOCH	NY RANGERS	53	31	20	51	22	11		4	2
PHIL ESPOSITO	NY RANGERS	53	24	27	51	23	9		3	0
LANNY MCDONALD	TORONTO	48	29	21	50	44	3		5	2
TOM WILLIAMS	LOS ANGELES	49	24	26	50	10	10		4	0
JACQUES LEMAIRE	MONTREAL	45	21	28	49	16	4		2	2
JEAN RATELLE	BOSTON	46	21	28	49	8	3		2	0
GUY CHARRON	WASHINGTON	49	22	26	48	16	2		1	2
ERIC VAIL	ATLANTA	47	22	26	48	18	2		3	2
TOM LYSIAK	ATLANTA	47	11	36	47	14	3		2	2
SYL APPS	PITTSBURGH	47	11	36	47	14	3		2	0

PLAYERS BY TEAM

PLAYERS	TEAM	GP	G	A	PTS	PIM	PP	SH	GW	GT
ERIC VAIL	ATLANTA	46	22	26	48	18	2		3	2
TOM LYSIAK	ATLANTA	47	11	33	44	11	1		2	1
RICHARD MULHERN	ATLANTA	32	18	24	33	55	2		3	0
WILLI PLETT	ATLANTA	43	9	16	32	66	1		3	0
GUY CHOUINARD	ATLANTA	44	15	20	29	4	4		3	2
CURT BENNETT	ATLANTA	44	14	13	27	27	2		2	0
KEN HOUSTON	ATLANTA	37	10	17	27	16	4		1	0
BILL CLEMENT	ATLANTA	48	8	12	20	4	1		1	0
JOHN GOULD	VAN.-ATL.	47	7	12	19	6	3		0	0
REY COMEAU	ATLANTA	48	5	14	18	18	0		0	0
TIM ECCLESTONE	ATLANTA	45	3	15	17	12	1		0	0
BARRY GIBBS	ATLANTA	47	3	11	14	38	0		0	0
ED KEA	ATLANTA	43	3	11	14					

HOCKEY

PLAYERS	TEAM	GP	G	A	PTS	PIM	PPG	SHG	GW	GT
GUY LAFLEUR	MONTREAL	50	37	38	75	18	10	0	6	2
MARCEL DIONNE	LOS ANGELES	49	28	44	72	8	7	0	1	2
STEVE SHUTT	MONTREAL	50	38	29	67	24	5	0	6	1
TIM YOUNG	MINNESOTA	47	20	40	60	42	9	0	2	2
PETER MCNAB	BOSTON	48	30	28	58	11	6	0	7	0
DARRYL SITTLER	TORONTO	46	18	38	56	39	5	1	5	2
ROD GILBERT	NY RANGERS	48	18	38	56	40	4	0	2	0
GILBERT PERREAULT	BUFFALO	47	22	33	55	18	4	2	6	0
RICK MARTIN	BUFFALO	47	29	25	54	43	10	0	5	2
BOBBY CLARKE	PHILADELPHIA	48	18	36	54	45	5	5	2	0
BUTCH GORING	LOS ANGELES	47	17	36	53	4	9	0	2	0
LARRY ROBINSON	MONTREAL	47	11	42	53	28	2	0	2	1
BORJE SALMING	TORONTO	47	8	45	53	22	1	0	0	0
DON MURDOCH	NY RANGERS	50	31	20	51	33	11	0	5	0
PHIL ESPOSITO	NY RANGERS	50	24	27	51	28	11	0	1	5
LANNY MCDONALD	TORONTO	48	29	21	50	46	9	3	3	1
TOM WILLIAMS	LOS ANGELES	49	24	26	50	10	10	0	3	2
JACQUES LEMAIRE	MONTREAL	45	21	28	49	16	4	1	3	0
JEAN RATELLE	BOSTON	46	21	28	49	10	6	1	3	0
GUY CHARRON	WASHINGTON	49	24	24	48	6	3	1	1	2
ERIC VAIL	ATLANTA	46	22	26	48	16	9	1	2	2
TOM LYSIAK	ATLANTA	47	18	30	48	31	2	0	1	0
SYL APPS	PITTSBURGH	47	11	36	47	14	2	2	1	2

PLAYERS BY TEAM

PLAYERS	TEAM	GP	G	A	PTS	PIM	PP	SH	GW	GT
ERIC VAIL	ATLANTA	46	22	26	48	16	9	1	2	2
TOM LYSIAK	ATLANTA	47	18	30	48	31	2	0	1	0
RICHARD MULHERN	ATLANTA	47	9	24	33	55	1	1	1	2
WILLI PLETT	ATLANTA	32	18	14	32	66	4	0	3	1
GUY CHOUINARD	ATLANTA	48	9	20	29	6	2	0	0	0
CURT BENNETT	ATLANTA	44	15	12	27	12	2	1	2	1
KEN HOUSTON	ATLANTA	48	14	13	27	27	1	0	2	0
BILL CLEMENT	ATLANTA	37	10	17	27	16	1	4	0	1
JOHN GOULD	VAN.-ATL.	48	8	12	20	4	1	0	2	1
REY COMEAU	ATLANTA	48	7	12	19	12	0	1	3	0
TIM ECCLESTONE	ATLANTA	48	5	14	19	18	0	0	0	0
BARRY GIBBS	ATLANTA	47	1	14	15	37	0	0	0	0
ED KEA	ATLANTA	40	3	11	14	38	0	0	0	0
BOBBY SIMPSON	ATLANTA	45	6	7	13	23	0	0	1	0
RANDY MANERY	ATLANTA	41	4	9	13	18	0	0	2	0
DAVID SHAND	ATLANTA	36	3	6	9	48	0	0	1	0
PAT QUINN	ATLANTA	34	0	9	9	37	0	0	0	0
PHIL MYRE	ATLANTA	26	0	2	2	2	0	0	0	0
LARRY ROMANCHYCH	ATLANTA	3	1	0	1	0	0	0	0	1
DANIEL BOUCHARD	ATLANTA	24	0	0	0	2	0	0	0	0

* *

RECORD OF GOALTENDERS FOR 1976-77 SEASON

ALL GOALS AGAINST A TEAM IN ANY GAME ARE CHARGED TO THE INDIVIDUAL
GOALTENDER OF THAT GAME FOR PURPOSES OF AWARDING THE VEZINA TROPHY

CODE- GPI--GAMES PLAYED IN. MINS--MINUTES PLAYED. GA--GOALS AGAINST.
SO--SHUTOUTS. AVE--60 MINUTE AVERAGE. EN--EMPTY NET GOALS. (NOT
COUNTED IN PERSONAL AVERAGES BUT INCLUDED IN TEAM TOTALS.)

WON-LOST-TIED RECORD BASED ON WHICH GOALTENDER WAS PLAYING WHEN
WINNING OR TYING GOAL WAS SCORED

GOALTENDERS	TEAM	GPI	MINS	GA	EN	SO	AVE	W	L	T
KEN DRYDEN	MONTREAL	38	2195	81	1	6	2.21	27	5	5
MICHEL LAROCQUE	MONTREAL	14	805	32	0	3	2.39	9	2	2
MONTREAL	TOTAL	50	3000	114		9	2.28	36	7	7
GLENN RESCH	NY ISLANDERS	27	1597	63	1	3	2.37	16	6	4
BILLY SMITH	NY ISLANDERS	21	1223	51	1	1	2.50	13	5	3
NY ISLANDERS	TOTAL	47	2820	116		4	2.47	29	11	7
GERRY DESJARDINS	BUFFALO	42	2468	103	1	3	2.50	28	10	4
BOB SAUVE	BUFFALO	2	104	7	0	0	4.04	0	2	0
AL SMITH	BUFFALO	6	248	18	0	0	4.35	0	3	0
BUFFALO	TOTAL	47	2820	129		3	2.74	28	15	4
WAYNE STEPHENSON	PHILADELPHIA	6	320	12	0	1	2.25	4	0	1
GARY INNESS	PHILADELPHIA	5	200	9	0	0	2.70	1	0	2
BERNIE PARENT	PHILADELPHIA	41	2360	111	1	4	2.82	22	10	8
PHILADELPHIA	TOTAL	48	2880	133		5	2.77	27	10	11
GERRY CHEEVERS	BOSTON	27	1620	78	0	2	2.89	19	5	3
GILLES GILBERT	BOSTON	20	1200	59	3	0	2.95	10	9	1
JIM PETTIE	BOSTON	1	60	3	0	0	3.00	1	0	0
BOSTON	TOTAL	48	2880	143		2	2.98	30	14	4
PHIL MYRE	ATLANTA	26	1493	72	0	3	2.89	12	8	5
DANIEL BOUCHARD	ATLANTA	24	1387	80	1	1	3.46	10	9	4
ATLANTA	TOTAL	48	2880	153		4	3.19	22	17	9
MIKE PALMATEER	TORONTO	28	1660	78	2	2	2.82	16	9	3
WAYNE THOMAS	TORONTO	20	1100	66	1	1	3.60	7	9	2
GORD MCRAE	TORONTO	2	120	9	0	0	4.50	0	1	1
TORONTO	TOTAL	48	2880	156		3	3.25	23	19	6
DUNC WILSON	PITTSBURGH	31	1828	85	1	3	2.79	14	12	5
DENIS HERRON	PITTSBURGH	14	739	40	2	0	3.25	5	4	3
GORD LAXTON	PITTSBURGH	6	253	26	0	0	6.17	1	3	0
PITTSBURGH	TOTAL	47	2820	154		3	3.28	20	19	8
ROGIE VACHON	LOS ANGELES	41	2439	122	1	2	3.00	17	16	8
GARY EDWARDS	LOS ANGELES	10	501	39	0	0	4.67	0	6	2
LOS ANGELES	TOTAL	49	2940	162		2	3.31	17	22	10

TEAMS' PENALTY MINUTES AND POWER-PLAY AND PENALTY-KILLING STATISTICS

	GP	PEN MINS	BMI	AVG	ADV	PPG	PP PCTG	TIMES SHORT	PPGA	PK PCTG	SHORT-HAND GF	GA
PHIL	48	958	2	20.0	142	31	21.8	201	37	81.6	8	2
DET.	47	745	4	15.9	169	28	16.6	184	47	74.5	8	5
L.A.	49	732	10	14.9	155	39	25.2	181	34	81.2	4	4
NY.R	50	694	12	13.9	185	46	24.9	175	37	78.9	1	10
CHI.	49	667	10	13.6	161	39	24.2	168	30	82.1	4	4
CLEV	48	653	14	13.6	194	38	19.6	156	33	78.8	1	9
TOR.	48	648	6	13.5	167	30	18.0	174	36	79.3	6	3
COL.	48	616	10	12.8	167	26	15.6	148	38	74.3	7	4
VAN.	50	632	8	12.6	165	28	17.0	162	42	74.1	2	5
WASH	49	613	14	12.5	183	18	9.8	157	28	82.2	6	13
BOS.	48	600	8	12.5	132	28	21.2	159	21	86.8	3	4
NY.I	47	566	4	12.0	135	34	25.2	163	28	82.8	11	2
ATL.	48	538	4	11.2	135	24	17.8	162	33	79.6	8	4
ST.L	48	516	4	10.8	158	28	17.7	159	31	80.5	4	5
BUFF	47	474	12	10.1	154	33	21.4	165	22	86.7	3	4
MINN	47	474	4	10.1	201	41	20.4	129	34	73.6	5	5
MTL.	50	490	8	9.8	151	41	27.2	146	21	85.6	3	1
PITT	47	378	6	8.0	158	29	18.4	123	29	76.4	4	4
TOTAL	434	10994	140	25.3	2912	581	20.0	2912	581	80.0	88	88

(AVE. PER GAME FOR BOTH TEAMS IN PENS. MINS.)
(BENCH MINORS (BMI) INCLUDED IN TOTAL PENALTY MINUTE.)
(BMI COLUMN INDICATES MINUTES FOR BENCH MINORS.)
(PK-PENALTY-KILLING EFFECTIVENESS)

-30-

202

the season, the results of all the games for the previous week, and the schedule of
games for the current week.

They list the top twenty to twenty-five scorers in the league, the leading
contenders for the Art Ross Trophy. You can see that Guy Lafleur of Montreal is
leading with 75 points ("PTS") on 37 goals ("G") and 38 assists ("A"). For
individual scoring records, every goal or assist is worth a point. Marcel Dionne
of Los Angeles is in second place with 72 points on 28 goals and 44 assists, Steve
Shutt of Montreal is third with 67 points on 38 goals and 29 assists, and so on
down the list.

Next to the player's name and team are columns for the games he's played
("GP"), goals ("G"), assists ("A"), points ("PTS"), penalties in minutes
("PIM"), power-play goals ("PPG"), short-handed goals ("SHG"), game-
winning goals ("GW"), game-tying goals ("GT").

A power-play goal is one scored when your team has either a one- or
two-man advantage over the other team as a result of a penalty call. A short-
handed goal, which doesn't occur nearly so often, is one scored when your team
is playing short-handed. If one of your teammates is in the penalty box while
your opponents are skating at full strength, and you score a goal, you're credited
with a short-handed goal.

To give you an example of how credit is awarded for a game-winning goal,
let me cite an actual game in which the Rangers beat the Colorado Rockies, 5–3,
on October 8, 1976. The Ranger goals, in order, were scored by Carol Vadnais,
Ken Hodge, Mike McEwen, Don Murdoch and Ken Hodge again. Since the
other team scored three goals, the Ranger who scored the fourth (Murdoch) was
credited with the game-winning goal. His was the last goal they needed to win.

As far as crediting a game-tying goal is concerned, it's given only when the
game ends in a tie. And although a tie game may have been evened up several
times, only the men who score their respective team's last goal get credit for
game-tying goals. For example, on December 14, 1976, the Rangers and Islanders played to a 4–4 tie. Phil Esposito, who scored the Rangers' fourth goal and
Bryan Trottier, who scored the last goal for the Islanders, got credit for game-
tying goals.

Players by Team

On the league stat sheets, after the leading scorers are listed, there is a listing of
all players (except goaltenders) by team. Within a given team, the players are

listed in order of their scoring, the highest-point man on top. Teams are given in alphabetical order by city. The abbreviations at the head of the columns are the same as those used for the league scoring leaders.

Eric Vail and Tom Lysiak lead Atlanta with 48 points each. Peter McNab leads Boston with 58. Where a man has been traded during the season, he is listed with his current team, and his point total reflects his combined point accumulation for both clubs. On the Atlanta roster, for example, you'll notice that John Gould, who had been acquired from Vancouver, had played a total of 48 games, and has a total of 20 points on 8 goals and 12 assists. Rick Smith, who played for St. Louis before coming to Boston, played 32 games and has 5 points, all on assists.

Goaltender Stats

Next comes a listing of goaltenders, by team, and their achievements.

You'll notice that alongside a man's name and team are columns for the number of games he's played in ("GPI"), the total minutes he's played ("MINS"), goals scored against him ("GA"), and empty-net goals ("EN")— those scored when he has been taken out of the game in the last few moments of play when his team is behind and wants to put an extra forward on ice; this leaves his team's net unguarded, and if the other team gets control of the puck, it's a pretty easy matter to score.

Next comes shutouts ("SO"), then the goaltender's average ("AVE") and how many games he's won ("W"), lost ("L") and tied ("T"). A goaltender's average refers to the average number of goals he's allowed per sixty minutes of playing time.

If you look at the figures for the first man listed, you'll see that Ken Dryden of Montreal has played in 38 games for a total of 2,195 minutes (he did not play a full sixty minutes in every game in which he appeared). There were 81 goals scored against him, one additional goal came when he had been removed from the game for a forward and he had six shutouts. His average was 2.21, a figure arrived at by multiplying the 81 goals he allowed by 60, and dividing that figure (4,860) by his 2,195 minutes. Dryden's record was 27 wins, 5 losses and 5 ties.

After Dryden, you'll find the record for Montreal's other goalkeeper, Michel Larocque. Then his figures and those of Dryden are tallied, to give you Montreal's total goaltending record. The fact that the number of games Montreal has played (fifty) does not equal the total of the games that Dryden and Larocque appeared in (fifty-two) means simply that they both appeared in two of their team's games. Their total won-lost record adds up, of course, to the team's record.

Penalty Minutes, Power Plays and Penalty Killing

The league's weekly stats also include the records of each team in penalty minutes, as well as their power-play and penalty-killing statistics. Teams are listed in order of per-game average of penalty minutes, starting with the team with the highest average.

The Philadelphia Flyers had played 48 games ("GP"), and Flyer players had amassed a total of 958 penalty minutes ("PEN MINS"), including two minutes for bench minors ("BMI"). Philadelphia, the most penalized team, had averaged ("AVG") 20 penalty minutes per game. Pittsburgh, the least penalized team, averaged only eight minutes per game.

The Flyers had a one-man or two-man advantage ("ADV") 142 times, and scored a power-play goal ("PPG") during these opportunities 31 times. Philadelphia's power-play percentage ("PP PCTG"), therefore, was 21.8. Montreal, next-to-last in the listing, had the best power-play percentage, 27.2, having scored 41 goals in the 151 times they had a numerical advantage. Minnesota also had 41 power-play goals, but since they had the advantage many more times (201), their power-play percentage was only 20.4.

The next three columns deal with the number of times a team was short-handed ("TIMES SHORT"), how many power-play goals were made against it ("PPGA") and its penalty-killing percentage ("PK PCTG")—in other words, the portion of the occasions that it was short-handed that the team managed to keep the opposition from scoring a power-play goal.

Philadelphia, for example, was short-handed 201 times, during which 37 power-play goals were scored against the Flyers. They managed to kill penalties and keep the other team from scoring power-play goals on 164 of those occasions, for an 81.6 percentage. You arrive at the penalty-killing percentage by subtracting the power-play goals (37) from the times the team was short-handed (201), and then dividing the remainder (164) by the times-short figure (201).

I had always felt that just looking at how many times a team scored a power-play goal didn't tell you too much without relating that figure to the number of opportunities. There's often a great discrepancy between teams, depending on how often a team is penalized. The same applies to penalty killing.

So about five years ago, on my own, I began figuring out the weekly power-play and penalty-killing percentages of each team. I think I was the first one to do this regularly.

The final two columns deal with short-handed goals for ("GF") and short-handed goals against ("GA") each team. The Islanders scored eleven short-handed goals and allowed just two of that variety. The Rangers scored only one short-handed goal and allowed ten.

Players' Interest
in Stats

HOCKEY PLAYERS, like other athletes, are naturally interested in knowing about their milestones.

Rod Gilbert achieved several during the 1976–77 season. On December 12, 1976, he played the one-thousandth game of his NHL career. Later in the season he scored his four-hundredth lifetime goal and then his one-thousandth career point. There was great public interest, so of course, we followed his approach to these marks over the course of the season and built up to it day-by-day. I also kept Rod informed.

On March 9, 1977, the Rangers scheduled a well-deserved Rod Gilbert Night. To prepare for it I went back through Rod's sixteen years with the Rangers to find whatever interesting and relevant stats and information I could. I went through scrapbooks and other books that were kept, many from before I joined the Rangers in 1967.

The sheet shown here is from the program for Rod Gilbert Night, and it shows that Gilbert held by himself or shared twenty-two different club records.

Rod Gilbert, who retired in November, 1977, was the type of player who did not exult about his own achievements when the team lost. When he scored his one-thousandth point, he gave the Rangers a lead over the Islanders, but unfortunately the game ended in a loss for the Rangers, and it took some of the glitter and joy away from his noteworthy achievement. He didn't even want to

ROD GILBERT RECORDS

(22 New York Ranger Records Held or Shared by Rod Gilbert)

CAREER RECORDS

(Including Game of March 3, 1977)

MOST LIFETIME GOALS — 400
MOST LIFETIME POWER PLAY GOALS — 107
MOST LIFETIME ASSISTS — 604
MOST LIFETIME POINTS — 1,004
MOST 20 GOAL SEASONS — 12
MOST 20 ASSIST SEASONS — 13
MOST 30 POINT SEASONS — 14

SEASON RECORDS

MOST GOALS BY A RIGHT WING — 43 (1971-72)
MOST ASSISTS BY A RIGHT WING — 61 (1974-75)
MOST POINTS BY A RIGHT WING — 97 (1971-72 & 1974-75)
MOST POINTS BY A LINE — 302, Gilbert (96), Ratelle (109) & Hadfield (97), 1971-72
MOST GOALS BY A LINE — 133, Gilbert (42), Ratelle (46) & Hadfield (45), 1971-72
LONGEST CONSECUTIVE POINT SCORING STREAK — 14 Games (Oct. 7, 1972-Nov. 8, 1972)
MOST ASSISTS, ONE GAME — 5 (Twice in 1974-75 and once in 1976-77 — Shared with Walt Tkaczuk)
MOST SHOTS, ONE GAME — 16 (Feb. 24, 1968 at Montreal)

PLAYOFF RECORDS

MOST LIFETIME GOALS — 34
MOST LIFETIME ASSISTS — 33 (Shared with Jean Ratelle)
MOST LIFETIME POINTS — 67
PARTICIPATED IN MOST PLAYOFFS — 10 (Shared with four other players)
MOST PLAYOFF GAMES — 79
MOST POINTS, ONE PLAYOFF GAME — 4 (1971-72—Shared with seven other players)
FASTEST TWO GOALS IN PLAYOFF GAME — 6 seconds (Scored at 9:32 and 9:38 of second period against Chicago, Apr. 11, 1968)

talk about it much after the game, because the game—and the loss—was an important one.

(Incidentally, I was disappointed that the Islanders' public relations staff didn't flash on the scoreboard at the Nassau Coliseum the fact that the point was Gilbert's one-thousandth. The significance of the achievement can be judged from the fact that he was only the eleventh man in the 51-year history of the NHL to score that many points. It would have been very much in order to notify the fans of what was taking place. Unfortunately, when you're in someone else's building, you have no control over things like that.)

Players are doubly happy when they can achieve a personal triumph in a game their team wins. For Gilbert, it happened that his one-thousandth game was a Ranger victory over the Canadiens in December, and thus a cause for real celebration.

208

A Little Help for My Friends

Rod Gilbert and Jean Ratelle had long been teammates in junior hockey, in the minor leagues and with the Rangers until Ratelle was sent to Boston in 1975–76 in one of the biggest trades in hockey history. The following season Ratelle was also approaching his one-thousandth NHL game and Gilbert asked me to let him know when Jean got close to the mark because Rod wanted to send him a congratulatory telegram.

I calculated that Ratelle would play his one-thousandth game on March 21, 1977 and advised Gilbert of this fact a few days before, and Rod sent a telegram on his friend's achievement of the same milestone he had reached three months earlier.

A statistician gets this kind of request from players now and then, and if it's someone you like and respect, you don't mind keeping an eye on something and keeping the player informed.

Wrong Number

Another player approaching a milestone on the Rangers in the 1976–77 season was Greg Polis, who started the season with appearances in 448 games. You don't need a statistician to tell you he needed only fifty-two more games to reach the five-hundred mark. He was well aware of it, and in fact, apparently kept his own records.

On January 30, 1977, the Rangers played their fifty-second game of the season, defeating the St. Louis Blues at Madison Square Garden. When I went into the locker room to talk to Polis after the game, he was angry. He scolded me about giving all the other players publicity while ignoring his five-hundredth NHL game. His wife, mother and other relatives had come to see him play that night, he said, because it was his five-hundredth game. "How come you didn't include that on your note sheet and stat sheet?"

"Hold on a second, Greg," I said. "The reason it wasn't on the sheets was because this isn't your five-hundredth game."

"What do you mean," Polis demanded angrily. "I played 448 games coming into this year. I needed fifty-two games to reach five hundred, and this was the fifty-second game of the season."

"You're right. It *is* the 52nd game of the season—for the Rangers, but not for you. You forgot you missed three games earlier in the season with your ankle injury. So the game is only your forty-ninth of the season, and the four-hundred ninety-seventh, not the five-hundredth, of your career. You still have three games to go.''

He was embarrassed about it, as he should have been. Three games later, he did play his five-hundredth game, and I did note that fact on the sheets. But whether his family came to watch him that night, I don't know.

Nicknames and a Living Legend

When expansion first came to the National Hockey League, I started making up nicknames for players, primarily to give them some identity in their first year in the league. Among them: Garnet Bailey became "The Carnation"; Gene Ubriaco, "The Little Old Winemaker"; Myron Stankiewicz, "The Brat"; Peter Mahovolich, "The Rabbit"; Nick Harbaruk, "The Herring"; Brit Selby, "The Snail," and Gerry Pinder, "The Person.''

Although there were logical nicknames, such as "The Golden Jet" for Bobby Hull, there was no good reason for most of the nicknames—just to give identity to some of those obscure players hardly anyone knew. Why should somebody be called "The Rabbit" or "The Snail"? Why not?

(I was nicknamed a few things myself—among them, "Dognose" and "Art the Dart.'' The latter, I think, was somebody's way of complimenting me for my alleged ability to hit the bulls-eye in assessing a player's worth to a team.)

Giving recognition to an unknown was the motivating idea behind a little fun we cooked up in December, 1973. When I do the stats, I spend all my time looking at names like Esposito and Cournoyer. I always wanted to know who the guys were at the other end. So I decided to start a Bottom Ten list. I also decided to figure out who the most anonymous guy in the Bottom Ten was.

One name that popped out at me was Morris Mott of the California Golden Seals. You couldn't find a more anonymous hockey player than that. He had only one goal and one assist, and was playing for the team with the worst record in hockey. If anyone needed recognition, it was Morris Mott.

There was no intention to poke fun at Morris, just to give him some recognition. So one night, for the heck of it, I told the TV director that Mott would score in the third period. The word was passed to our TV announcers, Jim Gordon and Bill Chadwick, and they suggested that Mott was a third-period player. To the shock of everyone—including myself and probably Morris—he got a goal and an assist in the third period that night. He became a living legend.

210

By his next appearance in Madison Square Garden, he was the toast of the town. The electric message board outside the Garden carried the promotional message: "Coming March 3, the California Seals with Morris Mott." A Morris Mott Fan Club was started by students at Brooklyn's Tilden High School. In the Garden there were more than a dozen bedsheet banners with his name. Inside our TV studio truck were pictures and newspaper articles of Mott, and from the ceiling hung a blowup toy player, on which Morris's number, twenty, was scribbled. The San Francisco *Chronicle* ran a feature story headlined: HOW HOCKEY FAME HIT MORRIS MOTT.

"The whole thing took me by surprise," said Mott, then a second-year, third-line forward. "I was really kind of embarrassed. I didn't know what to make of it."

When he came to the Garden, he told a reporter, "I wasn't sure what to do . . . whether in pre-game I should warm up with everyone else or come over and sign autographs. I've never had that problem before. . . . Now I know how Bobby Hull must feel. I'm a little embarrassed. But I hope it doesn't stop for a while."

On telecasts of Ranger games, the announcer would make frequent references to Mott, and when the Rangers played the Seals, any time Mott was on the ice one camera followed him almost exclusively. When word reached the West Coast, one reporter wrote, the little forward became something of a folk hero, and management was said to be considering a Morris Mott Banner Night at Oakland Coliseum. By this time, incidentally, he had scored seven goals and made a dozen assists, enough to get him out of the Bottom Ten.

I must emphasize that it was all in good fun. We weren't trying to demean him in any way. He was just a guy with a great-sounding name, playing for a bad team, hustling all the time without any recognition. With our TV technicians, I toasted Morris and his new fame with apple juice—Mott's, of course.

But now that he was no longer obscure, we had to search around for an alternate. We were happy to discover that Morris had a brother in the Western League at Phoenix, Darwin Mott. That was an even more anonymous name. We had to start helping him out.

FOOTBALL

Football

ON A SINGLE-GAME BASIS, football is the most difficult major sport for keeping records and stats. You run into all sorts of obstacles that you don't encounter in baseball, basketball or hockey.

The action is so fast in football that you have only about thirty seconds between plays, which gives you very little time to update your records and be ready for the next play. For instance, suppose Richard Todd completes a pass to Richard Caster. First, you note where the line of scrimmage was. Now, as soon as Caster has caught the ball and is tackled, you write down for the announcer how many yards were gained on the play. Then you've got to update Todd's passing stats and the receiver's stats, the number of completions and receptions, as well as the yardage for both. If it was a first down, you have to update that figure. And you've got to keep a running summary of the yardage picked up on the current march, so that if a touchdown results, you can quickly compute it and be able to report, for example, that the TD drive went eight plays for sixty yards. You may also be keeping track of tackles, so that you have to note who made the tackle on the play, and update his totals.

Occasionally, you've no sooner computed all these statistics than you look up and find there was a penalty and the play was called back. Because that nullifies everything that happened, you've got to erase all your updating—and, of course, add the penalty to your figures in that category.

The weather can be a *big* problem, especially when you're working a game in November or December in a winter wonderland like Buffalo or Boston (where I used to travel for some of the Jet games). It's not easy to keep all the necessary pieces of paper and index cards in front of you when the wind is howling and the snow is blowing on you. As it's too difficult to work with gloves on, there have been occasions when before the first quarter of the game was over I had lost all feeling in my hand. I've dropped my pencil without realizing it, and gone on "writing" with nothing in my hands, because my fingertips were frozen.

I once worked a Giant-Eagle game in Franklin Field, Philadelphia, where the wind-chill factor was 15°–20° below zero! An abundance of incomplete passes stopped the clock and made the game last longer than normal. Long before it was over, I'd lost all feeling in my extremities, and the only thing louder than my chattering teeth was Howard Cosell.

When you keep statistics for a football broadcaster, you're often expected to serve as spotter, too. In other words, it's your responsibility to identify who carried the ball on a particular play, who made the tackle and so forth. On a rainy, muddy or snowy field, it's often difficult to make out numbers. Most running backs, for example, wear similar numbers on their jerseys. The halfback is number 35, the fullback, 36; pass receivers usually have numbers in the eighties. By midgame, you can't tell one set of figures from the other. When you can't read the numbers, you've got to rely on following a man out, by position. You've really got to be on the alert to get it right.

What eases the burden of the football statistician is the fact that while each team has eleven men on the field, you're keeping statistics, in most cases, for just the running backs, the passer and the pass receivers (though sometimes you also keep track of tackles made, keying on a few individuals who are likely to accumulate a lot of tackles in the course of the game). Otherwise, you make almost no notation of the other players at all, except to point them out on the spotting board.*

*The spotting board is an item to help broadcasters identify players. The names of players and other pertinent information about them are laid out according to their position on the field. In some cases I make up the board, but most broadcasters prefer to set up their own. Spotting boards are all different, varying from simple to complex, from neat to messy, from permanent pegboard to one-use oaktag. Some go so far as to include each player's up-to-date stats, his height and weight, the name of his college team and any other significant data, such as a career high. Usually there is a board for each team, with the offensive squad on one side, the defensive on the other. In certain booths, you might find yourself holding one team's board on your lap while the other rests on the table in front of you. Football is a sport where extreme care is taken by broadcasters to spot players. Some announcers spend hours preparing their spotting boards.

So while just about every baseball player gets a turn at bat, every basketball player will usually shoot and in hockey anyone can get a goal or an assist, in football you're concerned, statistically, with only about one-third of the players on the field.

Not a Science

Of course, football stats are not an exact science, and a lot of judgment calls are involved. For instance, weather or normal wear-and-tear may sometimes obliterate the line markers on the field, and on a carry, you'll have to use your judgment as to whether it was a four-yard or five-yard gain. There have been times when I judged it to have been a four-yard gain but the official scorer called it five yards. Who's to say who was right? (I'd always go with the official scorer's decision, to keep the record uniform.)

Sometimes the ball is between yard lines, and since you can't award a man a half-yard, you have to decide whether the ball is considered to be at the 29-yard line or the 30. In instances like that, too, the statistician's judgment and the scorer's may differ.

Complicating your task, too, are the differences between college and professional rules. In the pros, for instance, it's necessary for the pass receiver to have both feet inbounds for a catch to count as a reception; at the college level, one foot inbounds at the time of the catch is sufficient. Even high school football has its own regulations. No broadcaster or statistician can know every single rule.

The only way to keep the records of all the individuals involved in the play up-to-date is to erase the previous figure. As the game wears on, your papers get worn out from all the erasing. You need total concentration, or else you may find—as I have—that you've erased the running back's last figures and neglected to put in the new total, because you've been distracted by a commercial cue or by someone pointing out something about the play. Then the player's card doesn't have a rushing total for the game. It can be tricky.

Meaningful Football Stats

Meaningful statistics are really anything that can give you an accurate insight into a player's contribution to a game. The logic of many stats used in football is still questionable.

The standards—yardage, the number of passes thrown and caught, punts, fumbles, interceptions—are fine as far as they go, but they really don't tell you the whole story.

For example, the leading pass receiver is usually someone who catches between seventy and eighty passes a season. But it's quite possible that the tenth-ranked receiver, who may have caught only fifty passes, scored more touchdowns than the leader did. So despite the fact that he caught fewer passes, he might have been more valuable to his team than the leading receiver. The tenth-ranked receiver caught passes for longer gains and scored more touchdowns, which is what a football game is all about. There are discrepancies like this in other football categories, too, which we'll talk about a little later.

In baseball, any one pitch, hit or fielding play is an isolated event involving one player doing one thing at a time. Because no one can help a hitter hit the ball, a pitcher throw the ball or a fielder catch and throw the ball, counting the successes and failures of each player in baseball gives valid information about his effectiveness. But football is entirely different. Eleven men, each of whom has a specific function, are involved offensively in every play. No ball carrier can gain ten or twelve yards without a handoff from the quarterback and blocking from others. Football is such a team effort that individual statistics can be misleading. I don't want to take anything away from the performance of O. J. Simpson—he's unquestionably one of the great running backs of all time—but his statistics can be manipulated, and so can anyone else's.

What I mean is this: every football play is made in the huddle, called either by the quarterback or coach. Every player is supposed to contribute to winning the game, but if things aren't equal—if the game isn't close and if rushing and passing records are at stake—then the winning or losing strategy of that contest becomes secondary to the real focus of attention, those records. While the rules prevent a baseball manager from having one of his players with a shot at the season home-run record go to bat a dozen times in a game, there's nothing to prevent a football coach or quarterback from having the same man carry the ball play after play after play. The defense may even "help" him; if they're ahead, they're glad to concede a little running yardage, since runs help kill the clock and running isn't anywhere near as quick a way of scoring as passing can be.

In short, a quarterback on a team that's way ahead or way behind can help a teammate to a running or pass-receiving record by constantly handing off or passing the ball to him.

At the end of the season, the rushing total is based strictly on how many yards the runner gained, the passing record on how many yards the passer accumulated in completed passes and the pass-catching record on how many the pass receiver caught—all without regard to how many attempts there were, or the circumstances.

Rushing

O. J. Simpson led the American Football Conference in rushing in 1976, and what makes that so remarkable is that he did it with Buffalo, one of the worst clubs in the league that year. His team was almost always trailing in the game, and when a team is behind, it usually has to pass a lot to try to get back in contention. Obviously, a lot of passing reduces the number of attempts at rushing. (Again, contrast this with baseball, where no matter how far your team is behind, you're going to get an opportunity for a base hit.)

One of O. J.'s best games in 1976 took place on Thanksgiving Day against the Detroit Lions. The Buffalo Bills, out of the game early and blitzed by a wide margin, had to pass often. Yet Simpson gained 270-odd yards in that game and broke the record for rushing in an individual game. So he deserves extra gold stars for accumulating the great totals he did, despite the fact that, with his team so far behind, he couldn't run as often as his team would have liked him to.

Rushing statistics fall short of giving an accurate picture in that a player given thirty or forty chances to run in a game may make only very short gains but still amass an impressive total of yards gained rushing, while a man with fewer chances may gain significantly each time but have a lower total for the game. So, "true" figures can sometimes mislead.

These qualifications aside, a man who averages over four yards gained each time he carries the ball, or gains as much as one hundred yards in a single contest, can be considered to have had a fine rushing game. Over a season, I'd say what distinguishes a good runner from an average runner is if he's able to gain one thousand yards. Like a .300 batting average to a baseball hitter or twenty points a game to a basketball player or thirty goals a season for a hockey player, that's the hallmark of a rusher.

For a team, 150–175 yards in a game is good, but this figure has to be judged in conjunction with how many yards it gained passing. A team might gain only 100 yards rushing, but if its passing attack netted 250 yards, you certainly can't fault the offense.

Comparing Rushing Records of Different Years

Comparison of rushing records from one season to another can be misleading. It's not fair to talk about a 1,000-yard rusher for a fourteen-game season in the same breath with a 1,000-yard rusher in a ten-game schedule—which is what the schedule was before 1960. It would probably be better if all-time rushing records (and some of the others, too) were kept on a per-game basis rather than on the basis of a cumulative season's total.

(This is different from comparisons of baseball records for various seasons because four extra games represent a greater proportion of a football schedule.)

Passing Statistics

Runners in the league are ranked according to the total yardage gained; receivers, by their total catches; punters; and kick returners, by their average. But at this point, nobody is quite sure of the best way to rate passers.

Some passers have high completion ratios; some aren't intercepted very often; some throw a lot of touchdown passes, yet don't have a very high completion ratio. It's possible to have a different quarterback leading in each of six or seven passing categories. One could be tops in passes completed, another in TD passes, a third in lowest interception percentage, and so on.

Some passing stats are misleading. For example, a quarterback may have a lot of pass completions in a game, but what isn't evident from the statistical summary is that he got the bulk of his completions in the last minutes of the game, when his team was behind and he was throwing a lot more passes than he normally would. In other words, to put completion stats in perspective, you should know what the score was when the passer got the bulk of his yardage. In the closing stages of a game, the defense will often concede short passes rather than risk the long bomb, so that a losing quarterback may end up with many completions he wouldn't have had if his team weren't losing.

Another weakness of passing statistics is that the yardage on a completed play is never broken down into how much was accounted for by the pass itself, and how much came from the receiver running after he caught the pass. A quarterback can lay a little screen pass or safety pass into the hands of a receiver, who then shakes off three tacklers and goes fifty yards. Or the quarterback can unload a long bomb that travels fifty yards from the line of scrimmage to a receiver, who catches it and is tackled on the spot. In both cases, the passer is credited with a fifty-yard completed pass.

All these factors—completions, touchdown passes, yardage, interceptions, among others—are taken into account in computing a quarterback's value.

Third-Down Performance

There are glaring omissions in the stats of a quarterback's effectiveness.

For instance, some observers of football say the real tipoff to a quarterback's ability is how often he converts a critical third-down play into a first down. If he does it 40 percent or 50 percent of the time, he's terrific. Yet other aficionados of pro football point out that some passers are so effective on first and second downs, they can run up a big, winning score without ever having to cash in a single third-down situation.

So while third-down performance is a nice statistic to play around with, it isn't anywhere near the whole answer in evaluating a quarterback's worth. But it's certainly important enough to be one of the factors considered.

Evaluating Kickers

When it comes to punting, the leader has always been the man with the highest average in yardage kicked. But the NFL recently came up with a new and more accurate way of evaluating a punter's effectiveness.

Under the new system, two basic categories are used to calculate a punter's value: his average yardage per kick, and his average net yards per kick. Net yards are figured on the basis of distance minus return.

As a result, while Buffalo's Marv Bateman led the NFL in punting in 1976 with a 42.8-yard average, John James of Atlanta was judged to be the league's *most effective* punter. The reason: when deductions were made for the yardage that Bateman's punts were returned, his average effectiveness was 29 yards per kick. But James, whose gross average per kick was 42.1 yards, had a net of 36.2 yards after touchbacks and punt returns.

To figure out the new category of judging punters, let's take the example of David Lee of Baltimore. In 1976 his punts went a total of 2,342 yards. When you deduct 60 yards lost on three touchbacks and 231 yards in punt returns, you're left with a total of 2,051 yards. When you divide that figure by his fifty-nine punts, the result is a net 34.8 yards, good enough to lead the American Football Conference in 1976.

In my opinion, this is a fairer way to estimate a punter's worth, because it takes into account field position as a result of the kick. A team punts to get the best possible field position, and a good punt is high enough to give the punter's team adequate time to cover the kick.

Evaluating Kick-Returners

The men who return punts and kickoffs have relatively little control over their destinies as far as leading the league in their categories.

If a man develops a reputation as an excellent runback man on kickoffs, the kicker on the opposing team will either try to kick the ball away from him, thus reducing his chances of gaining yardage, or will make an extra effort to boot the ball out of the end zone, so there's no opportunity for a runback by anyone. In baseball the best you can do against a man who's damaging you is pitch around him or throw carefully, but you can only do that so many times in the course of a game or season. In football, though, you can avoid the tough kick-returner almost indefinitely. A man who makes his living returning kicks—and is good at it—will get fewer and fewer chances to return a kickoff or punt as his reputation grows around the league.

Time of Possession

One category of statistics you're not likely to see in the papers, but one that's a very good reflection of which team dominated play, is *time of possession.*

Coaches, players, writers and broadcasters are always talking about the importance of ball control, but there wasn't a common statistic to indicate it until we started doing it on "Monday Night Football" telecasts. (More about those broadcasts later.)

If in the sixty minutes of playing time, one team had the ball for thirty-seven minutes and the other for twenty-three, I think that tells you a lot more about the game than, for instance, that one team outgained the other by a hundred yards.

It would really be helpful if something like this were to be a part of the printed summary of a pro football game.

Systems for Evaluation

When Johnny Majors was the coach at the University of Pittsburgh, he had a simple system of grading his defensive players. As he looked over films of the game, he'd give a player three points for a tackle, two points for assisting on a tackle, five for causing a fumble, five for recovering a fumble and ten for sacking the quarterback. He would deduct points from a player for missing a tackle. After studying the films, he'd give each player a grade; a middle linebacker, for example, might have a total of forty points.

Each pro team has its own way of rating players. Most of their systems are similar to the method Majors used at Pittsburgh.

Statistics as Strategy

One of the most noted statistical analysts, someone used as a consultant by at least a half-dozen pro football teams, is Bud Goode of Los Angeles. Working with computers, he has come up with all sorts of information for the teams that utilize his services. For instance, before the start of the 1976 season, he told George Allen that if the Redskins did not run the ball approximately forty times a game, there was no way for Washington to get into the playoffs. They did make it.

Long Way to Go

THERE'S STILL A WAY to go for football statistics to become complete.

About 1969 the Xerox Company began to recognize the need for football stats to be more incisive, and the company started handing out little analysis sheets to people in the press boxes during games. These sheets would contain such data as a runner's performance in each of the four downs, a breakdown of a passer's performance according to downs and how he did in the last two minutes. But it proved to be a little too complicated for many of the sportswriters, who were too busy to try to dissect the new, meaningful stats. The only stories written about the innovation were offbeat pieces about the lengths Xerox would go for a little publicity. It's unfortunate that nobody took them seriously; the idea was abandoned by the following season.

Some writers who have regularly covered football for a number of years have tried to come up with more meaningful stats on their own.

The primary object of a football game is to score. Of secondary importance is how you move the ball forward. We've still got to work out ways of establishing leaders in various categories—judging rushers on more than just the number of yards gained, pass receivers on more than just the number of passes they caught. Quarterbacks, the most difficult to evaluate, are probably the most fairly judged, by a complicated formula that combines all the separate categories now used.

224

Any worthwhile changes in statistics will have to originate with the NFL. Pro football has the machinery and the personnel to implement changes in the way records and stats are kept. Anything that proves valuable after a trial period will eventually filter down to college football and then maybe even to high school football.

Football Reports

The home football team usually hires three or four men to handle stats during the game. At the end of the game, the figures are tallied and either sent or phoned in to the Elias Sports Bureau.

It used to be that the Elias Sports Bureau would have everything computed in time for all the league's up-to-date stats to be printed in Tuesday's newspapers. With the advent of National League football games on Monday night, everything has been pushed back a day, so usually, up-to-date NFL stats don't appear until Wednesday or even Thursday.

From the official reports sent in by scorers for the football teams, the Elias Sports Bureau compiles an extensive weekly release, which is sent to clubs in both conferences and to sportswriters and broadcasters. It is an invaluable aid. The clear, thorough reports provide the information for the listings of standings and category leaders that appear in the papers.

The bureau's work with football, Seymour Siwoff says, begins on Sunday at 4:00 in the afternoon and doesn't end until 2:00 on Tuesday morning (because of "Monday Night Football").

Each team has a scoring crew that phones in pertinent data to the bureau immediately after the game, either Sunday or Monday. " 'Monday Night Football,' " according to Siwoff, "just caused a little more creative effort on our part, but we solved it by doing the mailing right here on the premises."

He explains that no mailing house would do the work at 2:00 A.M., so "we print, promulgate and mail here." More than three thousand addressees are involved in the Tuesday morning mailing.

Official NFL Scoresheet

The official National Football League scoresheet, filled in by the official scorer and submitted after each NFL game to the Elias Sports Bureau, is a mammoth

225

OFFICIAL NATIONAL FOOTBALL LEAGUE SCORE SHEET

GAME NO.

DATE:_____ AT:_____

OFFICIAL ATTENDANCE:_____

WEATHER:_____ TIME:_____

SCORE BY PERIODS				
	1ST	2ND	3RD	4TH	TOTAL
VISITING TEAM					
HOME TEAM					

	VISITORS	HOME		VISITORS	HOME
First Downs-Total			Total Fumbles		
-Rushing			Fumbles Lost		
-Passing			No. of Penalties		
-Penalty			Yards Penalized		
Total Yards Gained (Net)			Punts Returned By		
Total Offensive Plays			Punt Return Yardage		
Average Gain per Play			Kickoffs Returned By		
Net Rushing Yardage			Kickoff Return Yardage		
Total Rushing Plays			Passes Intercepted By		
Average Gain per Rush			Interception Return Yardage		

	VISITORS	HOME
Net Passing Yardage		
Gross Passing Yardage		
Tkd./Yds. Lost Att. Pass	TKD / YDS	TKD / YDS
Passes Attempted		
Passes Completed		
Passes Had Intercepted		
Avg. Gain per Pass Play		
Total Punts		
Total Yards on Punts		
Average Yards per Punt		

	VISITORS	HOME
Touchdowns-Total		
-Rushing		
-Passing		
-Runbacks		
Extra Points		
Field Goals		
Safeties		
Third Down Efficiency	MADE / ATT	MADE / ATT

NOTE—COMPUTE ALL YARDAGE FROM LINE OF SCRIMMAGE, EXCEPT FIELD GOALS

CIRCLE LONG RUN, IN EACH INDIVIDUAL CATEGORY BELOW, IF TOUCHDOWN SCORED.

RUSHING

VISITORS	ATT'S	YARDS	LONG	TD

HOME	ATT'S	YARDS	LONG	TD
TOTAL				

PASSING

VISITORS	ATT.	COMP.	YARDS	TKD/YDS LOST PASS	TDS	LONG	HAD INT.
TOTALS							

HOME	ATT.	COMP.	YARDS	TKD/YDS LOST PASS	TDS	LONG	HAD INT.
TOTAL							

KICKING CONTROL

KICKER & TEAM	PUNTS			KICKOFFS		
	BLK OR TB	D	NO.	TB	MISC
HOME						
TOTALS						

*KICKOFFS misc: ON-SIDE KICKS

PASS RECEIVING

VISITORS	NO.REC	YARDS	Long	TDs
TOTALS				

HOME	NO.REC	YARDS	Long	TDs

PASS INTERCEPTIONS

VISITORS	NO.	YARDS	Long	TDS	HOME	NO.	YARDS	Long	TDS
TOTALS					TOTALS				

PUNTING

VISITORS	NO.	YARDS	TB	IN-20	LONG	HOME	NO.	YARDS	TB	IN-20	LONG
TOTALS						TOTALS					

PUNT RETURNS

VISITORS	NO.	FC	YARDS	Long	TD	HOME	NO.	FC	YARDS	Long	TD
TOTALS						TOTALS					

KICKOFF RETURNS

VISITORS	NO.	YARDS	Long	TD	HOME	NO.	YARDS	Long	TD
TOTALS					TOTALS				

SCORING

VISITORS	TDS	X PT	F.G.	SAFE.	T.PTL.	HOME	TDS	X PT	F.G.	SAFE.	T.PTL.
TOTALS						TOTALS					

EXTRA POINTS (KICKS) MISSED BY

FIELD GOALS

LIST ALL YARDAGES IN SEQUENCE. CIRCLE SUCCESSFUL ATTEMPTS.

	MADE	ATTS.	YARDAGES
VISITORS			
TOTALS			
HOME			
TOTALS			

ATTEMPT BLOCKED BY_____

FUMBLES

VISITORS	NO.	OWN REC.	YARDS	LONG	TD'S	OP'S REC.	YARDS	LONG	TD'S
TOTALS									
HOME									
TOTALS									

FUMBLES OUT OF BOUNDS _____

BE SURE TO COMPLETE REVERSE SIDE

yellow form, about two feet long and one foot wide. It's a lot more complicated than the scoresheet the baseball official scorer sends in after a game.

Filled in on both sides, the NFL scoresheet lists just about everything that can take place in a game, except what a player mutters after he fumbles the ball or misses a tackle. It contains a listing of all players who were in the game and tells what each player did in such categories as yards rushing, interceptions, kickoff returns, field-goal attempts, passes thrown and caught, etc.

To complete the form properly requires a great deal of effort in terms of proofreading and checking. Usually, all the statisticians will work on the material during the course of the game. When the report is completed, it's sent to Elias, and it is on reports such as this that the Sports Bureau bases its weekly statistics.

NFL Final Stats

This report contains the final stats for the 1976 regular season in the National Football League.

The playoff matchups on page one give all the pertinent statistics—first downs, yards gained, rushing and passing stats, as well as punt returns, kickoff yardage, penalties, fumbles and every other category involving the teams that are in the first round of the NFL playoffs. The matchups given are Washington-Minnesota, New England-Oakland, Pittsburgh-Baltimore, Los Angeles-Dallas.

The remaining pages concern the final cumulative stats on all the teams in the NFL, with the teams listed alphabetically, beginning with Atlanta, Buffalo, Chicago, and so on.

The fourth page gives the rankings of the teams on offense and defense against rushing and passing. Among the interesting material is the scoring differential among the fourteen teams in each of the two conferences comprising the NFL—that is, the margin by which each team won or lost its games. Pittsburgh, as you can see, won its games by an average of more points than any other team. Tampa Bay ("TB"), meanwhile, didn't win a game, and lost by the largest scores of any team in the league.

Conference News Releases

Each of the conferences in the National Football League—the American Football

Playoff Matchups
OFFENSE

	NFC		AFC		AFC		NFC	
	WASH.	MINN.	N.E.	OAK.	PITT.	BALT.	L.A.	DALL.
GAMES (W-L)	10-4	11-2-1	11-3	13-1	10-4	11-3	10-3-1	11-3
FIRST DOWNS	255	294	260	303	271	301	265	269
Rushing	114	125	150	137	163	133	143	111
Passing	122	150	95	146	94	144	111	140
Penalty	19	19	15	20	14	24	11	18
YDS GAINED (total)	4096	4858	4694	5190	4637	5236	4869	4884
Avg per game	292.6	347.0	335.3	370.7	331.2	374.0	347.8	348.9
RUSHING (net)	2111	2003	2957	2285	2971	2309	2528	2147
Avg per game	150.8	143.1	211.2	163.2	212.2	164.9	180.6	153.4
Rushes	548	540	589	557	653	564	613	538
Avg Yds	3.9	3.7	5.0	4.1	4.6	4.1	4.1	4.0
PASSING (net)	1985	2855	1737	2905	1666	2927	2341	2737
Avg per game	141.8	203.9	124.1	207.5	119.0	209.1	167.2	195.5
Passes Attempted	370	442	309	361	277	361	315	390
Completed	187	270	146	232	143	215	171	222
Pct Comp	50.5	61.1	47.2	64.3	51.6	59.6	54.3	56.9
Yds Gained	2288	3117	1910	3195	1935	3221	2629	2967
Tackled	38	31	21	28	27	31	32	30
Yds Lost	303	262	173	290	269	294	288	230
Had Intercepted	20	10	20	18	12	10	15	13
Yds Opp Ret	149	85	380	185	106	146	211	155
Opp TDs on Int	0	0	0	0	0	1	0	1
PUNTS	90	69	67	67	76	59	79	74
Avg Yds	38.9	38.8	40.1	41.6	39.2	39.7	38.1	37.0
PUNT RET	52	40	48	50	71	40	52	45
Avg Ret	13.2	6.8	13.1	11.1	9.0	7.9	9.2	10.9
Ret for TD	1	0	2	0	0	0	0	0
KICKOFF RET	50	42	46	46	41	52	44	42
Avg Ret	21.3	20.5	23.6	22.3	20.9	20.6	23.3	24.5
Ret for TD	0	0	0	0	0	0	1	0
PENALTIES	90	77	102	107	111	92	83	94
Yds	868	615	914	957	836	786	754	761
FUMBLES BY	36	33	28	21	40	25	29	26
Fumbles Lost	23	19	16	11	19	18	21	16
Opp Fumbles	38	24	37	26	42	32	31	32
Opp Fumbles Lost	21	13	27	9	24	21	16	12
TOUCHDOWNS	32	36	48	47	43	51	44	34
Rushing	10	18	24	14	33	26	23	16
Passing	20	17	18	33	10	24	17	17
Returns	2	1	6	0	0	1	4	1
EXTRA POINTS	31	34	42	40	40	49	36	34
FG/FGA	22-34	19-31	15-25	8-19	14-26	20-27	17-26	18-23
TOTAL POINTS	291	305	376	350	342	417	351	296

DEFENSE

	NFC		AFC		AFC		NFC	
	WASH.	MINN.	N.E.	OAK.	PITT.	BALT.	L.A.	DALL.
OPP POINTS	217	176	236	237	138	246	190	194
OPP FIRST DOWNS	215	207	258	261	182	229	213	246
Rushing	109	103	102	98	69	83	79	113
Passing	91	91	134	138	96	126	118	111
Penalty	15	13	22	25	17	20	16	22
OPP YDS GAINED	4122	3671	4022	4379	3323	4187	3656	3730
Avg per game	294.4	262.2	287.3	312.8	237.4	299.1	261.1	266.4
OPP RUSHING (net)	2205	2096	1847	1903	1457	1848	1564	1821
Avg per game	157.5	149.7	131.9	135.9	104.1	132.0	111.7	130.1
Rushes	555	487	462	478	452	437	429	484
Avg Yds	4.0	4.3	4.0	4.0	3.2	4.2	3.6	3.8
OPP PASSING (net)	1917	1575	2175	2476	1866	2339	2092	1909
Avg per game	136.9	112.5	155.4	176.9	133.3	167.1	149.4	136.4
Passes Attempted	354	323	437	389	373	372	397	391
Completed	146	158	229	197	158	192	199	187
Pct Comp	41.2	48.9	52.4	50.6	42.4	51.6	50.1	47.8
Tackled	44	45	47	46	41	57	45	44
Yds Lost	324	322	429	370	313	465	395	327
INTERCEPTED BY	26	19	23	16	22	15	32	16
Yds Ret	190	213	505	128	262	211	376	133
Ret for TD	0	0	3	0	0	0	3	0
OPP PUNT RET	44	40	37	38	36	33	39	28
Avg Ret	7.3	7.2	7.8	6.9	5.7	7.0	7.2	9.0
OPP KICKOFF RET	63	66	71	61	61	77	70	62
Avg Ret	16.3	18.3	22.1	18.4	21.0	22.3	19.8	20.6
OPP TOUCHDOWNS	23	22	29	31	14	29	22	25
Rushing	12	14	12	17	5	11	11	12
Passing	11	8	16	13	9	16	11	12
Returns	0	0	1	1	0	2	0	1

OFFENSE	NFC ATL.	AFC BUFF.	NFC CHI.	AFC CIN.	AFC CLEV.	AFC DEN.	NFC DET.	NFC G.B.
GAMES (W-L)	4-10	2-12	7-7	10-4	9-5	9-5	6-8	5-9
FIRST DOWNS	191	250	201	238	260	239	259	210
Rushing	78	135	115	114	119	106	123	99
Passing	93	102	67	110	112	114	120	94
Penalty	20	13	19	14	29	19	16	17
YDS GAINED (total)	3103	4404	3843	4300	4542	4136	4353	3452
Avg per game	221.6	314.6	274.5	307.1	324.4	295.4	310.9	246.6
RUSHING (net)	1689	2566	2363	2109	2295	1932	2213	1722
Avg per game	120.6	183.3	168.8	150.6	163.9	138.0	158.1	123.0
Rushes	470	548	578	481	533	500	516	485
Avg Yds	3.6	4.7	4.1	4.4	4.3	3.9	4.3	3.6
PASSING (net)	1414	1838	1480	2191	2247	2204	2140	1730
Avg per game	101.0	131.3	105.7	156.5	160.5	157.4	152.9	123.6
Passes Attempted	354	383	278	360	373	353	356	357
Completed	157	156	123	187	209	168	201	164
Pct Comp	44.4	40.7	44.2	51.9	56.0	47.6	56.5	45.9
Yds Gained	1809	2084	1705	2443	2399	2510	2630	2105
Tackled	44	33	24	37	19	48	67	41
Yds Lost	395	246	225	252	152	306	490	375
Had Intercepted	24	17	15	15	15	22	12	22
Yds Opp Ret	469	246	213	102	123	260	121	362
Opp TDs on Int	4	0	0	0	0	1	0	3
PUNTS	101	87	100	76	69	84	85	84
Avg Yds	42.1	42.3	37.3	39.5	37.4	35.1	38.8	36.6
PUNT RET	60	33	43	54	49	51	31	40
Avg Ret	6.4	6.7	6.3	6.4	7.5	12.5	6.7	7.5
Ret for TD	0	1	0	0	0	4	0	0
KICKOFF RET	60	75	51	49	54	46	47	65
Avg Ret	21.2	21.3	21.3	21.3	21.9	23.4	21.0	20.9
Ret for TD	0	0	0	1	0	0	0	0
PENALTIES	84	91	114	79	107	105	97	87
Yds	714	797	984	700	1037	986	819	791
FUMBLES BY	30	45	24	38	45	23	38	37
Fumbles Lost	17	26	13	20	22	12	21	23
Opp Fumbles	30	37	37	34	24	23	27	27
Opp Fumbles Lost	20	23	23	15	11	13	15	15
TOUCHDOWNS	20	30	31	42	32	39	32	27
Rushing	10	11	20	15	9	14	9	15
Passing	10	16	9	21	21	15	20	10
Returns	0	3	2	6	2	10	3	2
EXTRA POINTS	20	26	27	39	28	36	28	24
FG/FGA	10-21	13-24	12-25	14-27	15-28	15-21	14-24	10-19
TOTAL POINTS	172	245	253	335	267	315	262	218

DEFENSE

	NFC ATL.	AFC BUFF.	NFC CHI.	AFC CIN.	AFC CLEV.	AFC DEN.	NFC DET.	NFC G.B.
OPP POINTS	312	363	216	210	287	206	220	299
OPP FIRST DOWNS	257	262	250	234	244	222	191	262
Rushing	143	128	104	116	109	90	94	132
Passing	95	110	128	103	111	104	76	107
Penalty	19	24	18	15	24	28	21	23
OPP YDS GAINED	4578	4730	4201	3675	3793	3734	3587	4123
Avg per game	327.0	337.9	300.1	262.5	270.9	266.7	256.2	294.5
OPP RUSHING (net)	2577	2476	1984	1917	1761	1709	1901	2288
Avg per game	184.1	176.9	141.7	136.9	125.8	122.1	135.8	163.4
Rushes	574	531	522	520	445	496	496	546
Avg Yds	4.5	4.7	3.8	3.7	4.0	3.4	3.8	4.2
OPP PASSING (net)	2001	2254	2217	1758	2032	2025	1686	1835
Avg per game	142.9	161.0	158.4	125.6	145.1	144.6	120.4	131.1
Passes Attempted	340	337	401	364	392	391	313	354
Completed	184	163	200	177	225	214	137	196
Pct Comp	54.1	48.4	49.9	48.6	57.4	54.7	43.8	55.4
Tackled	35	30	49	46	32	32	28	43
Yds Lost	275	221	395	444	321	240	218	357
INTERCEPTED BY	18	19	24	26	21	24	24	11
Yds Ret	207	293	215	330	234	452	445	197
Ret for TD	0	1	2	3	1	4	3	2
OPP PUNT RET	52	52	44	41	45	43	39	48
Avg Ret	6.9	16.9	7.9	7.9	11.5	8.7	7.1	5.6
OPP KICKOFF RET	38	48	54	66	57	50	55	44
Avg Ret	24.6	25.1	17.9	24.5	23.6	24.2	21.6	17.8
OPP TOUCHDOWNS	40	41	25	25	37	25	25	34
Rushing	22	19	10	11	15	14	13	17
Passing	14	18	15	13	18	8	11	13
Returns	4	4	0	1	4	3	1	4

OFFENSE	AFC HOU.	AFC K.C.	AFC MIA.	NFC N.O.	NFC N.Y.G.	AFC N.Y.J.	NFC PHIL.	NFC ST.L.
GAMES (W-L)	5-9	5-9	6-8	4-10	3-11	3-11	4-10	10-4
FIRST DOWNS	199	275	267	226	216	220	220	307
Rushing	71	103	122	92	98	104	109	140
Passing	110	152	125	111	97	93	91	142
Penalty	18	20	20	23	21	23	20	25
YDS GAINED (total)	3570	4802	4386	3758	3696	3535	3572	5136
Avg per game	255.0	343.0	313.3	268.4	264.0	252.5	255.1	366.9
RUSHING (net)	1498	1873	2118	1775	1904	1929	2080	2301
Avg per game	107.0	133.8	151.3	126.8	136.0	137.8	148.6	164.4
Rushes	416	498	491	431	530	438	505	580
Avg Yds	3.6	3.8	4.3	4.1	3.6	4.4	4.1	4.0
PASSING (net)	2072	2929	2268	1983	1792	1606	1492	2835
Avg per game	148.0	209.2	162.0	141.6	128.0	114.7	106.6	202.5
Passes Attempted	423	419	346	403	326	393	369	392
Completed	227	229	193	206	175	180	182	220
Pct Comp	53.7	54.7	55.8	51.1	53.7	45.8	49.3	56.1
Yds Gained	2429	3303	2604	2352	2104	1989	1844	2967
Tackled	39	42	37	51	44	45	43	17
Yds Lost	357	374	336	369	312	383	352	132
Had Intercepted	19	17	15	14	24	28	18	13
Yds Opp Ret	197	243	128	140	239	430	189	134
Opp TDs on Int	0	1	0	1	1	3	1	0
PUNTS	100	68	62	101	77	81	97	66
Avg Yds	35.3	41.1	38.2	39.3	39.7	39.7	35.5	35.3
PUNT RET	48	34	35	42	41	40	41	36
Avg Ret	10.5	12.6	11.9	8.9	4.8	7.2	10.4	9.7
Ret for TD	1	0	1	0	0	1	0	0
KICKOFF RET	58	65	59	62	53	73	58	54
Avg Ret	21.2	23.7	24.5	18.9	19.7	21.9	19.8	20.4
Ret for TD	0	0	0	0	0	0	0	0
PENALTIES	99	97	70	103	86	71	91	84
Yds	776	789	582	901	734	627	722	683
FUMBLES BY	25	32	14	32	27	44	33	44
Fumbles Lost	14	16	8	18	12	25	14	24
Opp Fumbles	33	35	31	38	32	36	31	32
Opp Fumbles Lost	17	20	18	27	15	21	15	20
TOUCHDOWNS	25	33	31	29	21	20	19	36
Rushing	6	18	15	16	11	10	8	17
Passing	17	15	15	8	9	7	11	18
Returns	2	0	1	5	1	3	0	1
EXTRA POINTS	24	27	29	25	20	16	18	33
FG/FGA	16-27	21-38	16-23	18-23	8-21	11-16	11-16	20-27
TOTAL POINTS	222	290	263	253	170	169	165	309

DEFENSE	AFC HOU.	AFC K.C.	AFC MIA.	NFC N.O.	NFC N.Y.G.	AFC N.Y.J.	NFC PHIL.	NFC ST.L.
OPP POINTS	273	376	264	346	250	383	286	267
OPP FIRST DOWNS	226	309	268	275	251	277	262	239
Rushing	117	161	125	129	120	135	113	111
Passing	90	132	131	121	119	127	129	105
Penalty	19	16	12	25	12	15	20	23
OPP YDS GAINED	3986	5357	5081	4491	4191	4916	4603	4089
Avg per game	284.7	382.6	362.9	320.8	299.4	351.1	328.8	292.1
OPP RUSHING (net)	2072	2861	2411	2289	2203	2592	2053	1979
Avg per game	148.0	204.4	172.2	163.5	157.4	185.1	146.6	141.4
Rushes	540	555	525	554	560	582	532	491
Avg Yds	3.8	5.2	4.6	4.1	3.9	4.5	3.9	4.0
OPP PASSING (net)	1914	2496	2670	2202	1988	2324	2550	2110
Avg per game	136.7	178.2	190.7	157.3	142.0	166.0	182.1	150.7
Passes Attempted	345	375	347	367	330	374	404	342
Completed	173	215	195	200	189	204	237	176
Pct Comp	50.1	57.3	56.2	54.5	57.3	54.5	58.7	51.5
Tackled	50	22	20	39	31	16	19	31
Yds Lost	344	188	193	312	242	144	138	248
INTERCEPTED BY	11	23	11	12	12	11	9	19
Yds Ret	176	161	144	212	62	146	195	243
Ret for TD	0	0	0	3	0	0	0	1
OPP PUNT RET	60	39	34	64	45	55	53	33
Avg Ret	11.0	9.6	8.0	11.6	11.1	8.3	7.6	9.2
OPP KICKOFF RET	53	55	57	54	39	39	44	66
Avg Ret	21.2	23.0	21.9	25.2	18.6	23.1	20.7	24.6
OPP TOUCHDOWNS	31	51	34	44	27	45	35	34
Rushing	13	24	14	22	14	14	16	19
Passing	17	25	20	18	11	25	17	13
Returns	1	2	0	4	2	6	2	2

OFFENSE	AFC S.D.	NFC S.F.	NFC SEA.	AFC T.B.
GAMES (W-L)	6-8	8-4	2-12	0-14
FIRST DOWNS	256	242	239	191
Rushing	111	131	75	71
Passing	127	91	141	93
Penalty	18	20	23	27
YDS GAINED (total)	4456	4085	4065	3006
Avg per game	318.3	291.8	290.4	214.7
RUSHING (net)	2040	2447	1416	1503
Avg per game	145.7	174.8	101.1	107.4
Rushes	473	576	374	433
Avg Yds	4.3	4.2	3.8	3.5
PASSING (net)	2416	1638	2649	1503
Avg per game	172.6	117.0	189.2	107.4
Passes Attempted	388	306	480	376
Completed	223	155	229	181
Pct Comp	57.5	50.7	47.7	48.1
Yds Gained	2687	1963	2874	1926
Tackled	46	34	28	50
Yds Lost	271	325	225	423
Had Intercepted	18	21	30	20
Yds Opp Ret	185	253	388	490
Opp TDs on Int	1	2	4	4
PUNTS	82	91	82	92
Avg Yds	38.7	39.9	37.4	39.3
PUNT RET	45	65	37	43
Avg Ret	10.9	8.6	6.6	8.5
Ret for TD	0	2	0	0
KICKOFF RET	52	38	79	70
Avg Ret	20.7	20.4	20.3	21.3
Ret for TD	0	0	0	0
PENALTIES	78	102	80	109
Yds	576	848	684	875
FUMBLES BY	28	30	30	30
Fumbles Lost	13	12	18	17
Opp Fumbles	24	37	24	33
Opp Fumbles Lost	11	16	11	19
TOUCHDOWNS	32	32	29	15
Rushing	13	14	14	5
Passing	17	15	13	9
Returns	2	3	2	1
EXTRA POINTS	26	26	26	11
FG/FGA	10-20	16-28	9-16	8-17
TOTAL POINTS	248	270	229	125

DEFENSE	AFC S.D.	NFC S.F.	NFC SEA.	AFC T.B.
OPP POINTS	285	190	429	412
OPP FIRST DOWNS	259	218	323	284
Rushing	113	94	166	136
Passing	132	102	136	124
Penalty	14	22	21	24
OPP YDS GAINED	4676	3562	5400	4801
Avg per game	334.0	254.4	385.7	342.9
OPP RUSHING (net)	2048	1786	2876	2560
Avg per game	146.3	127.6	205.4	182.9
Rushes	516	487	614	588
Avg Yds	4.0	3.7	4.7	4.4
OPP PASSING (net)	2628	1776	2524	2241
Avg per game	187.7	126.9	180.3	160.1
Passes Attempted	386	374	367	321
Completed	219	180	223	178
Pct Comp	56.7	48.1	60.8	55.5
Tackled	23	61	27	24
Yds Lost	194	573	246	171
INTERCEPTED BY	20	9	15	9
Yds Ret	299	93	218	99
Ret for TD	1	0	1	0
OPP PUNT RET	45	52	56	71
Avg Ret	13.4	6.8	9.6	10.6
OPP KICKOFF RET	49	46	47	35
Avg Ret	21.9	20.1	22.1	20.5
OPP TOUCHDOWNS	34	25	53	50
Rushing	10	10	20	23
Passing	21	13	27	19
Returns	3	2	6	8

TEAM RANKINGS

AMERICAN FOOTBALL CONFERENCE

	Offense			Defense		
	Total	Rush	Pass	Total	Rush	Pass
Balt.	*1	4	2	7	5	10
Buff.	8	3	10	10	11	8
Cin.	10	8	8	2	7	1
Clev.	6	5	6	4	3	5
Den.	11	10	7	3	2	4
Hou.	12	14	9	5	9	3
K.C.	3	12	*1	14	14	12
Mia.	9	7	5	13	10	14
N.E.	4	2	11	6	4	6
N.Y.J	13	11	13	12	13	9
Oak.	2	6	3	8	6	11
Pitt.	5	*1	12	*1	*1	2
S.D.	7	9	4	9	8	13
T.B.	14	13	14	11	12	7

SCORING DIFFERENTIAL RANKING

1. Pitt.	8. Clev.
2. Balt.	9. S.D.
3. N.E.	10. Hou.
4. Cin.	11. K.C.
5. Oak.	12. Buff.
6. Den.	13. N.Y.J.
7. Mia.	14. T.B.

NATIONAL FOOTBALL CONFERENCE

	Offense			Defense		
	Total	Rush	Pass	Total	Rush	Pass
Atl.	14	13	14	12	13	8
Chi.	9	3	13	10	6	12
Dall.	2	6	3	5	3	5
Det.	5	5	6	2	4	2
G.B.	13	12	10	8	11	4
L.A.	3	1	5	3	1	9
Minn.	4	9	1	4	8	*1
N.O.	10	11	8	11	12	11
N.Y.G	11	10	9	9	9	7
Phil.	12	8	12	13	7	14
St.L.	1	4	2	6	5	10
S.F.	7	2	11	1	2	3
Sea.	8	14	4	14	14	13
Wash.	6	7	7	7	10	6

* = League leader

SCORING DIFFERENTIAL RANKING

1. L.A.	8. Chi.
2. Minn.	9. N.Y.G.
3. Dall.	10. G.B.
4. S.F.	11. N.O.
5. Wash.	12. Phil.
6. Det.	13. Atl.
St.L.	14. Sea.

American
Football
Conference

410 Park Avenue, New York, N.Y. 10022 (212) 758-8606
Jack Hand, Director of Information
AFC-Ind-14
12/13/76

FOR RELEASE 6:30 A.M., EASTERN STANDARD TIME, THURSDAY, DECEMBER 16 - THURSDAY PMs

NFL'S TOP TWO PASSERS: KEN STABLER, BERT JONES TO BE SEEN IN AFC DIVISIONAL PLAYOFF

The National Football League's two top-rated passers will be featured this
weekend in the American Football Conference Divisional Playoffs which open on
Saturday when the New England Patriots, the AFC's Wild Card, oppose the Western
Divisional Champion Oakland Raiders in Oakland. Pittsburgh, which captured its
third straight Central title, travels to Baltimore Sunday to play the Colts,
winners of two successive Eastern crowns under Coach Ted Marchibroda. Both games
will be nationally televised by NBC.

Oakland quarterback Ken Stabler overtook Baltimore's Bert Jones on the 13th
weekend and maintained his narrow margin despite not playing on the final Sunday
to win the first NFL passing title in his seven seasons as a Raider. Stabler completed 194 of 291 for 2,737 yards, 27 touchdowns, 17 interceptions and finished
with a 103.7 passer rating. Jones, who led the AFC in passing from the fifth
through the 12th weekends, finished with 207 completions in 343 attempts, 3,104
yards, 24 touchdowns, nine interceptions and a 102.6 rating.

Stabler's 66.7 completion percentage was the second highest in league history,
topped only by Washington's Sammy Baugh, who had a 70.3 percentage in 1945.
Oakland's team mark of 64.3 (232 completions in 361 attempts) is an NFL record.
Stabler's 27 touchdown tosses were the most in pro football since Oakland's Daryle
Lamonica threw 34 in 1969.

Although Buffalo's O.J.Simpson will not be in the playoffs, he took his fourth
NFL rushing title in the last five years with 1,503 yards on 290 carries. He finished with seven 100-plus games, including a record breaking 273-yard performance
on Thanksgiving Day, and now has 9,626 yards in eight seasons. Jim Brown remains the
all-time leader with 12,312 yards in nine years.

Baltimore's Lydell Mitchell and Pittsburgh's Franco Harris, who finished second
and third respectively in the AFC rushing race, will be seen on the same field Sunday in their playoff game. The former Penn State running mates each carried 289
times; Mitchell gained 1,200 yards while Harris ran for 1,128. It was the second
straight year that Simpson, Mitchell and Harris were one, two and three in the AFC
rushing race.

A total of seven AFC backs, the most ever, rushed for 1,000 or more yards this
season. Pittsburgh's Rocky Bleier finshed fourth with 1,036 yards, Oakland's Mark
van Eeghen was next with 1,012, Denver's Otis Armstrong had 1,008 and Cleveland's
Greg Pruitt gained 1,000 even.

Baltimore's Toni Linhart was the top scorer with 109 points. He was successful
on 49 of 50 extra point attempts and kicked 20 of 27 field goals. Franco Harris, who
set a club mark with 14 touchdowns, was the AFC leader in that category followed by
New England quarterback Steve Grogan's 13 touchdowns and Oakland's Cliff Branch with
12. Grogan's 12 rushing TDs were the most ever by an NFL quarterback; he also
returned one fumble for a score.

Roger Carr, Baltimore's speedy pass-catcher, finished with 1,112 yards receiving,
one better than Branch's 1,111. San Diego's Charlie Joiner also topped the 1,000
yard mark with 1,056. Kansas City's MacArthur Lane, oldest NFL running back at age
34, took the AFC receiving title with 66 catches followed by Buffalo's wide receiver
Bob Chandler with 61.

Cornerback Ken Riley had three interceptions in Cincinnati's final game and was
the conference leader in that category with 9. Mike Haynes, New England's Rookie-
of-the-Year candidate, was second with 8 steals.

Haynes also finished second behind Denver's Rick Upchurch in punt returns.
Upchurch led with a 13.7 average. Haynes' 608 yards were the most in Patriots'
history and his 13.5 average also set a club mark. Miami rookie Duriel Harris was
the AFC's leading kickoff returner with a 32.9 average.

Buffalo's Marv Bateman was the leading punter with a 42.8 average while Baltimore's David Lee won the first net punting game race with a 34.8 mark.

Following are the AFC's final individual statistics:

LEADING SCORERS

TOUCHDOWNS

	TDs	Rush.	Rec.	Ret.	Pts.
Harris, Pitt.	14	14	0	0	84
Grogan, N.E.	13	12	0	1	78
Branch, Oak.	12	0	12	0	72
Carr, Balt.	11	0	11	0	66
McCauley, Balt.	11	9	2	0	66
Casper, Oak.	10	0	10	0	60
Chandler, Buff.	10	0	10	0	60
Johnson, N.E.	10	6	4	0	60
Simpson, Buff.	9	8	1	0	54

KICKING

	EP/A	FG/A	LG	Pts.
Linhart, Balt.	49/50	20/27	41	109
Stenerud, K.C.	27/33	21/38	52	90
Smith, N.E.	42/46	15/25	49	87
Gerela, Pitt.	40/43	14/26	47	82
Bahr, Cin.	39/42	14/27	51	81
Turner, Den.	36/39	15/21	47	81
Yepremian, Mia.	29/31	16/23	53	77
Butler, Hou.	24/24	16/27	54	72
Cockroft, Clev.	27/30	15/28	51	72

BEST PERFORMANCE: 18 pts. on 3 TDs:
Reggie Rucker, Clev. vs N.Y.J. 9/12
Roger Carr, Balt. vs Cin. 9/19
Bob Chandler, Buff. vs K.C. 10/3

Morris Owens, T.B. vs Mia. 10/24
Rocky Bleier, Pitt. vs T.B. 12/5
Freddie Solomon, Mia. vs Buff. 12/5
Ed Podolak, K.C. vs Clev. 12/12

LEADING PASSERS
(140 attempts)

	Att.	Comp.	Pct. Comp.	Yds Gnd	Avg Yds Gained	TD Pass	Pct. TD	LP	Int.	Pct. Int.	Rating
Stabler, Oak.	291	194	66.7	2737	9.41	27	9.3	88	17	5.8	103.7
Jones, Balt.	343	207	60.3	3104	9.05	24	7.0	79	9	2.6	102.6
Ferguson, Buff.	151	74	49.0	1086	7.19	9	6.0	58	1	0.7	90.0
Griese, Mia.	272	162	59.6	2097	7.71	11	4.0	47	12	4.4	78.9
Livingston, K.C.	338	189	55.9	2682	7.93	12	3.6	57	13	3.8	77.9
Sipe, Clev.	312	178	57.1	2113	6.77	17	5.4	52	14	4.5	77.1
Anderson, Cin.	338	179	53.0	2367	7.00	19	5.6	85	14	4.1	77.0
Fouts, S.D.	359	208	57.9	2535	7.06	14	3.9	81	15	4.2	75.3
Pastorini, Hou.	309	167	54.0	1795	5.81	10	3.2	67	10	3.2	68.6
Bradshaw, Pitt.	192	92	47.9	1177	6.13	10	5.2	50	9	4.7	65.3
Ramsey, Den.	270	128	47.4	1931	7.15	11	4.1	71	13	4.8	65.1
Grogan, N.E.	302	145	48.0	1903	6.30	18	6.0	58	20	6.6	60.8
Spurrier, T.B.	311	156	50.2	1628	5.23	7	2.3	38	12	3.9	57.1
Namath, N.Y.	230	114	49.6	1090	4.74	4	1.7	35	16	7.0	39.7
Todd, N.Y.	162	65	40.1	870	5.37	3	1.9	44	12	7.4	33.4
Marangi, Buff.	232	82	35.3	998	4.30	7	3.0	39	16	6.9	30.7

LONGEST: 88 yds., Ken Stabler (to Cliff Branch), Oak. vs G.B. 10/24 - TD
Rating based on Pct. Comp.; Avg. Yds. Gained; Pct. TD; Pct. Int.

LEADING PASS RECEIVERS

	No.	Yards	Avg.	Long	TDs
Lane, K.C. (rb)	66	686	10.4	44	1
Chandler, Buff.	61	824	13.5	58	10
Mitchell, Balt. (rb)	60	555	9.3	40	3
Casper, Oak.	53	691	13.0	30	10
Burrough, Hou.	51	932	18.3	69	7
Joiner, S.D.	50	1056	21.1	81	7
Rucker, Clev.	49	676	13.8	45	8
White, K.C.	47	808	17.2	41	7
B. Johnson, Hou.	47	495	10.5	40	4
Young, S.D. (rb)	47	441	9.4	33	1
Branch, Oak.	46	1111	24.2	88	12
G. Pruitt, Clev. (rb)	45	341	7.6	27	1
Carr, Balt.	43	1112	25.9	79	11
Biletnikoff, Oak.	43	551	12.8	32	7
Curtis, Cin.	41	766	18.7	85	6
Gaines, N.Y. (rb)	41	400	9.8	27	2
Doughty, Balt.	40	628	15.7	41	5
Coleman, Hou. (rb)	40	247	6.2	19	3

BEST PERFORMANCE: 12 (136 yds.), Dave Casper, Oak. vs N.E. 10/3
12 (64 yds.), Lydell Mitchell, Balt. vs N.Y.J. 11/28 - 1 TD

INTERCEPTION LEADERS

	No.	Yards	Long	TDs
Riley, Cin.	9	141	53	1
Haynes, N.E.	8	90	28	0
Jackson, Den.	7	136	46	1
Darden, Clev.	7	73	21	0
Edwards, Pitt.	6	95	55	0
Goode, S.D.	6	82	27	0
Blount, Pitt.	6	75	28	0
McCray, N.E.	5	182	63	2
Greene, Buff.	5	135	101	1
Casanova, Cin.	5	109	33	2
Wallace, Balt.	5	105	41	0
Whittington, Hou.	5	103	50	0
Reardon, K.C.	5	26	22	0

LONGEST: 101 yds., Tony Greene, Buff. vs K.C. 10/3 - TD

LEADING RUSHERS

	Att.	Yards	Avg.	Long	TDs
Simpson, Buff.	290	1503	5.2	75	8
Mitchell, Balt.	289	1200	4.2	43	5
Harris, Pitt.	289	1128	3.9	30	14
Bleier, Pitt.	220	1036	4.7	28	5
van Eeghen, Oak.	233	1012	4.3	21	3
Armstrong, Den.	247	1008	4.1	31	5
G. Pruitt, Clev.	209	1000	4.8	64	4
Cunningham, N.E.	172	824	4.8	24	3
Young, S.D.	162	802	5.0	46	4
Malone, Mia.	186	797	4.3	31	4
Gaines, N.Y.	157	724	4.6	33	3
Calhoun, N.E.	129	721	5.6	54	1
Johnson, N.E.	169	699	4.1	69	6
Coleman, Hou.	171	684	4.0	39	2
Clark, Cin.	151	671	4.4	24	7
Griffin, Cin.	138	625	4.5	77	3
Miller, Clev.	153	613	4.0	21	4

BEST PERFORMANCE: 273 yds. (29 att.), O.J. Simpson, Buff. vs Det. 11/25 - 2 TDs
LONGEST: 77 yds., Archie Griffin, Cin. vs Hou. 11/21 - TD

LEADING PUNTERS

	No.	Yds.	Lg	Avg.	TB	Blk	Ret.	Ret Yds	In 20	Net Avg.
Bateman, Buff.	86	3678	78	42.8	14	1	52	878	16	29.0
Wilson, K.C.	65	2729	62	42.0	8	1	38	365	14	33.4
Guy, Oak.	67	2785	66	41.6	15	0	38	323	13	32.3
West, S.D.	38	1548	57	40.7	5	0	22	223	9	32.2
Patrick, N.E.	67	2688	52	40.1	12	0	37	288	12	32.2
Carrell, N.Y.	81	3218	72	39.7	6	0	55	463	13	32.5
D. Lee, Balt.	59	2342	56	39.7	3	0	33	231	21	34.8
McInally, Cin.	76	2999	61	39.5	6	0	41	323	12	33.6
Green, T.B.	92	3619	56	39.3	3	0	71	754	12	30.5
Walden, Pitt.	76	2982	58	39.2	13	0	36	206	22	33.1
Cockroft, Clev.	64	2487	51	38.9	4	3	44	503	9	28.4
Seiple, Mia.	62	2366	56	38.2	4	0	35	272	14	32.5
Hoopes, Hou.	49	1849	57	37.7	7	2	27	404	8	25.6
Pastorini, Hou.	70	2571	74	36.7	4	0	39	511	12	28.3
Weese, Den.	52	1852	55	35.6	1	0	25	226	5	30.9

LONGEST: 78 yds., Marv Bateman, Buff. vs Hou. 9/19

PUNT RETURN LEADERS

	No.	Yards	Avg.	Long	TDs
Upchurch, Den.	39	536	13.7	92	4
Haynes, N.E.	45	608	13.5	89	2
Fuller, S.D.	33	436	13.2	43	0
Brunson, K.C.	31	387	12.5	48	0
Colzie, Oak.	41	448	10.9	32	0
B. Johnson, Hou.	38	403	10.6	46	0
Moody, Buff.	16	166	10.4	67	1
Bell, Pitt.	39	390	10.0	35	0
Moore, Oak.	20	184	9.2	23	0
Deloplaine, Pitt.	17	150	8.8	36	0
Piccone, N.Y.	21	173	8.2	60	1
Stevens, Balt.	39	315	8.1	44	0
Shelby, Cin.	21	162	7.7	30	0
Reece, T.B.	20	143	7.2	30	0

LONGEST: 92 yds., Rick Upchurch, Den. vs S.D. 10/3 - TD

KICKOFF RETURN LEADERS

	No.	Yards	Avg.	Long	TDs
Harris, Mia.	17	559	32.9	69	0
Phillips, N.E.	14	397	28.4	71	0
Perrin, Den.	14	391	27.9	43	0
Williams, K.C.	25	688	27.5	64	0
Jennings, Oak.	16	417	26.1	55	0
Shelby, Cin.	30	761	25.4	97	1
Holden, Clev.	19	461	24.3	44	0
Davis, Mia.	26	617	23.7	47	0
Stevens, Balt.	30	710	23.7	83	0
Upchurch, Den.	22	514	23.4	64	0
Moody, Buff.	26	605	23.3	41	0
Feacher, Clev.	24	551	23.0	46	0
Giammona, N.Y.	23	527	22.9	34	0
Hooks, Buff.	23	521	22.7	79	0
Deloplaine, Pitt.	17	385	22.7	39	0

LONGEST: 97 yds., Willie Shelby, Cin. vs Clev. 10/3 - TD

Conference and the National Football Conference—issues weekly news releases, based in part on statistics amassed by the Elias Sports Bureau.

In the example shown here—the AFC release for the week ending December 13, 1976—summarizes the highlights of what had taken place and what events were coming up. (The NFC has similar information in its release for the same period.) The first page offers a few interesting notes on the leaders in each department, pointing to forthcoming confrontations of leaders in the playoffs. On subsequent pages are listings of the leading players in touchdowns, kicking, passing, pass reception, interceptions, rushing, punting, punt returning, etc.

Releases are sent not only to each of the teams, but to newspapers and broadcasters as well. This provides raw material for many of the stories you see in your daily papers.

Monday Night Football

THE MOST TRYING experience I've ever had in my career as a statistician was working with "Monday Night Football," the weekly ABC program, in 1970. Because it was the first time that pro football had ever been regularly scheduled for prime-time television, we wanted to make a big impression on the viewing public. Consequently, there was a lot of pressure, not only on me, but on everyone connected with the broadcasts, including the announcers—Don Meredith, Keith Jackson and the incomparable Howard Cosell. The tension was especially thick in the control booth where people would be screaming at each other, trying to get everything exactly right.

We'd go through all sorts of rehearsals in the afternoon, and discuss what types of data and stats would be pertinent to the particular game. Then I'd get into the booth at about 8:00 P.M., an hour before game time, and because those games ran longer than most pro football contests, I very often didn't leave my seat until midnight. With three play-by-play announcers, a spotter and myself crammed into a small broadcast booth, it was awfully congested, and tempers were put to the test.

It took two or three hours for us to unwind after those games. We'd go out for a drink and talk about how the game had gone, what kind of job we thought we had done, what the ratings were likely to be, whether the game was close enough to be interesting, etc. It wasn't until the wee hours of the morning that everyone connected with the broadcast could loosen up.

In all sports broadcasts, the big ingredient is the mutual respect that a statistican has with his announcer. In the case of "Monday Night Football," we weren't used to working with each other; we got together only once a week. Also, there were the special demands of football—national, prime-time-TV football, at that—so it got rough at times.

I wore two different sets of headphones. On one I'd be hooked up to the official statistician in the press box, getting information from him. The other phone connected me to the videograph room. To the people there, I'd keep sending updated information so that when O. J. Simpson was shown in a close-up, we'd flash on the screen that he had carried the ball 16 times for 72 yards and two touchdowns. Or that Roger Staubach had completed 12 out of 18 passes for 65 yards, with one touchdown and two interceptions.

As I mentioned earlier, on a completed pass you'd have to mark down a reception for the receiver, the yards gained, a pass completion for the quarterback and how many yards he got on the completion. You have to make sure you put down a first down for him and add on yards to the particular march. And I'd have to get updated information like this down to the videograph room within a matter of seconds after every play, while keeping our play-by-play and color broadcasters constantly informed.

On "Monday Night Football" we kept all kinds of stats:

On each *passer,* we kept pass attempts and completions, how many yards his passes gained, how many touchdowns they accounted for and how many of his passes were intercepted.

On each *receiver,* we kept how many passes he caught and for how many yards, and how many touchdowns were involved.

On each *running back,* we kept the rushing attempts, the yardage, the touchdowns and number of fumbles.

On each *punter,* we kept how many times he punted, how many yards each punt went and his average yardage per punt. Sometimes we'd also keep a record of how many yards each of his kicks was run back. (You've always got to keep in mind where the line of scrimmage was, so that you can compute instantly the yardage the punt traveled from scrimmage.)

On each *punt returner,* we kept a record of how many punts he returned, the yardage on each, his total yardage and the average return per punt.

On each *kickoff returner,* we kept a record of how many kickoffs he returned, the yardage on each, his total yardage and the average return per kickoff.

I also kept the number of *penalties* for each team, and how much each team was penalized.

238

Also recorded were the number of *turnovers* by each team, how many yards were involved, how many of the turnovers were fumbles and how many were interceptions.

We also kept track of all the *first downs;* how many times each quarterback was tackled while passing *(sacks);* and how each team did in *third-down situations,* that is, whether or not they made first downs on those plays.

An important record, of course, was an up-to-the-minute chart of how the scoring went in the game. For instance, the Jets scored first on a seven-yard run by John Riggins. In parentheses, we might add the number of plays and yardage gained on the touchdown march—for example, "17 plays for 81 yards."

Some of this material never got used, but a lot of it was. In any event, it was necessary to be prepared for just about any kind of request at any time. We were, after all, working with network people, and they're heavy hitters.

Keeping stats for a network TV presentation of the "Monday Night Football" variety is the ultimate job for a statistician. The pay was good and the prestige was gratifying. Despite that, and though I enjoyed being part of that first-year experiment, it really wasn't fun for me.

I was on a whirlwind schedule, working and traveling too much. In 1970 I'd work a Knick basketball game in Madison Square Garden on Saturday night. Next morning I'd get up about eight o'clock and go into the Ranger office in the Garden, where I'd get all my hockey stats updated for the Ranger game that night. At about 11:30 in the morning, I'd hop on the Flushing train and go out to Shea Stadium to work the Jets football game. After the Jets were finished, at about 4:30 in the afternoon, I'd shoot back on the train in order to get back to the Garden about an hour and a half before that night's Ranger game. I'd work the Ranger game, go home, sleep fast and wake up with the roosters the following morning. A driver would be waiting for me to hustle me in his taxi to the airport, where I would catch the earliest possible plane to whatever city was the site of that night's "Monday Night Football" game. Sometimes it might be a relatively nearby city, such as Philadelphia, Washington or Baltimore, but often it was as far away as Dallas or Houston.

After the game I'd stay overnight in the football city, and Tuesday morning, after a few hours' sleep, get up to catch the earliest available plane back to New York, where I'd go directly to the Ranger office. I'd spend the day there, then work a Knick game that night—and finally, after that was over, go home. On Wednesday I'd put in another fifteen-hour day because usually there was a hockey game I'd have to work that night. Good thing there are no baseball games played that time of year.

239

I suspect the frantic pace set a record for most games, miles and statistics computed by one man in the most major sports within a week—but I'd rather do without it.

The pressure and traveling were too much, and I gave up "Monday Night Football" at the end of the year. Until 1973 I continued with Jets games and an occasional freelance football stats assignment, but since '73, I do stats almost exclusively for baseball and hockey.

BASKETBALL

Basketball

THE FIRST PROFESSIONAL statistical work I did was at a basketball game between the Knicks and the Detroit Pistons in 1961. I was paid five dollars for my services.

As I mentioned, Marty Glickman was doing the Knick games, while Marv Albert was Marty's protegé, waiting in the wings to get his crack at broadcasting. On this particular day, Marty had another commitment, so Jim Gordon did the broadcast.

For five or six years, I worked a lot of basketball games, serving the out-of-town announcers, most of whom did not carry their own statisticians with them.

Too much happens too fast in a basketball game—especially a professional one, where more than two hundred points are scored—for an announcer to keep his own stats. As a result, there are many opportunities for a statistician to break into basketball. This is especially true in New York, where there are so many college games in addition to the pros. Eventually I did stats for the Knicks, including the years they won their championships (1970–71 and 1972–73). As enjoyable as it was, I had to give it up, because my workload was too heavy.

Much of my time with the Knicks, I worked the games down in the control room with the videograph. It is of prime importance that the score of the game is updated and flashed after every basket. This saves the broadcaster the trouble of announcing the score all the time.

243

When you work in the TV control room, you also have to update all the other stats. In addition, you have to make sure that the operator of the videograph machine knows who scored the points and has updated his scoreboard accordingly. It's very embarrassing to give a score that's not correct.

Non-Stop Action

Keeping basketball stats is not easy, because there's constant change of figures—almost every thirty seconds (especially with the 24-second clock in the pro game, which requires a team to shoot within that time or give up the ball). As with football, you can't lose your concentration for a moment, or you're going to miss a basket or rebound, turnover or assist.

In the space of ten seconds, you might have to make a half-dozen different notations. A player brings the ball up and misses the shot; you enter that on the player's record as an attempted shot. One of his teammates grabs the rebound, takes a shot and misses; now he must be given credit for a rebound plus another shot attempt. This time, someone on the other team brings down the rebound; he is credited for a rebound. He throws upcourt to a teammate, but the ball is stolen. The player who makes the steal has to be given credit for that, while the other team is charged with a turnover. The player who made the steal throws the ball downcourt to a teammate, who feeds another teammate cutting across the key for an easy lay-up. You have to record the basket, change the team's point total, change the basket-maker's point total and credit the man who fed him with an assist.

And don't take too much time doing all this, because the other team is racing downcourt and shooting.

At the end of the half and the end of the game, of course, broadcasters will run down the scoring. At the end of the half, if eight or nine players have made it to the scoring column, you don't have much time to get everything tallied, correct and legible.

In baseball there isn't much crossing out or erasing to do—you just keep score of the game as it goes along and simply cross out and update batting averages as players have their turn at bat. In basketball, though, you're continually crossing out and erasing to update a player's totals. Even if you're only dealing with his points scored, you have to leave yourself a lot of room; you never know when someone is going to erupt with a forty-point game.

Keeping Score

There are different ways of keeping score of a basketball game and its various components. In the Field Goals Attempted (FGA) and Field Goals Made (FGM) columns, I draw a vertical line for each marker. When the number reaches five, I draw a slash through the preceding four vertical lines.

Field Goals Attempted   Field Goals Made

-ͱͱͱ ͱͱͱ ͱͱͱ I I   -ͱͱͱ I I

I do the same thing with assists.

For the points that each player and both teams score, I merely put a slash through the already printed number corresponding to the most recent score.

Points

1 2 3 4 5 6 7 8 9 10
11 12 13 14 15 16 17 18
19 20 21 22 23 24 25 26

When working a basketball game, I number individual index cards ten through thirty, so that when a player reaches a high point total, I just put the appropriate index card in front of the announcer. If Earl Monroe has just scored his twentieth point I'll put the card with number twenty on it in front of the announcer, so he can report, "That basket brought the Pearl's point total to twenty."

Scoring Championship

The scoring championship in the National Basketball Association is based on per-game average (providing the player has scored at least 1,400 points during the regular season).

The contest for top scoring honors came down to the very last day of the 1977–78 regular season, with spectacular performances by the two top contenders forcing statisticians to take their per-game averages to an extra decimal point.

On the afternoon of Sunday, April 9, 1978, David Thompson of the Denver Nuggets poured in 73 points against the Detroit Pistons. This gave him a season's total of 2,172 points in 80 games, an average of 27.15 points per game. It looked as if Thompson had locked up the scoring title.

That night, however, George Gervin of the San Antonio Spurs responded with 63 points against the New Orleans Jazz. This gave him a season's total of 2,232 points in 82 games, an average of 27.22 points per game—and the championship.

Thompson's 73 points tied as the third-highest total for a single game in the league's thirty-two-year history. Wilt Chamberlain, while playing for the Philadelphia Warriors in a 1962 game against the Knicks, scored 100 points, the highest single-game total in NBA history.

Until the last day of the 1977–78 season, Chamberlain's 31 points in one quarter had been a league record. Then Thompson scored 32 points in the first period, which broke Wilt's record, and a few hours later Gervin broke Thompson's record, with 33 points in the second period of his game.

Both Gervin and Thompson were helped by their teammates, who fed them the ball at every opportunity. However, when Gervin scored enough to clinch the title (59 points, one more than needed) he was given an eight-minute rest. The Spurs played a normal game in the fourth period, without trying to feed him.

Even if another player has a higher point total, the scoring championship would go to the man with the best per-game average. For example, in 1977–78, Calvin Murphy outscored Kareem Abdul-Jabbar, 1949 points to 1600. But Abdul-Jabbar did his scoring in 62 games, for a per-game average of 25.8, while Murphy averaged 25.6 in 76 games. Abdul-Jabbar thus finished fourth and Murphy, fifth. Bob McAdoo was third with a 26.5 per-game average.

Definition of Terms

Let's go over the definitions of some of the terms used in basketball statistics.

Turnover. A relatively new statistic, a turnover is charged whenever the offensive team loses possession of the ball without attempting either a field goal or a free throw. It's not considered a turnover when a quarter expires before a team can get off a field goal or free throw. Usually, the team with a lot of turnovers will lose the game.

There are twenty different ways a team can be charged with a turnover. Among them are losing the ball on a *three-second violation,* meaning one of its players was in the offensive foul lane for at least three seconds; a *five-second violation,* charged when a team does not throw the ball in-bounds within five seconds; a *ten-second violation,* not getting the ball across the midcourt line in ten seconds; a *24-second violation,* not attempting a field goal within the twenty-four seconds allotted in pro ball after a team has gained possession of the ball; *palming the ball; double-dribble; discontinued dribble; a back-court violation; stepping out of bounds; offensive goaltending; losing the ball with a bad pass.*

Steal. A steal is another relatively new statistic, and many fans aren't quite sure under what circumstances a player is credited with one.

According to the NBA rules, a player shall be credited with a steal whenever he takes the ball away from an opponent by any legal means, whether it's intercepting a pass or deflecting a dribble away from an opponent. (If he bats the ball away and it goes out of bounds and remains in possession of the other team, it's obviously not a steal.)

There are times when two players cooperate in a steal. For instance, supposing player A taps a ball away from player Z, and the ball is recovered by player B, who is A's teammate. The scoring on that would be a turnover for player Z and a steal for player A, since he is the one who caused the turnover and created the opportunity for his teammate to recover the loose ball.

Field-Goal Attempt. A field-goal attempt is charged to a player anytime he shoots, throws or taps the ball at the basket when, in the opinion of the scorer, he is attempting to score a field goal. If he should be fouled in the act of shooting and not make the field goal, he is not charged with a field-goal attempt. If he is fouled on the shot and the basket is made and counts, he is charged with a field-goal attempt and, of course, credited with the basket.

If a player passes the ball to a teammate and the pass inadvertently hits the rim or the backboard, it does not constitute a shot, and therefore the player is not charged with an attempted shot. This is another case of official scorer's judgment, which develops with experience.

Should a player take a shot that doesn't hit either the rim or the backboard (something that happens only occasionally), and if, in the opinion of the scorer, it was obviously a field-goal attempt, you would charge the shooter with a field-goal attempt. In addition, the player who recovers the ball would be credited with a rebound, even though in this kind of situation the 24-second clock is not reset.

A blocked shot is also counted as an attempted field goal.

When a player who is under the basket when a shot is missed by a teammate tries to tip the ball up and score a basket in one motion, he is credited with a rebound on the play, but also is charged with a field-goal attempt, since he tipped the ball up with the intention of scoring.

If a player tips in a missed free throw by a teammate, he is credited with a rebound and a successful field-goal attempt.

Once in a while, a player accidentally puts the ball into his own basket (Earl Monroe of the Knicks did it in the final second of a game late in the 1976–77 season). When this happens, you credit the opponent nearest the goal with a basket *and* field-goal attempt. (A player can't logically score more baskets than the number he attempted.) If two players were equally close to the basket, award the field goal to the more pleasant one or the one who needs the points more.

Free-Throw Attempt. Anytime a player has a chance to score on a foul shot, he is charged with a free-throw attempt, with certain exceptions. In a situation where he is given three chances to make two (foul shots), he is charged with three free-throw attempts (unless he makes his first two). If he makes a free throw, but it's nullified because a teammate stepped into the foul lane too soon, you do not charge the shooter with a free-throw attempt. But you *do* charge his team with a turnover. When the defensive team is called for a free-throw violation (say, a defensive player has moved into the foul lane too soon), and if the foul shot is made despite the violation, the shooter is charged with an attempt and credited with the point. If the shot is not made, he is not charged with a free-throw attempt, since the violation entitles him to another free throw.

Assists. An assist is credited to a player tossing the *last* pass that leads directly to a field goal—and only if the player receiving the pass scores in response to it, as evidenced by his immediate action toward the basket. This is one more instance where a scorer's keen judgment comes into play. In other words, if Dave Cowens whips a pass to Jo Jo White, who immediately drives toward the hoop and scores, Cowens gets an assist. But if Jo Jo takes Cowens's pass, dribbles over to the corner, stops and then, with the 24-second clock running out, takes a successful jump shot, Cowens does not get an assist.

The same principle applies to the player feeding a pivot man, who then scores. Say Earl Monroe passes the ball into Bob McAdoo, who dribbles once, gives a head fake, and scores. You would credit Monroe with an assist because the continuity had not been broken by the one dribble and head fake. But if Doug Collins passed the ball to Julius Erving, who dribbled the ball more than once, stopped, faked and then scored, you would not credit Collins with an assist because the continuity was broken by the action Erving took to get position on his opponent. There has to be *immediate* reaction on the part of the shooter attempting to score.

An in-bounds pass can involve an assist if it leads directly to a goal. A good example is the "alley-oop" play where the player in-bounding throws a high pass to a teammate near the basket. The teammate goes up, takes the ball and scores in virtually one motion. In that instance, the player throwing the ball in would be credited with an assist.

Only one assist may be credited on a field goal.

Rebounds. A statistical category that sometimes requires perceptive judgment by the scorer is rebounding. A rebound is credited to a player or team each time a ball is retrieved after a field-goal attempt or free-throw attempt is missed. An *offensive rebound* is credited to a player each time he retrieves the ball after a missed field-goal or free-throw attempt by one of his teammates. A *defensive rebound* is credited when the ball is retrieved after an opponent misses a field-goal or foul-throw attempt.

If a player should go up for a rebound and, instead of catching the ball, tap it, volleyball style, to an opponent, he would be credited with a rebound.

As mentioned, a player who tips up the ball and scores after a teammate misses a shot is credited with a rebound as well as a basket. If he tips it up and it doesn't go in, he is credited with the rebound.

Blocked Shots. Another relatively new official statistic kept by the National Basketball Association is the category called blocked shots. You would credit a player with a blocked shot when he deflects the course of an obvious attempt at a field goal by an opposing player, causing the shot to be missed. In such an instance, the shooter would be charged with a field-goal attempt, and the player on either team who retrieved the ball would be credited with a rebound—an offensive rebound if the ball is retrieved by a teammate of the shooter.

If the ball is blocked and knocked out-of-bounds with the shooting team retaining possession, the blocker still gets credit for a blocked shot, but no rebound is credited.

It was in the 1973–74 season that a player's rebounds, which had previously been carried in a lump sum, were broken down into offensive and defensive rebounds. That same season, in response to demands from the public and members of the media, two other interesting statistics—steals and blocked shots—were added to the official league stats. The top ten NBA players in those categories are now listed along with leaders in categories kept prior to 1973–74: a player's games, minutes played, field goals attempted and made, percentage of field goals made, free throws attempted and made, free-throw percentage and rebounds. Many newspapers now also print the leading teams in defense, with how many points they allow each game, and the leading teams in offense, including how many points they average per game.

All the new statistics make things more interesting but also more difficult for the statistician, who has to keep track of that many more items during a basketball game.

Jump-Ball Records. Some clubs keep records of how each team does in jump balls. Like records of success in hockey face-offs, this is an inexact, almost intangible kind of statistic. If a player appears to win the tap and gets it to a teammate, who immediately loses control of the ball, should the first player receive credit for winning the tap? Similarly, on a hockey face-off, a player may appear to win the puck, but the teammate he taps it to gets pushed off the puck or outraced for it and loses control. Statistics like these have some meaning, but not very much.

Basketball Plus-Minus. I suppose the premier statistician as far as the NBA is concerned is Harvey Pollack in Philadelphia. He keeps more basketball stats than anyone I know. He has even devised a plus-minus system for pro basketball players. Simply, it measures a player's all-around efficiency by crediting him with a point every time his team scores when he's on the floor (field goal or foul shot), and charging him with a point every time the opposition scores when he's on the floor.

I like the idea and I think fans will like it, too. It has value because all of a team's players have probably done something right in order for the team to score. Eventually, I think, the idea will be adopted—not necessarily as an official item, but as something individual clubs will use for the fans and media.

Minutes Played. An official record kept is of the number of minutes a player is in the game. Time is computed by full minutes only and rounded off to the nearest minute. Seconds added to one player's time, in order to bring his total to a full figure, are subtracted from the time of the man he replaces. For example, if Earl Monroe replaced Jim Cleamons with 2:15 left in the quarter, and played out the quarter, Cleamons would be credited with ten minutes of playing time and Monroe with only two minutes of playing time. Or if Bob McAdoo replaced

Spencer Haywood with 2:45 remaining in the quarter and played the remainder of the period, McAdoo would be credited with three minutes of playing time, Haywood with nine minutes.

The only exception to rounding off time to the nearest minute is when a player comes into a quarter for just a few seconds. He's then given credit for a full minute, even if he plays just a second or two. There is no carry-over of partial minutes from one quarter to another. In each twelve-minute quarter, a team's minutes played must add up to sixty (twelve minutes multiplied by five players), and must add up to twenty-five minutes for any five-minute overtime period.

There are fans and others who would like to see some formula worked out whereby you can tell a player's scoring productivity per minute played, rather than per game. Their contention is that a player may have only a seven-point-per-game scoring average, but if he's only playing fifteen minutes per game, his scoring production is pretty good.

Obviously, this doesn't tell the whole story either. Among other factors, you'd have to consider shooting effectiveness. One man may score eight points on ten shots, while another scores twenty but has taken thirty shots.

Official Scorer

Just as in hockey, the official scorer at an NBA game is selected by the home team, subject to the approval of the Commissioner. The scorer usually has three or four assistants working the game with him.

Under his direction, summaries and scoresheets are distributed to all members of the media at halftime, and sometimes after each quarter. At the conclusion of the game, final-summary scoresheets are given out, which include all the categories mentioned earlier. Copies of the summary are mailed into the league office, and it is from these that the league compiles its statistics.

The Elias Sports Bureau is the official statistician for the NBA, and as such, receives a copy of the official scoresheet. League stats are updated on the basis of these official scoresheets.

There are going to be instances when one scorer will award an assist, blocked shot or even a rebound where another scorer might not.

As a result, when I work basketball games, I'm usually busy at halftime, checking my stats against the official scorer's. In some cases, I might not agree with his decisions, but since his records are official and mine are not, I will change mine to the way the official scorer has decided the play should be scored.

Decisions as to whether a player has been given an assist or blocked shot are almost never announced in basketball arenas.

Elias Basketball Reports

Once a week—usually on Mondays—the Elias Sports Bureau issues weekly stat sheets that report on the performance of every team and player in the National Basketball Association in every conceivable basketball category. The NBA then disseminates the stat sheets, which are preceded by a news or feature story relating to a recent statistical accomplishment (such as McAdoo scoring his ten-thousandth NBA point).

Team standings are given, along with a breakdown of what each team has done against every other team in the league. All the team statistics are given, including shooting percentages, rebounds on offense and defense, steals, blocked shots, turnovers, disqualifications (fouled out of game), points and average. Also given is the differential between the per-game average of points scored by a team and the per-game average of points scored against it. Thus, San Antonio, which in fifty-four games had averaged 114.1 points while its opponents had averaged 114.2 points against it, had a −0.1 scoring differential.

Individual scoring leaders are given in a variety of categories—most-points-per-game average, highest field-goal percentage, highest free-throw percentage, as well as leaders in rebounds, blocked shots, assists and steals. Individual and team highs are given in various categories.

Then, listed by team, is every player in the NBA and his season record in every conceivable basketball statistical category—games and minutes played, field goals made and attempted, foul shots made and attempted, offensive and defensive rebounding, assists, personal fouls, disqualifications (''DQ'') or times fouled out of a game, steals (''ST''), blocked shots, cumulative point total for the season and per-game point average. If you look at the Atlanta listings, you'll note that John Drew is averaging 22.6 points per game. In the last column ''HI'' refers to the player's high point total of the season, which in Drew's case was 42. He had hit on 49.1 percent of his field-goal attempts. He was making his foul shots at a rate of 71.5 percent.

In addition, there are assorted notes of interest that might be picked up by sportswriters and broadcasters.

NATIONAL BASKETBALL ASSOCIATION

TWO PENNSYLVANIA PLAZA ● SUITE 2010 ● NEW YORK, N.Y. 10001 ● 212-594-3000

FOR RELEASE: 6:30 PM (EST), Monday, Feb. 14, 1977

McADOO'S 10,000th POINT PLACES HIM IN EXCLUSIVE COMPANY

NEW YORK--On Feb. 9, Bob McAdoo played the 358th game of his NBA career and scored his 10,000th point. The historic event took place when McAdoo and his New York Knick teammates were playing the Indiana Pacers at Market Square Center in Indianapolis.

Only four players in the history of the Association have reached the 10,000-point plateau in fewer games than it took "Big Mac" to reach it.

Of course Wilt Chamberlain heads the list having scored his 10,000th in his 236th game. Next comes Elgin Baylor who reached the mark in his 315th game. It took the number three man on the list, Kareem Abdul-Jabbar, 319 games to get there and Oscar Robertson, number four, needed 334 games.

McAdoo's mark of 358 games just nosed out Rick Barry who took 360 games to break into five figures.

McAdoo, Abdul-Jabbar of Los Angeles and Golden State's Barry are all in the top twenty in scoring according to NBA statistics released today.

Pete Maravich of New Orleans continues to lead the league in scoring with a 29.9 average based on 1463 points scored in 49 games.

Abdul-Jabbar is the field goal percentage leader with a mark of .586 and Ernie DiGregorio leads in free throw percentage with .943.

Portland's Bill Walton held on to his leadership in rebounds and blocked shots with 15.3 rebounds per game and 3.46 blocked shots. Abdul-Jabbar is second in both categories with marks of 14.1 and 3.02 respectively.

Don Buse of Indiana continues to lead the league in assists and steals, averaging 8.7 assists per game and 3.49 steals.

STANDINGS
(Including games played Friday, February 11, 1977)

	Atl.	Bos.	Buf.	Chi.	Cle.	Den.	Det.	G.S.	Hou.	Ind.	K.C.	L.A.	Mil.	N.O.	NYK.	NYN.	Phi.	Pho.	Por.	S.A.	Sea.	Was.	WON	LOST	PCT.	G.B.
ATLANTIC																										
Philadelphia	2	3	1	1	1	2	1	1	2	2	2	2	-	3	2	2	-	1	1	-	-	2	33	20	.623	-
Boston	2	-	3	1	-	2	-	2	1	1	2	3	1	2	2	-	-	1	2	1	-	2	26	27	.491	7
Knicks	2	1	1	1	2	1	1	3	2	-	-	3	1	-	1	-	2	1	1	1	-	2	24	29	.453	9
Buffalo	-	1	-	1	1	3	-	1	-	1	2	1	1	2	2	1	-	2	-	-	-	2	19	33	.365	13½
Nets	1	1	1	1	-	1	2	-	-	-	1	2	1	-	1	1	-	1	-	1	-	1	17	36	.321	16
CENTRAL																										
Washington	2	2	1	1	1	2	1	1	3	2	-	2	1	1	2	-	2	2	1	1	-	-	30	22	.577	-
Houston	3	1	1	3	1	-	2	1	-	2	1	1	2	-	1	1	1	2	2	2	2	2	29	23	.558	1
Cleveland	-	2	1	1	-	1	1	1	2	2	2	4	1	2	2	1	1	-	1	1	1	1	28	24	.538	2
San Antonio	-	3	1	1	1	2	2	1	2	2	-	1	1	2	1	2	2	2	2	-	2	1	29	25	.537	2
New Orleans	3	2	1	-	1	-	3	2	1	1	-	1	-	2	1	-	1	1	1	1	1	2	24	30	.444	7
Atlanta	-	3	2	2	1	-	-	1	-	1	1	2	1	-	2	-	-	3	2	1	-	-	22	34	.393	10
MIDWEST																										
Denver	-	1	3	2	-	1	1	1	2	2	1	3	3	1	2	1	2	1	1	4	2		34	19	.642	-
Detroit	3	2	1	2	2	1	-	2	1	2	4	-	2	3	1	2	1	1	1	-	1	-	32	23	.582	3
Kansas City	2	1	2	2	1	-	2	1	1	-	1	1	1	3	2	1	2	1	1	1	1	1	28	28	.500	7½
Indiana	2	2	2	2	1	-	1	-	-	-	1	1	1	3	2	1	-	2	1	-		2	25	30	.455	10
Chicago	1	1	1	-	1	-	1	-	1	1	1	3	3	1	1	1	1	-	3	1	1	2	23	32	.418	12
Milwaukee	1	-	1	1	-	-	-	2	1	-	2	-	-	-	-	3	1	1	2	1	1	-	17	42	.288	20
PACIFIC																										
Los Angeles	1	2	1	1	2	2	1	1	2	3	-	3	2	1	2	1	1	3	2	1	2		35	19	.648	-
Portland	1	2	3	2	2	1	1	1	3	2	-	1	1	3	1	1	2	1	1	1	-	1	35	21	.625	1
Golden State	3	2	2	2	1	2	1	-	1	2	-	1	1	1	1	1	1	3	1	1	1	2	30	24	.556	5
Seattle	2	1	1	2	1	-	2	2	-	2	1	1	2	2	1	2	2	1	1	1	-	2	29	26	.527	6½
Phoenix	3	2	1	2	1	1	1	-	1	2	-	1	2	1	1	1	1	-	-	1	2	1	25	27	.481	9

		FIELD GOALS			FREE THROWS			REBOUNDS			MISCELLANEOUS			Blk	Turn		SCORING	
Team	G	Made	Att.	Pct.	Made	Att.	Pct.	Off.	Def.	Tot.	Asst	PF	Stl	Sh.	Over	DQ	Pts.	Avg.
S.A.	54	2396	5038	.476	1369	1708	.802	750	1684	2434	1304	1330	594	329	1190	25	6161	114.1
Den.	53	2343	4867	.481	1283	1788	.718	888	1763	2651	1436	1350	620	302	1317	10	5969	112.6
G.S.	54	2449	5134	.477	1123	1477	.760	858	1730	2588	1390	1379	599	292	1115	14	6021	111.5
Det.	55	2572	5253	.490	960	1282	.749	775	1682	2457	1389	1498	594	308	1144	28	6104	111.0
Port.	56	2461	5117	.481	1276	1684	.758	848	1894	2742	1341	1490	606	346	1235	28	6198	110.7
L.A.	54	2436	5052	.482	995	1326	.750	777	1764	2541	1325	1225	510	294	1034	9	5867	108.6
Phil.	53	2226	4652	.479	1303	1776	.734	814	1809	2623	1210	1336	521	380	1275	8	5755	108.6
Mil.	59	2606	5662	.460	1115	1493	.747	880	1776	2656	1375	1526	558	247	1199	22	6327	107.2
Knicks	53	2348	4905	.479	968	1281	.756	660	1718	2378	1274	1272	430	206	1061	10	5664	106.9
Ind.	55	2356	5322	.443	1154	1558	.741	989	1773	2762	1324	1379	604	330	1112	28	5866	106.7
K.C.	56	2403	5241	.459	1151	1421	.810	815	1738	2553	1367	1486	585	274	1095	24	5957	106.4
Buff.	52	2150	4790	.449	1229	1624	.757	777	1692	2469	1151	1432	443	231	1132	10	5529	106.3
Sea.	55	2348	5187	.453	1102	1582	.697	938	1615	2553	1245	1487	639	338	1209	16	5798	105.4
Hou.	52	2227	4571	.487	1019	1310	.778	763	1616	2379	1245	1359	389	250	1035	21	5473	105.3
Bos.	53	2232	5001	.446	1082	1445	.749	819	1900	2719	1260	1313	328	179	1110	34	5546	104.6
N.O.	54	2255	5001	.451	1130	1468	.770	822	1845	2667	1204	1402	413	220	1142	19	5640	104.4
Wash.	52	2194	4712	.466	1019	1431	.712	789	1721	2510	1193	1246	402	279	1085	10	5407	104.0
Phoe.	52	2120	4618	.459	1157	1525	.759	716	1598	2314	1271	1334	479	219	1164	19	5397	103.8
Atl.	56	2273	4968	.458	1237	1653	.748	855	1699	2554	1271	1547	533	230	1208	42	5783	103.3
Clev.	52	2172	4900	.443	946	1256	.753	864	1661	2525	1161	1225	368	298	907	17	5290	101.7
Chi.	55	2139	4826	.443	1037	1403	.739	888	1795	2683	1269	1281	453	209	1077	23	5315	96.6
Nets	53	1999	4648	.430	1108	1489	.744	719	1611	2330	920	1424	520	264	1001	32	5106	96.3

TEAM STATISTICS - DEFENSE

Allowed by:	FIELD GOALS			FREE THROWS			REBOUNDS			MISCELLANEOUS			Blk	Turn		SCORING		
Team	Made	Att.	Pct.	Made	Att.	Pct.	Off.	Def.	Tot.	Asst	PF	Stl	Sh.	Over	DQ	Pts.	Avg.	Dif.
Chi.	2205	4680	.471	1008	1343	.751	696	1731	2427	1299	1437	528	308	1071	36	5418	98.5	-1.9
Clev.	2071	4674	.443	1099	1459	.753	784	1723	2507	1064	1217	449	262	998	11	5372	100.8	+0.9
Nets	2066	4481	.461	1240	1653	.750	739	1909	2648	1162	1304	485	328	1138	13	5372	101.4	+1.8
Phoe.	2045	4512	.453	1216	1596	.762	727	1672	2399	1123	1499	553	271	1187	25	5306	102.0	+1.8
Wash.	2233	4864	.459	950	1258	.755	736	1600	2336	1198	1318	518	214	972	21	5416	104.2	-0.2
Phil.	2262	5133	.441	997	1313	.759	932	1564	2496	1246	1421	548	232	1129	26	5521	104.2	+4.4
Port.	2308	5096	.453	1218	1639	.743	850	1716	2566	1224	1532	585	315	1217	28	5834	104.2	+6.5
L.A.	2313	5182	.446	1000	1319	.758	899	1707	2606	1239	1211	493	211	1049	16	5626	104.2	+4.4
Hou.	2185	4650	.470	1093	1415	.772	723	1375	2098	1186	1257	325	221	878	20	5463	105.1	+0.2
K.C.	2299	4899	.469	1303	1714	.760	752	1868	2620	1151	1389	505	265	1225	22	5901	105.4	+1.0
Sea.	2267	4955	.458	1268	1683	.753	870	1743	2613	1367	1426	490	309	1330	17	5802	105.5	-0.1
N.O.	2260	5026	.450	1232	1642	.750	880	1823	2703	1108	1442	544	250	1137	24	5752	106.5	-2.1
Bos.	2331	5153	.452	995	1331	.748	738	1778	2516	1227	1277	459	246	904	17	5657	106.7	-2.1
Den.	2345	5064	.463	975	1361	.716	825	1570	2395	1315	1469	612	311	1254	20	5665	106.9	+5.7
Ind.	2389	5142	.465	1149	1516	.758	923	1869	2792	1383	1389	493	326	1217	14	5927	107.8	-1.1
Atl.	2362	4926	.479	1316	1750	.752	807	1782	2589	1369	1489	533	285	1177	34	6040	107.9	-4.6
Knicks	2314	4938	.469	1100	1468	.749	782	1770	2552	1169	1262	491	269	1017	9	5728	108.1	-1.2
G.S.	2374	5014	.473	1134	1534	.739	828	1711	2539	1404	1287	519	263	1184	14	5882	108.9	+2.6
Buff.	2403	5058	.475	937	1252	.748	805	1732	2537	1343	1409	476	291	1081	24	5743	110.4	-4.1
Det.	2411	5104	.472	1275	1690	.754	896	1741	2637	1327	1220	530	264	1222	12	6097	110.9	+0.1
Mil.	2681	5602	.479	1251	1688	.741	941	1905	2846	1587	1408	518	303	1205	18	6613	112.1	-4.9
S.A.	2581	5312	.486	1007	1356	.743	871	1795	2666	1391	1458	534	281	1255	26	6169	114.2	-0.1

DQ = Individual players disqualified (fouled out of game).

INDIVIDUAL SCORING LEADERS
(Minimum 46 games played) or 920 points

	G	FG	FT	PTS	AVG.		G	FG	FT	PTS	AVG.
Maravich, N.O.	49	567	329	1463	29.9	Tomjanovich, Hou.	52	487	192	1166	22.4
Abdul-Jabbar, L.A.	54	609	250	1468	27.2	Boone, K.C.	56	517	218	1252	22.4
Knight, Ind.	51	540	274	1354	26.5	Westphal, Phoe.	51	429	242	1100	21.6
Lanier, Det.	54	581	221	1383	25.6	Barry, G.S.	54	447	267	1161	21.5
Thompson, Den.	54	506	306	1318	24.9	McGinnis, Phil.	51	421	252	1094	21.5
McAdoo, Knicks	45	432	228	1092	24.3	Kenon, S.A.	52	457	188	1102	21.2
Issel, Den.	52	459	285	1203	23.1	Dandridge, Mil.	52	427	206	1060	20.4
Gervin, S.A.	54	470	300	1240	23.0	Lucas, Port.	53	427	213	1067	20.1
Hayes, Wash.	52	473	248	1194	23.0	Walton, Port.	48	386	194	966	20.1
Drew, Atl.	48	420	243	1083	22.6	Monroe, Knicks	50	408	185	1001	20.0

FIELD GOAL LEADERS (Minimum 195 FG Made)	FG	FGA	PCT.	FREE THROW LEADERS (Minimum 82 FT Made)	FT	FTA	PCT.
Abdul-Jabbar, L.A.	609	1039	.586	DiGregorio, Buff.	83	88	.943
Jones, Den.	331	587	.564	Barry, G.S.	267	292	.914
Mix, Phil.	206	372	.554	Bridgeman, Mil.	155	171	.906
Lanier, Det.	581	1072	.542	Russell, L.A.	137	154	.890
Gervin, S.A.	470	871	.540	Gross, Port.	119	135	.881
Collins, Phil.	220	409	.538	Newlin, Hou.	187	213	.878
Meriweather, Atl.	233	437	.533	Brown, Sea.	121	138	.877
Issel, Den.	459	865	.531	van Breda Kolff, Nets	125	144	.868
Gross, Port.	270	510	.529	Collins, Phil.	110	127	.866
Monroe, Knicks	408	772	.528	Eakins, K.C.	141	163	.865

REBOUND LEADERS
Minimum 46 games or 525 rebounds

	G	OFF	DEF	TOT	AVG.
Walton, Port.------48		161	573	734	15.3
Abdul-Jabbar,L.A.-54		178	586	764	14.1
McAdoo, Knicks----45		137	440	577	12.8
Gilmore, Chi.------55		224	479	703	12.8
Hayes, Wash.------52		185	444	629	12.1
Lucas, Port.------53		190	441	631	11.9
Nater, Mil.------52		193	417	610	11.7
McGinnis, Phil.---51		202	385	587	11.5
Lanier, Det.------54		162	457	619	11.5
Malone, Hou.------52		234	352	586	11.3

BLOCKED SHOTS LEADERS
Minimum 46 games or 66 blocked shots

	G	NO.	AVG.
Walton, Port.------------	48	166	3.46
Abdul-Jabbar, L.A.------	54	163	3.02
Hayes, Wash.------------	52	143	2.75
Jones, Phil.------------	53	129	2.43
Malone, Hou.------------	52	116	2.23
Johnson, Buff.----------	48	107	2.23
E. Smith, Clev.---------	40	86	2.15
Jones, Den.-------------	53	112	2.11
Gilmore, Chi.-----------	55	116	2.11
Lanier, Det.-----------	54	110	2.04

ASSISTS LEADERS
Minimum 46 games or 265 assists

	G	NO.	AVG.
Buse, Ind.----------------	55	479	8.7
Watts, Sea.--------------	52	421	8.1
K. Porter, Det.----------	55	435	7.9
Van Lier, Chi.-----------	55	427	7.8
Henderson, Wash.--------	57	421	7.4
Barry, G.S.-------------	54	339	6.3
White, Bos.-------------	53	303	5.7
Gale, S.A.-------------	54	295	5.5
Westphal, Phoe.---------	51	277	5.4
Frazier, Knicks--------	49	264	5.4

STEALS LEADERS
Minimum 46 games or 82 steals

	G	NO.	AVG.
Buse, Ind.--------------	55	192	3.49
Taylor, K.C.------------	54	150	2.78
Watts, Sea.------------	52	127	2.44
Ford, Det.-------------	55	131	2.38
Buckner, Mil.----------	56	127	2.27
Gale, S.A.-------------	54	121	2.24
Jones, Den.------------	53	118	2.23
Hollins, Port.---------	50	111	2.22
Kenon, S.A.-----------	52	113	2.17
Barry, G.S.-----------	54	116	2.15

INDIVIDUAL HIGHS

Most Minutes Played, Season	:2165, White, Bos.
Most Points, Game	: 51, Smith, G.S.vs Hou. 12/11; Maravich, N.O. vs K.C. 12/14
Most Field Goals, Game	: 23, Maravich, N.O. vs Wash. 12/26
Most Free Throws, Game	: 16, McAdoo, Buff. vs Ind. 12/7
Most Rebounds, Game	: 33, Nater, Mil. vs Atl. 12/19
Most Offensive Rebounds, Game	: 15, G. Johnson, G.S. @ Hou. 11/24; Nater, Mil. vs Atl. 12/19
Most Defensive Rebounds, Game	: 23, Abdul-Jabbar, L.A. vs K.C. 11/7; McAdoo, Buff. vs Ind. 12/7
Most Offensive Rebounds, Season	: 234, Malone, Hou.
Most Defensive Rebounds, Season	: 586, Abdul-Jabbar, L.A.
Most Assists, Game	: 20, K. Porter, Det. vs Bos. 11/20
Most Blocked Shots, Game	: 9, Smith, Mil. @ Den. 12/7; Walton, Port. @ Den. 1/26; Lanier, Det. vs Den. 2/4
Most Steals, Game	: 11, Kenon, S.A. @ K.C. 12/26
Most Personal Fouls, Season	: 236, Shelton, Knicks
Most Games Disqualified, Season	: 17, Meriweather, Atl.

TEAM HIGHS & LOWS

Most Points, Game	: 150, Port. vs S.A. 1/9
Fewest Points, Game	: 73, Nets @ Ind. 1/8
Most Points, Half	: 80, by three teams
Fewest Points, Half	: 28, Nets vs Wash. 1/21
Most Points, Quarter	: 48, Bos. vs K.C. 11/24; Port. vs S.A. 1/9
Fewest Points, Quarter	: 10 by five teams
Most Field Goals, Game	: 61, L.A. vs Bos. 12/28
Fewest Field Goals, Game	: 27, Chi. vs Port. 12/28
Most Free Throws, Game	: 44, Buff. vs Atl. 1/12
Fewest Free Throws, Game	: 2, Knicks vs Chi. 1/25
Most Rebounds, Game	: 71, Ind. vs Bos. 1/26
Fewest Rebounds, Game	: 24, Atl. @ Hou. 1/28
Most Assists, Game	: 45, Chi. vs G.S. 11/30; Den. vs S.A. 1/2
Most Steals, Game	: 23, Port. vs Knicks 11/7
Most Personal Fouls, Game	: 42, Port. @ Atl. 1/16
Fewest Personal Fouls, Game	: 11, Buff. vs L.A. 2/9
Most Blocked Shots, Game	: 15, Buff. @ Nets 2/11
Most Turnovers, Game	: 38, by three teams
Fewest Turnovers, Game	: 7, Clev. vs Mil. 11/4; Nets vs Bos. 2/2

ATLANTA	G	MIN	FGM	FGA	PCT.	FTM	FTA	PCT.	OFF REB	DEF REB	TOT REB	AST	PF	DQ	ST	BLK SH	PTS	AVG.	HI
Drew	48	1671	420	855	.491	243	340	.715	167	258	425	96	172	4	74	20	1083	22.6	42
Hudson	48	1576	390	838	.465	123	143	.860	43	78	121	139	138	2	60	16	903	18.8	39
Robinson (Tot)	51	1720	344	713	.482	178	252	.706	152	323	475	64	160	0	45	21	866	17.0	33
Robinson (Atl)	10	392	80	161	.497	50	63	.794	33	76	109	19	37	0	17	3	210	21.0	32
Meriweather	51	1499	233	437	.533	146	203	.719	171	269	440	49	229	17	31	52	612	12.0	27
Charles	56	1509	230	558	.412	145	178	.815	26	84	110	166	141	1	94	33	605	10.8	25
Barker	54	1315	181	427	.424	110	162	.679	109	281	390	58	218	11	33	40	472	8.7	21
Hawes	18	318	55	114	.482	23	29	.793	28	56	84	17	45	1	10	8	133	7.4	19
Brown	51	983	120	266	.451	81	101	.802	59	126	185	74	146	4	36	4	321	6.3	20
Denton	43	679	100	248	.403	33	47	.702	77	134	211	32	95	1	14	15	233	5.4	25
Hill	55	869	111	246	.451	71	88	.807	20	58	78	185	131	0	45	3	293	5.3	21
Willoughby	39	549	75	169	.444	43	63	.683	65	105	170	13	64	1	19	23	193	4.9	16
Sojourner	32	347	57	123	.463	30	46	.652	34	61	95	13	40	0	10	5	144	4.5	18
Terry (Tot)	38	402	66	142	.465	27	32	.844	7	26	33	45	35	0	15	0	159	4.2	22
Terry (Atl)	5	98	17	38	.447	9	9	1.000	3	2	5	12	8	0	4	0	43	8.6	22
N.W.T. (2)	-	1635	204	488	----	130	181	----	20	111	131	388	83	0	86	8	538	----	--

BOSTON

	G	MIN	FGM	FGA	PCT.	FTM	FTA	PCT.	OFF REB	DEF REB	TOT REB	AST	PF	DQ	ST	BLK SH	PTS	AVG.	HI
White	53	2165	407	962	.423	230	269	.855	57	200	257	303	134	5	81	19	1044	19.7	38
Scott	53	1378	293	652	.449	116	148	.784	46	119	165	168	133	3	50	12	702	19.0	31
Havlicek	50	1774	360	783	.460	153	190	.805	71	174	245	245	135	3	52	10	873	17.5	33
Wicks	53	1777	307	677	.453	218	321	.769	182	376	558	123	208	8	42	40	832	15.7	25
Cowens	21	736	132	295	.447	47	61	.770	68	208	276	101	77	5	20	19	311	14.8	30
Rowe	50	1450	217	433	.501	104	148	.703	129	240	369	63	127	0	14	30	538	10.8	22
Boswell	45	822	129	256	.504	78	106	.736	79	152	231	66	170	7	19	7	336	7.5	22
Saunders	40	492	90	191	.471	16	25	.640	38	72	111	48	93	2	11	5	196	4.9	21
Kuberski	49	637	94	231	.407	50	66	.758	55	116	171	30	68	0	6	4	238	4.9	16
Ard	50	896	92	237	.388	43	68	.632	72	201	273	51	114	1	17	28	227	4.5	14
Stacom	50	580	96	230	.417	20	29	.690	17	29	46	57	33	0	10	2	212	4.2	16
Cook	19	92	15	45	.333	7	14	.500	5	12	17	2	19	0	6	3	37	1.9	6
Wilson	5	21	0	9	.000	0	0	----	0	0	0	3	2	0	0	0	0	0.0	0

BUFFALO	G	MIN	FGM	FGA	PCT.	FTM	FTA	PCT.	OFF REB	DEF REB	TOT REB	AST	PF	DQ	ST	BLK SH	PTS	AVG.	HI
Dantley	48	1655	300	593	.506	274	337	.813	153	213	366	83	132	1	53	9	874	18.2	32
Smith	53	1844	394	868	.454	152	209	.727	75	199	274	270	174	2	102	6	940	18.1	33
Shumate	48	1834	301	580	.519	227	332	.684	120	408	528	110	139	1	67	69	829	17.3	26
DiGregorio	51	1404	240	559	.429	83	88	.943	32	81	113	215	105	0	36	2	563	11.0	36
Adams	50	1223	160	375	.427	101	126	.802	100	162	262	111	150	0	48	9	421	8.4	28
Gianelli (Tot)	46	1252	159	358	.444	62	80	.775	104	215	319	47	117	0	23	65	380	8.3	19
Gianelli (Buff)	27	622	73	176	.415	27	32	.844	44	97	141	21	63	0	9	37	173	6.4	16
Averitt	45	700	144	384	.375	79	110	.718	11	30	41	72	88	2	20	3	367	8.2	26
Gerard (Tot)	39	635	132	296	.446	51	74	.689	58	82	140	66	100	1	31	39	315	8.1	21
Gerard (Buff)	15	179	31	86	.360	13	18	.722	20	20	40	17	27	0	10	9	75	5.0	12
Johnson (Tot)	48	856	104	222	.468	37	47	.787	122	193	315	35	144	5	21	107	245	5.1	16
Johnson (Buff)	9	259	31	72	.431	12	16	.750	35	69	104	9	39	3	6	34	74	8.2	16
Foster	43	578	90	211	.427	26	37	.703	29	36	65	34	81	0	15	0	206	4.8	14
Williams (Tot)	41	612	61	168	.363	54	69	.783	16	52	68	90	47	0	26	1	176	4.3	14
Williams (Buff)	20	301	26	75	.347	24	30	.800	8	26	34	46	21	0	18	1	76	3.8	8
N.W.T. (8)	-	1931	360	811	----	211	289	----	150	351	501	163	213	1	59	52	931	----	--

CHICAGO

	G	MIN	FGM	FGA	PCT.	FTM	FTA	PCT.	OFF REB	DEF REB	TOT REB	AST	PF	DQ	ST	BLK SH	PTS	AVG.	HI
Gilmore	55	1906	377	722	.522	244	395	.618	224	479	703	125	186	4	29	116	998	18.1	32
Johnson	54	1845	361	792	.456	217	261	.831	195	348	543	118	213	9	73	37	939	17.4	30
May	45	1450	263	593	.444	104	128	.813	85	194	279	86	126	2	45	7	630	14.0	24
Holland	52	1467	302	702	.429	80	96	.833	41	92	133	132	118	2	90	8	682	13.1	30
Van Lier	55	2138	201	501	.401	159	197	.807	78	187	265	427	188	3	83	10	561	10.2	26
Mengelt	34	602	123	254	.484	47	59	.797	13	49	62	53	52	1	17	1	293	8.6	20
Marin	29	500	92	201	.458	18	22	.818	20	27	47	34	47	0	8	2	202	7.0	18
Laskowski	41	530	69	195	.354	26	28	.929	14	46	60	42	22	0	30	2	164	4.0	15
Pondexter	52	797	85	209	.407	35	54	.648	58	124	182	31	58	0	28	8	205	3.9	12
Kropp	40	434	64	137	.467	26	38	.684	20	23	43	26	71	1	17	1	154	3.9	18
Boerwinkle	55	750	84	181	.475	23	46	.500	68	147	215	124	96	0	14	12	195	3.5	16
Hicks (Tot)	16	136	22	54	.407	2	2	1.000	14	23	37	13	20	0	4	0	46	2.9	10
Hicks (Chi)	14	129	22	52	.423	2	2	1.000	13	23	36	12	19	0	3	0	46	3.3	10
Starr	17	65	6	24	.250	2	2	1.000	6	4	10	6	11	0	1	0	14	0.8	4
N.W.T. (4)	-	687	89	264	----	54	75	----	53	52	105	43	74	1	15	5	232	----	--

CLEVELAND

	G	MIN	FGM	FGA	PCT.	FTM	FTA	PCT.	OFF REB	DEF REB	TOT REB	AST	PF	DQ	ST	BLK SH	PTS	AVG.	HI
Russell	52	1606	330	777	.425	221	286	.773	116	208	324	142	152	2	54	17	881	16.9	31
Carr	52	1497	356	777	.458	134	166	.807	73	140	213	138	133	3	39	6	846	16.3	29
B.Smith	52	1281	333	731	.456	83	103	.806	57	155	212	82	111	1	30	21	749	14.4	27
Chones	52	1390	266	572	.465	96	127	.756	119	275	394	63	170	3	21	37	628	12.1	23
Cleamons	51	1802	234	531	.441	100	134	.746	95	164	259	261	108	0	62	19	568	11.1	25
Snyder	52	1033	183	427	.429	74	87	.851	24	64	88	108	118	2	27	24	440	8.5	18
Brewer	52	1716	186	420	.443	65	109	.596	177	328	505	132	135	2	68	58	437	8.4	20
E.Smith (Tot)	40	889	132	287	.460	72	124	.581	63	180	243	32	128	3	21	86	336	8.4	21
E.Smith (Clev)	6	100	19	34	.559	11	19	.579	11	24	35	2	19	1	2	17	49	8.2	13
Brokaw (Tot)	51	1023	150	375	.400	122	160	.763	15	65	80	134	106	1	23	28	422	8.3	27
Brokaw (Clev)	10	132	20	51	.392	17	23	.739	5	11	16	23	21	1	1	5	57	5.7	14
Thurmond	49	997	100	246	.407	68	106	.642	121	253	374	83	128	2	16	81	268	5.5	13
Walker	34	471	56	127	.441	34	46	.739	25	35	60	104	53	0	31	1	146	4.3	14
Lambert	35	243	31	70	.443	16	18	.889	29	42	71	16	29	0	8	7	78	2.2	10
Williams	15	44	10	29	.345	4	4	1.000	2	0	2	5	6	0	1	0	24	1.6	6
N.W.T. (2)	-	243	48	108	----	23	28	----	12	33	45	12	37	0	8	5	119	----	--

N.W.T. = Not With Team
DQ = Individual Players Disqualified (Fouled out of Game)

DENVER	G	MIN	FGM	FGA	PCT.	FTM	FTA	PCT.	OFF REB	DEF REB	TOT REB	AST	PF	DQ	ST	BLK SH	PTS	AVG.	HI
Thompson--------53	1906	506	1003	.504	306	415	.737	99	117	216	196	162	1	76	27	1318	24.9	40
Issel-----------52	1711	459	865	.531	285	360	.792	147	330	477	129	151	1	61	23	1203	23.1	38
Jones-----------53	1594	331	587	.564	140	203	.690	117	335	452	193	141	1	118	112	802	15.1	27
McClain---------49	1361	179	407	.440	82	107	.766	39	124	163	227	172	4	74	12	440	9.0	18
Wise------------46	896	146	296	.493	100	153	.654	47	110	157	91	114	0	38	9	392	8.5	20
Silas-----------52	1357	137	412	.333	110	171	.643	172	259	431	93	109	0	41	15	384	7.4	20
Price (Tot)-----52	1007	152	334	.455	57	67	.851	31	103	134	138	141	0	77	10	361	6.9	20
Price (Den)-----26	563	87	189	.460	33	38	.868	22	65	87	85	75	0	45	4	207	8.0	14
Webster---------51	705	123	246	.500	79	130	.608	89	186	275	33	81	1	13	63	325	6.4	17
Beck------------37	388	89	200	.445	30	37	.811	34	39	73	26	51	1	14	1	208	5.6	16
Taylor----------53	1134	105	245	.429	34	56	.607	68	87	155	204	147	0	97	6	244	4.6	11
Towe------------40	338	45	114	.395	16	23	.696	8	23	31	66	48	0	14	0	106	2.7	8
N.W.T. (2)------ -	767	136	303	----	68	95	----	46	88	134	93	99	1	29	30	340	----	--

DETROIT																			
Lanier----------54	2068	581	1072	.542	221	270	.819	162	457	619	186	151	0	57	110	1383	25.6	40
H.Porter--------52	1451	318	658	.483	62	74	.838	109	193	302	36	138	0	37	47	698	13.4	27
Carr------------55	1710	298	605	.493	125	173	.723	148	259	407	131	190	7	96	30	721	13.1	25
Ford------------55	1696	285	586	.486	87	110	.791	59	118	177	238	139	1	131	12	657	11.9	22
Simpson---------54	1152	263	610	.431	100	131	.763	33	98	131	123	76	0	54	5	626	11.6	25
K.Porter--------55	1483	219	422	.519	58	82	.707	15	50	65	435	195	6	67	7	496	9.0	25
Money-----------48	931	189	355	.532	48	60	.800	26	42	68	121	121	2	58	10	426	8.9	23
Barnes----------33	513	114	248	.460	63	81	.778	34	105	137	21	79	1	23	19	291	8.8	33
Eberhard--------46	842	127	267	.476	69	89	.775	46	106	152	37	130	4	27	10	323	7.0	19
Douglas---------55	973	123	278	.442	73	139	.525	113	208	321	41	202	6	24	51	319	5.8	16
Sellers---------30	204	38	109	.349	40	51	.784	14	14	28	13	39	0	13	0	116	3.9	13
Brown-----------25	153	8	20	.400	11	16	.688	8	26	34	6	30	1	5	6	27	1.1	6
N.W.T. (1)------ -	49	9	23	----	·3	6	----	8	8	16	1	8	0	2	1	21	----	--

GOLDEN STATE	G	MIN	FGM	FGA	PCT.	FTM	FTA	PCT.	OFF REB	DEF REB	TOT REB	AST	PF	DQ	ST	BLK SH	PTS	AVG.	HI
Barry-----------54	2033	447	1046	.427	267	292	.914	47	244	339	140	2	116	37	1161	21.5	42
Smith-----------54	1909	421	873	.482	216	272	.794	64	154	218	223	159	0	68	21	1058	19.6	51
Wilkes----------50	1646	346	730	.474	150	194	.773	104	270	374	131	145	0	86	11	842	16.8	31
Williams--------54	1305	222	467	.475	75	99	.758	51	114	165	189	159	4	82	15	519	9.6	26
Parish----------49	793	174	349	.499	85	116	.733	113	202	315	41	119	2	34	53	433	8.8	24
Ray-------------50	1241	171	284	.602	71	137	.518	131	260	391	69	155	2	52	48	413	8.3	18
Dickey----------34	628	120	260	.462	36	49	.735	79	103	182	47	71	1	15	7	276	8.1	20
Johnson---------52	781	186	396	.470	33	43	.767	28	58	86	51	87	0	50	4	405	7.8	22
Dudley----------52	1102	147	271	.542	74	119	.622	77	114	191	216	106	0	44	3	368	7.1	19
Davis-----------29	487	49	111	.441	46	68	.676	31	51	86	25	82	1	9	8	144	5.0	12
Parker----------39	419	69	130	.531	37	49	.755	42	30	72	28	32	0	23	10	175	4.5	13
Rogers----------14	94	24	67	.358	8	8	1.000	4	2	6	5	19	0	5	2	56	4.0	10
N.W.T. (1)------ -	597	73	150	----	25	31	----	87	124	211	26	105	2	15	73	171	----	--

HOUSTON																			
Tomjanovich-----52	2088	487	929	.524	192	230	.835	120	346	466	120	132	0	35	18	1166	22.4	40
Murphy----------52	1771	375	755	.497	153	179	.855	35	75	110	245	184	5	93	2	903	17.4	30
Newlin----------52	1378	254	572	.444	187	213	.878	38	95	133	205	141	1	40	2	695	13.4	35
Malone (Tot)----52	1423	219	451	.486	143	223	.641	234	352	586	53	166	1	41	116	581	11.2	25
Malone (Hou)----50	1417	219	451	.486	143	223	.641	234	351	585	53	165	1	41	116	581	11.6	25
Johnson---------52	1300	259	507	.471	81	110	.736	53	141	194	122	152	1	30	19	559	10.8	30
Lucas-----------52	1457	219	440	.498	84	105	.800	28	90	118	266	99	0	69	6	522	10.0	25
Kunnert---------51	1169	184	382	.482	49	62	.790	132	256	388	106	216	10	23	57	417	8.2	23
Ratleff---------28	446	60	134	.448	20	32	.625	19	42	61	33	33	0	18	5	140	5.0	12
Jones-----------45	708	81	174	.466	51	67	.761	52	105	157	37	96	0	28	12	213	4.7	16
Owens-----------37	395	59	112	.527	43	66	.652	33	81	114	17	83	2	3	12	161	4.4	13
White-----------32	261	34	75	.453	12	18	.667	11	19	30	22	23	0	6	0	80	2.5	14
Kennedy---------14	121	9	21	.429	0	1	.000	6	13	19	3	16	0	2	1	18	1.3	6
N.W.T. (2)------ -	69	7	19	----	4	4	----	2	4	6	16	19	1	1	0	18	----	--

INDIANA																			
Knight----------51	1964	540	1112	.486	274	337	.813	148	209	357	178	119	0	67	10	1354	26.5	43
Williamson (Tot)45	1520	377	844	.447	165	209	.789	24	98	122	101	153	3	66	6	919	20.4	37
Williamson (Ind) 3	94	20	41	.488	4	5	.800	0	3	3	11	10	0	7	0	44	14.7	26
Roundfield------53	1459	313	661	.474	139	202	.688	161	297	458	63	213	7	52	102	765	14.4	33
Jones-----------53	1832	314	736	.427	122	159	.767	148	264	412	128	202	7	64	68	750	14.2	26
Hillman---------55	1622	271	605	.449	117	173	.676	164	347	511	117	235	13	68	74	659	12.0	27
Robisch---------53	1057	190	459	.414	130	163	.798	91	202	293	71	103	0	26	21	510	9.6	27
Buse------------55	2086	200	463	.432	83	106	.783	43	147	190	479	93	0	192	12	483	8.8	19
Flynn-----------52	981	190	438	.434	71	101	.703	65	92	157	126	82	0	47	4	451	8.7	24
Green-----------49	748	146	351	.416	68	89	.764	62	77	139	39	123	1	29	11	360	7.3	24
Bennett---------42	585	62	185	.335	70	121	.579	72	79	151	38	97	0	21	18	194	4.6	19
Elmore----------- 6	46	7	17	.412	4	5	.800	7	8	15	2	11	0	0	4	18	3.0	7
Anderson--------16	102	14	32	.438	2	5	.400	3	3	6	8	15	0	2	1	30	1.9	4
N.W.T. (4)------ -	651	89	224	----	70	92	----	25	45	70	64	76	0	19	5	248	----	--

N.W.T. = Not With Team
DQ = Individual players Disqualified (Fouled out of Game)

KANSAS CITY	G	MIN	FGM	FGA	PCT.	FTM	FTA	PCT.	OFF REB	DEF REB	TOT REB	AST	PF	DQ	ST	BLK SH	PTS	AVG.	HI
Boone	56	2058	517	1081	.478	218	255	.855	87	135	222	223	177	0	88	12	1252	22.4	37
Taylor	54	1887	350	712	.492	178	216	.824	61	122	183	249	151	0	150	14	878	16.3	34
Wedman	55	1829	347	741	.468	139	165	.842	126	198	324	166	149	3	71	15	833	15.1	38
Washington	56	1501	297	694	.428	117	164	.713	138	324	462	61	219	8	39	58	711	12.7	26
Lacey	56	1722	211	498	.424	141	175	.806	115	356	471	251	199	7	79	96	563	10.1	21
Robinzine	54	1126	210	462	.455	93	128	.727	94	213	307	72	203	5	55	11	513	9.5	27
Johnson	55	977	156	327	.477	56	62	.903	49	96	145	69	117	1	34	16	368	6.7	18
Eakins	56	970	122	259	.432	141	163	.865	49	179	273	92	136	0	20	38	365	6.5	23
Hansen	22	158	37	84	.440	13	16	.813	15	18	33	19	22	0	5	1	87	4.0	11
McCarter	40	437	67	159	.421	22	33	.667	10	23	33	59	40	0	13	0	156	3.9	12
Barr	50	735	71	167	.425	26	35	.743	19	60	79	103	60	0	29	12	168	3.4	14
Bigelow	19	115	28	57	.491	7	9	.778	7	14	21	3	13	0	2	1	63	3.3	11

LOS ANGELES	G	MIN	FGM	FGA	PCT.	FTM	FTA	PCT.	OFF REB	DEF REB	TOT REB	AST	PF	DQ	ST	BLK SH	PTS	AVG.	HI
Abdul-Jabbar	54	2032	609	1039	.586	250	349	.716	178	586	764	210	180	3	68	163	1468	27.2	40
Russell	54	1685	369	756	.488	137	154	.890	55	130	185	132	113	1	49	7	875	16.2	35
Allen	52	1705	345	738	.467	129	163	.791	36	130	166	271	120	0	68	15	819	15.8	30
Washington	53	1342	191	380	.503	132	187	.706	182	310	492	48	183	1	43	52	514	9.7	20
Tatum	40	621	135	296	.456	43	58	.741	34	67	101	59	92	1	44	12	313	7.8	23
Lamar	50	859	165	418	.395	40	56	.714	25	47	72	128	53	0	40	1	370	7.4	22
Ford	54	1092	167	360	.464	49	68	.721	56	154	210	78	105	0	39	12	383	7.1	19
Chaney	53	1636	149	358	.416	37	51	.725	80	137	217	206	147	3	89	23	335	6.3	16
Neumann (Tot)	39	560	100	239	.418	33	49	.673	17	30	47	89	71	0	22	6	233	6.0	24
Neumann (L.A.)	35	511	85	205	.415	28	43	.651	12	26	38	85	64	0	19	4	198	5.7	24
Abernethy	42	664	88	174	.506	47	65	.723	51	75	126	44	56	0	25	2	223	5.3	14
Kupec	54	576	92	204	.451	55	71	.775	51	74	125	37	73	0	13	2	239	4.4	13
Roberts	16	75	10	27	.370	3	4	.750	6	3	9	6	13	0	2	0	23	1.4	4
N.W.T. (3)	-	262	31	97	----	45	57	----	11	25	36	21	26	0	11	1	107	----	--

MILWAUKEE	G	MIN	FGM	FGA	PCT.	FTM	FTA	PCT.	OFF REB	DEF REB	TOT REB	AST	PF	DQ	ST	BLK SH	PTS	AVG.	HI
Dandridge	52	1831	427	916	.466	206	268	.769	113	217	330	177	165	0	66	20	1060	20.4	37
Winters	55	1873	438	897	.488	125	152	.822	48	111	159	283	152	1	78	18	1001	18.2	43
Bridgeman	59	1818	364	827	.440	155	171	.906	90	218	308	158	170	3	64	17	883	15.0	41
Nater	52	1321	257	505	.509	131	172	.762	193	417	610	76	152	6	37	34	645	12.4	30
Carter (Tot)	43	861	153	385	.397	52	72	.722	39	49	88	93	92	0	34	7	358	8.3	26
Carter (Mil)	29	624	110	284	.387	42	53	.792	29	35	64	72	63	0	23	5	262	9.0	26
Buckner	56	1434	205	459	.447	49	99	.495	71	108	179	244	205	5	127	11	459	8.2	21
Meyers	27	508	61	146	.418	47	75	.627	46	84	130	34	59	0	16	7	169	6.3	22
Lloyd	54	848	128	270	.474	74	100	.740	69	103	172	26	127	5	21	12	330	6.1	22
Restani	41	720	112	215	.521	9	19	.474	51	111	162	51	66	0	21	7	233	5.7	22
English	48	553	113	237	.477	37	49	.755	60	87	147	21	69	0	14	14	263	5.5	21
Garrett (Tot)	43	403	77	168	.458	29	37	.784	25	51	76	17	60	0	13	8	183	4.3	12
Garrett (Mil)	14	188	37	75	.493	11	15	.733	15	21	36	10	30	0	6	5	85	6.1	12
Walton	32	432	53	111	.477	30	40	.750	10	23	33	85	38	0	27	0	136	4.3	12
N.W.T. (5)	-	2035	301	720	----	199	280	----	85	241	326	183	230	2	58	97	801	----	--

NEW ORLEANS	G	MIN	FGM	FGA	PCT.	FTM	FTA	PCT.	OFF REB	DEF REB	TOT REB	AST	PF	DQ	ST	BLK SH	PTS	AVG.	HI
Maravich	49	1981	567	1320	.430	329	397	.829	58	178	236	251	127	0	47	13	1463	29.9	51
Goodrich	27	609	136	305	.446	68	85	.800	25	36	61	74	43	0	22	2	340	12.6	28
James	43	970	218	440	.495	87	106	.821	49	119	168	46	113	1	19	4	523	12.2	36
Williams	53	1149	262	578	.453	91	122	.746	65	139	63	138	0	56	10	615	11.6	30
Boyd	47	1212	194	406	.478	79	98	.806	19	71	90	147	78	0	44	6	467	9.9	24
Behagen	43	874	150	384	.391	70	96	.729	117	233	350	60	118	1	35	14	370	8.6	19
Coleman	51	1505	188	388	.485	52	70	.743	102	254	356	54	186	6	38	24	428	8.4	21
McElroy	49	1153	145	318	.456	81	109	.743	37	68	105	136	69	1	41	4	371	7.6	26
Moore	54	1409	144	353	.408	59	88	.670	123	319	442	131	154	3	34	78	347	6.4	17
Kelley	48	864	101	212	.476	89	115	.774	122	201	323	123	152	5	31	37	291	6.1	21
Stallworth	27	229	59	125	.472	10	21	.476	12	26	38	8	47	1	10	7	128	4.7	15
Griffin	53	871	66	117	.564	102	142	.718	84	189	273	99	150	3	29	19	234	4.4	15
Walker	20	159	25	55	.455	13	19	.684	9	17	26	12	27	0	7	2	63	3.2	11

KNICKS	G	MIN	FGM	FGA	PCT.	FTM	FTA	PCT.	OFF REB	DEF REB	TOT REB	AST	PF	DQ	ST	BLK SH	PTS	AVG.	HI
McAdoo (Tot)	45	1722	432	901	.479	228	312	.731	137	440	577	129	169	3	46	71	1092	24.3	42
McAdoo (Knicks)	25	955	250	501	.499	118	154	.766	71	242	313	64	95	2	30	37	618	24.7	36
Monroe	50	1737	408	772	.528	185	225	.822	25	105	130	238	130	0	53	14	1001	20.0	37
Frazier	49	1778	346	728	.475	154	208	.740	32	157	189	264	118	0	80	5	846	17.3	32
Haywood	26	864	174	384	.453	96	116	.828	69	174	243	36	57	0	11	26	444	17.1	35
McMillian	40	1355	193	422	.457	52	65	.800	42	158	200	80	62	0	36	2	438	11.0	25
Shelton	53	1345	242	514	.471	93	128	.727	154	252	406	96	236	6	78	66	577	10.9	31
McMillen(Tot)	48	983	182	365	.499	68	93	.731	76	198	274	47	97	0	8	4	432	9.0	31
McMillen(Knicks)	28	713	137	273	.502	42	57	.737	47	155	202	31	68	0	7	2	316	11.3	31
Layton	44	648	121	238	.508	47	62	.758	11	28	39	130	68	0	16	5	289	6.6	24
Burden	38	407	106	249	.426	27	49	.551	17	24	41	46	50	0	27	0	239	6.3	21
Bradley	38	554	72	154	.468	24	31	.774	20	50	70	67	68	0	16	4	168	4.4	20
Beard	43	571	73	152	.480	36	56	.643	28	59	87	73	72	0	27	1	182	4.2	15
Jackson	49	641	68	157	.433	29	40	.725	45	100	145	51	122	2	19	12	165	3.4	19
Meminger	12	95	3	12	.250	2	4	.500	4	4	8	9	5	0	3	0	8	0.7	2
N.W.T. (3)	-	1107	155	349	----	63	86	----	95	210	305	56	121	0	27	32	373	----	--

N.W.T. = Not With Team
DQ = Individual Players Disqualified (Fouled out of Game)

NETS	G	MIN	FGM	FGA	PCT.	FTM	FTA	PCT.	OFF REB	DEF REB	TOT REB	AST	PF	DQ	BLK ST	SH	PTS	AVG.	HI
Archibald-------	34	1277	250	560	.446	197	251	.785	22	58	80	254	77	1	59	11	697	20.5	34
Hawkins---------	23	585	173	362	.478	88	123	.715	23	36	59	35	59	0	33	10	434	18.9	44
Skinner---------	53	1371	227	553	.410	150	184	.815	81	140	221	161	180	5	65	31	604	11.4	24
van Breda Kolff-	45	1444	155	364	.426	125	144	.868	97	182	279	74	124	1	42	41	435	9.7	21
Bantom (Tot)----	50	1004	182	379	.480	83	114	.728	105	139	244	57	140	5	39	28	447	8.9	32
Bantom (Nets)---	6	209	45	98	.459	25	30	.833	22	36	58	5	27	2	4	7	115	19.2	32
Bassett---------	53	1725	192	463	.415	70	131	.534	115	336	451	73	173	8	66	35	454	8.6	20
Fox-------------	45	729	115	253	.455	53	62	.855	66	143	209	28	113	1	16	14	283	6.3	21
Davis (Tot)-----	30	522	69	188	.367	32	48	.667	47	103	150	37	68	0	16	1	170	5.7	14
Davis (Nets)----	8	180	28	78	.359	10	17	.588	17	33	50	13	23	0	7	0	66	8.3	14
Terry-----------	40	712	83	212	.392	32	39	.821	25	67	92	27	77	0	29	5	198	5.0	19
Wohl (Tot)------	29	467	56	133	.421	25	36	.694	9	34	43	63	54	1	17	4	137	4.7	22
Wohl (Nets)-----	15	405	49	116	.422	21	32	.656	8	30	38	48	36	0	17	4	119	7.9	22
Hughes----------	52	1368	111	242	.459	9	48	.188	134	243	377	52	215	8	77	74	231	4.4	14
N.W.T. (7)------	-	2775	571	1347	---	328	428	---	109	307	416	150	320	6	105	32	1470	---	--

PHILADELPHIA

	G	MIN	FGM	FGA	PCT.	FTM	FTA	PCT.	OFF REB	DEF REB	TOT REB	AST	PF	DQ	BLK ST	SH	PTS	AVG.	HI
McGinnis--------	51	1796	421	929	.453	252	369	.683	202	385	587	189	177	1	105	20	1094	21.5	37
Erving----------	53	1841	403	814	.495	249	324	.769	116	353	469	187	168	0	102	82	1055	19.9	32
Collins---------	30	1006	220	409	.538	110	127	.866	30	65	95	124	87	2	35	7	550	18.3	33
Free------------	52	1562	326	723	.451	226	322	.702	72	93	165	177	148	1	45	16	878	16.9	39
Mix-------------	47	1271	206	372	.554	150	184	.815	88	171	259	87	104	0	63	13	562	12.0	37
Bibby-----------	52	1683	209	460	.454	143	178	.803	54	117	171	227	128	0	67	2	561	10.8	28
Jones-----------	53	1266	130	258	.504	32	66	.485	116	286	402	59	183	1	31	129	292	5.5	16
Dunleavy--------	22	270	46	103	.447	26	35	.743	7	20	27	34	49	1	5	2	118	5.4	32
Barnett---------	11	196	24	55	.436	8	12	.667	6	7	13	22	21	0	4	0	56	5.1	10
Dawkins---------	31	312	63	102	.618	21	40	.525	19	85	104	9	73	1	4	26	147	4.7	12
Bryant----------	40	428	69	162	.426	37	48	.771	33	51	84	32	55	0	24	11	175	4.4	22
Catchings-------	41	721	47	94	.500	28	39	.718	48	146	194	26	108	1	20	68	122	3.0	16
Furlow----------	24	131	19	70	.271	11	13	.846	13	16	29	16	6	0	5	2	49	2.0	8
N.W.T. (1)------	-	237	43	101	---	10	19	---	10	14	24	21	29	0	11	2	96	---	--

PHOENIX	G	MIN	FGM	FGA	PCT.	FTM	FTA	PCT.	OFF REB	DEF REB	TOT REB	AST	PF	DQ	BLK ST	SH	PTS	AVG.	HI
Westphal--------	51	1633	429	846	.507	242	294	.823	33	87	120	277	111	0	88	17	1100	21.6	32
Adams-----------	43	1270	281	608	.462	149	205	.727	104	243	347	179	152	3	46	46	711	16.5	34
Sobers---------	51	1339	256	544	.471	152	184	.826	55	89	144	155	168	2	70	11	664	13.0	28
Perry-----------	44	1391	179	414	.432	112	142	.789	149	246	395	79	163	3	49	28	470	10.7	20
Heard-----------	43	1346	172	454	.379	100	138	.725	118	316	434	88	136	2	55	55	444	10.3	28
Lee-------------	52	1010	196	450	.436	79	121	.653	62	124	186	153	172	8	85	19	471	9.1	30
Erickson--------	21	416	76	148	.514	19	27	.704	12	38	50	44	51	0	10	2	171	8.1	19
D. Van Arsdale-	52	1085	156	344	.453	95	112	.848	21	62	83	91	62	0	26	5	407	7.8	19
T. Van Arsdale-	52	1025	131	297	.441	70	102	.686	39	102	141	50	112	0	14	2	332	6.4	20
Terrell---------	48	646	118	227	.520	35	60	.583	41	103	144	23	70	0	17	12	271	5.6	20
Awtrey---------	52	1200	106	239	.444	68	91	.747	70	171	241	118	120	1	16	19	280	5.4	14
Feher-----------	27	88	16	36	.444	30	42	.714	9	10	19	11	8	0	2	2	62	2.3	17
Schlueter-------	13	56	4	11	.364	6	7	.857	3	7	10	3	9	0	1	1	14	1.1	5

PORTLAND

	G	MIN	FGM	FGA	PCT.	FTM	FTA	PCT.	OFF REB	DEF REB	TOT REB	AST	PF	DQ	BLK ST	SH	PTS	AVG.	HI
Lucas-----------	53	1912	427	898	.476	213	272	.783	190	441	631	143	205	6	55	35	1067	20.1	41
Walton----------	48	1776	386	739	.522	194	280	.693	161	573	734	189	140	4	52	166	966	20.1	30
Hollins---------	50	1409	266	643	.414	132	177	.746	34	108	142	198	175	3	111	28	664	13.3	28
Gross-----------	56	1568	270	510	.529	119	135	.881	116	160	276	182	175	6	85	38	659	11.8	23
Twardzik--------	48	1242	168	270	.622	151	184	.821	49	79	128	158	148	4	89	6	487	10.1	23
Steele----------	55	1092	200	409	.489	113	143	.790	50	66	116	108	145	3	78	7	513	9.3	28
Davis-----------	56	1184	187	415	.451	126	159	.792	40	49	89	114	96	1	31	10	500	8.9	25
Gilliam---------	55	1149	213	501	.425	56	75	.747	44	105	149	115	99	0	54	4	482	8.8	23
Neal------------	41	705	119	249	.478	56	87	.644	60	118	178	54	104	0	7	29	294	7.2	20
Walker----------	46	441	98	213	.460	40	65	.615	31	42	73	36	64	0	8	2	236	5.1	19
Jones-----------	37	489	65	142	.458	28	45	.622	45	23	85	30	57	0	22	17	158	4.3	20
Calhoun---------	45	520	62	128	.484	48	62	.774	28	70	98	25	81	1	14	4	172	3.8	16
Mayes (Tot.)----	5	31	3	10	.300	3	7	.429	4	6	10	3	8	0	0	2	9	1.8	4
Mayes (Port.)---	1	3	0	0	---	0	0	---	0	0	0	0	1	0	0	0	0	0.0	0

SAN ANTONIO

	G	MIN	FGM	FGA	PCT.	FTM	FTA	PCT.	OFF REB	DEF REB	TOT REB	AST	PF	DQ	BLK ST	SH	PTS	AVG.	HI
Gervin----------	54	1735	470	871	.540	300	358	.838	101	236	337	129	198	10	68	80	1240	23.0	42
Kenon-----------	52	1948	457	959	.477	188	230	.817	192	387	579	129	131	0	113	46	1102	21.2	41
Paultz----------	54	1762	322	713	.452	150	195	.769	117	332	449	131	170	3	42	103	794	14.7	28
Silas-----------	14	278	47	115	.409	75	90	.833	5	22	27	41	26	0	13	3	169	12.1	28
Bristow---------	54	1361	251	521	.482	140	179	.782	85	160	245	158	131	0	62	2	642	11.9	25
Gale------------	54	1695	227	476	.477	92	111	.829	36	134	170	295	154	2	121	30	546	10.1	24
Olberding-------	54	1188	185	365	.507	145	183	.792	111	166	277	67	179	4	39	14	515	9.5	23
Calvin (Tot)----	47	813	120	319	.376	164	194	.845	17	30	47	125	74	0	34	2	404	8.6	24
Calvin (S.A.)---	35	606	93	237	.392	123	146	.842	11	20	31	104	58	0	23	1	309	8.8	24
Dietrick--------	54	1152	178	391	.455	79	112	.705	71	167	238	80	181	6	69	37	435	8.1	20
Dampier--------	52	999	136	296	.459	42	57	.737	13	38	51	137	58	0	33	11	314	6.0	21
Ward-----------	12	85	12	42	.286	13	13	1.000	5	10	15	4	15	0	2	2	37	3.1	16
Karl-----------	13	135	10	35	.286	17	25	.680	1	5	6	24	17	0	7	0	37	2.8	8
N.W.T. (2)------	-	66	8	17	---	5	9	---	2	7	9	5	12	0	2	0	21	---	--

N.W.T. = Not With Team.

SEATTLE	G	MIN	FGM	FGA	PCT	FTM	FTA	PCT	OFF REB	DEF REB	TOT REB	AST	PF	DQ	ST	BLK SH	PTS	AVG	HI
Brown---------51	1492	389	797	.488	121	138	.877	54	115	169	136	98	0	91	11	899	17.6	42
Watts---------52	1683	262	622	.421	111	187	.594	48	138	186	421	169	3	127	17	635	12.2	37
Seals---------54	1366	265	584	.454	86	121	.711	86	166	252	69	178	5	34	39	616	11.4	34
Green---------49	1299	190	442	.430	110	154	.714	137	220	357	85	132	0	33	86	490	10.0	21
Burleson------55	1183	202	452	.447	136	188	.723	115	228	343	58	161	1	44	72	540	9.8	26
Weatherspoon(Tot)37	863	157	348	.451	48	69	.696	68	168	236	25	93	1	30	18	362	9.8	25
Weatherspoon(Sea)26	711	130	272	.478	43	61	.705	57	155	212	23	74	1	27	13	303	11.7	25
Love (Tot)------32	787	121	331	.366	70	89	.787	57	71	128	32	76	1	13	4	312	9.8	22
Love (Sea)------ 5	63	4	24	.167	2	4	.500	4	13	17	5	6	0	4	0	10	2.0	4
Norwood--------51	1234	166	349	.476	122	164	.744	99	126	225	80	142	1	51	1	454	8.9	21
Johnson--------55	1058	185	372	.497	110	179	.615	110	93	203	82	146	1	84	46	480	8.7	23
Tolson--------37	386	95	176	.540	61	112	.545	52	52	104	19	53	0	22	12	251	6.8	19
Wilkerson------54	944	135	358	.377	50	69	.725	60	94	154	109	87	0	50	3	320	5.9	20
Oleynick-------38	433	72	190	.379	33	43	.767	8	27	35	50	39	0	10	4	177	4.7	19
N.W.T. (3)------ -	1448	253	549	----	117	162	----	108	188	296	108	202	4	62	34	623	----	--

WASHINGTON

	G	MIN	FGM	FGA	PCT	FTM	FTA	PCT	OFF REB	DEF REB	TOT REB	AST	PF	DQ	ST	BLK SH	PTS	AVG	HI
Hayes---------52	2112	473	943	.502	248	376	.660	185	444	629	84	192	1	58	143	1194	23.0	45
Chenier-------48	1786	399	904	.441	158	185	.854	38	148	186	180	107	0	82	25	956	19.9	35
Bing----------47	1274	219	484	.452	107	140	.764	49	66	115	233	119	1	46	4	545	11.6	32
Henderson (Tot)-57	1784	229	525	.436	146	200	.730	26	126	152	421	82	0	87	9	604	10.6	27
Henderson(Wash)-11	216	33	72	.458	20	32	.625	8	20	28	35	8	0	8	1	86	7.8	14
Gray (Tot)------54	1156	193	427	.452	100	135	.741	54	141	195	92	168	3	45	21	486	9.0	23
Gray (Wash)-----29	513	79	165	.479	41	57	.719	31	57	88	37	84	2	18	8	199	6.9	16
Kupchak--------52	844	178	316	.563	99	139	.712	92	181	273	36	133	2	14	22	455	8.8	26
Wright--------52	1078	193	437	.442	61	76	.803	25	53	78	180	127	0	42	2	447	8.6	25
Unseld--------52	1801	160	339	.472	70	116	.603	165	369	534	230	170	3	55	31	390	7.5	18
Grevey--------46	584	95	234	.406	40	54	.741	39	52	91	26	75	1	12	4	230	5.0	19
Weiss---------38	514	41	94	.436	23	29	.793	12	43	55	91	44	0	31	.2	105	2.8	10
Pace----------17	71	12	28	.429	13	19	.684	9	13	22	4	21	0	1	12	37	2.2	12
Jones---------- 3	33	2	9	.222	2	4	.500	1	3	4	1	4	0	2	0	6	2.0	4
Riordan--------32	174	19	59	.322	4	7	.571	5	12	17	9	20	0	2	2	42	1.3	8
N.W.T. (2)------ -	1480	291	628	----	133	197	----	130	260	390	47	142	0	31	23	715	----	--

SCORES OF GAMES OF WEEK ENDING FEBRUARY 13

Tuesday, February 8
Knicks 125, Los Angeles 107
Houston 97, Cleveland 81
Chicago 111, San Antonio 89
Milwaukee 100, Nets 97
Golden State 128, Washington 104
Phoenix 117, Atlanta 104
Denver 119, Portland 111
Buffalo 99, Philadelphia 89

Wednesday, February 9
Los Angeles 105, Buffalo 90
Nets 93, New Orleans 89 (ot)
Philadelphia 107, Milwaukee 104
Houston 108, Chicago 103
San Antonio 135, Detroit 129
Indiana 110, Knicks 109
Atlanta 99, Seattle 98

Thursday, February 10
Cleveland 116, Indiana 101
Milwaukee 112, Kansas City 102
Golden State 114, Denver 101
Washington 109, Phoenix 103

Friday, February 11
Boston 119, Knicks 111
Buffalo 96, Nets 94
Philadelphia 118, Indiana 109
Chicago 110, New Orleans 92
Detroit 101, Cleveland 94
Atlanta 121, Portland 108
Kansas City 120, Washington 106
Los Angeles 117, Denver 109
Seattle 114, Golden State 107 (ot)
San Antonio 107, Houston 104

Sunday, February 13

West All-Stars 125
East All-Stars 124

THIS WEEK'S SCHEDULE

Tuesday, February 15
Detroit vs. Boston at Hartford, 7:30
Washington at Buffalo, 7:30
Portland at Cleveland, 8:00
Seattle at San Antonio, 7:30
Nets at Chicago, 7:30
Phoenix at Kansas City, 8:05
New Orleans at Milwaukee, 8:00
Atlanta at Golden State, 7:30

Wednesday, February 16
Chicago at Knicks, 7:30
Buffalo at Philadelphia, 8:05
Seattle at Houston, 8:05
Boston at Washington, 8:05
Portland at Detroit, 8:05
Phoenix at Indiana, 8:05
Nets at Denver, 7:35

Thursday, February 17
Boston at Kansas City, 7:35
Houston at San Antonio, 7:30
Golden State at Milwaukee, 8:00
Cleveland at Buffalo, 7:30

Friday, February 18
Seattle at Nets, 8:05
Phoenix at Philadelphia, 8:05
Portland at Chicago, 7:30
Washington at Detroit, 8:05
Knicks at Milwaukee, 8:00
Golden State at Indiana, 8:05
Atlanta at Los Angeles, 8:00

Saturday, February 19
Seattle at Buffalo, 9:00
Nets at Knicks, 8:00
Phoenix at Cleveland, 8:05
Detroit at Washington, 8:05
Houston at Kansas City, 8:05
Portland at Denver, 7:35

Sunday, February 20
Knicks at Nets, 1:45
Cleveland at Philadelphia, 1:45 (CBS-TV Reg.)
New Orleans at San Antonio, 12:45 (CBS-TV Reg.)
Los Angeles at Washington, 1:45 (CBS-TV Reg.)
Phoenix at Detroit, 6:45 (CBS-TV Reg.)
Seattle at Indiana, 7:05
Atlanta at Denver, 1:35
Boston at Golden State, 1:00 (CBS-TV Nat.)

HENRY BIBBY FEATURE

This past summer was not a pleasant one for Henry Bibby. The 6-1 guard was unable to reach contract terms with the New Orleans Jazz and then the club signed Gail Goodrich as a free agent to join Pete Maravich in the backcourt.

"I was concerned about my future," recalls Bibby. "I knew I could play in this league but I didn't know if I'd get the opportunity."

Then his chance came. The Philadelphia 76ers purchased his contract from New Orleans on Sept. 17 and he was one of 11 guards in the Sixers' camp, certainly not an ideal situation, but Henry made the most of it.

"We were looking for a good outside shooter and defensive player and he was available," said Philadelphia coach Gene Shue, hardly going overboard about his new player.

General manager Pat Williams almost echoed his coach's thoughts. "He was a known item," says Williams. "He was no longer needed in New Orleans and we decided to bring him to camp and see what he could do."

What he's done is even more than the 76ers could have anticipated. As the player cuts were made, Bibby remained and, when the season started, he was the Sixers' third guard behind Doug Collins and Lloyd Free. In the third game of the season, Bibby replaced Free in the starting lineup and he's been there ever since, teaming lately with Free while Collins was sidelined for a lengthy period with a pulled groin muscle.

One familiar with Bibby's NBA past may have had to do a double-take when watching him perform for Philadelphia. No longer is he the guard who comes off the bench to provide "Instant Offense."

He's now the playmaking guard. "This team doesn't need me to score," says Henry. "There are other things I can do to help us win. It's my job to get everyone into the offense. I can't be concerned about scoring. I have to concentrate on other parts of my game."

That's not as easy as it sounds. "I have to really concentrate on my ball handling and defense. It's a matter of adjusting my thinking both in practice and in the game. I have to think more about making the play. I'm not looking for my shot but I'll take it, when it's there."

Not that the playmaking role is entirely new, either. "I quarterbacked at UCLA, adds Henry who starred on Bruin national championship teams before joining the Knicks as a fourth round draft choice in 1972. "But when I came into the pros, I realized that, as a substitute, there was no way I could do everything I wanted to."

His role with the 76ers is different than the ones he had with the Knicks and Jazz and, besides, when you are fighting for your life in professional basketball, you do what's asked of you.

Lately, his scoring has picked up, along with his playmaking. Collins has been hampered since the first of the year and Henry's playing time has increased to the point where he's third on the club in minutes played, trailing only Julius Erving and George McGinnis. And his scoring has shown a corresponding increase, over 15 points a game in 1977.

Now Shue is talking more enthusiastically about his new guard. "It took him sometime to get used to our system," says Gene. "He was new to our team and he's feeling more comfortable as the season goes on. He's working all the time and playing great."

Perhaps playing so well that he'll help the 76ers gain the NBA championship, something new to every current Philadelphis player but Bibby, who was a rookie on the Knicks' title team in 1972-73.

                                                    more....

And how do the teams compare?

"Two completely different types of teams," says Henry. "The Knicks had a lot of experience and were team oriented. They played well together but were basically an outside shooting team.

"This team could be great. We have the ability to score from the inside that makes it so much easier to win."

To score from inside, you have to get the ball there. That's Henry Bibby's job and he's doing it well.

FOUR REGIONAL GAMES AND CELTICS-WARRIORS ON CBS SUNDAY

A national game, featuring the Boston Celtics at the Golden State Warriors, and four regional games will be televised by CBS Sports this Sunday (Feb. 20).

The regional games are: Cleveland at Philadelphia, Los Angeles at Washington, New Orleans at San Antonio and Phoenix at Detroit.

In the national game, which starts at 4 p.m., Eastern time, the Celtics will be looking for their first victory over the Warriors this season after two defeats.

Golden State won at home, 105-98, Jan. 2, with five players scoring in double figures paced by Rick Barry's 29 points. Boston's backcourt duo of JoJo White and Charlie Scott combined for 64 points, 33 by White, but the Celtics' other three starters, Steve Kuberski, Sidney Wicks and Jim Ard scored a total of only nine points.

Four weeks later, Jan. 30 in Boston, Golden State won again, 109-92, outscoring the Celtics 30-16 in the final quarter to break open a tight game. Phil Smith led the Warriors with 35 points, while John Havlicek had 20 for the Celtics.

The lineups for the national game:

No.	Boston Celtics	Ht.	No.	Golden State	Ht.
10	Jo Jo White	6-3	00	Robert Parish	7-0
12	Sidney Wicks	6-8	1	Gus Williams	6-2
17	John Havlicek	6-5	10	Charles Johnson	6-0
18	Dave Cowens	6-8	11	Marshall Rogers	6-1
20	Fred Saunders	6-7	15	Charles Dudley	6-2
27	Kevin Stacom	6-5	20	Phil Smith	6-4
31	Tom Boswell	6-9	22	Sonny Parker	6-6
33	Steve Kuberski	6-8	24	Rick Barry	6-8
34	Jim Ard	6-9	40	Derrek Dickey	6-7
41	Curtis Rowe	6-7	41	Jamaal Wilkes	6-6½
42	Bobby Wilson	6-3	42	Dwight Davis	6-8
52	Norm Cook	6-9	44	Clifford Ray	6-9

THURMOND NOTES THE DIFFERENCE

Is the style of play among league centers different than 10 years ago? "Yes," says Cleveland Cavaliers' 14-year veteran Nate Thurmond, who suffered a knee injury last week. "Centers now have more agility and shoot from both inside and outside. They're tougher to guard because they run so much more now."

BRAVES' GAME RESCHEDULED

The February 4 Indiana at Buffalo game, which was postponed because of the blizzard in Buffalo, has been rescheduled there for Monday night, February 21, at 7:30 p.m.

PLAYER TRANSACTIONS

Feb. 4: Philadelphia reinstated Dave Collins from injured list.

Feb. 8: Portland placed Lloyd Neal on injured list.

Feb. 10: Cleveland placed Nate Thurmond on injured list and reinstated Foots Walker from injured list.

Feb. 11: San Antonio waived Mack Calvin.

Feb. 11: Portland signed Clyde Mayes.

NATIONAL BASKETBALL ASSOCIATION
OFFICIAL SCORER'S REPORT

DATE _____ AT _____ ATTENDANCE _____

OFFICIALS: _____ TIME _____

VISITORS	Min	FGM	FGA	FTM	FTA	REBOUNDS			Ast	PF	Steals	Points
						OFF	DEF	TOTAL				
TOTALS												

FG % _____ FT % _____ TURNOVERS: _____ Team Rebounds: _____

HOME	Min	FGM	FGA	FTM	FTA	REBOUNDS			Ast	PF	Steals	Points
						OFF	DEF	TOTAL				
TOTALS												

FG % _____ FT % _____ TURNOVERS: _____ Team Rebounds: _____

BLOCKED SHOTS			Score By Periods	1	2	3	4	OT	OT	OT	TOTAL
VISITORS:	HOME:										
			REMARKS: _____								
			_____								
			_____								
			_____								
TOTALS	TOTALS										

NATIONAL BASKETBALL ASSOCIATION

OFFICIAL SCORER'S REPORT

DATE Feb. 10, 1977 AT Phoenix, Ariz. ATTENDANCE 11,352

OFFICIALS: Bob Rakel, Jesse Kersey TIME 2:03

VISITORS WASHINGTON	Min	FGM	FGA	FTM	FTA	REBOUNDS OFF	DEF	TOTAL	Ast	PF	Steals	Points
35 Grevey, F	19	1	6	0	0	1	2	3	1	2	1	2
11 Hayes, F	40	10	17	2	4	3	13	16	2	5	3	22
41 Unseld, C	41	4	8	2	2	5	8	13	5	3	3	10
45 Chenier, G	35	9	25	3	3	2	2	4	2	4	1	21
32 Wright, G	29	5	11	1	1	1	2	3	4	3	1	11
12 Gray	22	4	6	5	6	0	1	1	3	5	0	13
14 Henderson	23	3	6	2	2	0	2	2	1	1	0	8
25 Kupchak	21	9	14	4	8	4	9	13	1	3	0	22
8 WEISS	10	0	2	0	0	0	1	1	3	0	0	0
6 RIORDAN	DNP		COACHS	DECISION								
21 BING												
44 PACE												
TOTALS	240	45	95	19	26	16	40	56	22	26	9	109

FG% 474 FT% 731 TURNOVERS: 21 Team Rebounds: 9

HOME PHOENIX	Min	FGM	FGA	FTM	FTA	REBOUNDS OFF	DEF	TOTAL	Ast	PF	Steals	Points
32 Terrell, F	23	3	11	1	1	1	5	6	1	3	0	7
4 T. Van Arsdale, F	19	1	3	0	0	0	2	2	1	1	0	2
33 Adams, C	32	6	12	2	2	2	9	11	6	4	2	14
30 Lee, G	20	2	5	2	2	0	1	1	4	3	1	6
44 Westphal, G	36	11	21	7	9	1	2	3	5	0	3	29
40 Sobers	19	3	8	0	0	0	4	4	4	1	0	6
14 Erickson	27	5	12	1	2	1	5	6	3	1	2	11
21 Awtrey	27	3	7	6	6	0	3	3	3	2	0	12
5 D. Van Arsdale	21	6	8	0	0	0	0	0	2	2	1	12
24 HEARD	11	1	3	2	2	0	4	4	2	4	0	4
7 FEHER	DNP		COACHS	DECISION								
54 SCHLUETER	4											
TOTALS	240	41	90	21	24	5	35	40	31	21	9	103

FG% 456 FT% 875 TURNOVERS: 16 Team Rebounds: 4

BLOCKED SHOTS

VISITORS:	TOTAL 4	HOME:	TOTAL 4
HAYES	2	ADAMS	2
GRAY	1	HEARD	2
UNSELD	1		

Score By Periods	1	2	3	4	OT	OT	OT	TOTAL
WASHINGTON	21	27	31	30				109
PHOENIX	21	31	36	15				103

REMARKS: TECHNICAL FOULS: Chenier, Wash. 5:02 of 1st Q

Lee, Phx. 4:58 of 1st Q

Erickson, Phx. 1:06 of 3rd Q

264

Official Scoresheet

The blank sheet shown here is filled in by the official scorer after every NBA game and sent into the Elias Sports Bureau. It doesn't require as much work as a football or baseball scoresheet. You don't have pitching changes, pinch-hitters or extra-inning games, and though you can have overtime basketball games, it doesn't happen very often.

Washington-Phoenix

This example of a filled-out official scorer's report is from a game played at Phoenix on February 10, 1977, between the Suns and Washington Bullets.

Two copies are generally made up; one is done hastily to accommodate the writers who need the stats immediately after the game. That one, on orange paper, is checked over and proofread quickly. Photocopies are given to everyone who needs one. They provide the raw material for the box scores that appear in the next day's newspaper. If it's done quickly enough, the play-by-play announcer might have the official stats in front of him for use at the end of his broadcast.

Then the material is checked more thoroughly, copied over neatly on the white sheet provided for the official report and sent in to the Elias Sports Bureau.

Of all the sports I have worked, I probably relate most closely to basketball, which I played as a youngster and which I still play (though with slower steps and shorter breath). I hated to give up working basketball games, but my tight schedule forced me to. Basketball is still the best sport for a young person to break into a statistics career with, because just about every high school and college has a basketball team, and there's always a need for statistical help.

BETTING
AND STATS

Stats and Sports Betting

WE'VE TALKED about what sports statistics mean to fans, players, broadcasters, coaches, managers and general managers. One segment of the population we haven't discussed that has a profound interest in sports stats is the gambler. From professional oddsmaker to casual bettor, stats are of deep concern to gamblers. Much valuable, sought-after information is non-statistical, but something the statistician could, if he wanted to, pass along.

When I first started with the Mets, I'd get calls in the broadcast booth or hotel room from people who would identify themselves as a local sportswriter or broadcaster—one man even said he was a cartoonist—wanting to know about scheduled pitchers, injuries and the like. Calls would be especially frequent about fifteen minutes before the start of a double-header, when pitchers for both games had already been announced, but it was unclear who would start which game. In my naïveté, I'd answer these "media" people, until co-workers told me my callers were, in fact, bookmakers or other gamblers looking for an extra edge in betting.

For instance, if the Mets had a twin-bill scheduled and Seaver was slated to pitch one game and someone out of the bullpen was due to start the other, a bettor knowing which game Seaver was pitching would be able either to bet heavily on the Mets in the game Seaver was pitching or back the Mets' opponents in the game that the lesser pitcher was due to start.

Once I realized that my callers were gamblers, I deliberately started giving them wrong information. "Is Seaver pitching the first game?" they'd ask. And knowing that he was, I'd say, "No, he's pitching the second." After a while, those phone calls stopped coming, the gamblers either figuring that I had gotten wise to them or that I had the wrong information. I still get calls, of course, from legitimate media people, though occasionally a phony one may get by me.

Once, when Tommie Agee had been injured and out of the Mets' line-up for a few days, I got a long-distance call from someone who identified himself as being with a particular New York radio sports show. He asked whether Agee was going to play and I gave him the correct answer, that Tommie was still hurt and wasn't going to play. Something about the call struck me as odd, and when we got back to New York after the road trip, I checked with the man whose name the caller had given as his own. The announcer said he had never called me. It was obviously either a bookmaker or somebody else betting on the game. This helped get me in the habit of screening my calls, and I don't think they try any more.

We don't give starting line-ups even to the broadcasters doing our pregame show on radio or television. They find out when the people listening at home do—right before the start of the game. Then it's too late for anybody to change the odds on a game, or alter a bet.

Big Business

I'd estimate that gambling on sports is a better than sixty-*billion*-dollar business in the United States. Still, many sports bettors keep their own records and statistics.

You probably have heard the story about the incurable gambler who goes to a bookie every day and bets on every single pro basketball game, and loses every one of his bets. The same pattern continues for a week, but he still wants to bet. So he asks his bookie what's on the NBA schedule, and the bookmaker replies, "There are no basketball games today, but there are four hockey games."

"What the hell do I know about *hockey?*" the bettor demands.

Betting Line

Professional bookmakers go by a betting line, which consists of the odds on a game and the point spread, the number of points by which one team is likely to defeat another.

270

Most bets are made on a 6–5 or 5½–5 basis, which means you stand to win five dollars, but if you lose you pay six dollars or five dollars and fifty cents on your five-dollar bet. The edge goes to the bookmaker as his profit for handling the action.

The only official football line in the country is the Las Vegas line, which is the one that most bookmakers use in determining point spreads on both college and professional games. In basketball and baseball the line comes from a dozen different sources across the country.

Especially for football games, which are played once a week (college on Saturday and pros generally on Sunday), the line will constantly change, according to the information made available about injuries and other matters.

Information Sources

There are a great many publications and services offered to sports bettors. They may be as generalized as a weekly newsletter or as refined as telephone services that offer last-minute information.

Many of these services try hard to know their business and many have been able to operate with a degree of success. But a knowledgeable sports fan can do about as well with his own handicapping of a sports event. Regardless of the extent of their operations, I believe the sports services can't win much more than 50 percent of the time, which means they're wrong close to 50 percent of the time.

Football:
The Most Popular
Sport for Betting

AS FAR AS BETTING is concerned, football is probably the number-one sport. There are all sorts of betting cards and pools conducted in offices, as well as man-to-man and man-to-bookmaker betting. Accordingly all sorts of football handicapping services have developed. In addition, because so many fans can't sit down to watch a football game without betting on it, many of them keep a lot of their own records.

The point spread is vital to the football bettor, for it often determines whether he'll win or lose his bet. Often the question isn't which team is better than the other—there's a near-unanimous agreement on that—but by how many points.

Let's assume, for example, that Ohio State is playing Michigan on a particular Saturday afternoon, and the point spread has Michigan a ten-point underdog to Ohio State. What this means, in essence, is that at least on paper, Ohio State is ten points better than Michigan and should win by that margin or very close to it. If you bet on Ohio State, therefore, for you to win your bet, Ohio State has to win by at least eleven points. You've given a ten-point handicap. If Ohio State wins by nine points or less, you've lost your bet, even though you backed the winning team. If Ohio State wins by exactly ten points, which was the point spread, the bet is off.

Because they don't want to have to return the bettors' money, some bookies eliminate the possibility of a deadlock by adding an extra half-point to the spread

272

quoted by the professional linemaker. In the case cited, they might make Ohio State a 10½-point favorite, so that even a 10-point victory for Ohio State would give the bookie the win from those who bet on Ohio State. It sometimes pays for a bettor to shop around for a bookie who hasn't added on that half-point. And there are instances where a bettor, finding bookies who quote slightly different odds, will bet one team with one bookie and the opponent with the other—and on rare occasions, win both bets!

In wagering on professional football, the bettor, to be successful, can't have enough statistical data available. Items such as the past performance of a football team and its ability to beat the point spread over the course of a season are essential.

There's really no magic formula for selecting winners of a football game, because there are so many unpredictable factors, such as injuries to key players, weather conditions and psychological reactions of a team to where they're playing. But statistics and trends remain fairly constant from year to year, and the wise bettor relies on careful analysis of these factors in determining which team to bet on.

Injuries

The biggest winning edge the bettor can develop is knowing the extent of injuries to players. Knowing that a couple of big players are hurt helps the bettor decide whether to give points and bet on the favorite or take points and bet on the underdog.

However, there are many ways of evaluating players' injuries as listed in the club's injury report. Some are listed as "doubtful starters," some "questionable," some "possible" and some "probable." This is rather hazy terminology that sometimes can lead to confusion. Sometimes a player listed as "doubtful" will see more action than a "probable" starter. Only if a player is hurt really seriously will he be designated beforehand as being out of a game.

Weather

Weather conditions play an important part in the betting considerations of some fans. There are teams—perhaps Los Angeles or Dallas or Miami—that do not play well late in the season in cold-weather areas like Minnesota, Green Bay or Detroit. From your own records, or those kept by others, you'll see that as a

273

season wears on, teams used to playing in warm weather don't do well in northern climates. This will affect the outcome of either late-season or post-season games, and the bettor who has kept track of these things will bet accordingly.

Some bettors believe you should give extra consideration to the underdog, either in a college or pro game, if the weather is going to be particularly bad. Especially in a college game, bad weather would be a good time to bet on a four-touchdown underdog, because it might be a very difficult day for scoring points. Betting on the underdog, you have twenty-eight points in your pocket, and they have a better chance of losing by less than twenty-eight on a wet, sloppy field, where it's hard to score, than on a dry surface.

Other Betting Factors

Some football bettors—bookmakers among them—keep track of how a team has done historically vis-à-vis the point spread: in other words, how often its winning margin exceeded the spread when it was the favored team, and how often it came within the spread when it was the underdog.

After studying the stats made available through publications and broadcasters, sophisticated football fans will go beyond those factors and take into consideration such matters as the home-field advantage; the career competition records between teams from the same conference, which play each other year after year; the record of a particular quarterback against a given team; and so on.

Some bettors will keep records not only of how, say, the Minnesota Vikings and Detroit Lions (both in the same conference) have done against each other over the years, but how they've done on their home field and their opponent's field. And they'll study how Fran Tarkenton, the Minnesota quarterback, has done against Detroit over the years.

There are various factors a football bettor has to be aware of. For example, it's important to know that one of the front four on the defensive team isn't going to play in the game. This is important because it means the pass rush will be less intense, and if you give even the worst quarterback in the league a couple of extra seconds to throw, he'll perform like the best quarterback in the league. Similarly, if you give a so-so running back a couple of extra steps to the outside—as would happen if the opposing starting defensive end is hurt and not playing—he could operate with the high-class quality of O. J. Simpson. So you can see how little bits of information can make a difference to the bettor.

Basketball Betting

IN BETTING on basketball, neither the bookmaker nor the bettor has much information from which to draw. Certainly there's not as much as in football. Yet the gambling action is second only to football.

Except for the statistical nuts who keep their own records and follow every game in detail, it's impractical to develop adequate stats on which to make "scientific" betting judgments. Remember, the average college team plays about thirty games a season, and pro teams play eighty-two games in the regular season. Keeping records for a pro basketball team is a lot different from doing it for a pro football team, which plays only sixteen regular-season games. Handicapping the hundreds of college and professional basketball games that take place every week is an almost impossible task.

Another problem is the time lag between games. In football you ordinarily have a full week between games and nothing of importance (such as injuries) is likely to escape the attention of the news media. But basketball games are played every day of the week, and there isn't sufficient time between games for the fan to digest and analyze the stats thoroughly. And because there are so many games on the schedule, no single game can possibly get the kind of detailed exposure an individual football game does. You don't go into a basketball bet with as much information as you have for a football bet. It's more of a helter-skelter situation. Nevertheless, there are certain factors that ought to be considered in making a bet.

Home-Court Advantage

In the 1976–77 season, the home-court advantage played an important role in who won a large percentage of basketball games, both college and professional. The home records of teams were too good for it to be considered mere coincidence.

Point Spread

As with football, the astute basketball bettor will keep track of how each club does in relation to its point spread. If a team has been failing to make the point spread constantly, a linemaker will be a little leery about posting the spread for that team's next game. In some instances, he might take the team off the books.

Often you'll see sportswriters comment sarcastically that the only patrons who stayed until the end of a one-sided basketball game were bettors who wanted to know if they'd beaten the point spread. The boos or cheers that accompany a basket late in a one-sided game usually come from bettors for whom the spread is all-important.

Pro Games Preferred

A lot of people prefer to bet on pro basketball games rather than college games. I think that's primarily because in pro basketball the bettor, the linemaker and the bookmaker are privy to just about everything going on, whether it's an injury to a key player, a winning streak or anything else pertinent to a bet. With that knowledge, the linemaker can establish his line accurately (and profitably), and the others can call their bets accordingly. No one is likely to make as many mistakes in wagering on pro games as on college games, where conditions in far-off places like New Mexico or Kansas may change overnight without the linemaker or bettor knowing anything about it. The line will be set only according to what the linemaker knows.

Almost every college in the country has a basketball team, and it's a physical impossibility to keep up on what's happening all over, no matter how many records and statistics you keep.

276

Polls Don't Help

Even the polls are not a great help in determining how to bet. When a team is high in the weekly ratings, you're likely to think, "They're winning, so they must be good"—and bet on them. But if you don't know what the team's schedule has been, and it's beaten only lesser teams, its won-lost record is a bit deceiving. If it's going up against a good team and you bet on it because of its record, you're making a mistake.

By the same token, if you don't realize that all of a team's victories have been at home and this game is on the road, where it does badly, you'd be mistaken to bet on this team. The opposites also apply, of course. A team might be better than its won-lost record because it has played a very tough schedule. Or it might lose a lot on the road but still be a worthwhile bet today, because tonight's game is at home.

Actually, you should probably disregard the ratings as a basis for making a bet. The weekly ratings that come in from the two wire services, AP and UPI, are probably the worst possible guides. The Associated Press poll is compiled by sportswriters from member newspapers across the country, but how can a fellow in Arkansas, who hasn't seen any eastern teams play in weeks, give an accurate appraisal when he votes? And the United Press rankings are based on the votes of college coaches throughout the land, but each one sees only a few of the top teams play, and their knowledge is mainly of what's happening in their own respective geographical locations, or based on what they've read.

Baseball Betting

To bet on baseball, you don't really need elaborate scouting reports or the guides or other printed material that bettors in football and basketball rely on. The reasons are that there's so much information available daily in the newspapers and the average baseball fan is much more aware of what's happening in his sport than other fans.

The betting line may be given simply in terms of which team is favored. Say the Mets are a 6–5 or 8–5 favorite, which means that you risk six or eight dollars to win five. Sometimes the line is a point spread given according to runs. For example, Cincinnati may be a two-run favorite to win a game; if you bet on the Reds and they win by one run, you lose the bet. Rarely does a wager involve both odds and a run margin.

Wait until June

Don't make a baseball bet until June, when the teams have leveled off at their own ability. Too many strange things can happen in April and May—.200 hitters hitting .350, last year's pennant-winners playing below .500, rookie pitchers blowing the ball past seasoned batting stars. Unlike other sports, a lot of baseball games are postponed until later in the season because of bad weather, and so it takes a longer time for a pattern to emerge that accurately reflects the talent you're betting on.

278

Betting on Pitchers

Baseball betting is essentially pitcher betting. In fact, some bookmakers quote the names of opposing hurlers rather than opposing teams. Connie Mack used to say that pitching is 80 percent of the game, but many bettors feel the figure is even higher than that.

Since pitching is the most important factor in determining which team to bet on, knowledgeable fans will keep records of how each pitcher has done over the season, both overall and against particular teams. Some pitchers, of course, perform well against some teams and poorly against others, just as some teams have their patsies and their nemeses. You have to consider what side the pitcher throws from, whether the team he's facing has mostly left-handed or right-handed batters, and how that pitcher does against hitters from either side of the plate.

Occasionally, the starting pitcher's name is incorrectly listed in the newspaper, so the bettor has to be ever alert. It helps in this instance to know whether that team calls for a four-day or five-day pitching rotation.

Injuries

As in all other sports, it's helpful to know what players are sidelined by injuries (or slumps), information that's readily available in the daily papers.

Other Factors

The home advantage usually is not so important in baseball as it is in basketball or football.

Streaks give a team a winning edge. The mental attitude of a team is usually better when it's won its preceding game.

Many baseball bettors clip out the box scores and other printed statistics from the papers and study them carefully, hoping to uncover a surprise angle. For example, they might learn that a certain pitcher loses most of his night games, or that a particular team seems to have trouble scoring runs in a particular ball park, or that a team always has problems the first couple of days on a road trip, especially after traveling a long distance.

Gimmicks

There are a lot of popular gambling gimmicks around for baseball, including office pools and daily and weekly pools on the runs scored by a group of teams. These ordinarily don't involve a lot of money. They're usually run by a small, dollar-volume bookie, or perhaps just by a co-worker looking for a pastime. There are baseball pool cards, similar to football cards, in which you are given 4–1 or 5–1 odds that you can't pick the winners of, say, five games on a particular day. Sometimes the odds offered are higher.

Because baseball is played just about every day, it's hard to break the betting habit. If you're on a losing streak you figure, "Well, I can always come back and win tomorrow."

Hockey Betting

HOCKEY IS A tremendously exciting spectator sport, but there really isn't much gambling action listed, though in 1976–77 the line on hockey games was posted in New York papers for the first time. It's such a low-scoring sport, you need every possible edge to stay in the black when betting.

The price line on hockey games is usually based on the differential in goals. For instance, if the Canadiens are favored to beat the Rangers, the bookmaker's line might read, "Montreal, 1–1½ goals." This means that if you placed your money on Montreal, you would win only if they defeated the Rangers by two or more goals. As with football and basketball, the bettor is really laying the odds, and of course, the bookmaker comes out with the edge.

Home Advantage

One big factor in winning hockey games—and bets—is the home advantage. The home team wins a large percentage of hockey games—more so than in baseball and football, though not so much as in basketball.

Who's the Goalie?

The goaltender's record is probably the most important factor in deciding how to bet. Remember, the goalie is the last line of defense in a hockey game, and when he makes a mistake, that red goal light goes on.

Unlike baseball, where the newspaper is usually accurate on the expected starting pitcher, you almost never know for sure who the starting goaltender in a hockey game will be. A fan who follows hockey closely will usually have a pretty good hunch, though, and can bet accordingly, provided other factors are also taken into consideration.

In Canada, where more hockey betting goes on than in the United States, fans keep their own records of how goalies play against each team, how each player fares against particular teams, how certain teams do in given arenas.

Don't Ignore Scheduling

A big handicapping factor in hockey is the scheduling, and by that I don't mean just which team is playing which.

It's not unusual for a team to be in, say, Minnesota one night, and the West Coast the next night. A hockey fan who likes to bet will check the schedule a week in advance to see where clubs have played before and where they're heading. If there's a big travel jump after a hard home stand, you can usually bet against the club in the second or third game of its road trip—*no matter how easy the opposition may appear!*

Power-Play Record vs. Penalty Record

A good trick for a hockey bettor is to note whether a team with a good power-play record is facing a team that draws a lot of penalties. In such a match, you can figure that the good power-play team is going to get a lot of opportunities. Even if it's the weaker of the two teams, you might be swayed to bet on it because the stronger team gets so many penalties. Let's say the Philadelphia Flyers—a good club, but also the most penalized team in the league (averaging perhaps twenty minutes a game)—are playing the Minnesota North Stars, who are way down in the standings but have an unusually effective power play. You can assume that, based on past performance, Minnesota is going to have eight or nine opportunities to use a power play against the Flyers. If the North Stars come into the game a two-goal underdog, it might be a good idea to bet on them. Yet if Minnesota were playing Pittsburgh, which averages only eight penalty minutes a game, it's likely they'd get only three or four opportunities for power plays and you'd lose your betting edge.

Five-Dollar Bet, Hundred-Dollar Satisfaction

Some bettors keep such incredibly vast and complex records for themselves, you'd think they were employed as statisticians for a team. Often it's not so much a matter of money as it is sheer satisfaction. Many of them bet very small amounts. They know they're not going to get rich betting on sports events. For them it's just a specialized kind of game, and even if they win just five dollars in the course of a week, the effort is well worth it in terms of satisfaction.

In many cases, the five-dollar bettor will get more satisfaction than the plunger who bets hundreds of dollars on the game. Maybe it's the joy of outwitting the establishment.

Statistician's Edge

Obviously, as a professional statistician, I have an edge in betting on sports, especially baseball. But I haven't placed any bets since I've been in the business. I certainly wouldn't wager on games involving teams with which I've been associated. I'd never even consider wagering on a particular game, because I'd really have a problem preserving my objectivity. I have enough trouble keeping my emotions in check.

It's enough for me to hope that the teams I work for win, because I'm an employee *and* a fan. Because betting on them would adversely affect the way I did my job, I've never been involved in any kind of bet on any of the thousands and thousands of sporting events I've worked.

Also, I know from observing people who do bet that once you start, it mushrooms. It doesn't stop at being a one-shot or once-a-week deal; it gets into your blood and it's very, very difficult to stop.

NUMBERS FOR FUN AND PROFIT

Broadcasters

Broadcaster Temperament

Like any other group of people, broadcasters have a variety of temperaments. Some are high-strung and tend to come apart when things go wrong. Others can roll with the punches. The latter group knows that no one is perfect and that mistakes will be made. If you err, they'll correct the mistake and just go on.

Most of the broadcasters I have worked with could handle almost any situation that arose in the course of a ball game calmly. In critical situations or when something out of the ordinary happens that they may not even be able to see clearly because fans are blocking them or because it happened in a remote part of the field, they'll deal with it in a professional way, without panic, until I can pass on whatever information is appropriate.

Bob Murphy showed his cool in more ways than one when during the 1977 baseball season, I moved some papers in such a way that they interfered with some microphone wires and overturned a can of soda all over Murph. Without missing a syllable, he broadcast the whole inning standing up, while his pants dried.

Differences in personality really show up at the outset of a broadcast. Some broadcasters, no matter how many thousands of games they've announced in their careers, are always nervous when a broadcast begins. You know not to disturb their concentration at this point, because they're so tense and absorbed in

287

what they're going to say, they're probably going to jump at anything *you* say. If anyone so much as taps them on the shoulder, they'll just about go through the booth. With broadcasters of this type, you learn to have said anything you're going to say by ten or fifteen minutes before air time.

These broadcasters are a far different breed from the sportscasters who will laugh and joke and be loose as the proverbial goose right up to fifteen seconds before air time.

A statistician has to learn which broadcaster has which kind of personality, and deal with him accordingly. With those announcers he sees infrequently, he has to be extra careful because there are situations he hasn't seen them in, and he doesn't want to upset their concentration or pass them information when they're not prepared to use it. Therefore, he's got to be more alert and on guard.

There are personality differences, of course, even among the broadcasters I work with regularly. The three Met announcers each like certain kinds of items more than others. Bob Murphy, for example, tends to become a little more excited in some situations than Ralph Kiner or Lindsey Nelson would. When it's coming down to a tense part of the game, I make sure I've got a line on every pitch. Murph would also get into a little more detail on the out-of-town scores than the other two would. Ralph Kiner loves offbeat trivia—say, the fact (mentioned earlier) that Larry Christenson was the only pitcher to have hit two homers the previous season.

All three Met broadcasters are very dedicated, always well prepared. They get to the ball park very early, at least two hours before the game, and know what they're going to say before a game starts.

That's not the case with all broadcasters, by any means.

Unfortunately, some broadcasters (none I work with) don't let facts stand in the way of a good story. And they're content to bull their way through, rather than prepare. A typical exchange:

"Hey, who's out in the bullpen?"

"I don't know. Looks like a right-hander."

Or:

"Hey, haven't the Red Sox won a lot of games?"

"Seven or eight, I think. I don't know."

To me, this kind of broadcasting shows they're not taking pride in their work and, certainly, that they're ill-prepared.

I've worked with announcers over the years who were not prepared, but those I work with now are, without exception, *well* prepared. Lindsey Nelson is as thorough a broadcaster as you'll ever meet. Bob Murphy is always asking me

288

dozens of questions before a game: "Who's hurting on this team?" "Who's hitting?" "What was so-and-so's record in the minors?" Ralph Kiner and Marv Albert are also well prepared. These broadcasters, regardless of the number of years they've been well-regarded broadcasting professionals, do their homework as if they were just starting out.

For instance, Marv will be in the booth about forty-five minutes before a hockey game to check over the note and stat sheets, circling what he wants to use, crossing out what he thinks is not significant. This is someone who's made it to the top, so you might think he doesn't have to give it that much effort. But he does, because he takes pride in his work.

Others, some of the out-of-towners, aren't nearly so dedicated. Twenty minutes before the game, they're still in the pressroom, drinking a soda. As they're walking out, they might ask, "Hey, Artie, who's hurt for the Rangers?" But they do little beyond that—and it shows.

Some broadcasters change. One I worked with a long time was very conscientious when he first started. For years, he invariably gave extra effort. But then, whether it was because he thought he had it made or for some other reason, he started to change. It got to the point where his pregame preparation was almost nil.

His laxity affected my work, too. Before, I had put forth extra effort to match his because I wanted his broadcasts to be especially good. But now that he wasn't trying very hard, neither was I. It got to the point where I would do only what I had to.

His performance was almost an insult to my professional pride, because I felt that people who watch broadcasts I'm associated with over a period of time get to know that the statistics, scores and records given by the announcer are fed to him by me, in most cases. So when *no* information is forthcoming or erroneous information is given it's an affront to my professional integrity and reputation. This broadcaster either made mistakes in what I gave him, or invented "facts."

Luckily, this man is an exception; most broadcasters I've worked with are hard-working, well-prepared pros who take a great deal of pride in what they do.

Appreciation of Stats

Not all major league broadcasts employ statisticians, and in too many other instances the statistician is a working broadcaster, which means when he's on the air he can't be doing the job of a statistician. Montreal's French-language broad-caster does the stat sheets every day, but since he is broadcasting, he can't be available to the others in the course of a ball game.

Most broadcasters have a deep appreciation of statistics—certainly, the Met announcers do. Lindsey, for example, comments that you can't do a broadcast without statistics, especially in baseball, the most statistic-oriented of all sports. "The statistician may be the most important man in the booth," he declares.

Bob Murphy feels that the statistician is "terribly important" because, he says, "the one thing you want to do is impart as much information as you possibly can to a sports fan. The broadcaster is fully occupied in detailing the play-by-play, and so he has to rely on a statistician to be on top of the things that are happening while the game is going on."

Ralph Kiner comments that baseball is a game of statistics, and stats are part of its romance. The people who follow the game probably follow the numbers considerably more than do fans in any other sport, he says, "and so it's constant comparisons and constant chances for discussions and arguments."

According to Lindsey Nelson, a statistician can actually set the tenor of the whole broadcast, because, he says, his attitude will have a lot to do with the attitude of the broadcaster.

Sometimes I get compliments from the front office, and I appreciate the pat on the back. But the compliments that mean the most are those I get from the people with whom I work directly.*

* Bob Murphy, who has worked with men he considers outstanding statisticians, says that "as fine as other people are, they don't come close to doing the job that Art Friedman does." Murphy has gone so far as to say that in years to come, Art could be a successful general manager of a professional sports team, because, working as he does with statistics, Art is aware of the inner workings of a club, both on the field and in the front office.

Murphy has said of Friedman that he has the mind to handle his responsibilities and the personality that makes people want to be around him and work with him. Consequently Murphy observes, Art has the chance to do just about anything he wants to in sports. Lindsey Nelson has praised Art's "fantastic memory."

Ralph Kiner notes that Art is extremely fast and that he keeps up with everything. Kiner says Art listens to the broadcast, so if an announcer gets on to a subject that requires quick reference, he'll have it ready before the announcer needs it. "That in itself makes broadcasting so much easier for us," says Ralph, explaining that while a broadcaster might remember an approximate figure, he would not remember the exact one. (Did Aaron hit a homer every 16.2 times at bat, or every 16.3?) And if there wasn't a man to look it up for the broadcaster, he'd have to do it himself. "And you probably wouldn't even do a good job on your play-by-play because you can't do both. But he puts it right out there in front of you, which lets you continue your trend of thought, and it really makes for a much smoother, much easier broadcast."

290

Gaining Broadcaster's Confidence

One of the most important things a statistician has to do is gain the trust of the broadcasters with whom he's working. They have to have faith in the information he's given them because, in the heat of the game, they're not going to have the chance to check a fact out themselves.

Lindsey Nelson has said he has sufficient confidence in me to start a sentence on the air without knowing the ending, which requires a statistical fact, because he's certain that I'll supply it in time. For example, during a late-1976 at-bat for Joe Torre, Lindsey recalled that Torre had started the season with a lifetime average of close to .300, but, not knowing what it was precisely, he turned to me, and I told him immediately, ".298."

"It would have been horrible," Lindsey told an interviewer, "if Artie had come back and said, 'I don't know,' or 'Wait, I'll look it up.' But I knew he'd have it. You have to sort of leave things up to your statistician."

When a broadcaster and statistician work together a long enough time for confidence to develop, then the broadcaster can do a great many things he wouldn't otherwise. Lindsey remembers a national network broadcast of a football game on the West Coast where the statistician asked him, "Now, what kind of statistics do you want to have?" Lindsey compares his own reaction to the maxim, "If you have to ask about the cost of a yacht, you can't afford to own one." Lindsey didn't tell the statistician, but his feeling was that if he didn't know the kind of stats Lindsey would want, he probably wouldn't be of much help, because Lindsey didn't have time to sit down with him and lay out what he needed. "I need anything that's pertinent to this broadcast," Lindsey comments, "and he needs to know what is pertinent and give it to me."

Daily Contact Makes a Difference

Obviously, there's a big difference between working with the same broadcasters on a daily basis, as I do with the Mets, and the "Monday Night Football" sort of thing, where the statistician sees the broadcasters only once a week and there is little opportunity to learn how one another thinks and feels. That relationship, necessarily, is going to be cooler when the contact is occasional.

In contrast, the Met broadcasters and I know each other so well that we can easily perceive that one of the others isn't feeling well or is having a personal problem, without his mentioning it. There's a terrifically loose, relaxed relationship among us, and we've enjoyed many a laugh at situations that have developed over the years.

Some of the laughs have come from running gags. One I always think of involves Ralph Kiner's rugs. After we had won the 1969 World Series, the Met announcers and several of the players went on a tour that included Morocco. There, Ralph, who tends to purchase all kinds of unusual things, bought a couple of rugs. Winter went by and so did early spring, and Ralph hadn't received his rugs. In one particular game, which was carried by Armed Forces Radio, Ralph thought it would be fun to mention that if the rug dealer in Morocco was listening, he would appreciate receiving the floor coverings he had ordered more than six months earlier. Ralph did announce it, and a few days later he came to the park with a big smile, reporting that his rugs had arrived.

Trivia Experts

ONE OF THE BEST baseball trivia experts I've ever encountered is Lauren Matthews, promotion director and former public address announcer for the Mets.

To Lauren, baseball trivia comes naturally. Of course, the fact that he was deeply interested in the sport made it easy to absorb and retain obscure information.

He agrees that a prime reason for the widespread interest in baseball trivia is the fact that baseball has many more statistics than other sports. And, he says, it has a richer history. Baseball has had excellent records from the turn of the century on, and its early personalities were widely publicized. He makes the point that everyone knew Babe Ruth hit sixty homers one season, but few knew the yards gained by Red Grange.

Lauren has engaged in at least one major trivia "confrontation." It took place in the middle of the 1975 season, and started, as so many things do, as a joke. The bartender in a tavern frequented by electricians with whom Lauren works bills himself as "The Pope" and is something of a legend among people who know him. Patrons would come into the bar and swap trivia with him.

Somehow the idea of a trivia match developed, and Chip Cipolla, the WNEW-radio sportscaster, got interested in putting the match on the air. Participants would be "The Pope," Lauren and "Bill the Baker," a fan I get to see throughout the year.

Bill's real name is Bill Stimers and he's known as "the Baker" for the simple reason that he works for a bakery. A quiet, low-keyed man, Bill is invariably helpful. From his seat behind the broadcast booth, he'll keep me posted on what is transpiring in out-of-town games he listens to on his ever-present radio, and he'll give me programs from out-of-town games he's attended.

Bill is quite a fan. In addition to his Met tickets, he has tickets to Jets games and season's tickets to Ranger games. Along with his portable radio, he keeps programs, scoresheets and other paraphernalia with him in the ball park. He's such a baseball fan that one year when both the Mets and Yankees were involved in pennant races, he watched a game at Shea, then caught a bus to Cleveland in time to watch the Yankees play there, then rode a bus all night to come back to Shea for the Mets' game the following night.

So it was a worthy line-up of trivia experts. The questions were drawn up by Larry Kieran, controller for the Harry M. Stevens Co. Larry, after considerable research, came up with about one hundred tough but legitimate queries.

Chip emceed. He'd ask a question and the contestants had ten seconds to write down the answer. Lauren won the match, but he observes that he and the others could have asked one another questions that would have elicited only an intelligent guess, at best. Though he's read about the period before 1955, that year is when he really got into baseball seriously. An older trivia fan would probably be better at events that happened before 1955.

Lauren makes up the questions for the baseball quiz that goes on the Shea scoreboard at every Met home game. Some he just gets off the top of his head; others he finds in a record book. He considers *The Baseball Encyclopedia* (published by Macmillan) an excellent source.

Late in the '76 season, he had this question on the board: "Can you name three Met switch-hitters who have hit home runs from both sides of the plate?"

When he posted the answer, I called to tell him that I thought there were *four* (Bud Harrelson, as well as the three he had—Lee Mazzilli, Ken Singleton and Don Bosch). Lauren said he'd check with Bud, and Harrelson said the first of his four career homers was an inside-the-park job down the right-field line in Pittsburgh in 1967, which he said he hit right-handed. I could have sworn he hit it left-handed. Over the years, I have found that ballplayers are the worst judges of what happened to them. But Bud is an exception; he usually is very aware of what's happening. Next day I checked at Shea and found that he was correct: he had hit the homer off Juan Pizarro, a left-handed pitcher, and though he hit the ball down the right-field line, he was batting right-handed. Bud even remembers that the right-fielder was Al Luplow and that the fielder thought the ball was foul, so he didn't chase it right away.

294

A new scoreboard feature at Madison Square Garden is the posting of a nightly trivia question, drawn up by John Halligan and me for hockey games. The question will involve either the Rangers or that night's visiting team. We try to make it a good head-scratcher, but not so obscure that it's just utter frustration for even the most knowledgeable fan. Trivia should be fun.

Funny, You Don't Look Like a Statistician

WHEN I FIRST STARTED working full-time as a statistician, people meeting me for the first time seemed surprised. "Gee," they'd say, "we pictured a little old man with horn-rimmed glasses sitting over an actuarial table."

I'm sorry to bend the stereotype, but few if any statisticians are what people expect. As I mentioned, I was terrible at math in high school. I hated math so much, I got about as far as algebra and gave it up completely.

The only time I enjoyed arithmetic was when I applied it to the sports records I was keeping at home. Of course, I could remember the number of every player who was on the 1955 Dodgers, but I couldn't remember what I had learned the day before in math.

Maybe this is consoling news to some of you who entertain visions of becoming statisticians. You don't have to love math, and courses in advanced algebra and trigonometry aren't prerequisites, by any means. Similarly, being a whiz at math is no guarantee you'd be a good statistician.

I get letters from hundreds of people who hope to become pro sports statisticians. They come not only from youngsters, but also from older people, men in their thirties and forties making twice the money that I do, in jobs as CPA's or in the stock market. They're bored with their work and want to enter the world of sports statistics, which they think is glamorous. They want to travel all over the country, have people ask for their autographs, associate with sports heroes and all the rest. I hate to puncture any dreams, but the profession is far from a bed of

296

roses. It has its good points—as expressed by my oldest son, Jeffrey, who, when he was about six and couldn't even pronounce "statistician," let alone spell it, was engaged in conversation with a friendly neighborhood grocer. The man asked him the usual questions about his name, age, where he lived and went to school, then said: "Where does your daddy work?"

Jeffrey thought a minute and replied, "My daddy doesn't work; he just goes to baseball games."

(The day is not too far off when Jeffrey and then my middle son, Gregg, will be helping me do my work at home. Our youngest, Jonathan, is only five, but I'm pretty sure he'll be as deeply into the game as his brothers are.)

Yes, there is a glamorous, fun aspect to the job, but that's only one side of it. As I tell people who want to get into the business, you can forget about ever having a weekend off and must be prepared to work thirty-five or more days in a row. We had a stretch in 1976 when we went thirty-seven days without respite, then had one day off and went seventeen more in a row. In other words, in a fifty-five-day stretch we enjoyed one day off. And "enjoyed" is hardly the word, because that one day we were off in Chicago, it didn't stop raining until 4:30 in the afternoon.

There are times when I feel sorry for myself, even a little bitter. Suppose we've just played a tough double-header and we're hot and dirty. On the plane, we can't wait for that first drink and to sit back and just relax. Everybody is able to do that, except for a few writers—and the broadcast statistician. Just about everyone else can read, sleep, chat, play cards, whatever, but the statistician can't, because there's too much work to do. And it's not easy to work on an airplane, because the tables are small and the plane goes up and down like a rookie's batting average.

But it's primarily at home that I get to feeling sorry for myself, especially after a game in which there have been rain delays. I get home after midnight, and I've still got a couple of hours of work to do. I'm sometimes tempted to hang up my calculator and call it quits, but there's too much that's good about working as a sports statistician to give up the experience.

A statistician has to be prepared for a lot of work—in fact, more than most people in the business have. Of course, he's got to enjoy sports thoroughly. I've worked as a statistician at more than three thousand sports events—that's a lot of National Anthems to hear—and I've seen so many, I almost never attend a game that I'm not working.

Because of expansion, stats are more important now in all major sports— you're dealing with six hundred major league baseball players, as opposed to two hundred; with eighteen National Hockey League teams, instead of six; twenty-six NFL football teams, instead of twelve; and so on. And because statistics form more of a dimension than ever before for evaluating an athlete and giving him personality, there are more opportunities for statisticians. Yet opportunities are not unlimited. The chances of making it into the ranks of statistician for a professional sports club is less than the opportunity of making it as a pro athlete.

How to Break into Sports Statistics

Despite all this, if you're still determined to give it a whirl, I'd say the best place to start is at home. Keep your own records; learn to keep score and compile day-by-day records of teams and individual players. Set up your own systems. This will give you a feeling for the job and the experience of doing it, and will help you decide whether you really like doing it.

Seymour Siwoff of the Elias Sports Bureau says his organization receives hundreds of job applications each year, which is much more than they can handle. Elias is very selective about hiring, because, "as the result of our reputation, we can't afford to have anyone here who can't produce." Some who have tried out at Elias have failed, but those who do manage to land positions there, last. "We have very little turnover," Siwoff says.

An accountant himself, Siwoff remarks that you don't necessarily have to be an accountant to do a good job in statistics, "though it probably would help in some areas." It does take a particular type to do well, he adds.

Because of the great demands for Elias's services, the bureau does take on some part-time people. "Remember," he says, "on a Sunday sometimes we cycle in two different crews—one in the morning and one at night. So we need hands, but capable hands."

Accordingly, when he responds to young people who write in about jobs, he emphasizes that the field is limited. "We hate to sound discouraging," he'll write, "but we have to be realistic. If you can get a club to give you a chance, great, because there is an opportunity there." He always tells young people to get a good education, and if they like sports, to major in journalism as an avenue to get into it.

Expansion teams have asked Siwoff to help develop their statistical crews, and he's gone to places such as Tampa and Seattle, which added football teams in 1976, to interview candidates and run seminars.

Existing teams in different sports that were having trouble have also enlisted

Siwoff's help. "If we could get the same quality of people out in the field that we have in our office, it would be fantastic for us."

There are openings on a part-time basis with some of the expansion teams, so he recommends that people interested in becoming sports statisticians write local clubs. If possible, become a statistician for your high school or college teams.

Keeping stats for basketball games is a good way to break into the business. A person in college has ample opportunity to do this, because almost every college in the country has a basketball team, and there is a need for people to keep the records and statistics that have to be given to sportswriters and broadcasters (and sometimes to the league or conference in which the college plays). It's terrific experience.

Read as much as you can about sports, to give yourself the background to provide information beyond the figures.

Try to do as much baseball as you can, because baseball stats are the most involved, and if you can do *them,* you can do any sports statistics. There are ten times the stats kept in baseball as in football, basketball or hockey, and you have to update them every day, as opposed to the other sports, in which you have several days to a week to compile the figures.

There are some colleges that now give sports administration courses to men and women. (The University of Ohio is one.) Several women are now employed as sports statisticians, with more and more becoming interested in this field.

What Do You Need?

What qualities do you need? Well, the *basic* responsibility of a statistician in major league sports is to be accurate, because so many people depend on you. So, first of all you've got to have a respect for facts, and the willingness to ferret them out.

There's a saying in baseball broadcasting, "It's a small booth and a long season," which is especially true when you're traveling and working together, counting spring training, as many as 190 games a year. As Bob Murphy says, "That's a lot of togetherness, more togetherness than a lot of married people have, so it is terribly important that, in addition to your talents for the job you're doing, you have good rapport with the people you're spending so many hours with."

Obviously, then, a sense of humor is very important to keep the relationship pleasant and to brighten up the day-to-day routine.

As a statistician you must be able to accept criticism—sometimes you might even be yelled at. You're occasionally going to run into people who would like nothing better than to stump you. Occasionally, a writer, almost maliciously it seems, will demand some information of you in the middle of a tight situation, when you're obviously busy with something else. Despite this, you have to be able to maintain good relationships with everyone.

You can't be thin-skinned. The job isn't just sitting down with a ledger in a back office somewhere, where no one speaks to you. It's dealing with the public—management, players, broadcasters and press—so public relations is a major part of the job.

As a statistician, you're going to become involved with some broadcasters who are very high-strung. When I first started out, for example, and was freelancing basketball games, there was one announcer (who's still broadcasting for the same pro team) who was the nicest guy you'd want to meet before the game. But once the action got under way, he was such a fan of his team that he'd become irrational; and when things went wrong for the club, he'd blame everybody, from the referee to me. We didn't know each other very well, but we were on a first-name basis, and I worked for him over a period of a year and a half the three or four times his team came to Madison Square Garden.

One particular game went into overtime, and when a Knick scored a basket against his team, I indicated to him the fact that it was the player's thirty-fourth point. It was nothing to hide—the player had scored that many points, and it was worth mentioning on the air—but the broadcaster ignored it. When I persisted, thinking he hadn't noticed the first time I showed him the scoresheet with "34" circled across from the player's name, the broadcaster grabbed the stat sheet out of my hand, and just crumpled it up and threw it away.

After the game, when he had calmed down, he said very seriously: "We don't give those figures. I'm broadcasting for this team and I don't give this kind of information. You're being paid by me, and you'll give me positive figures on *my* team, and that's it."

I didn't work for him after that.

Nose for News

In Bob Murphy's opinion, a statistician has to be more than just a statistician—he has to have a nose for news. "He has to be able to write headlines almost before they happen." Bob has said that I have the ability to see something unfolding, even an obscure record that is about to be broken. There have been times, he recalls, that he's turned to me and said, "Will you check on something?" only to see me holding the item of information he was going to request. He contends I'm the only person he knows who, late in the season (when rosters have swelled to forty names, including minor league farmhands), can identify any player who comes into the game.

Knowledgeability about a sport makes it possible to provide information that is meaningful. The "nose for news" that Murphy and others treasure is a necessity, if you're going to answer the sometimes specialized questions of newspapermen and broadcasters, as well as those from within your own professional sports operation.

A good memory is a prime requisite, because there are situations where you just don't have the time to look things up or you'll lose the significance of a piece of information. For instance, the Mets had a series with the Padres in '76 during which, in two games in succession, the first innings were almost identical for San Diego—Johnny Grubb led off with a single, Enzo Hernandez sacrificed and the next two batters flied out to the outfield. Being able to remember in the second game that the same thing had occurred in the first enabled me to get that information to our broadcaster when it was pertinent. It wasn't a big deal, but interesting enough to mention on the air. If I had to take the time to look it up, we would have been in the next inning.

If we're playing Cincinnati and Ken Griffey keeps flying to center field, and I remember it, by the final game of the series I'll mention it to the broadcaster, who can then make the observation that Met pitchers haven't let him pull the ball very often in this series. In this instance, as in most cases, I'd just present the broadcaster with the facts, and let him make his own analysis of them.

You should know the relationship of one statistic to another, so that you can give the broadcaster stats he might not have thought of—say, a ballplayer's individual achievement in relation both to his own previous achievements and to the all-time record. The obvious statistics are not necessarily the most important ones.

Occupational Hazard

When I go to a party with people I haven't met and someone asks me what I do for a living, I'll tell them I'm a brain surgeon or something equally far-out. I try not to reveal my true occupation.

Maybe I'm gun-shy, but there's good reason. Telling a fan that you're a sports statistician is like a gunfighter in the Old West touting himself as the fastest gun in the West—everyone wants to challenge you. Eventually, someone will find an obscure item you don't know off the top of your head. There's an unlimited array of baseball facts. "Hey, let me ask you a question: 'Who was on deck when Bobby Thomson hit his famous home run?' 'What team did Carl Erskine pitch his no-hitter against for the Brooklyn Dodgers?' 'Who hit the first Met grand-slam home run?' " These, I happen to know the answers to (Willie Mays, Chicago Cubs, and Rod Kanehl), but there are plenty of questions I can't answer. There's always going to be some fanatic who spends twelve hours a day going through every baseball record book and who's going to come up with a stopper. When I confront one of these characters, I try to be polite, but there are times I show my annoyance. So I don't advertise my occupation. It helps me avoid these trivia showdowns, and besides, I like to think there's more to my life than statistics.

That's not to say I don't enjoy trivia—I love it—but I've never accepted an invitation to participate in a trivia contest, because there's nothing for me to gain. If I know the answers or can stump the others, it seems as if I'm blowing my own horn, and if I'm stumped, it comes off as if I don't know my business.

When people try to test the sports knowledge of Seymour Siwoff of the Elias Sports Bureau, he tells them, "I maintain a whole library in my office, and that's where I look up the information. I never try to retain it. If I do, it's just one of those fortunate things."

He doesn't deny a good memory helps, but as a general rule, when he's dealing with numbers, he abides by his office's popular saying: "Look it up."

Seymour acknowledges that in the case of a statistician dealing with a broadcaster on the air, information has to be provided spontaneously or the effect of it can be lost, but in the case of his bureau, he says, "We have the time. Hold on and we'll look it up." He tries to avoid being put on the spot. Should a stranger on a plane, for instance, ask Siwoff what business he's in, he'll simply say, "I'm in the sports business." Not that he's ashamed of his significant role, by any means. With the enormous romance surrounding sports, he says, "We never put ourselves above anything else. We realize our position. People are paying to see the athlete."